*John Bird Burnham (1869-1939)*

# JOHN BIRD BURNHAM —

## Klondiker, Adirondacker and Eminent Conservationist

*Warmest good wishes*

BY

MAITLAND C. DE SORMO

*Maitland de Sormo*

Adirondack Yesteryears Inc.
P.O. Drawer 209
Saranac Lake, N.Y. 12983

Books written or edited by same author:

*Told Around the Campfire*
*Noah John Rondeau, Adirondack Hermit*
*Old Times in the Adirondacks*
*Seneca Ray Stoddard, Versatile Camera-Artist*
*The Heydays of the Adirondacks*

First Edition

Library of Congress Catalog Number: 78-50 570
ISBN 0-9601158-5-4

Copyright May 1978 by Maitland C. De Sormo

All rights reserved. No part of this publication may be reproduced, stored in a retrieval system, or transmitted, in any form or by any means, electronic, mechanical, photocopying, recording or otherwise without the prior written permission of the publisher, except a reviewer who may quote brief passages in a review.

# Dedication

*To all those who have over the years earnestly and steadfastly struggled to protect and pass down God's greatest gift — the wild places and creatures of the world — and to those who nowadays seek solace, solitude and Nature's wholesome, recreative pleasures — this book is affectionately dedicated.*

## Table of Contents

| | Page |
|---|---|
| Dedication | 5 |
| "My Mountain Home," poem by John Bird Burnham | 8 |
| Biographical sketch from *Leaders in American Conservation* | 9 |
| Foreword by Robert F. Hall | 11 |
| List of Illustrations | 14 |
| Preface | 16 |

### Part I: The Delaware Days

| | | |
|---|---|---|
| Chapter 1 | — Ancestry and Early Days | 19 |
| Chapter 2 | — The Critical Years | 25 |

### Part II: The Klondike Gold Rush

| | | |
|---|---|---|
| Chapter 3 | — Skagway and the White Pass (Dead Horse) Trail | 35 |
| Chapter 4 | — Bennett Lake Ordeal and Tricky Tagish Crossing | 51 |
| Chapter 5 | — The Miles Canyon — White Horse Rapids Challenge | 57 |
| Chapter 6 | — Loss of the Boats and Encounter with River Thieves | 65 |
| Chapter 7 | — Near Tragedy of Renaud Party and Recovery of Boats | 75 |
| Chapter 8 | — Some Survival Suggestions and Demise of Two Wary Wolves | 81 |
| Chapter 9 | — Rumors and Reports from Dawson City | 89 |
| Chapter 10 | — More Survival Tactics and Houtchikoo Murders | 93 |
| Chapter 11 | — Indian Starvation and Last Lap — Outbound Trek | 100 |

### Part III: Burnham the Adirondacker

| | | |
|---|---|---|
| Chapter 12 | — Moving Along the Road to Success | 112 |
| Chapter 13 | — The Crater Club | 119 |
| Chapter 14 | — Acquisition of Highlands Property | 129 |
| Chapter 15 | — Wide Waters of Lake Champlain | 134 |
| Chapter 16 | — Surgery Survival and Subconscious Mind | 139 |
| Chapter 17 | — Some Thoughts About Prayer, Solitude, Practical Religion and Rev. George Webster | 143 |
| Chapter 18 | — Local Politics and Politicians | 149 |
| Chapter 19 | — Fateful Siberian Interlude and Some Environmental Concerns | 157 |
| Chapter 20 | — Washington's Birthday Meetings etc., | 163 |

## Part IV: Burnham the Conservationist

Chapter 21 — The Albany Years ................................. 172
Chapter 22 — The Campaign to Protect Migratory Birds ............ 178
Chapter 23 — The Migratory Bird Treaty with Great Britain for Canada ......... 182
Chapter 24 — The Campaign for Migratory Bird Refuges ............ 187
Chapter 25 — Burnham versus Hornaday ............................ 190
Chapter 26 — Burnham — Dilg Controversy over Game Refuge Legislation ....... 198
Chapter 27 — Three Score and Ten ................................ 203

## Appendix

Chapter  1 — Characteristics of Klondikers ...................... 211
Chapter  2 — Personal Opinions About Some Unusual Men ........... 214
Chapter  3 — Pioneers and Explorers ............................. 221
Chapter  4 — The Subjective Mind ................................ 224
Chapter  5 — Personalities of the Two Roosevelts ................ 228
Chapter  6 — Conservation's False Prophets ...................... 236
Chapter  7 — Thirty Years of Progress in Conservation ........... 242
Chapter  8 — Conservation's Debt to Sportsmen ................... 246
Chapter  9 — The Moose Shot 'Round the Corner ................... 250
Chapter 10 — Unpopular Game Laws and the Hunter's Questionnaire ........ 253
Chapter 11 — History of the Deer in New York State .............. 258
Chapter 12 — The Future of the Adirondack Park .................. 260
Partial List of Published Material by and about John Bird Burnham ............. 262

## MY MOUNTAIN HOME

*My heart is in the Highlands,*
*And though my semblance works*
*Inside four walls of brick and stone*
*The soul within me shirks.*

*My heart is in the Highlands*
*My thoughts are far away*
*From written word and printed page*
*And all that people say;*

*From city sound and city sight,*
*From ruck of men that strive,*
*From those that pull the groaning load,*
*From those that grimly drive.*

*Far from the haunts of strife and greed*
*My spirit rests today*
*Among the lichened mountain tops*
*Above a sun-kissed bay.*

*I see the white gulls' lazy flight,*
*The white boats sailing by,*
*The white clouds floating in between*
*The blue of lake and sky,*

*Ah me, the body is enslaved —*
*But never gaol of stone*
*Imprisoned keeps this soul of mine,*
*The spirit gains its own!*

*J. B. Burnham*

*From:* LEADERS IN AMERICAN CONSERVATION, *National Resources Council of America, Ronald Press Co., N.Y., 1971, page 51.*

## BURNHAM, JOHN BIRD (1869-1939)

Born March 16, 1869 in Newcastle, Delaware. Trinity College, Connecticut, B.A. 1891, D.Sc. (honorary) 1939. From 1891 to 1897 he was business manager of *Forest and Stream Magazine* in New York City, resigning his position to join the first Klondike Gold Rush. In 1898 he purchased a farm in Willsboro, New York, which he operated as the Highlands Game Preserve. Early in 1905 he was appointed chief game protector of the State of New York and three years later was named deputy commissioner of fish and game; in 1911 he became acting commissioner. In that year he was selected by the founders of the American Game Protective and Propagation Association to become its first president. In 1915 he was a member of a three-man committee selected to codify New York's fish and game law. One of the first objectives of the American Game Protection and Propagation Association was to secure the enactment of a strong federal law for the protection of migratory birds. He became the organizer of the public support for such a law, which became reality with the enactment of the Weeks-McLean Law on March 4, 1913. He was named chairman of the Advisory Committee to the Department of Agriculture on the Migratory Bird Law established by the new law. When the constitutionality of the Weeks-McLean Law was challenged, he again led the campaign to obtain the ratification of the Migratory Bird Treaty with Great Britain for Canada. He also served as chairman of a United States Forest Service Committee on Game in the National Forests and was a member of the Committee on Game and Fur-bearing Animals of the National Conference on Outdoor Recreation of 1924. In 1921 he led an expedition to Siberia to collect specimens of the unclassified Marco Polo sheep for American museums. His book, *The Rim of Mystery,* is an account of the expedition. In 1926 he was awarded the gold medal of the Camp Fire Club of America. Died September 24, 1939.

JAMES B. TREFETHEN

---

"John Bird Burnham, 1869-1939," *American Wildlife,* 28(6):244-46, November-December, 1939.
*Who Was Who in America,* 1897-1942.

*Portrait of John Bird Burnham done in Mexico in 1917. Media combination — charcoal, ink, crayon and paint.*

# Introduction

### By Robert F. Hall

Willsboro, N.Y.

My neighbors who 40 years ago were also neighbors of John Bird Burnham remember him as a very respected man, genial and accommodating, pipe-smoking, wise, witty, articulate, opinionated and very proud. Alton Wrisley, then a young farmer of 30, recalls visiting Burnham in his Essex office to offer for sale corner posts needed for the modular homes Burnham was constructing.

The old man puffed on his pipe, smoking more matches than tobacco and thumbed the spent matches into a large fire-wood box. "I've got enough corner posts laid end to end to reach from here to the Atlantic Ocean," Burnham said, but he kept young Wrisley in conversation for an hour, at the end of which he said, "Bring me all the corner posts you cut. I'll buy them."

Wrisley never doubted but that this was a generous gesture fully in keeping with the Burnham reputation for helping local people when they needed it, but he made haste to profit by the transaction.

It is always hard to reconcile the image of an old man with the youth he had once been. In Burnham's case, the mellow, confident, successful man of affairs at 65 is in sharp contrast to the young man of 27 who, suffering from severe depression, fled to the bitter winter of the Klondike gold rush where he recovered his identity in a long, and to my mind, heroic battle with sub-zero weather, ice jams, flooding water, violent criminals and, perhaps worst of all, the almost constant threat of death by starvation.

These chapters in the book which follows, written by Burnham in the graphic journalistic style which marked all his literary work, are its high point and will stand as a classic of its kind.

Burnham returned to civilization with enough energy, imagination and drive to explain his success as a farmer, pioneer builder and developer of recreational communities, an activist in local politics and a nationally known conservationist.

"The driving force of his life," his son Koert commented in later years, "was to assure the wise use of our natural resources so that future generations would be able to enjoy hiking, fishing, hunting, and photography."

Burnham was proud of the fact that in his lumbering he practiced scientific forestry so that in subsequent years the land was producing more merchantable timber than when he made the first cutting.

Of special interest to us who live in the Adirondacks was his campaign to enforce the state law against using hounds to hunt deer. It will surprise many modern-day hunters to learn that a law, long since taken for granted as essential to prevent extinction of the whitetail, was so bitterly opposed by local residents.

This fight launched him on the course of crusading conservationism which resulted in his appointment as chief game protector of New York State, three years later as deputy commissioner of fish and game, and in 1911 as acting commissioner.

As first president of the American Game Association he was involved with every important conservation measure considered or adopted by Congress during his lifetime. As a conservation journalist, he wrote for outdoor magazines the articles which built public support for the laws he insisted the nation needed.

Burnham's name is closely associated with the Migratory Bird Treaty with Canada and with the Migratory Bird Conservation Act which authorized the Federal Government to acquire land for waterfowl refuges. What is less known, however, was his role in promoting the duck stamp program which subsequently financed so many worthwhile conservation projects.

I cannot on my part accept Burnham's strictures against the Civilian Conservation Corps (CCC) and the New Deal; I think objective appraisals of these programs have since provided a view more balanced than his.

Koert Burnham suggests that the later split between his father and Franklin Roosevelt is only part of the story. When F.D.R. was a member of the New York State Senate, he turned to Burnham for advice and guidance, and it was Burnham who brought together young Roosevelt and Thomas Mott Osborne in a partnership which gave the state important prison reform legislation. Burnham parted with Roosevelt when the latter sponsored state legislation to prevent farmers from cutting and selling firewood unless they protected their employees with Workmen's Compensation Insurance.

In any case it seems that Burnham was surprisingly silent on President Franklin Roosevelt's outstanding contribution to the cause to which Burnham was devoted. In 1934, Roosevelt named a committee of three — Aldo Leopold, Thomas Beck and Burnham's close friend, J.N. "Ding" Darling — to establish a chain of waterfowl sanctuaries, a landmark action in conservation history.

It is widely believed in these parts that the reason why for many years the Adirondack Park did not include part of Westport and Willsboro and all of the town of Essex was due to influence exerted by Burnham. This is not, to my knowledge, documented, although his son concedes that as a member of the Whallonsburgh Grange he supported a resolution to keep these areas outside the Blue Line.

Burnham may have been motivated by his fear that including these towns in the Adirondack Park would have hindered farmers from hunting foxes and rabbits with dogs. However, my own surmise is that Burnham, with a prophetic sense as to the value of land-use planning, was practicing some premature zoning, designating this flat land lying along Lake Champlain as a future region for recreational development. Certainly it seemed to have little in common with the forests on the mountains that the constitutional principle of "forever wild" was designed to protect.

At the recommendation of the Adirondack Study Commission, the Legislature revised the Blue Line in 1972 to include the hitherto omitted lands, persuaded that lake front property also needed protection against inappropriate and unsightly development.

Whether Burnham would today agree with the revision, I do not know. He favored retention of open space; yet he had enormous dislike of bureaucracy. On the other hand, he never hesitated to seek governmental authority for conservation measures which would have been impossible without it.

High on my list of Burnham's contributions to the Adirondacks were his efforts to improve our local economy through promoting appropriate local industries. His log cabin industry, his modular homes, and his development of our wollastonite deposits are widely cited. This last one is still providing jobs for our people, thanks also to his son and daughter, Koert and Rose, who continued to promote it after the father's death.

Burnham lived at a time when the corporate yardstick of progress — bigness — was generally accepted. Yet I have the feeling that he would have been sympathetic to the more modern belief that there are limits to growth and that preservation of small industry has intrinsic value for society and especially for our smaller communities.

His efforts to save the Boquet Electric Company, which generated power from the river just south of Reber, might remind us that many hydroelectric plants along our rushing streams, now abandoned, would serve a most useful and strategic service if they could be restored.

I have been running through my mind the names of other distinguished men and women whose contributions to the Adirondack economy were similar to those of John Burnham. There was Elkanah Watson, John Milholland, Harold Hochschild, Richard Lawrence and the Paines. Common to all was this reverence for our mountains, forests and streams, and a desire to build, not to exploit.

Meanwhile for those who are engaged in research into the conservation movement from 1886 to 1939, the papers of John Bird Burnham will answer many questions. They are deposited with the Conservation History and Research Center of the University of Wyoming at Laramie.

For bringing Burnham's journals to public notice we are indebted to an old friend of the Adirondacks and for some years now its Boswell: Maitland DeSormo.

I suspect that Mait, as we call him, was attracted to this subject in part because of its Canadian implications. Mait's father and mother were Canadian-born and that great nation to our north has always had a strong appeal to him. The Klondike gold rush was Canadian, not Alaskan, and Burnham's ability to push the migratory bird treaty to its conclusion was due in part to the latter's friendship for Canada and Canadians.

Mait has more than one string to his bow. He researches, writes, edits, publishes and promotes.

It is easier to understand Mait when one learns that he is a graduate of Hamilton College, which nestles near the southern border of our region. This small college has produced far more than its share of literary professionals — Carl Carmer, Alexander Wolcott, Ezra Pound, John V. A. Weaver, David Beetle, Samuel Hopkins Adams, Paul Friedlander, and Maitland DeSormo.

This book on John Bird Burnham joins a shelf of five on Adirondack history written by Mait, constituting in itself a testimonial to his own dedication to our region.

Robert F. Hall<br>
Willsboro, N.Y.<br>
January 24, 1978

# List of Illustrations

| | |
|---|---:|
| John Bird Burnham (1869-1939) | frontispiece |
| Koert and Florence Burnham | 18 |
| Amstel House, New Castle, Del. | 19 |
| Van Leuveneigh House | 20 |
| V R (Wolcott) Ranch near Rawlins *(Courtesy of the University of Wyoming)* | 26 |
| Corral of V R Ranch *(Courtesy of the University of Wyoming)* | 27 |
| Henrietta DuBois Burnham and sister | 30 |
| Rev. George DuBois D.D. | 30 |
| Felsenheim Keene Valley | 31 |
| Burnham's Office at *Forest & Stream*, N.Y.C. | 32 |
| Map of Trail of '97 & '98 | 34 |
| Steamer "Islander" at Skagway September 3, 1897 | 36 |
| Skagway Harbor from "Islander" | 36 |
| Skagway | 36 |
| The Beach at Skagway | 36 |
| Jefferson R. (Soapy) Smith | 38 |
| "Soapy" Smith's saloon | 38 |
| Skagway River and Start of White Pass Trail | 39 |
| Loading a Pack Horse | 39 |
| Map showing White Pass & Chilkoot Trail | 42 |
| Chilkat Indian Packers | 44 |
| Rest Break on the White Pass Trail *(Hegg photo)* | 45 |
| Tough Going | 46 |
| Porcupine Hill, Dead Horse Underfoot | 46 |
| The Dead Horse Trail — White Pass | 46 |
| A Cache on the Trail | 46 |
| Approaching Summit of White Pass Trail | 49 |
| Packers in Sight of Summit of White Pass — August 1897 | 49 |
| Summit Lake Camp August 1897 | 49 |
| Camp at Deep Lake | 49 |
| Butchering Project | 50 |
| Whipsawing Boat Timbers | 50 |
| Miles Canyon-Side View | 56 |
| Miles Canyon | 57 |
| One of Hepburn's Barges in Rapids | 61 |
| Lumber Scow in Rapids *(Hamacher photo)* | 61 |
| Time Out for Reloading | 67 |
| Shooting White Horse Rapids *(Hamacher photo)* | 67 |
| Wreck Below White Horse Rapids — Men Overboard | 67 |
| Tramway By-Passing Rapids | 71 |
| Five Finger Rapids of Yukon River | 71 |
| McKercher Chopping Canoe Loose from Ice | 73 |
| Cabin Near Fort Selkirk | 83 |
| Interior of Burnham — McKercher Cabin | 83 |
| Burnham and Giant Wolf | 83 |
| Close-up of the Giant Wolf | 83 |
| Part of the Female Klondike Contingent | 88 |
| Dog Teams on the Trail | 88 |
| Heavy Sledding | 88 |
| Wolverine Family | 88 |
| Ancient Squaw and Smoke Spooks *(Stoddard photo)* | 91 |
| Kloochmen at Home *(Stoddard photo)* | 92 |
| One Who Didn't Make It | 96 |
| Burnham's Watch in Salve Box Carrier | 96 |
| Northwest Mounties and Teams | 96 |

| | |
|---|---|
| Packet Awaiting Spring Launching at Lake Bennett | 96 |
| Police and Canadian Customs Station at Summit of Chilkoot Pass | 105 |
| Above the Scales in Chilkoot Pass | 105 |
| Nearing Summit of the Pass | 105 |
| Typical Stampeders | 105 |
| Cache of Flour or Oats | 107 |
| The 35 Degree Ordeal on Lower Chilkoot Trail | 107 |
| Near View of Line of Packers | 107 |
| Carrying Timbers for Boat Building up the Pass | 107 |
| Sheep Camp — Chilkoot Pass | 109 |
| Trailside Camp in Chilkoot Pass | 109 |
| Crater Club Map of Grounds | 117 |
| Crater Club Map (Burnham) | 117 |
| The Sawmill | 117 |
| "Camp Bonnie" First Burnham Cottage at Club | 121 |
| Log House at Thirteenth Lake | 121 |
| Crater Club Double-Page Spread | 122-123 |
| Christopher Morley (1890-1957) | 125 |
| Steamer "Vermont" from the book *A Century of Progress* | 126 |
| Capt. Sherman of the "Vermont" | 126 |
| Willsboro Point from the Pinnacle *(Courtesy of Morris Glen)* | 130 |
| Burnham's First "Highlands" Home | 130 |
| Old P O and Tavern at Highlands Forge | 132 |
| Burnham's Second Home | 133 |
| The "Happy Jack" | 135 |
| Split Rock Over Whallon's Bay *(Courtesy of Morris Glenn)* | 136 |
| Split Rock Lighthouse and Tower *(Courtesy of Morris Glenn)* | 137 |
| Room Built by Burnham connecting lighthouse and tower *(Courtesy of Morris Glenn)* | 137 |
| Rev. George Webster (1866-1942) | 145 |
| J. B. Burnham and Andy Taylor | 158 |
| Interior of Chukotsk Peninsula | 158 |
| The Base Camp | 158 |
| The Unknown Sheep | 158 |
| The "Wislow" | 161 |
| Capt. Billy Thompson | 161 |
| U.S. Coast Guard Schooner "The Bear" | 162 |
| Burnham at "Highlands" 1935 | 163 |
| Mrs. Burnham in 1940 | 163 |
| Conservationists at "Highlands," February, 1919 | 165 |
| Group of Conservationists at "Highlands" in 1934 | 165 |
| Dan Beard and Trophy, Lake Kipawa, Ont. *(Photo by Joseph Van Vleck)* | 167 |
| Burnham Bookplate made by Dan Beard | 167 |
| N. Y. S. Conservation Dept. Hdqtrs. Albany | 176 |
| N. Y. S. Game Law Codification Comm. Left & right: John Burnham, Marshall McLean, George Lawyer | 176 |
| First Shipment at "Highlands" Deer Park | 191 |
| Raold Amundsen at Nome in 1921 *(Lomen's photo)* | 215 |
| Lincoln Ellsworth and Raold Amundsen over North Pole | 215 |
| Dr. Frederick A. Cook | 218 |
| Lieut. Robert E. Peary, U.S.N. | 218 |
| Vilhjalmur Stefansson at "Highlands" | 218 |
| F.D.R. as Secretary of Navy April 4, 1917 *(Courtesy of F.D. Roosevelt Library)* | 229 |
| F.D.R. at Lake Placid September 1935 | 231 |
| Teddy Roosevelt on Campaign Trail | 231 |
| Burnham and Mexican Mountain Sheep 1917 | 252 |
| Burnham on Mexican Hunting Trip | 252 |
| WE Never Sleep | 272 |

# Preface

This book, which should have been a straight autobiography, was in fact originally planned as such but never reached the point of publication. Therefore, a generation of readers has been denied the pleasure of enjoying what is obviously one of the most exciting and meaningful personal histories of our time.

This is the story of John Bird Burnham, (1869-1939), an exceptionally interesting man who was — like his friends Theodore Roosevelt, Gifford Pinchot and other distinguished colleagues — deeply concerned about and involved in the gamut of complex environmental problems which were already acquiring alarming dimensions even in his era. Because of his pronounced persuasive ability, persistence and strong leadership qualities he became the acknowledged spokesman for many causes connected with the various aspects of conservation and ecology.

To say that he was ahead of his time would be an accurate appraisal of his awareness of the perplexing problems generated by the universal misuse and abuse of our God-given heritage. The passing years have certainly provided ample proof that he and others with similar concerns were hardly guilty of exaggerating the urgencies and consequences which confronted his generation and — even more drastically — ours as well.

Throughout his lifetime he steadfastly represented and practiced what he and many others considered to be the soundest methods of managing and enjoying all forms of our natural endowment. To him all categories of animate and inanimate objects were important, destructible, exhaustible, interrelated parts of a great, mysterious pattern that should be respected, protected and intelligently used.

Nor did he limit his energetic attention and service to only the larger arenas: he was always available and eager to cope with state and local demands, issues, obligations and responsibilities. That he was true to his trust is the theme of this story.

Back in the Summer of 1932 James C. Derieux, an editor of the influential *American Magazine* and the author of two articles about his friend, John B. Burnham,[1] spent a month with the latter at his home, "Highlands," near Keeseville, N.Y. At that time the two men discussed an autobiographical project in considerable detail because shortly afterward Derieux sent along a suggested outline and format. Following these guidelines Burnham

---

[1] "John Burnham, Conservationist and Hunter." *Field and Stream* May, 1929 and "There'll Never Be A Time When Everybody's Broke." *American Magazine* May, 1932.

compiled a series of chapters which provide an absorbing account of an eventful and productive career which included, among many other callings, noteworthy accomplishments as a Klondiker, author, artist, Adirondack businessman, explorer, big-game hunter, scientist and eminent conservationist.

Since he was still working on the manuscript right up to the time of his death, in 1939, and since by then Derieux had other commitments, the collaborative effort regrettably never reached the publication stage.

His long-time friend and colleague Dr. E. W. Nelson, for many years chief of the Bureau of Biological Survey, described John Burnham as "one of the ablest and most successful conservationists of our wildlife and allied natural resources that America has ever produced." Among the more outstanding conservation measures in which his services were of prime importance were (1) The Migratory Bird Treaty, (2) the Migratory Bird Treaty Act (enabling legislation), (3) the New Alaska Game and Fur Laws and (4) the Upper Mississippi River Wildlife Refuge and subsequently the establishment of other sanctuaries in Canada as well as in the United States....

The brief biographical sketch on previous page, taken from the authoritative *Leaders in American Conservation,* provides the bare bones treatment of his impressive list of credits.

The book itself should furnish sufficient factual and personal details to enable the man to emerge from behind the impressive list of kudos and deeds.

A. R. Spofford, first Librarian of Congress, is credited with the rather obvious observation that books are made from books. That statement of course does apply regrettably often to contemporary biography because of the seeming scarcity of Grade A subjects and relevant material.

There certainly has been no dearth of material to work with on this particular project. In fact Burnham did his part so well that the work of this substitute editor consisted mostly of selection and organization. But just what and how much to use presented many problems to one whose knowledge of conservation history and its heroes leaves much to be desired....

Literary authorities seem to be in general agreement that the function of a modern biography or autobiography should not be the production of a magnified epitaph or an expanded tract. Its purpose should be the presentation of selected details which depict the faults and foibles as well as the attitudes and attributes which constitute the lights and shadows of his character.

Lambert, the Puritan general, stated that "the best of men are but men at their best" and in doing so refuted the sleazy theory that if you label a person as being good or great you are thereby honor-bound to consider him as great or good all through and upon every side and occasion. Apparently this is based on a subtle ethical law which decrees that a sensitive, noteworthy person must be "all things to all men."

Fortunately, many more knowledgable men have offered sound advice and constant encouragement and thus kept the project moving, however slowly. Among them are the following: the late Harry Hansen, editor of Hastings House; James Craig, editor of *American Forests* and James Trefethen, director of publications for Wildlife Management Institute.

Especially helpful have been George Crossette, formerly chief of geographical research for the *National Geographic Magazine* and William Carr, founder of museums at Bear Mountain State Park, the Arizona-Sonora Desert and Ghost Ranch Museums, near Tucson, Arizona and Abiqui, New Mexico respectively.

William Casselman of Elizabethtown, N.Y. also gave valued assistance in the format.

Many thanks also to Morris Glenn, author of *Story of Three Towns,* for photos and material on the Crater Club and Christopher Morley.

My deepest appreciation and thanks go to Bob Hall, whose introduction and prestigious name have greatly enhanced the acceptability of this writing venture.

Above all others, I am sincerely indebted to Koert and Florence Burnham because their whole-hearted cooperation, warm hospitality and endless patience have been the genuine motivating factor in the production of this book about his remarkably successful, many-sided father.

Maitland C. De Sormo<br>
Lower Lake<br>
Saranac Lake, N.Y.

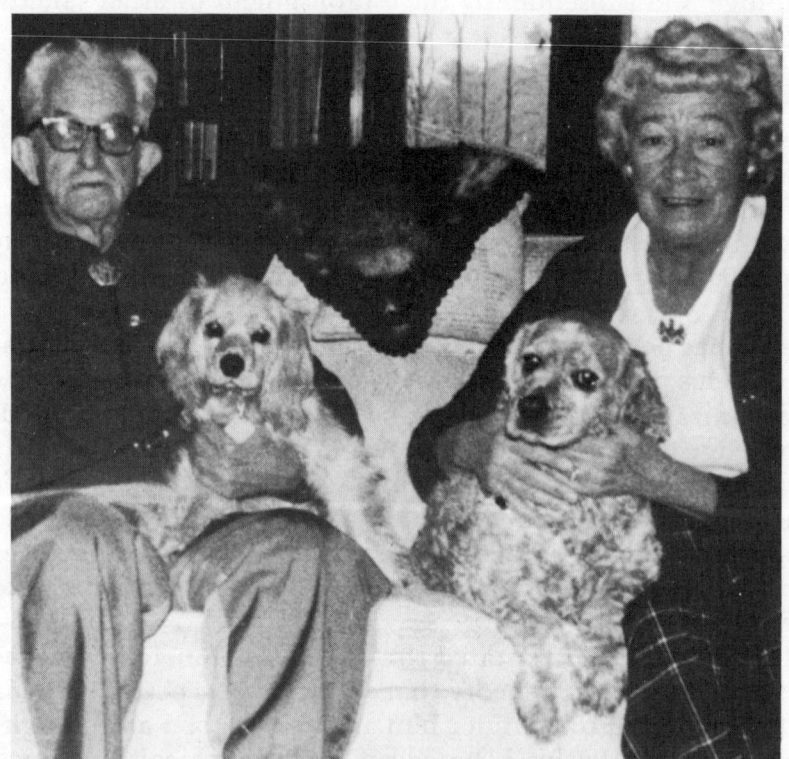

*Koert and Florence Burnham*

# Part I

# Chapter 1

**Ancestry and Early Days**

John Bird Burnham was born in New Castle, Delaware on March 16, 1869 in the Amstel House, a large stone and brick mansion built in 1698, which his mother — Elizabeth Van Leuveneigh Bird — had inherited. Previously, two of the signers of the Declaration of Independence had lived there, as had Caesar Rodney, whose vote made the Declaration possible. In recognition of this service Rodney was subsequently appointed as a committee of one to notify George Washington of his election to the presidency. Washington, La Fayette and many other distinguished men of that tumultuous era were entertained and sheltered under its rooftree.

*Amstel House, New Castle, Del.*

Traditionally, his mother's family had come from Ireland to Virginia with Lord Baltimore. Her colonial paternal ancestor was one of the two brothers of William Byrd of Westover. The story goes that an Irish tutor suggested changing the spelling of their surname in order to "differentiate them from the birds that fly." The older brother therefore adopted

*VanLeuvenigh House home of Mrs. John B. Burnham prior to marriage.*

the variation of Byrd. The next, Bird; this left for the son's direct ancestor only the original form of the name.

His father, John Burnham, a Yankee of Scottish ancestry, descended from one of three brothers who came to America in 1638 on an ill-fated ship named the "Angel Gabriel." Apparently the prophetic name sank the vessel because she met her doom on the reefs off Pemaquid, Maine. Fortunately all three Burnhams, two men named Andrews and two Storeys survived the wreck, as did a small boat, in which the survivors followed the coastline south until they reached the locality which later became the settlement of Ipswich, Massachusetts. Later on, their particular part of the region was set aside as the town of Essex.

Somewhat later one of the Burnhams migrated to the fertile northern part of Delaware, where John's father was born to the life of a gentleman farmer. His father was thirty-six and his mother thirty-two when they were married. Her father had long been a widower and she his devoted companion; for that reason she did not marry earlier.

Burnham senior, a pioneer peach grower, owned three farms, two of these entirely given over to extensive orchards. However, he spent most of his time in New Castle and made only occasional visits to his holdings except in the harvest season. Then he would make headquarters at Appoquinomink Farm in order to personally hire the pickers, who came from as far away as Philadelphia, and to supervise the shipment of the peaches to the best markets.

Harvest-time was a memorable event for his sister Eliza and the youngster, for at the height of the season his mother would take them there for a visit of several days. Tons and tons of the sweet-scented fruit would be brought in by wagon for sorting, packing and transportation to the railroad, while the piles of over-ripe peaches and culls kept growing in size. The nomad pickers, who camped in the barns and outbuildings, used the cull pile as their chief source of food. Since their free and easy way of life had a strong fascination for the boy, his mother was in constant fear that he would be kidnapped because of the numerous friendships he made.

So far as he had been able to learn all his ancestors were lovers of field sports. During the hunting season both his parents would drive out from New Castle nearly every good day for shooting quail in the stubble fields, and occasionally their trips would take them well down the little state.

There was something instinctive about the son's love of the chase. He recalled vividly in later years that when he was only four he had been awakened one night by his father's tossing a bunch of quail into his crib. The smell and feel of the birds roused from the depths of his being the wild inheritance of Nimrod. He could remember that he clung to the birds all the rest of the night and determinedly repulsed every effort of his mother to take them away.

Each Fall his father also visited Appoquinomink for the bird-shooting season and when he was eight he accompanied him on such a trip. Young as he was he could recall being deeply thrilled by the sight of the galloping dogs suddenly braking to a point, the sudden roar as the bevies took wing; and he never tired of watching as the dogs excitedly worked on the singles.

That was one of the very few quail hunts his father and he went on. Later he occasionally went with him by boat for rail and reed-bird shooting in the marshes near New Castle. But from that time on he had little difficulty keeping up with his father's pace when walking. The reason was that his parent was steadily losing ground to tuberculosis, which caused his death three years later. His last two summers were spent with his family at the old Worden Hotel in Saratoga; there most of the son's hours were spent learning to shoot with bow and arrow with the Indian boys at their nearby encampment. The father's final three Winters were passed at Ormond, Florida.

John was a husky, red-faced lad until he was nearly sixteen when in all probability he had a touch of the same disease. Eliza, his older sister, died from it at that age and Lucy, his other sister, had passed away when she was only two.

One phase of his youth was aptly described by the grown Burnham: "Even as a boy I rebelled against church and Sunday School. My father was Senior Warden of Immanuel Church in New Castle and my mother held things together in that communion not only by her tact when schisms arose against the rector, but practically by playing the organ and entertaining the Bishop on his visitations. My father and sister sat in the body of the church in their box-like pew, but to let me work off part of my boyish spirits I was allowed in the organ loft to pump the organ. This gave me a kind of standing with the other boys who had to sit in the pews, and if I happened to be sick there was no dearth of volunteers to take my place.

"Behind the organ, where the pump lever was, nobody in the choir could see what was going on. There was a back window which gave access to one of the great vertical tomb slabs bolted to the end of the church and, when the sermon began, I used to get through the window and shinny down the tombstone and amuse myself among the graves or hunt up boys who did not go to church. But I always managed to be back at the organ pump before air was required for the concluding music. Even then I respected my mother because she was not a snooper. Contrary to a common attitude among mothers she seemed to think I was older than my years rather than younger as most mothers seem to assume. I believe most men will agree that more boys go to the Devil through too much watching than through too little. I am sure that Mother knew the enforced inaction of a church service was highly unpleasant to her boy, so she made it as easy for him as possible with the object of establishing the habit of attendance. It was not her fault that for twenty years it failed."

In later years the son paid his mother this touching and eloquent tribute: "She radiated good-will to everyone and she put this universal affection to practical use. I cannot remember that she ever had an unkind word for anyone. Through all the bitter poverty of her later life she never failed to give a tenth of her pittance to charity. Her self-denial was supreme and the beauty of it was that her charities were personal and never realized as charity by the recipient, so adroitly and delicately was the service rendered.

"She delighted in bringing estranged people together and she was a genius in ironing out marital troubles. She was a rare combination of good sense and spirituality. It was this object lesson that founded my belief and trust in God and His goodness."

As John later described himself, he was not a bad boy. His mother unobtrusively influenced the direction of his associations and he naturally disliked sneaks and dirty-minded boys. Nevertheless, as he grew older he achieved a somewhat dubious distinction in the sissy circles which customarily shape the attitudes of small-town people. It was not that he was vicious but that he was over-venturesome. The old cats constantly criticized his mother for letting him stray too far away from her apron strings. Eventually they settled the subject as far as he was concerned by deciding that he would inevitably come to a bad end. He managed to survive a series of minor adventures which they did not consider to be desirable experiences for their own little Lord Fauntleroys. Their overall verdict was that since he apparently could not be drowned, he certainly must have been "born to be hanged!"

As far back as he could recall, water in wide reaches or in turmoil had always exerted over him a relentless fascination. Unfailingly, he wanted to be either on it or in it. He learned to swim by falling into the water from the slimy cribbing of a dock. Not more than seven at the time, he was exploring at low tide. He recalled that he was scared but not terrified as he should have been if water in the large had been an unknown quantity. Otherwise his story would have ended then and there for terror smothers action. But he did what the puppy dog does when his feet will not reach bottom — kicked his feet and flailed with his arms until the current swung him in to where he could grasp a timber. After he got to shore he divested himself of his clothes, laid them on the sand to dry in the sun and waded in over his head to try it over again. His mother could not believe that he had learned to swim until he had demonstrated in her presence.

One Winter he was overboard eight times and he had to swim for it each time in order to save his life. This was in the neighborhood of Wilmington, Delaware, where he attended the old Rugby Military Academy. The Baltimore & Ohio Railroad was building a high bridge over the Brandywine. Timber false-work had been erected from the bed of the stream to support the construction of a steel span 110 feet above the water, and the boys delighted to swarm over the false-work like monkeys. At times they would race to see which one would be the first to climb from the bottom to the top and vice versa.

Then came a day in the late Winter when a coastal low of unusual proportions produced an exceptionally heavy rainfall. The steel span had been completed except for the bolts at one end, but the riveters had left at night without finishing tying it in. Sometime in the night the ice in the creek broke up and jammed against the false-work, and the downpouring torrent carried the timbers away along with the steel. When morning came there was no bridge — nothing left to show for the months of labor the builders had expended. Burnham never found out why the contractor did not work a night shift to put in the few bolts needed to insure the safety of the steel work, and the incident forever after appealed to him as a dramatic example of lack of human foresight. Be that as it may, the oversight also paved the way for one of the thrills of his lifetime — and very nearly the final thrill for the venturesome lads.

That memorable day was a Saturday. The boys got the news before breakfast and though it was still raining in a subdued way, they gathered in force on the scene. With three other boys, his cousin John and himself, they walked on the railroad track to the edge of the void and peered over. They could see nothing in the raging waters below. The timbers, no doubt, had been carried to Delaware Bay by that time, but they could not understand why there was no sign of the fabricated steel work until they realized that the water almost reached the floor of the high suspension foot-bridge a short distance away, and the stream was everywhere over its banks and running with a deep current among the trees on the higher levels. The hill gorge was filled by an ominous roar that was an enticing challenge.

Close inspection showed that the fish-plates had not been fastened to one of the rails of the track that had run across the bridge, for this rail was straight-out ten or twelve feet beyond the supporting pier — straight and unbent above that alluring void. Frank Garrett dared the others to walk to the end, turn around and walk back; not a difficult feat if one ignored the space below. They all accomplished the stunt, but it was not so easy because each had to look down to make sure his next step would be on the rail. Finding nothing else worth-while to tackle at this level and drawn by the challenging roar of the water, the fifteen-year old lads gravitated down-hill and crossing the foot bridge arrived at Kilpatrick's near by, where Burnham kept a twelve-foot skiff. The boat had not been in the water for several months and leaked badly, but the cousins got a pair of oars and a paddle and headed out to cross the river. They wanted to look over the flotsam that had collected among the trees on the farther side to see if anything was salvageable.

This ordinarily still-water stretch above the fourth dam was by then no means placid. The volume of the freshet had turned it into wave-broken rapids. It required good seamanship to keep the boat from swamping. In midstream they heard shouts and looking up-river beheld a great mass of ice bearing down on them and reaching from shore to shore. A jam, which had formed higher up, had broken. In a jiffy it had caught the two boys and their boat was pinned by the ice, locked in hard and fast as if in a vise.

The youngsters did not need to be told that they were up against it for fair and that if they got out alive, it would be due solely to their own unassisted efforts. They could see the spume and the slather from the twelve-foot dam a few hundred yards below and knew that if the boat went over sideways it meant sure death. Burnham, at the oars, gave a strong heave in an attempt to turn the boat's bow, broke an oarlock and measured his length on the bottom of the boat. The skiff's position remained unchanged.

The situation demanded quick action. The water was in a hurry to get over the dam and be done with it. But there seemed to be no brilliant solution of the difficulty — at least the imperiled pair could think of none. However, they wasted no time in conference. Neither did they relive the events of their past lives. His cousin John slipped over the bow of the boat and proceeded to paw his way through the ice toward the timbered shore while Burnham, wanting to save his boat, made one last effort to turn her, intending to shoot the dam if he could get her head on. It was no use, however; the boat was locked fast so he, too, reluctantly took to the river.

Neither boy had taken the time required to strip off his coat — which was fortunate. The ice-cakes were honeycombed and rough and soon the skin was stripped from their wrists. Had it not been for the protection afforded by the coat-sleeves, their arms would have suffered likewise. The blocks among which they found themselves were more than a foot thick and of all sizes up to four or five feet across. The sole reason they were able to make progress among them was the fact that the cakes were in motion, rising and falling on the waves and, to a lesser extent, turning on their axes as a result of the friction of the shores. The lads did not attempt to dive under them for fear of not being able to force a way to the surface afterwards. At times, as the current drove the mass more closely together, the air was nearly squeezed from their lungs. It was punishing work but they were nerved by the knowledge that a dead-line time limit had been set. In just so many seconds they realized that they would be swept over the dam and ground to pulp on the rocks below by the tons of ice pouring over the barrier. In such situations the latent powers possessed by all humanity come into play: they drew on reservoirs of unsuspected strength.

The cousin gained the trees first. Burnham could see him hanging on to one of them and then letting go and making his way to another nearer the firm land of the hillside. By then men were running along the water's edge. Burnham could see that they carried ropes and that some were trying to throw one to his cousin. The first one fell short but soon after he was hauled safely to the shore.

Burnham reached for a tree trunk but an offset in the current threw him outward. Realizing that the wing of the dam on the inner side of the headgates to the raceway was deflecting and forcing the torrent to the river's channel, he redoubled his efforts.

He was filled with rage against the mercilessness of a mighty enemy but refused to be licked. It was not that he feared death, as he later explained it, nor was it really an escape. Just stubborn determination to conquer that gave him a second wind. Striking out with every ounce that he had, warmed by his efforts and with laboring lungs, he thrust the ice-cakes aside and behind.

As he saw the swirl that marked the location of the submerged headgates, he reached out as far as he could. The luck of those who refuse defeat was his for he caught the square edge of the outer timber and was swept in a semi-circle over the dam and around to the shelter behind. The next moment he had clambered up to the top of the headgates and, standing in water up to his waist, watched his boat go over. Down swooped a beautifully-modeled craft — but all that came to the surface were splinters of his treasured possession.

This hair-raising experience was presented in considerable detail, not only for its inherent interest but because it was a typical example of Burnham's courage, stamina, presence of mind and resourcefulness — qualities that he was to display many times during the course of his unusually eventful life.

# Chapter 2

## The Critical Years

Most men start lazy in the sense that they do not like set jobs. Industry and perseverance are acquired habits. Both are likely to be serious faults unless developed to last-ditch heroism and otherwise handled with intelligence. Every philosopher who ever lived has taught that the pursuit of success as an end is barren and destructive. It becomes merely a self-forged collar chained at the other end to something immovable. As Don Marquis said, "The bee, the beaver and the ant don't give up working 'cause they can't!" There is a happy medium between the self-imposed grind and a butterfly existence. Most people must work to live but, fortunately, if they first fit themselves for work, with a little courage they can make the opportunities to select the kinds of work they like. Instinctively Burnham knew all this, but like others he had a hard time getting started.

Burnham's own words aptly describe this stage of his life: "As a boy I had plenty of animal courage but craven desire to avoid trouble in the conflict with other minds. I always gave in to the boy who wanted to play marbles when I wanted to go in swimming. 'Aw, come on, the water's fine,' I would say — but we played marbles or did something else when every nerve in my body was tingling for the shock of the cool water, and I was dreaming of making a higher dive than I had the day before.

"I think I was fifteen before I realized that I had a mind of my own and made up the crude motto: The more I see of other fellows' ideas the better I like my own. Because I was not a physical coward, leadership had been thrust upon me in gang-fights with boys from other sections of town, but our bunch was regularly licked because I accepted the cautions of the more timid cohorts, who are always the most vociferous. Rough-and-tumble fighting is a great educator. Through it one learns that there is a limit to the time when he can lean on others, and that if he is to have any joy in himself he must cut loose and carry on in his own way. When the idea finally percolated we at once got the jump on "the muckers" and ran them all the way to their homes behind the Rising Sun Brewery."

Burnham's Military Academy classmates evidently recognized his leadership ability because he not only became colonel of the two companies but also their drill instructor on recommendation of the Regular Army officer who was leaving.

Continuing his recollections: "I have always been deficient in concentration. Old Professor Alcorn taught me at Rugby Military Academy, and it was the most valuable lesson I ever learned. He taught it at the expense of my knuckles and ears. Once he dragged me to the platform by one ear, meanwhile belaboring my knuckles with his hardwood ruler in retaliation for the kicks his shins were getting and when he had me there — if it had been a few feet farther he would have had only the ear — he set me up as a horrible example to the school as an incorrigible "wool gatherer."

"The ear had to be stitched on. Both it and its fellow, which had only less trying experiences at Alcorn's school, are bat-winged and serve to remind me of one of my weaknesses.

"At Trinity College the man who gave most help was Professor Johnson. If it had not been for Johnson my time in Trinity would have been wasted, because I was working my way through and my mind was occupied with material and unpleasant things. Aside from athletics and fraternity there was no glamor attached to my college days. The one thing I remember of Greek is the phrase "gnothi seauton," — know yourself. Of Latin the only undying memory is that I was given the opportunity to secure Mark Twain and Charles Dudley Warner as judges of a "prize-version declamation." Higher mathematics is a haze. But "Boohoo" Johnson in his English department was an inspiration.

"Johnson lived the life of his interests and forgot everything else. If ever there was a glorified "wool gatherer" it was he. I had to learn a lot about the virtue of concentration and the glory of keeping one's nose to the grindstone no matter how it hurt. Johnson taught us the love of life for the beauty that is in it. Above all he hated sophistication. The simplest tale of heroism would bring a mist to his eyes, and he would stand for ten minutes in the middle of Vernon Street, forgetful of all else except his enjoyment of a fine sunset. He was firm in his own convictions but he taught us when uncertain to try it out on the dog — to consult others before giving final expression. 'Maybe you will find you are wrong,' he said, 'but if you are right you will be more sure of the fact and in a position to hold your ground against all Hell.'"

Burnham had to be very frugal while attending Trinity because his father's early death from tuberculosis had left the family with large expenses and an appreciably diminished income. He met the challenge by full use of his resourcefulness and perseverance, qualities which he displayed continually throughout his later life. While the literary lights among the students were engrossed with French versification and other forms of artificial expression

*V R (Wolcott) Ranch near Rawlins (Courtesy of the University of Wyoming)*

*Corral of V R Ranch (Courtesy of the University of Wyoming)*

and therefore had no time to gather college news, Burnham took advantage of this opportunity by becoming the business manager of *The Tablet*. By hard work he built up the advertising revenue until it rivaled that of the prestigious *Harvard Crimson*.

Since the manager of such a publication is entitled to a sizeable share of the ad income, the enterprising Burnham was some $1,500 to the good at the end of his sophomore year and, while still finding time for athletics and fraternity life during the remaining two years, he graduated with honors in English and $900 in his pocket.

He also carried away a profound disgust for that element always found in collegians who cannot get over their college days. "Sentiment is only worthwhile when unselfish. The man who grows lachrymose over his college because of his part in it is just about as valuable to the world as the fellow who prides himself on his descent from a family who never worked."

In 1886, when he was seventeen and summering on the V.R. Ranch in southeastern Wyoming, a place which later became famous as the locale of Owen Wister's *The Virginian*, Burnham was hired to supply the entire ranch, which at round-up time numbered more than 75, with wild meat worth about .05¢ per pound or a couple of cartridges. Only once was it necessary to butcher a beef, which brought comparatively high prices on the Chicago market. On one of his hunting trips, accompanied by an old frontiersman, he had the opportunity to kill one of the last buffalo then left of the 60 million or so which had once roamed the prairies.

As they stalked the lone cow and soon got within point-blank range, the old-timer kept urging him to shoot. Up to this time the boy had never heard of a game law, but he still had no hankering to kill merely for the sake of being able to say that he had once shot a buffalo. He then asked his companion if the meat could be used and if the head and hide were worth saving. The old hunter replied that the animal was worthless for either of those purposes but characteristically remarked, "You'd better kill 'er, boy, 'cause it's the last chance you'll ever git to shoot a buffaler!"

The boy, who had not yet heard of conservation in the modern sense, nevertheless refused to kill the shaggy old creature. Later he sold his account of the trip, his first long article, to *Forest and Stream*....

In the six years of his first sojourn in New York City he learned all he wanted to about hard work. He started at 22 as an office boy on a salary of five dollars per week, but after a month's delivering of fire insurance policies in strange rookeries in the caverns of the lower city, he struck another job that paid $15.00 a week. This was with *Forest and Stream,* the greatest journal of hunting and fishing and outdoor sport of its day. He could have enjoyed life even in the City if his work had been more closely allied with the objectives of the magazine but he had been hired, on probation, to get advertisements. If he had not been in love he later declared that he would have either tried to get on the other part of the staff at a cut in wages or resigned then and there; but he knew the only chance he had to draw down $20.00 soon and so inveigle his fiancee Peggy to share his poverty was in the business end. Men who can sell tooth-paste or advertising space always get into the money more quickly than those in literary or pro-lines. Moreover, he had experience in his work and had brazenly boasted of his ability to "get business," so he was given the opportunity to demonstrate.

Love, laziness and pride alone kept Burnham at the job. Sometimes it required all three combined to keep him from sneaking away and finding a hole into which he could crawl.

The City was strange to him and inhumanly hard-boiled. At that time, the petty advertising solicitor was considered an unmitigated nuisance. In the country a book agent generally got a hearing and often a kind word if not a sale but, in the city, life seemed too short to waste precious time on such undesirables. He did not want to be found loafing in the office, which was then in an old building at 318 Broadway, across the street from the Remington Arms headquarters. Therefore, after a particularly cutting rebuff he would make his way to the slips of Fulton Market and sit on a string-piece of a dock, trying to get back his courage to approach another prospect with a grin on his face to hide the whipped feeling inside. He could get pleasure from watching the fishing boats, their plucky crews and their silvery cargoes.

The first month he escaped being fired by landing an eight-dollar advertisement from a little fellow who was almost as unsophisticated as himself.

George Bird Grinnell and E. R. Wilbur owned *Forest and Stream.* The former was the leading conservationist of his day. He founded the first Audubon Society and personally financed it. Burnham remembered Grinnell's surprise one day on receiving a contribution for the Society and his haste to return it to the donor. Dr. Grinnell used his journal to promote conservation, an entirely new thing in those days. He knew intimately the Rocky Mountain tribes and was their blood brother and powerful friend. Glacier and other National Parks came into being through his initiative. But he disliked business and therefore the new employee's contact was with E. R. Wilbur, the treasurer, a stern, uncompromising personality who never overlooked errors or accepted excuses. But he was a keen business man and in his way honorable. From him Burnham had invaluable training. He was a hard and sarcastic master who demanded results, not explanations. No one could get in a second sentence with him if it had to do with explaining a failure.

One day Burnham learned that H. C. Squire, proprietor of a sporting goods store on Cortlandt Street, had withdrawn his advertisement from *Forest and Stream* because of Wilbur's insistence that his bill should not run longer than thirty days. Angry with Wilbur's method of enforcing the decree, Squire had taken the Greenier gun with him, the two accounts amounting to eleven hundred dollars.

Burnham asked for the chance to retrieve the account, but Mr. Wilbur scoffed at him. All that day he fretted about the matter, every little while asking if anything had been heard from Rufus Peckham, the experienced and diplomatic solicitor on the staff who was on a mission among the gun manufacturers of Connecticut. The office failed to get in touch with Peckham and the next morning, after using all his stock of persuasion, Burnham received Mr. Wilbur's reluctant permission to try his hand at the problem of bringing the lost sheep back to the fold — on condition that he would not mess things up, so that when Peckham returned he could complete the job.

Burnham called on Mr. Squire at his place of business immediately. It was then ten in the morning, but despite the fact that his clerks were idle he was waiting on a customer. As soon as the customer left Burnham introduced himself as the representative of *Forest and Stream,* which gave Mr. Squire an opportunity to tell him in picturesque and uncomplimentary terms just what he thought of Wilbur. After he had freed his mind of this weighty subject, he told his visitor to run along as he had irrevocably decided that the name of H. C. Squire would never again appear in the pages of *Forest and Stream*.

Burnham was desperate, however, so he did not run along. When Squire returned from lunch and found Burnham still there, he threw several rhetorical fits and would have got a cop to bounce him had he been able to think of a good charge to prefer against him in Police Court. In the meantime Burnham had goaded his sluggish mind until an idea had evolved. He asked Mr. Squire if his contract for the Greenier gun agency in the United States had not included the amount and character of the advertising he was to place in the leading magazines devoted to sport, and if so would not the British manufacturers of the gun want to know why he had dropped the renowned publication? "Will you tell them," Burnham asked, "that you do not pay your bills on time?" Squire looked at him as though he had seen him for the first time, and he seemed to be genuinely surprised that Burnham had developed a business idea. At no time did he admit any possibility that the agency might be lost, but just before closing his store the pesky Burnham asked him what time he arrived in the morning. That did it. Squire turned on him in a fury and said he could not possibly endure another day like this, and that he would renew the contract if the pest agreed to stay away.

Mr. Wilbur was so worried over Burnham's continued absence that he remained late at the office. When the belated one brought back the eleven-hundred-dollar contract he nearly dropped dead. Before he recovered from the shock the young man told him that a raise in his salary from $15 to $20 per week only totaled $250 per annum, which was a reasonable commission on a difficult piece of work. And he agreed and on the strength of this Burnham got married.

Versatile and outstanding as John Burnham was, his wife — Henrietta Haines Du Bois Burnham — was also remarkably gifted. The sixth of eight children she was born on July 7, 1861 in Chillicothe, Ohio to George Washington DuBois, D.D., and his wife, Maria Coxe McIlvane, whose father was the Right Reverend Charles Pettit McIlvane, second Episcopal bishop of Ohio and a president of Kenyon College.

Henrietta was named after a cousin, Henrietta Haines, a daughter of a governor of New Jersey. Since she did not like the two given names and as she was sixth in direct descent from Col. Caleb Heathcote (1666-1720), early mayor of New York, Lord of the Manor of Scarsdale, ardent churchman and the man largely responsible for the establishment of famed Trinity Church, Henrietta substituted his distinguished name for that of Haines.

During the Civil War her father served as chaplain (rank of captain) with the 11th Ohio Regiment. Subsequently he was the Episcopal priest in twelve or more parishes before

*Rev. George DuBois D.D.*

*Henrietta DuBois Burnham (right) and her sister.*

becoming Canon of the Cathedral in Faribault, Minnesota in 1869. He had that post until 1878 besides being a missionary to the Chippewa Indians at Leech Lake.

One of Mrs. Burnham's oft-repeated stories was that in Winter the Indians, who furnished most of the family food, always brought the milk frozen either on a slab of birchbark or in a birchbark pail. Maple sugar or syrup served as the sweetener and using these two ideas, she invented a rather special candy.

Years later, just prior to her marriage, she wanted to give her groom a cash present and, since she had already spent the money earned from selling her paintings on her education, she decided to market her candy. The enterprise was so successful that she was able to make her husband a gift of several hundred dollars.

From early childhood she and the other DuBois children were fond of drawing and sketching. Her first formal instruction was during the summer of 1879, when she was vacationing near Ogdensburg on the St. Lawrence river. While at Cooper Union in 1883 she was awarded a medal for her work. Her artistic ability was further developed in Keene Valley, where members of the Summer colony of famous painters expressed interest and offered advice — particularly the renowned Robert Minor.

Of even more assistance was Abbott Thayer, with whose family she lived for a time in Woodstock, N.Y. His favorite pupil, he rated her as the most promising female artist in America. Before long her best-liked subject became trees — usually done in oils and invariably dominating the landscape. J. P. Morgan, Senior, who bought one of her paintings, was so fond of it that, taken to each of his residences, it was ordered to be hung opposite his seat in the dining room. Some of her best work was done on Long Island at Babylon and Mastic, while others were painted near Rye-on-the-Sound.

Her father's first trip to Keene Heights, now known as St. Hubert's and the Adirondack Mountain Reserve, was sometime prior to 1885. There he bought property and built the two Felsenheim cottages, an observatory, a studio for Henrietta and All Souls, his private

*Dr. DuBois at the gate of Felsenheim, St. Hubert's, Keene Valley, N.Y.*

chapel. A competent amateur astronomer with at least one patent he was also a published genealogist.

John Burnham, a friend of the DuBois family, while still in Rugby Military Academy, came to the lovely valley in 1885 and fell in love with the incomparable Marcy-Ausable region as well as with Henrietta. Right after his graduation from Trinity College in 1891 they were married by her father in his hillside sanctuary.

In the early 1890's, when John Burnham was associate editor for *Forest and Stream* both he and his wife were its featured illustrators. Both became honored members of the National Arts Club, to which prestigious organization she was elected on the supposition that the initials on her work were those of her brother Harry, but her ability and charm soon convinced the committee of the soundness of their selection.

Besides being an accomplished artist Mrs. Burnham was also an exceptional horse-woman — sidesaddle or astride. When her son Koert was a baby his daytime cradle was a saddlebag and, until he was strong enough to hold onto her, he rode in one. The other, the balancing bag, contained mail and groceries.

Undoubtedly her most spectacular feat — and the one of which she was the proudest — was holding a tea service on her fingertips while putting her steed through its five or six gaits. The amazed spectators thought that the service items must of course have been glued in place when they saw that scarcely a drop of cream or a pinch of sugar was ever spilled....

Burnham's active work in conservation had begun when he joined the staff of *Forest and Stream* in 1891. Besides semi-free-lancing as a newspaper reporter, artist and photographer in New York, Burnham served as associate editor, illustrator and business manager of the famous weekly periodical until his first trip to Alaska and the Klondike in August, 1897. The publication had already acquired a splendid reputation for its record in game protection. Many of the principles of wildlife conservation which are now considered orthodox were first proposed by *Forest and Stream*.

*Burnham's Office at Forest & Stream, N.Y.C.*

While there John Burnham wrote many articles on game protection and also for several years published annual reports dealing with American game preserves. Incidentally, he is credited with being the first person to advocate the idea of a buffalo census.

Such a work load meant almost total commitment for the eager young man who had not yet learned the limitations of physical strength. The wine of success was in itself a spur for increased effort. He worked many evenings and then took business to bed with him. Three children added to their joys and also their cares. He got grippe one winter and had six recurrences of it in rapid succession, but did not lose a day from the office. He survived, but only by paying the penalty in the form of shattered senses and sleepless nights. Their maid diagnosed his condition as nervous "prosperation." Burnham was rapidly reaching the point where living hardly seemed worth the effort, and he considered himself a burden to his wife and children. Moreover, since he providently had enough insurance to tide them over temporarily, he seriously felt that they would be far better off without him.

His perceptive wife, while deeply sympathetic, knew her husband's nature and rightly suggested the unfailing remedy: the spiritual and physical therapy provided by wilderness scenery and a complete change of pace.

"But what shall I do and where shall I go?" he asked.

"Anything, but by all means do something drastic! What's going on?" she inquired.

"The Klondike Gold Rush is the biggest thing, I guess."

"Well, what are you waiting for?"

Very shortly afterward Burnham was on his way to Alaska, where he joined the first thousand eager Argonauts jammed together on the narrow mudflats of Skagway.

# Part II

## The Klondike Gold Rush

*Although the 19th century had already experienced three greater gold rushes — in California, Australia and South Africa — none of them shook the world as dramatically as did the 1897-1898 Klondike stampede. While the other international spectaculars produced more gold and attracted more men, none could come close to matching the traumatic frenzy created by the gigantic gold-brick scheme which infected and affected the minds and imaginations of the entire continent — and the rest of the world as well.*

*Even during Russian occupation days in Alaska it was well known that there was considerable gold in the basin of the Upper Yukon, but at that time fur-trading was considered to be of more available and predictable importance. By 1879 a few hundred prospectors had filtered in and were diligently combing the region but it was not until that fateful August 17, 1896 when George W. Carmack, the drifter squawman and his Indian in-laws — Skookum Jim and Tagish Charley — hit the eventual 3 million-dollar jackpot on Rabbit, later and aptly called Bonanza Creek, near Dawson.*

*Understandably the prospectors already in the area immediately flocked to the scene, staked the productive claims and some struck it rich, but it was not until the following July, when the returning fortunate Argonauts reached Portland and San Francisco with more than three tons of dust and nuggets, that the world went wild with gold fever. Before the contagion was over — a little more than a year later — nearly 35,000 ill-equipped Klondikers swarmed over the stormy Chilkoot and White Passes or crammed themselves, their cattle and their gear into scarcely seaworthy steamers and assorted floating tubs for the lengthy, dangerous all-water trip up the Yukon via St. Michael.*

*The gold-seekers didn't have much choice of overland routes to the Yukon headwaters because each was a formidable obstacle course. The White Pass option, while 600 feet lower than Chilkoot, was ten miles longer and even more precarious for horses and men because in many places it was extremely narrow, boulder-strewn and bog-pocked. The 35-mile Chilkoot trail featured an agonizingly slow, thousand-foot ordeal up a 35-degree slope which proved to be pure torture for the over-dressed, over-loaded and inexperienced gold-crazy men and women.*

*Before the Klondike fever had died down it was conservatively estimated that 50,000 participants had spent at least 1,000 dollars each — about half the production of all the Yukon goldfields. However, it is noteworthy that some of the claims proved to be the richest in mining history.*

*By 1932, the big dredging companies operating in the Canadian Klondike, on the Seward Peninsula and at Nome, Fairbanks, Circle, Iditerod etc., extracted a grand total of 321 million dollars in placer gold.*

*Nevertheless, the fact remains that about one in a hundred of the individual prospectors ever struck it even reasonably rich. The disillusioned others gained only a wealth of experience and memories that set them apart from other men for the rest of their lives.*

*Even though the Yukon encounter represented what must have been their sternest testing ground and personal highwater mark of excitement, relatively few of the deluded gold-seekers and finders had either the inclination or the ability to record their gripping* and sometimes gory experiences. John Burnham, however, drawing on his varied background as writer, associate editor and staff artist-photographer for Forest and Stream was well prepared to recount his eventful seven months in the Northland.

He also used his old diaries and letters to refresh his memory. Except for the publication of his Yukon Notes, a series of six articles which were published in Forest & Stream, he never actually finished writing up this segment of his life and was working on it right up to the time of his death in 1939.

Since his verbal and pictorial recollections constitute an obviously important contribution to American and Canadian history, it is with great pleasure that I present in the first person these highlight chapters of a fascinating, productive and distinguished career.

[The Editor]

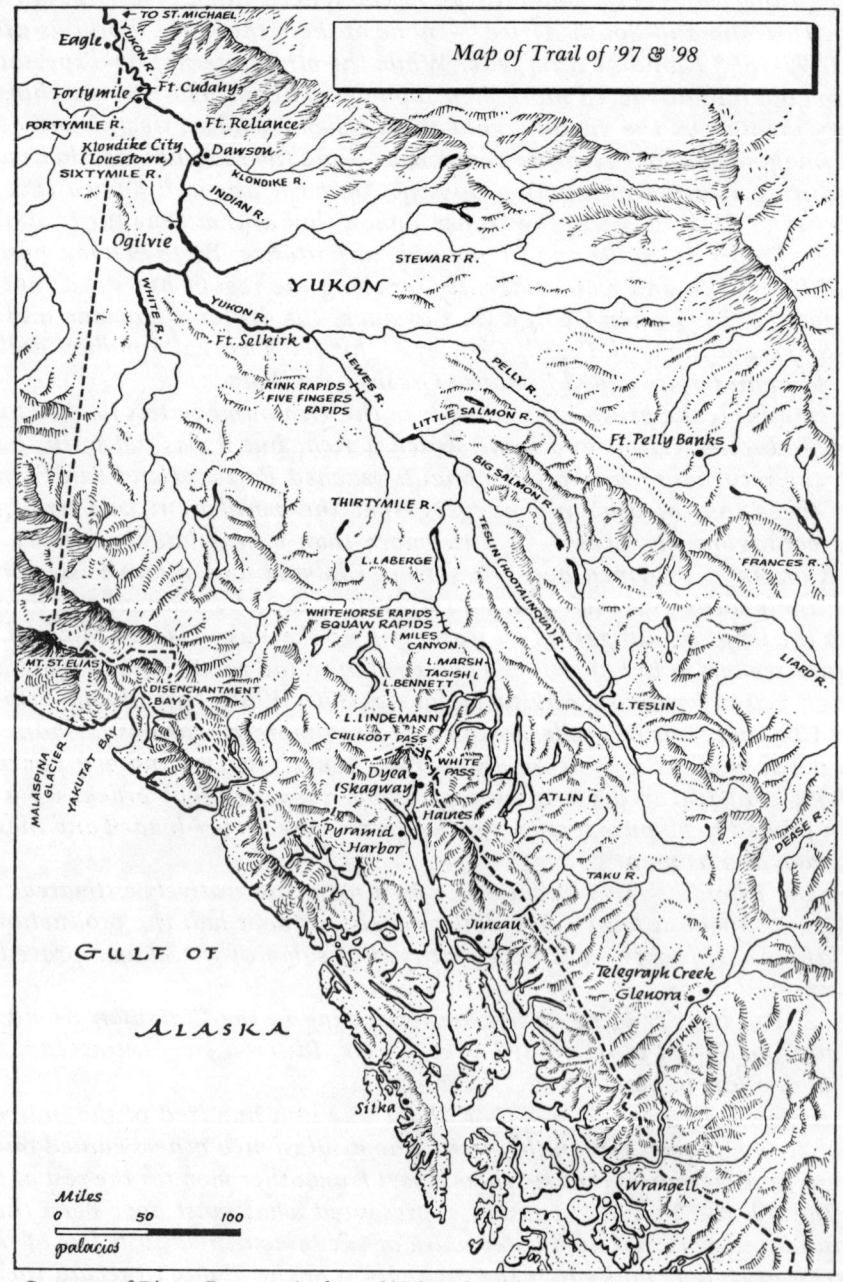

Courtesy of Pierre Berton, Author of "The Klondike Fever," Knopf, N.Y.C. 1967

# Chapter 3

## Skagway and the White Pass (Dead Horse) Trail to Summit Lake

Leaving war out of the reckoning, just about once in a lifetime there comes a great adventure which fires the mind of a nation. Canada had such an adventure in the quest for precious metals in her Northland, and I was determined to take advantage of it. The United States had it in '49 in the trek for gold in California, somewhat before my time, and in '97 came the Klondike Gold Rush. This one was for me. Primal instincts were stirred such as sent the Mongols westward to Europe, the Vikings to Vinland and the Phoenician sailors beyond the gates of the world — Gibraltar and Abyla.

Contradictory as it may seem, the main-spring of the Klondike Rush was not just the lust for riches, but rather the age-old urge for taking a fall out of Man's hereditary enemy as exemplified by the implacable forces of Nature. Men who were discharged in unending streams from sea-going vessels on the flats below Chilkoot and White Passes were bright-eyed for trouble. They knew they were up against a Herculean job before they could cross the mountains to the Promised Land, and that this land was shrouded with terror and guarded by genii of hunger and cold. But they were in a perverse mood and would have stormed Hell with equal joy. They did not know the geography of the country nor the first thing about their route — and seemingly they didn't care. It was of conflict they dreamed, not maps. They were sick of an ordered life and sick of hanging onto life just because it was life.

Many of them had never before slept in the open and few were provided with clothes suitable for the approaching winter, but nothing dashed their exuberant spirits. Their opportunity had come and it was a great adventure, a great gamble!

The Argonauts were landed by ship's boats in the glacial mud flats at the head of a hundred-mile-deep fjord like a new creation from an ark after the Old World had perished in the flood. It was just as new to them. They were mostly young, with a considerable percentage of college boys, though every class and condition was represented, from Negroes and Indians to pack peddlers, gamblers and divinity students. The only kind of men not there were the cautious men — the "Safety First" kind.

On August 3, 1897, when I was dumped from the steamer *"Islander"* on the Alaskan beach that afterwards became Skagway, I had no interest in the wild and rugged scenery of that fjord-head and only a feeling of antipathy for the gold seekers who thronged about. But I could not sit forever on a duffle bag in the rain. Soldiers talk more of the hardships of war than of its dangers, and similarly while I welcomed death I could not stand water running down the back of my neck. So I helped put up a tent and, once inside, realized for

*Steamer "Islander" at Skagway—
September 3, 1897*

*Skagway Harbor from "Islander"*

*The Beach at Skagway*

*Skagway*

the first time in a long while that I was actually hungry. The keen air from the sea and from the snow-clad mountain tops and the glaciers between them was already working and I was kicked into doing things to supply my bodily wants.

The next thing I realized was that one J. R. Smith,[1] who claimed to be a U.S. marshal, had annexed this part of Alaska for himself and his pocketbook. It was not as primitive a country as we had thought. Smith had husky guards on the beach who searched our dunnage and, when the inevitable whiskey was found, notified us to appear at the "Marshal's" headquarters uptown.

Jefferson R. held court in a frame building, the only such shelter as yet erected, the balance of the population being housed in tents. It looked like a country district schoolhouse both inside and out. When I got there the building was jammed with prospective Klondikers, all anxious to know what had become of their liquor. The only chairs, which were on the platform, were occupied by the "Marshal" and a few of his friends, who sat there passing the time of day and paying no attention whatever to the rest of us, who were classed by the generic term of "Miners."

Looking around, I saw the man who had told me I was under arrest circulating among the crowd. He would talk impressively with someone for a minute or two and then the man would give him some money, which went into a fat billfold and, when this had been restored to his hip pocket, he would circulate some more. I saw some of the victims paying the collector as much as fifty dollars, so when he reached me and, after a short scouting, told me mine would be twenty dollars, I made no delay in paying. As he was turning away, I put my hand on his arm and asked when I would get my whiskey back. He gave me a fishy look as he replied. "Never, son, never! This is Injun country; you have violated the territorial law!"

When the last dollar had been given up and Smith adjourned court, we walked back to the beach. Every other tent on both sides of the street was a saloon in full blast. We had to buy our whiskey back at the rate of .50¢ a drink, but this was cheap compared with prices down-river. We were being broken gently to the primitive law that might makes right. Later on the lesson proved of value to many of us.

Even here, however, Smith had to do something to save his face. Each Monday night, by schedule, he raided the saloons and it got to be monotonous to see the colored water dumped in the street. Saloon-men paid for protection and the suckers paid the so-called fines and also furnished the whiskey. It was a profitable game as long as it lasted.

Our experience was at Skagway, which was said to be the gateway to White Pass. At Dyea, on the Chilkoot Route five miles away, no doubt things were the same. In his short day Jefferson R. Smith flourished like a green tree.

When we landed, no one had yet been able to find White Pass. There was a legend that an Indian had told someone who had told somebody else that there was an easy route here across the mountains to the headwaters of the Yukon River. This route was said to be passable for horses, and so everyone who had brought pack-horses, including myself, had our horses dumped into the sea to swim ashore at Skagway, rather than at Dyea, because it was well-known that nothing short of a goat could negotiate Chilkoot.

Later we found that the information about White Pass had been press-agented by a promoter who was trying to sell a prospective railroad and who desired to get free advertising

---

[1] Jefferson R. Smith, the infamous "Soapy," landed at Dyea in 1897 and quickly made himself the leader of a band of nearly 300 assorted crooks, cardsharps and cutthroats unequaled since vigilante days in Virginia City. An ingratiating, hale-fellow well-met type, descended from a prominent Georgia family and very generous with stolen money, he completely dominated both Dyea and Skagway as well as the White and Chilkoot Pass trails as far as the uncontrollable Canadian summit boundary. His reign of intimidation and terror ended abruptly and violently in a bloody showdown with town-surveyor and ex-Indian fighter Frank H. Reid only four days after the self-appointed Colonel had presided over the July 4, 1897 celebration.

*Jefferson R. (Soapy) Smith*

*"Soapy" Smith's saloon*

*Skagway River and Start of White Pass Trail*

*Loading a Pack Horse*

for his scheme.[1] There was a trail for five miles up the Skagway River, but after that it degenerated from bad to worse until it finally ran up a tree and ended in a knot-hole. Three thousand of us worked making a trail to Lake Bennett on the Yukon, but before it was completed its fifty-mile length was corduroyed with the bodies of dead horses and enough profanity had been released to pave a road to Hell and back again.

The first part of the way we made the road as we went along. If one man got into a hole he could not get out of the others went around him. We followed the river up, fording it when we came to precipices on one side we could not get around and keeping up the other side till we got trapped again. But finally the river went the wrong way to oblige a dissolute glacier and we were obliged to climb up through the cul-de-sac of mountains which hemmed us in, and do what we would, could not get out of White Horse Gulch. It was then that the New York *World* came to the relief of the pack. Otherwise we might have left our bones with the dead horses in the Gulch.

Pulitzer really did a mighty fine thing. With horse-shoe nails costing a dollar each and oats eighty dollars a sack, everybody was strapped, and we could have no more purchased powder and drills to do the necessary blasting than we could have financed a first mortgage on the Empire State Building in New York. Pulitzer sent us the drills and dynamite. A Miner's meeting was held and laws to cover the situation enacted. Each party was to stay where it was camped even if the horses starved, and each was to give eighty percent of its strength to the work of trail building. Certain men were selected as police on the basis of owning rifles and knowing how to use them. These officers were instructed to shoot to kill in case of any infraction of the law. Some that I ran up against gave every indication of having uneasy trigger fingers.

We had five men in our party and one had to remain in camp to look after the horses. I was anxious to find out what lay ahead after we got out of the Gulch. Eighty percent of five men is four men which, minus the camp guardian, is three; but I decided to go ahead on the basis that I was worth more as a pathfinder than a pick and shovel man. It was too important a matter to quibble over.

In the morning I put a sandwich in my shirt and walked up to the foreman of the first gang above our camp and asked for a job. I got as far in front as possible and, when no one was looking my way, I dropped my tool and advanced to the next gang. The plan worked rapidly until I came up with a group of hard-rock miners, old-timers from Aspen, Colorado, who had just finished drilling a set of holes in boulders high up on the Hog Back and were about to start a new set lower down. They gave me the job of packing a fifty-pound case of dynamite to the holes already drilled and as an after-thought instructed me to shoot them. I had never seen a blast set off, but they said it was easy, as it proved to be; and they gave me fuse, exploders and a tin can to dip up the all-too-abundant water and pour it into the holes, after loading, for tamping. "And don't you slip, buddy," said one of them, "because if you do, you're apt to land that box of powder on us!"

I cut my fuses different lengths and lighted the longest first and set off four or five shots at a time, first yelling "Fire," at the top of my lungs. I was so interested in the work that I forgot the real reason for my trip, with the result that darkness overtook me long before the summit came in sight. I ate my sandwich and camped beneath the boughs of the last tree at timber line. This was a scrubby fir with branches clear to the ground like the feathers on ptarmigan's legs. It sleeted or rained all night and the temperature was about the freezing point. Just above me was a great snow-bank. I had no blanket and no fire but I

---

[1] The White Pass and Yukon Railway — Michael Heney, chief engineer — extending 111 miles from Skagway to Whitehorse below the rapids, was funded by Canadian capitalists and completed in early 1900.

slept soundly. There was a lot of litter about the base of the tree which made a fairly soft couch and the drooping evergreen boughs shed most of the rain. But the main thing that made it possible to get a refreshing rest was the fact that I had grown accustomed to living in the open and had acquired the art of sleeping when cold. Also I was dog-tired and had a peaceful mind.

I was up next morning as soon as it was light enough to see and in an hour's time had reached the head of a narrow lake at the point where now stand the coal-sheds of the White Pass Railroad. I felt sure I had surmounted the divide because I could see the Tooshi Mountains, blue in the distance, to the north and the land appeared, on the whole, to drop in that direction. I therefore called the lake Summit Lake, a name which it bears today.

Traveling along the east side of the lake six miles, I came to its end, but two miles farther on the way was blocked by a broader lake, to which later I gave the name Middle Lake. Going around the south and west sides of this lake, I found where it discharged through a considerably rocky stream into what we called Shallow Lake which, having forded the stream, I followed two miles to a point where I became convinced this watershed would have to be abandoned for a course more to the westward. In that direction the flanking mountains ended and there was a broad, tree-less, beaver-meadow plain for many miles before it was blocked by mountains. This gave the opportunity to strike west to intercept the Chilkoot trail in the neighborhood of Lake Lindeman, or Bennett, whereas the outlet of Shallow Lake, from where I stood, seemed to run by the easterly side of the Tooshi Mountains.

I was certain I had come far enough, and that, aside from the boggy character of the ground, there were no further obstacles to block our passage to the Yukon.

I had a short-barreled, .38 caliber revolver in my pocket and all around were flocks of ptarmigan. It was the disease year for rabbits, and none were to be seen, or otherwise I could have gotten food more easily. The ptarmigan were more wary than in Winter and I fired half my ammunition before I hit a bird. The ptarmigan took a short flight and fell dead in a glacial pot-hole with ten feet of water in it. At first I thought of taking off my clothes and swimming for it, but then a better idea came and I began tossing stones beyond it. At each resulting wave the bird floated nearer and, before long, it drifted to my feet. I had the feathers off in a jiffy but I had trouble to find sufficient roots to make a fire to broil it. One can eat a grouse without missing salt for seasoning, just as he can enjoy the liver from a big-game animal. Other meat tastes very flat without salt. One thing to remember about game killed this way is to cook it while still warm, or, if necessary, eat it raw. Otherwise, it soon becomes very tough and impossible to masticate. However, tough meat can be cut in pieces and swallowed as a dog bolts his food without producing indigestion. Other foods must be chewed but raw meat is so easily digested that chewing is not essential for the outdoor man.

I spent three days alone above timber line, before returning to camp on the Ocean side of the Pass. It was very still up there with little to break the breathless silence except the cackle of ptarmigan and the short whistle of the marmots.

Much of the time was devoted to laying out a trail which could be used by horses. I marked the trail by cairns of stones and led it by the easiest available grades to Summit Lake.

Just before the work was completed I was startled by the sight of a human being who had approached to within fifty feet without attracting attention because I was so deeply engrossed in my work. He was a man of large frame between sixty and seventy years of age,

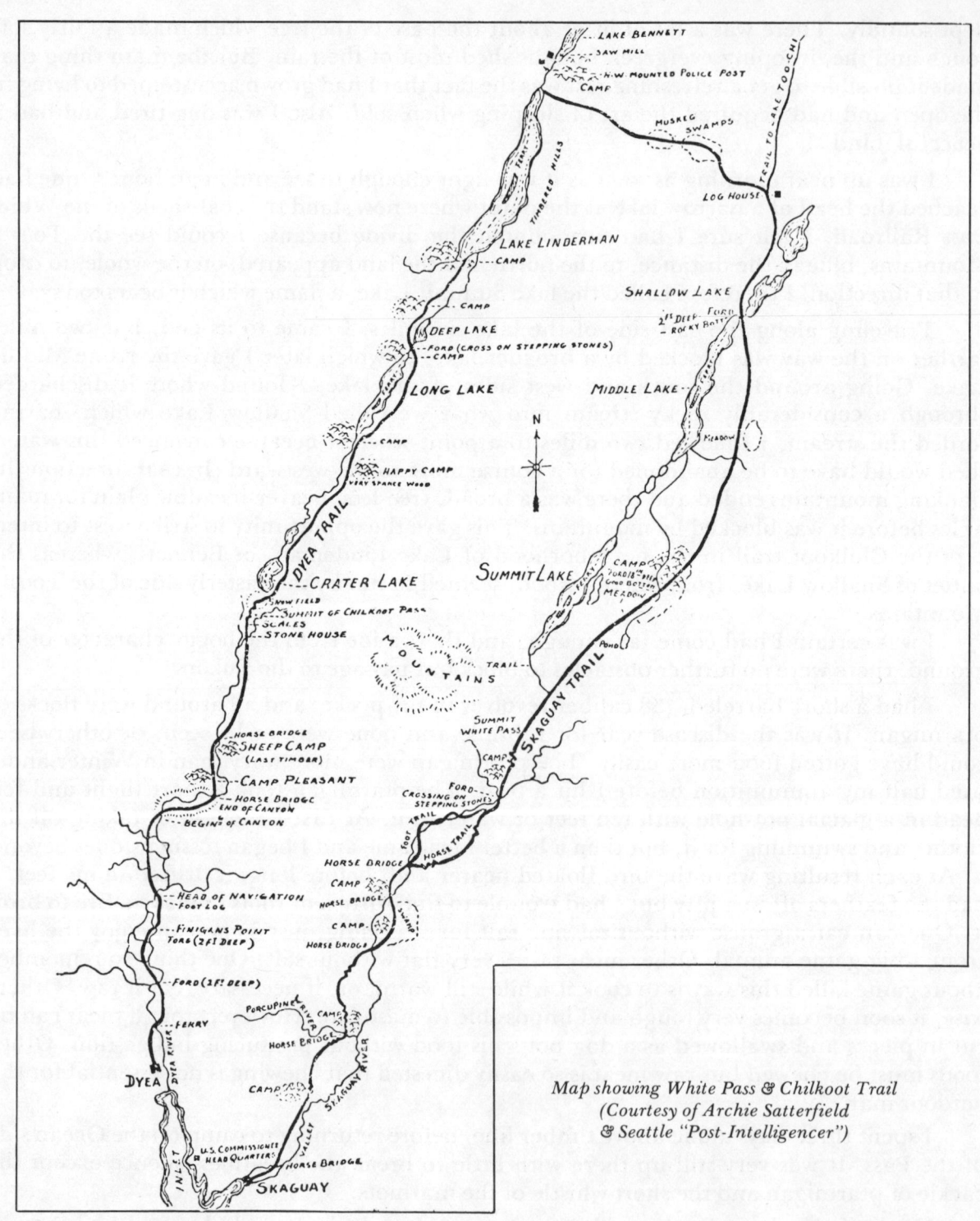

*Map showing White Pass & Chilkoot Trail
(Courtesy of Archie Satterfield
& Seattle "Post-Intelligencer")*

shaggy, grizzled, mackinaw-clad and evidently an old-timer. He told me his name was John Hepburn and asked what I was doing.

I explained that I was marking a horse trail and told Hepburn of the twelve miles of potential water travel and of a plan I had evolved to utilize it. At our camp behind we had six folding canvas boats which, while only twelve feet long, had sufficient beam and freeboard to float a load of half a ton. I intended bringing up two boats and, by rowing one and towing the second, would be able to transport fifteen hundred pounds of supplies at a trip, using horses only at the portage between Summit and Middle Lakes. Eight or ten pack-horse loads for that country at one time. The plan had the further advantage that it would materially shorten the time the horses had to be kept above the timber line, where conditions were bad for them.

Hepburn set to and helped me erect the last markers. As we worked our way back over the Pass, he told me he had followed gold rushes for years, including Omenacre, Caribou and Cassiar, and that he had made money and did not need to work, but had joined the Klondike Rush because he could not stay home when anything like this was going on. He figured it would be worth a dollar a pound to boat supplies across the lakes and, before we parted, had made up his mind to hire men at Skagway to whipsaw lumber and carry it to the summit for the construction of a fleet of scows. He put the plan into effect and he and I were, for weeks afterward, the boat-freighters in the Pass.

During my absence the trail had been completed from the Gulch on up the Hog Back Mountain, and I soon met the advance of the miners with their pack-trains. I talked with each party and informed them of what lay ahead. To each I made the offer to boat their supplies across the lakes on a trade basis. Summit Lake could be reached in a day from our camp, and I told them that for every pound of our supplies they packed there I would take an equal amount of theirs across the lakes. The plan worked and our packing capacity on many days was doubled.

Our party included an ex-foreman and Donald McKercher, a Canadian farmer's son who had just graduated from Toronto University. It was merely a set of acquaintants picked up on the trans-continental train. We had no partnership agreement. The understanding was that, while we hung together, each man would do his share of the work, but that when any man wished to strike out for himself he was free to do so. It was highly primitive but it worked. Each man naturally did the thing for which he was best adapted. The sales manager had a liking for horses and understood them and he rubbed them down at night, fed and humored them and also tended camp; while the rest of us carried on the trail work.

I had learned packing in Wyoming as a boy in 1886 and soon the other three caught on and we became fair wranglers. Despite the continuous rain on the Coast side of the Range we never had a horse with a sore back. In this we were an exception to ninety percent of the others.

All through August and September three thousand men and as many horses were packing on that "Trail of Agony and Dung," to paraphrase a trifle its unprintable title then in universal use. The men who did not understand packing and would not learn soon wrecked their horses. Approaching pack-trains could be smelled long before they could be seen. The poor animals' backs progressed from one set of sores to another until the flesh rotted away and only the bony frame-work supported the load. Such horses, naturally, wanted to lie down and die, but their inexperienced masters would not permit them the luxury. The men hated themselves for what they did, but grim necessity was in the saddle. They did not spare themselves anymore than they spared their horses. There was a task to be completed and they set their teeth to it. Seven nights in the week these mud and sweat-soaked Argonauts turned into soggy, wet blankets, unable to sleep for raw, cracked hands acquired in their jobs of packing. And seven mornings they got up stiff and sore and vengeful at the leaden skies, the mire and the cliffs that blocked their progress.

*Chilkat Indian Packers*

Occasional moments when the clouds lifted a scene of wild beauty was disclosed. Above the spruce and fir-clad valley of the Skagway River were noble mountains, suggestive of aspiration to untroubled minds, great snow banks and picturesque glaciers. This austere beauty was in stark contrast to the petulance of the thin line of human ants with their horses, toiling up the trail.

Mountain goats made snow-white dots on the rock slides just above the timber line and big bears were frequently encountered. Once, while packing a rifle, the clouds lifted and I saw two bears feeding on berries just across a deep ravine from the trail. I left our pack train and went after them. When I had reached their locality, I stopped and looked over the ground momentarily, expecting to get a shot.

Behind me I could smell that train of living death and I could plainly hear an unending stream of profanity. I knew that each bunch of six or eight horses was followed by a clean-up man with a club, and that any horse that faltered or fell out of line would get an unmerciful beating on the sorest part of its anatomy.

The bears were oblivious to the tainted air and the sounds from the men so near. Evidently they took it as a phase of the crudity of Nature and were as unmoved as the mountains. I did not add the touch of bloodlust to the picture, because just then a dense fog rolled over the place like night and I had to return to the trail.

One day I saw a suffering horse, to escape punishment, dodge into a tent, where a man was engaged in cooking. The tent came down on top of the horse and man and, when they pulled the tent off the wreckage, there stood the poor animal, head down and quivering in every muscle; a tragic picture of dejection. The leader of the outfit explained, "He's got this one more trip in him and, by the Almighty, he's going to make it!" But the horse knew better. Later in the day I saw this same man staggering along under the weight of that horse's pack. All three thousand horses died before Winter came, but the men lasted longer. However, of the thousands that started, only hundreds reached their objective.

*Rest Break on the White Pass Trail (Hegg photo)*

When I did not have a rifle with me, I always carried a .38 revolver and I became the un-official horse-killer of the trail. While the owners did not spare their horses, their cruelty was chiefly a matter of grievance and, strange as it may seem, many of the men developed strong affection for their animals. Frequently men who had asked me to kill horses down for the last time would turn their backs and even shed tears while the act of mercy was performed. It is easier to become inured to suffering than to face the finale.

The trail was so narrow that travel could not be carried on except in one direction at a time. In the morning the miners fell in line going towards the interior and advanced just as far in that direction as they could, or until the tide turned backward. Then they cached the loads and joined the returning procession. That was the idea but it received constant jolts. Even the stronger horses were continually falling down and blocking the trail. Their packs had to be taken off before they could be yanked to their feet, and often the tie-knot was under several feet of black mire. The rope amalgamated the slime into its substance and so it passed into men's hands, causing the flesh to crack and fester. Across the beaver-meadows to Linderman the top crust of the alluvial plain broke through, like rotten ice, and there was no bottom until the trail was filled with the bodies of dead horses. It was said that, finally, one could walk the entire fifty miles of the trail stepping from one dead horse to another. And then too, fool horses or their fool masters were continually bucking the tide of travel by coming in the wrong direction. When horses met on precipices, the weaker ones were pushed off and became carrion for the ravens.

One day, while fording a stream in the Log Cabin — Linderman stretch, one of our horses was carried by the current into deep water, floating on its side on account of the overbalancing of its pack, and unable to swim. The water was ice-cold but somebody had to get the horse and I jumped in and towed it to the bank. While the other men held on to the pack, I slacked and released the rope, having to dive under more than once to accomplish my object. Horse and I clambered up the bank together — in fact, I had hold of his tail —

*Tough Going*

*Porcupine Hill, notice dead horse underfoot.*

*A Cache on the Trail*

*The Dead Horse Trail — White Pass*

but that immersion resulted in the foundering and death of the animal while I never even caught cold. It was a horse in good condition and not the crow-bait of the trail.

The incident caused me to reflect that it was no great shakes to be "tough as a horse." As a matter of fact, horses are delicate animals, while men are the most tenacious of life of any of God's creatures. If a cat has nine lives, a man, by the same reasoning, has ninety-nine. The misery that one man can successfully endure would annihilate the whole of the rest of the kingdom!

*[Jack London vividly described the plight of the pack-horses on the White Pass route: "The horses died like mosquitoes in the first frost and from Skagway to Bennett they rotted in heaps. They died at the rocks, they were poisoned at the summit and they starved at the lakes. They fell off the trail — what there was of it — and they fell through it. In the river they drowned under their loads or were smashed to pieces against the boulders. They snapped their legs in the crevices and broke their backs falling backward with their packs.*

*"In the sloughs they sank from sight or smothered in the slime. They were disemboweled in the bogs where corduroy logs turned end-up in the mud. Men shot them, worked them to death, and when they were gone went back to the beach and bought more. Some did not bother to shoot them, stripping the saddles and shoes off and leaving them where they fell. Their hearts turned to stone — those which did not break — and they became beasts, the men of the Dead Horse trail."]*

The day following my return from the exploration trip we loaded four of our folding boats on two horses, feed on another, and supplies on the rest and started for Summit Lake, so that I would be able to start the boat-packing for the first animals. I led and Billy, the Cop, had charge of the white horse carrying the feed in the middle of the outfit; while Mac brought up the rear as clean-up man. We got to the head of the advance column shortly after noon, where the packers were shedding their loads preparatory to returning, with only my newly-marked trail beyond. Then, to our consternation, we found that we had lost Billy and his lead. I ran back a long way asking every outfit I met if they had seen Billy the Cop, who was well-known on the trail, but could learn nothing of his whereabouts. I figured that he had fallen behind at one of the numerous fords, which were broken up in many trails, and that he had lost sight of us. After I had gone two miles, however, I knew this could not be the case, because I had then reached a point where Billy had to be helped out of a minor trouble. So I returned to the head of the used trail, and there Mac and I held consultation. We decided it would be unwise to take the risk of weakening or losing our horses on the uncertain chance of catching up with the horsefeed for, if we failed, there was nothing in Nature, otherwise, the horses could profitably eat. Moreover, we had nothing for food for ourselves. As it was it would be long after dark before Mac could hope to get back to camp, but he was willing to handle the outfit alone. So it was decided that I should push on at once in an endeavor to head Billy off somewhere short of the Klondike — and, afterwards, carry the boats myself to Summit Lake. Neither of us wanted to lose another day in the pack-train schedule. Mac asked what I would do for food and I told him the lighter outfits would be arriving any day at Summit Lake and I would make them support me.

After parting from Mac I realized I was hungry and experienced some misgivings as to the wisdom of my plan. Pork and beans or whistleberries, as the latter were called, seemed much more attractive than half-raw ptarmigan and Alaskan woodchucks. Before I got very downhearted, however, I sighted a tent below my marked trail and, going to it, found a man inside baking bread. He told me he was cook for a survey party, which had just reached this point, making a reconnaissance of the Pass. I tried to buy some food but he said the party was short of supplies and he could not let me have anything. He had not seen a stray white horse with a man, but as I had found the track of a horse in my trail, I was not worried on this subject.

That man was not only baking but also cooking beans and dried fruit on the top of his light, sheet-iron Alaskan Stove, and no physiologist can tell me it is the taste of food alone that starts the gastric juice flowing! We argued the subject of a square meal 'til I got excited by his obstinacy and began thinking of the .38 in my pocket. I must have been telepathic and he read my mind, for after he had taken a careful look through the tent flaps to see that none of his party was near, he gave me a good-sized loaf of hot bread, and, after tucking this in my shirt front and parting with a dollar, I left. Outside I tore off large fragments of the bread and consumed half the loaf as I walked. I knew Billy would need the other half.

It was nearly dark next day when I spotted Billy coming at a snail's pace towards me. At his heels was the white horse, following like a very tired dog. There never was a more complete picture of woe. Billy's face was black with mud, except for vertical lines under his eyes, where the tears had cut twin channels. Ordinarily, Billy was a fine figure of six-foot manhood and he had been a star athlete, but his shoulders drooped in sympathy with the void in his digestive apparatus. His clothes were torn and filthy, his hair matted, and he had lost his hat. S.O.S. was written all over his face and figure and his horse was equally pathetic.

I gave Billy the bread and he sank down and wolfed it. I can see him now. I climbed a ledge above and, with my penknife, cut an armful of coarse grass, but the horse was too far gone to even sniff it. Grain and sawbuck alike had disappeared from the horses's back. Billy said he did not know how he passed us on the trail, but that it must have been at the last ford. He thought he had fallen behind and he speeded his efforts to catch up. He climbed higher and higher and over the crest of the Pass — with the old rhymes of "Excelsior" running in his tired mind, but he never came to the place where "The shades of night were falling fast....In happy homes he saw the light of household fires gleam warm and bright." He fell over the rock rim of a glacial tarn and dragged his horse with him. The horse had his back nearly broken and could not get up, so Billy and the horse lay there together in the mud and water until dawn. The balance of the time had been spent getting back.

We lay on the grass cut for the horse with some more added to it to complete the bed and, despite the cold and lack of fuel for a fire, slept soundly. In the morning the poor horse died and Billy and I walked down the trail to the place the boats were cached. Here we had two pieces of good luck: The first was a good meal with the Cunningham Brothers, a couple of big Irishmen who, lacking horses, were engaged in back-packing their supplies.

Billy had left for camp and I was standing by the boats figuring out a packing rig that would not be too much of a man-killer when they hove in sight, swinging along under loads of three fifty-pound sacks each which, as it happened, was the standard horse-load for the trail.

They stopped for a rest and a "visit" and, when I told them of twelve miles of water travel in the heights above, it first seemed to them a fairy story too good to be true.

One of the brothers sighed and remarked, "If we had the bacon we could have bacon and eggs if we had the eggs," which gave me a Yankee opportunity for a trade. "You have the beef which can do for bacon," I said, "and I have some eggs. Pack the four boats to the water and I will lend you two of them to carry your outfit across. That will give us all bacon and eggs."

*Packers in Sight of Summit of White Pass — August, 1897*

*Approaching Summit of White Pass Trail*

*Summit Lake Camp August, 1897*

*Camp at Deep Lake*

*Butchering Project*

*Whipsawing Boat Timbers*

# Chapter 4

## The Bennett Lake Ordeal and the Tricky Tagish Crossing

A day later, just as I finished putting the parts of the boats together, the first pack-train reached Summit Lake. This happened to be a party I had not notified, and they were a mean outfit and abusive. They did not like my idea of leading a trail to a blank end, as they called it, and the air was sulphurous for a time until the Cunninghams pitched in and threatened to throw the whole caboodle into the lake. After that we got down to cases and it ended by my getting $100 in gold to freight their supplies to the terminus at Shallow Lake, plus grub while the job was on. From that time on, until Winter blanketed the Pass, I was kept busy and never had to wait for a cargo. In fact, each time I returned to the head there would be several outfits bidding against each other for my services. I preferred the trade agreement to speed our supplies through but, if I could not get a party who would lend us their pack-train for a day, I took cash, which was increasingly useful to pay for horse-feed and the other expenses of our party. Our horses were re-shod constantly with shoes taken from dead horses, but horseshoe nails were hard to get and always high-priced. There were blacksmiths on the trail who charged ten dollars for shoeing, and they naturally frowned on competition.

Mac, who was now in charge of our pack-train, sent me up my sleeping bag. The weather on the inner side of the Coast Range was steadily growing colder and storms in the Pass developed in intensity. On the Ocean side there had been no marked fall in the temperature, due to the ameliorating influence of the warm Japan Current. At times the conflicts of the warm and cold currents became titanic, and we poor mortals suffered.

One morning I started from the head of Summit Lake in company with four of Hepburn's big freight scows, but my two boats were the only ones to get through. Two of the Hepburn scows were wrecked and the others storm-bound in coves. The return trip against the wind was the hardest piece of rowing I ever negotiated. The wind lashed the water to the fury of a cataract, and it was only by closely hugging the shore-line that any progress could be made. In the attempt to round one rock shoulder the boats were hurled back six times. The seventh attempt, however, was blessed by a momentary vacuum in the wind. As I rested in the partial shelter beyond, a golden-eyed duck on the water was tossed against the boat right by my hand. I caught it and threw it quickly into the boat and got my hand on the oar again just in time to prevent losing the position so hardly won.

The exhausted duck lay quite still, but every little while it emitted a mournful note that suggested the mew of a cat. I am ashamed to admit the fact but when the situation permitted I killed the duck and afterward ate it.

No one who has not experienced it knows how ravenously hungry a man becomes when he is living outdoors in cold weather and working to the limit of his strength. He lives to eat and thinks of little else.

I worked by no set schedule and, like a wild animal, ate and slept when chance favored me. The hardest part of the game was the return trip, because this was made without eating. Besides the twelve-mile row against the invariable head-winds, it involved eight miles of walking across the two-mile portage. Four of these miles were under the weight of seventy-pound boats, as I could not carry two at one trip. Naturally, I was ravenous by the time the head of Summit Lake was reached but, under my self-imposed terms, I could not eat until I had made a contract — including food — with a new party for freighting their goods. These parties were always in a hurry and if I did not get in contact with them at mealtime I had to defer eating.

One afternoon I started from the landing with a load thrown into my boats the moment they got to shore. I had not tasted food for twenty-four hours, but "rush" was the word if we were to beat the freeze-up and so I started. It was dark before I reached a cove where I knew there were some firs the size of the dwarfed trees of China and Japan. Unlike the potted trees, however, these hundred-year-old dwarfs had large roots and, being full of resin, the roots would burn. I quickly threw out a sack of flour and a side of bacon and started a fire. I mixed water with flour in a can with the aid of a little wooden paddle and then baked the dough on the paddle and ate it off before repeating the process, meanwhile broiling on skewers innumerable slices of bacon to be similarly annihilated. The night was as black as ebony. It was spitting snow from the wild heights above, but in the yellow glow of the fire I was warm with happiness and pleasure. There were no worries to mar the keen enjoyment of stowing away that delicious food!

I had to wait for the horses at the portage and fire several shots before the packers found the place in the dark, and it was afternoon the next day before the trip was completed. As I was throwing the fifty-pound packs out of the boats, I could not fail to notice the cook of the party was making preparations for dinner. The job completed, I sat down on a sack and waited. Some of the party were already loading their tin plates with food when the leader walked over to me and curtly said, "Here's your money." "I'm waiting for dinner." "Your job's finished. Get out!" The thought of the weary miles back to food enriched my vocabulary and I told him things about himself and his ancestry that cannot be repeated — and the skunk accepted it. It is only fair to say that such instances were of rare occurrence on the trail and exclusively confined to city-bred men.

I would leave the incident at this point were it not for the fact that truth compels me to state I did not make the trip back hungry. The Cunningham brothers had a tent at the short portage above Middle Lake and they had finished their dinner but, when I told them my story, they immediately started cooking another for me, meanwhile commenting on the depravity of human nature as a mother croons to her babe.

I had a fishhook in my hat and there were willows that would make fish-poles growing in hollows at Shallow Lake. The Cunninghams said that since they had erected their tent by the portage they had seen fish jumping in the black water just below where the wide stream fell over the last rocks and mingled with the lake. It carried them back to their boyhood days and they talked of the trout in the Shannon. Around the camps were scattered ptarmigan feathers and, with the aid of sewing thread, a fly was manufactured and I soon was whipping the pool while the brothers watched with an interest not to be denied. Those fish rose to the first cast, leaping clear of the water, but it was several minutes before I hooked one. Realizing that I was not allowing enough time, I slowed my action before setting the hook and at once was fast to a pound-and-a-half fish, which fought like a crazy thing, darting and leaping as if possessed before it was landed. It was iridescent and looked like a herring but, on account of its great dorsal fin, we decided the fish was a grayling. The Cunninghams had fished with bait for these grayling but without success. They were fly-crazy, however, and any number could be taken by this method of fishing.

On a later date one of the Cunninghams, using for bait part of the head of a marmot I had shot, caught with a handline a salmon-like trout at this place which it was estimated would weigh twenty-five pounds. It was in this same pool that later on the Mayor of Seattle was drowned, having been swept from his feet while fording the stream after dark.

One evening when I was returning light, the leader of an outfit offered me fifty dollars to take his supplies the two miles across Shallow Lake to the Bennett Trail. I had the cargo stowed and was pushing off when I was halted by two men with an enormous lashed roll of fur robes, which they insisted must go with the load. They said their horses had already been sent around with the tent as they were going to camp at Log Cabin to get an early start in the morning. I told them if the wind came up they were apt to lose their whole outfit with a top-heavy load like that, but they pointed to the placid water and said they would take the chance.

Half a mile from shore what I had feared happened. Of a sudden an opaque curtain was drawn across the sky and, with a howl, the Wind God let loose hit us and slapped that robe roll 'til the towed boat careened half her side under water. My two boats were separated by only eighteen inches of tow-line. With a flirt of an oar, I jack-knifed them head and tail together from the windward side and immediately threw all my weight on the raised side of the towed boat and then, with the free arm, pulled a side of bacon and some fifty-pound sacks to hold it down. The low gunwale came above the water and I got the load stabilized and lashed before the waves became too high to make the task impossible. It was a close shave. When I came ashore forty rods on the leeward side of the landing, the owners made never a kick over the soaked condition of their packs. They said when the boats disappeared from sight in the squall, they had given up everything for lost and were ready to make track back to the Coast for a new outfit.

The skyline of the trail now was dark with pack-trains. Tent villages had sprung up at the head of Summit Lake and at Log Cabin, the landing at Shallow Lake. Just before dark one evening I pulled my boats out of water at the Summit Lake encampment and, with an oar, cleared away a foot of snow under one of them, and then spread my sleeping bag in its shelter. It dawned on me that a man standing in the doorway of a nearby tent was watching my movements. Catching my eye, he asked what I was doing and, upon my replying that I was making ready to turn in for the night, he invited me to his tent, saying that he could not let a dog sleep out on such a night. His manner was so friendly that his words carried no offense. After that Judge Green of Great Falls, Montana, was my host each time I returned from a freighting trip.

In company with Judge Green was a famous oculist from Kansas City, whose name I have forgotten. I was told that he was a leader in his profession and that he had developed an exact mechanical plan for measuring the curvature of the eyeball. Both men were well along in years, but youthful in spirit and fine sportsmen. Their chief packer, whose name was Williams, was recuperating from a nasty stab-wound he had received in a fight at a card game. Things were coming Williams' way and he was riding his luck and pleasantly joshing his opponents to help out his bluffs when, without warning, one of the losers reached across the table and jabbed a knife between Williams' side ribs. Most men would have been unnerved by the suddenness of the attack, but Williams had drawn and shot his assailant dead before the latter could recover to strike again.

Our pack-train had now come up and Billy the Cop volunteered to help me carrying the boats over the long portage. One day of the work, however, was enough for him. While he weighed fifty pounds more than I, he could not acquire the knack of balancing a boat on his shoulders against the shifting winds of the mountains. I became fearful that our boats would be smashed with Billy's dives and so the partnership was abandoned. Billy had a sweet-tooth and liked candy and pastry. Once, when we sent him to Skagway to get a treat of fresh meat, Billy returned with a load of cakes, pies and sweets — but no meat. He sure got the ugly look about camp that night!

I shall never forget the day that Mac and I cut loose from the White Pass trail and started down-river on the Yukon end of the trip. The others in the party had given up and decided to return and winter at Skagway. All hands were up several hours before daylight at our camp near Log Cabin and, before the East had paled, we were on the trail with our last load for Lake Bennett. The stars snapped overhead and the snow crunched under the horses' feet. Little was said but every man was thinking of the chances. Winter was on us and only the winds and the swift current of the Yukon kept a way open. The others thought it a reckless gamble on our part, and that one or another of the big lakes through which the River passed in its upper reaches would be closed or that ice-jams would stop us, but deep down Mac and I were happy with the shift of the scene to a new type of adventure. We had negotiated the climb over the mountain and now had a coast down-hill before us with favoring currents!

The Yukon is the only great river in the world which has its source near an ocean. By the Chilkoot route it begins only fifteen miles from the same ocean it travels twenty-six hundred miles around in a great circle to empty into. By the same route, thirty miles from salt water, boats may be launched for the long drift with the current to the Klondike or beyond. We had come the longer way, but even so had only fifty miles of land travel. This was the reason the great influx to the Klondike was by the back door.

On the way to Bennett one of our horses died and Mac and I carried his load the last eight miles of the trip. We had one of the best pack-trains on the trail and this big roan was the pride of our outfit. He was strong, spirited and intelligent, and the only horse in the lot who seemed to have interest in what was going on and affection for his human co-laborers. Without warning the fine animal sighed, sank down on his belly in an upright position and died, faithful to the end. It always seemed to me that this horse stayed in an upright position instead of rolling over to save us trouble in removing his pack.

On the sand beach at the head of Lake Bennett Mac and I bade farewell to our companions and, in the falling darkness, began the work of putting our knocked-down canvas boats together. They were a round-bottomed type, called "Eureka," made by the Acme Folding Canvas Boat Company of Miamisburg, Ohio. They proved so practical and satisfactorily well-adapted to our purpose that years later I tried to get one for a trip down the largest tributary of the Yukon with my youngest son, Koert, only to be told that the company which made them was no longer in existence.

By midnight our job was completed so with loaded boats we pushed out into the thirty-mile lake to take advantage of a fair wind then blowing. Each of us had two boats connected by eighteen-inch tow-lines. The rear freight boats were loaded to within three inches of the water-line and covered with canvas tarpaulins fastened to the gunwales with single nails to keep the waves out. In the boats which we rowed were tents, rifles, blankets and cooking utensils and supplies for immediate use. We had lashed masts in the bows of our lead boats and spread to the wind tiny sails, and soon were slipping along at a satisfactory pace, considering the dead weight towed behind.

It was then that I learned for the first time that Mac had never sailed a boat in his life and could not swim, having grown up in a country devoid of lakes and rivers....

Lake Bennett occupies the bottom of a V-shaped trough in the mountains and the wind naturally blows in line with the lake but, for some perverse reason, Mac's boats seemed drawn as if by a magnet towards the easterly side. Maybe it was the drag of the freight boat that caused the trouble, but I think more likely the difficulty he experienced was in steering with an oar. Whatever the cause we had not gone two miles before his boats were in under some black cliffs against which the waves were breaking with sufficient force to smash the frail craft. I got alongside and we furled our sails, which was by no means an easy job in such small boats in rough water. After that we hitched all four boats in tandem and started rowing to get away from the shore, but Mac knew no more about rowing than sailing so, as we were up against the rocks, I had him pull in his oars and lie down to lessen the drag of the wind. It took every ounce of strength I possessed to get the boats to the open lake, and the strength had to be judiciously applied to prevent breaking the oars but eventually we got around the cliffs which, being a point, had made a lee shore. An hour later, just at daylight, we found a cove with a nice sand beach where we landed and had a snooze, the first rest in twenty-four strenuous hours.

For several days thereafter we rowed the boats in tandem of four, so that I could watch Mac the better and coach his oarsmanship. He soon got the knack and did very well except in the roughest water.

We had our next buffet from old Boreas when crossing Tagish Lake. We had camped at the head of the lake the night before on the same camp-ground where a murder had been committed in the morning. That day we caught up with the boat carrying the murderer. He was lying in the bottom, bound with a log-chain and unconcernedly using the corpse of his victim as a pillow. His companions and captors were in search of a detail of police said to be somewhere on the lake. Their faces were stern and they certainly appreciated the gravity of the offense even though their prisoner did not.

Tagish Lake is shaped like a corkscrew. We were following the left side of the handle, going north. Midway of the handle, the screw part runs at right angles to the eastward through a twenty-mile cleft in high mountains. It is called the "Windy Arm" and has an evil reputation.

The day was brilliantly clear and the lake placid as we skirted its west shore at mid-day and we were just congratulating ourselves upon our good fortune when a roar smote the air like the sound of a fog siren. Looking over our shoulders we saw black terror hit the waters of the "Windy Arm" and blot them out. Our boats rocked and then the hurricane of wind and snow struck us like all the Norse devils. I yelled to Mac that we must get off that lee shore and we turned our boats to the wind and bucked the storm in the same spirit it had shown us. It was "Damn your dirty tricks! I'll show you you can't put it over on me!" uttered from heaving lungs through clenched teeth.

With our heavily-loaded boats, clawing up that lee shore was grueling work. The force of the wind kept down the swell, but at times Mac's boats went clear out of sight with the water above them. We did not want to make the mistake of rowing directly into the mouth of the "Windy Arm," but good seamanship required that we head our boats very close to it in order to prevent breaching. We could see nothing of the land and were dependent for direction on the feel of the wind on our necks.

Late in the afternoon rowing became easier and just at night-fall we reached smooth water at the edge of the ice. Skirting this with a few strokes of the oars, we found the mouth of a stream where the ice was easily broken and soon reached an ideal camp-site among thick spruces....

*Miles Canyon-Side View*

# Chapter 5

## The Miles Canyon — White Horse Rapids Challenge

The next morning the jaws of death I looked into were not red, but white; white as a corpse, white and cruel as the fangs of a tiger. They were the leaping waves of one of the world's great rapids with a record that year of more than three hundred human victims. In short, this is the story of my troubles in the canyon at the White Horse Rapids of the Yukon.

*Miles Canyon*

The Yukon is one of the world's great rivers. It is two thousand miles long and, at its delta, where it empties into Bering Sea, it is a hundred miles wide. The Yukon has a peculiarity shared by no other great river. It is like a snake with its tail in its mouth in that its headwaters are very near to the same ocean into which it empties. Only fifteen miles from the salt waters of the Pacific in Chilkoot Pass the sweet waters of the Yukon begin, and fifteen miles farther on the prospector can launch his boat on Lake Linderman and never take it out, if he has the nerve, until its keel is lapped by the salt waters of the Sea of Vitus Bering. If he has the nerve, however, it covers quite a contract.

A couple of hundred miles inland, where the river has accumulated volume from the snows of innumerable mountains until in places it reaches a width of half a mile, its way is disputed by a basaltic dyke; and here the Yukon goes crazy for the stretch of three miles which includes Miles Canyon and White Horse Rapids. This is the only serious obstacle to navigation in all the length of the river's course to the sea. It presents a real, man-sized argument, however. The berserk flood bucks and plunges like a wild thing beating out its brains against the rocks. Those who have seen the lower Whirlpool Rapids at Niagara will have a very fair idea of these Yukon rapids.

The reason men went into the Klondike in the Gold Rushes of 1897 and '98 across Chilkoot and White Passes to gain the River's head was that after a short though agonizingly punishing climb they could, as it were, slide down-hill the rest of the way. Few, in those days, had ever heard of White Horse Rapids.

That memorable morning McKercher and I were gliding in our boats over the swift but placid current of the river between gravelly shores, flanked by pleasing groves of spruce and cottonwood when, rounding a bend, we were startled to see our way apparently blocked by a two-hundred-foot-high dam of black rock reaching across the river. For all the world it seemed the river ended at that rock wall. We became aware of an ominous rumbling deep in the bowels of the rock. Wild ducks, which had drifted near the wall, took wing and flew back toward us. As there was no visible way of going farther, we put it at a beach on the right bank where a number of other boats were moored, and here we learned that we had reached the Rapids.

The basalt dyke is highest on its up-river edge, where it encloses the Canyon. From above you look down on a succession of goose-flight V-shaped rows of white-caps two hundred feet below. From wall to wall the width of the Canyon is similarly about two hundred feet. A thirty-foot Yukon double-ender boat was making the passage with four oarsmen pulling at the oars and a steersman standing erect in the stern, hauling and shoving with his long steering oar to hold the boat head-on in her course. The craft shot through the gloomy tunnel like a bat out of Hell — at times in plain sight but was often blotted out by a smother of foam. Fore and aft, the boat had been covered with tarpaulins to keep the water out. From landing to landing the distance is a mile and boats made it in three minutes. The Canyon proper, however, is only five-eighths of a mile long and, in the swiftest current, the speed must have been thirty miles per hour; no great shakes of a speed on smooth water perhaps but, in that pounding torrent, enough to smash any craft not of the stoutest construction.

About the middle of the Canyon the walls of the chute widen into a circular bowl, called by the Stampeders "The Eye," and in it, turning counterclockwise, the water swirls in a great whirlpool. We studied the water carefully and I made up my mind I could run it with our little craft.

Food supplies had to be freighted through and we just could not take the chance of their loss through incompetent handling.

Mac and I were making the trip with twelve-foot folding canvas boats which had been carried across the Pass. If we had taken time to build a wooden boat, the river would have been solid ice before we could have started. As a single boat would not carry sufficient supplies for one man, each of us had two. We rowed one and towed another more heavily-laden boat behind. I had to get them through with a maximum amount of freight.

In the Canyon I carried 450 pounds with each boat, but through White Horse the load had to be reduced to 350. Twenty years later I was told by Hamaker, the historical authority at White Horse, that I still held the record for being the only man who had ever taken a boat through these rapids alone, and also the record for the smallest boat to get through safely.

Before committing my boats to them I studied every foot of the rapids, picked my course, and decided on the action necessary to be taken in the worst places. The first two trips through the Canyon went off like clockwork but on the third my foot slipped. Failure to remember to tie in my left oarlock almost cost me my life.

The slip-up came from conceit. On my mind, as a result, there is now deeply etched an old copy-book maxim, "Pride *cometh* before a fall."

I was getting my boat ready for the trip through when some old friends, the Montgomery party, dropped in at the landing. They began asking questions as to how to get through the rapids and I told them to run around on top where they could see, and I would show them how it was done. I was strutting so much that I forgot to get under the canvas and tie fast the oarlock.

At both ends of the boat I had lashed poles fastened to tripods in the cock-pit and had drawn a tarpaulin over the boat from stem to stern, nailing it with shingle-nails around the gunwales, and this served to keep the waves out as long as the boat traveled end-on to the rapids. Amidships, however, where I rowed, the canvas had to be brought down to the level of the sides of the boat. The oarlocks were flimsy, being insecure, provided with chains about four inches in length; but it was my custom to tie them quite tightly with cod-line so they could not jump out of the sockets. Each fifty-pound sack comprising the cargo was likewise lashed to the frame of the boat to prevent shifting, and the weight arranged so that at the bow the keel was clear of the water.

Shod with moccasins to facilitate swimming should that become necessary, I knelt on the bottom of the boat facing downstream so that I could see what was coming. Sacks of flour lashed to the ribs opposite my thighs served to hold me in the boat. No one could have handled so light a boat without ballast and stayed in it through all its crazy gyrations.

In order to maintain control in the lightning-quick changes of current in a rapid of the first order it is necessary to have steerage-way, which means that the boat must be propelled at a greater speed than the water. The common plan, however, could not be followed with such small and fragile boats because the waves were too high and their upstream fronts too vertical. My cockle-shells would never have come up again after their first dive.

Waves in rapids, unlike sea waves, are produced by obstructions on the bottom or sides. The water in them curls from behind up towards you and then drops vertically downward. A small boat cannot successfully dive through such waves. It must have time for its bow to climb over the waves so that, in due course, the rest of the boat can follow over the top. The description of course is set at slow-motion tempo. Therefore, I reversed the usual procedure and, when I could get my oars in, rowed backward with a fury against the current.

The Montgomery party walked up the hill above the Canyon and I cast loose, going first upstream in the current of the clockwise backwash until I was carried downward in a great circle and down the slit in the rock-wall opening to a long vista of white-capped waves like dancing ghosts. The gearshift smoothly slipped into high and the boat shifted forward like a skier at the jump.

Smash! The boat bounded upward and almost over and, with that first blow, the left oarlock jumped the socket and hung useless by its flimsy chain. In one split second I was repentent, scared, profane and praying — and all the while holding the balance of the boat with one oar. I pulled and I pushed and changed from one to the other in mid-action as the lightning-like water-shifts demanded. Experience had made the motions automatic. My prayer was that I could keep the boat right-side up long enough to reach the smooth water of "The Eye." I should have asked for something more.

I was soon out of the elephant kicks and among the myriad lesser slappings of "The Eye." The time had come to replace the oarlock. I reached over and caught it and, with the continuation of the movement, placed it back in the socket; but in that wink of an eye one of the secondary whirlpools, formed in the proximity of all larger ones, developed from the depths, shot upwards and capsized the boat and the green water came in over the gunwale six inches deep. I threw all my weight on the upper side and slowly, far too slowly, the grip of the water relaxed and the boat righted. My body hit the oar in the convulsive action, the chain of the left oarlock snapped, and the oarlock slid to the end — and disappeared!

Whatever my feeling before, now I knew I was in bad. The water inside the boat sloshed first one way and then the other, and it was like riding a bicycle without pedals to keep her afloat. The second chute of the rapid is much worse than the first and I was being sucked into it. I could see the Montgomery party watching from the rim above and I could fancy their saying "Too bad! Just too bad!"

I read one fool story awhile ago based on the perverted theory that the whirlpool in "The Eye," like the Maelstrom,[1] holds for all time whatever is consigned to it. I do not think the writer ever saw the whirlpool and I know he never was in it. My life and 450 pounds of food depended on keeping in it, and it scares me to recollect the flimsy margin by which this was accomplished.

Whatever saved me was the trifling fact that the lost left oarlock had not been properly smoothed after casting. As a result the oar had been roughened and it did not slide off when held against the upper part of the socket, which projected a quarter of an inch above the gunwale. I began pushing with the oars in unison and to my great relief found I could propel the boat through the choppy waves at a fair rate of speed.

But it was little better than a snail's pace in opposition to the downward drag of the rapids. I was hanging on the brink of another world for a period all too long.

The fingers of the whirlpool pulled me from the clawing grasp of the chute. The boat gathered headway and swept to and along the west wall of "The Eye."

An uprooted spruce tree had fallen from above and lodged with its branches sweeping the waves. To this I made fast and baled the water out of the boat with my slicker hat. In my then frame of mind I would have been glad to have abandoned the boat, but this was not possible. I scanned the rock above me but could find no place where it could be climbed. I looked across to the east side and saw my friends, with others who had joined them, standing at the edge staring at me. There was a gulf separating us that could not be bridged. I did not like it but I would have to finish, as I had begun, by water.

The boat's painter was too large to go through the oarlock socket and I unraveled one of its three strands, ran that through the socket and inserted the oar into the loop. I found it worked as well as an oarlock and I let go, circled the whirlpool and entered the second rapid.

---
[1] E.A. Poe's *"Descent into the Maelstrom"*

*One of Hepburn's Barges in Rapids*

*Lumber Scow in Rapids*

The boat handled better than I had dared hope, but there was still the worry of making the landing at the foot of the Canyon.

Where the walls of Miles Canyon ended, the river immediately widened out between sloping, wooded banks which extended down to and beyond Squaw Rapids before being again constricted at White Horse Rapids. The rush of water from the Canyon shot through the pool below at about thirty miles per hour, its edges marked by a long reach of indescribably tumbling water on both sides, and beyond were currents running in the reverse direction. In order to gain the landing, which was on the east side, it was necessary to make a quick traverse from one current to the other, and to do this successfully required forward speed and a charge through the reach at exactly the right angle. The slightest mistake meant being snuffed out. The boat's responsive action had restored my confidence. I gauged the angle properly and, as the boat shot through the ruff, threw myself forward almost on my face, with oars held vertically to save them from being snapped off — and the next second I was pushing easily to the shore.

As we carried one of our boats back to freight the camp outfit through, I made the Canyon trip five times. Through White Horse Rapids, however, I made four trips only. Here I avoided part of the worst chute by ducking through a wave at the west side into the choppy water behind. Waves in rapids are fixed as to location. This particular wave was caused by a submerged mass of basaltic rock.

White Horse is a glorious spectacle. Most of the volume of the river is gathered and shot through a rock-constricted funnel in a mad chute not over fifty feet in width.

John Hepburn had reached the Canyon before us and had at once taken up the work of piloting boats through the Rapids. Most of the Klondikers came down-river in five-ton boats which they had built on the shores of Lake Bennett. The standard boat was thirty feet long and double-ended, a dory model. From four to five men rowed this boat, two men to a seat, while the steersman directed its course with a long oar at the stern. At the head of the Canyon, from half to two-thirds of the cargo was taken out and back-packed around. Protected with canvas and then manned with its full complement of oarsmen, the professional pilot took charge. For both rapids, the pilot received a fee of fifty dollars, and he could make from three to four trips per day. As there were not enough pilots to go around, with an increasing number of boats coming down each day, I had often been requested to take boats through but had steadily refused. Many of the parties were obliged to strip their boats and cut them loose, and quite a business developed below the rapids picking up the derelicts and bringing them to shore for ten dollars per boat. Also, a few of the men who had previous experience and yet dreaded to shoot the rapids, lined their partly-loaded boats down with long ropes, but this was a tedious and highly risky process.

As I walked back across the portage, I ran into Hepburn in company with a number of men on his way to the Canyon landing. It was evident he had seen the accident, for he conscientiously set about giving me a dressing for risking my life in a "cockleshell." I stood it as long as I could and then I jumped him. My argument was that the chance I was taking was a personal matter, but that he was gambling for the money he could make and was therefore less of a sportsman. Really I knew this was not so, that it was the game and not the profit that interested old John.

Hepburn seemed perturbed when he took charge of his next boat at the Landing. I hope I am not to blame for the fact that, at the last pitch of White Horse, he ran her under and drowned one of the crew, Freedman, for whom Freedman's Point was named. Hepburn never piloted another boat after that but went on through to Dawson.

I had trouble with Mac also over the rapid-shooting after the Hepburn incident. Heretofore, he had allowed me to monopolize it on the basis that it was an easier job than backpacking, which was entirely true, but now that the hazard had been emphasized, he was determined to do his share. The only way I could handle Mac was to tell him that, while neither of us cared a darn for his life, in course of duty we were both bound in honor to preserve the basis of that life, as represented by our supplies. It was only because of longer experience that I was permitted to continue. I assured Mac I could swim ashore if a boat went under and no doubt this could have been done, provided the accident happened in the lower part of a rapid, where the struggle would not be too long-drawn-out. I wore just trousers and shirt and a light pair of moccasins so as not to be handicapped by too many clothes. As a boy I had delighted in swimming rapids and had learned that the way to do it with safety is to keep on top of the water, except when diving through waves. It is the deeper currents that grip and pull the body under, and not the froth on the surface.

No one knows the depth of the water in the Canyon, but it must be more than a hundred feet. Just below, however, where the river broadens, it becomes shallow once more and, as the channel is rocky and the current swift, it is by no means easy to navigate. In fact, at Squaw Rapids, half-way between the Canyon and White Horse, several men were drowned.

It was necessary to cross the river because the White Horse portage is on the opposite side from the Canyon carry. Mac insisted on taking his two boats across and, beyond the minor adventure of hitting a rock near the farther shore, which scarcely more than knocked the paint fom the canvas, we got through without incident. At Squaw Rapids we let the boats down the short pitch with ropes and soon had our camp made at the White Horse carry.

The danger of White Horse is the bottle-neck at the lower end. A part of the basaltic ledge on the west side has fallen in and shunted the main volume of the river through a fifty-foot-wide opening down which it dashes like water projected against a pavement from a mammoth fire hose. There is no logic to such water, and no buoyant power, and a boat must perforce ride through it and not over it. After watching some of the large boats dive under like submarines, it seemed evident it was no place for tiny craft like ours, which had to breathe to live.

The rapids fascinated me and, as we passed backward and forward over the portage, I studied them as a lover studies the face of his beloved. With growing understanding the rapids became more friendly but infinitely more tantalizing. They danced and flirted and seemed to say, "We are yours for the taking — only beware!" For Mac too they sang a swan song — a tragic song for you, dear fellow, but that came later on —.

My plan was to drop down through the center of the rapids, retarding the speed of the boat as much as possible with the oars until I was just above the wave precipitated from the submerged rocks. Then I would push hard on the oars and gain speed and dive through this wave, in the way I had just changed currents at the foot of the Canyon. This permitted the boat to skirt the edge of the dangerous last chute without taking its worst buffets. My strategy turned out to be the right solution to the problem.

I took the four boats through in one day with 1400 pounds of supplies, 350 to a load. So far as I have been able to find out, these are the smallest boats which ever made the trip — and the only boats that shot the rapids successfully with a single occupant. Frank Slavin, the Australian heavy-weight pugilist, with one companion, took a sixteen-foot boat through White Horse in '97; and later on, at an exceptionally low stage of the water, three men made the trip in a boat about the same as Slavin's.

*******

Jan Welzl, in his book *Thirty Years in the Golden North*[1] supplied further vivid details of this treacherous stretch of whitewater. "At one place half the width of the river drops suddenly in a cataract as high as a house, while in the other half the water dashes down at a terrific rate along its slanting bed seething as if it were in a boiler. I estimated that we were moving at a speed of fifty miles an hour.

"I was sitting on the bottom of the boat quite overwhelmed with fear. At one moment the branch of a tree flicked my head like a whip and I thought that my last hour had come. We whizzed through the air as though flying, and I kept saying to myself that never again as long as I lived would I embark upon such a venture.

"But Captain Tamarak was sitting at the helm, his face rigid and his eyes fixed with the utmost concentration and watchfulness upon the white rapids and whirling waves. Not until we had reached the foot of the rapids were our tongues unloosed.

"The Captain told us that four boats had capsized there in a single day and not a soul was saved. On another occasion twenty prostitutes on their way to Dawson City had perished. When the gold-diggers heard about this there were great rejoicings because so many of the miners had squandered the results of their labors on such females.

"Still another tragedy took the lives of a boatload of Negroes. In all, from 1897 to 1901 nearly five hundred people were drowned at White Horse."

In 1958 a dam created Schwatka Lake, raised the waters of Miles Canyon and buried the rapids.

---

[1] Welzl, Jan., *Thirty Years in the Golden North*, Macmillan, N.Y., 1932 pp. 158-9.

# Chapter 6

**The Loss of the Boats and the Encounter with the River Thieves.**

The Thirty-Mile River, as the stretch between White Horse and Lake Labarge is called, was bad in the days before Williams and his fellow steamboat captains dynamited out the boulders and made a channel. One had to zigzag between, or "play checkers" with the boulders, as we called it. Actually in places the boulders were placed in staggered form like the squares on a checkerboard. I have a poor snap-shot taken of one of the thirty-footers whose dazed steersman in dodging one rock, laid her sideways against another with the result that both men and supplies were swept out of the boat by the racing current. The picture shows the boat on edge, and heads of men and sacks floating down-stream. Fortunately no one on this occasion was drowned.

Water sense is gained, I think, only in boyhood days and cannot be developed later on in life. It is the same with many things connected with the outdoors; the sense of direction for example. If a man does not cultivate early that telepathic sense, he will never have it. Such senses are born in people but if not exercised in childhood are atrophied and lost.

Mac was a good horseman because he had grown up with horses and understood their fine qualities and loved them, but the vagaries of water were always a closed book to him. As he had never experienced the thirst of a current against his naked body, it was not to be expected he could gauge its force on a boat. It amazed me to see him, one night as we were making a landing, reach out and grasp with a vise-like grip a snag whose top projected above the foam-flecked current of the Thirty-Mile. The deadweight of the boats was nearly a ton and that current had a good part of the authority of the law of gravitation. It was like reaching out of a train window and grabbing a signal tower with the object of bringing the train to a standstill. Mac's train went right along and he stayed....

It was impossible to row against such a current, so I could not go back to help him. All I could do was to bunt his boats to shore and try to retard their progress until he could get there and make them fast. Mac saw the emergency and never hesitated. He drew up his feet against the snag and gave a push, disappeared in the deep water but was thrown in to shore, scrambled out and, with hip-boots full of water to add to the weight of his water-soaked clothes, came ploughing along through two feet of snow. As Mac later on dried out by an open fire, neither of us commented on his act or, in fact, on anything except the supper which was cooking over the coals; but I always thought that nicely-timed action of his was one of the bravest things I ever saw. He feared the water and could not swim yet, when needed, took no thought of his life.

The thermometer, which had steadily been going down, now averaged from zero to five degrees below. One gradually became accustomed and hardened to the cold. The air was bracingly dry and charged with ozone.

We feared that a still night would cement the ice-bridge across Labarge, the last of the big lakes on the Yukon. We entered the lake, however, in a driving gale of snow from the south.

It was just getting dark but, as the ice danger was so imminent, we decided to keep going so we drove steadily through the black night with the waves rolling over our two boats, and only occasionally showing their presence by the ghostly gleam of the breaking crests.

About one in the morning, as we were skirting the dim face of a wall-like rock formation, the sea let down that hoodoo freight-boat of mine on a sharp snag of rock coming up from the depths. The boat hung a moment before the next roller carried her off. I *felt* her rip. Calling to Mac to stand by, I headed for the shore a hundred yards away.

I had two worries: First, that the boat would sink and pull me down before I could reach the shore, as it had a lot of hardware and heavy things in it. And second, that there was no break in the rock wall and no place to get ashore where the boats and cargoes could be saved. But we had our rabbit's foot with us. No one can tell me that there is no such thing as Luck! We found the only sand beach within two miles in either direction along that precipitous shore! Just before we reached it, the last of the air from under the canvas in the freight-boat went out with a "whiff," as she turned on her side and sank to the bottom.

The wind was suggestive of the open sea and there was a double line of miniature breakers on the beach. We both promptly jumped overboard to hold the boats off so they would not be smashed. The first sea that hit us went right on over our heads and carried with it our hats, but fortunately the drag of the sunken boat held that pair off for a time.

When the bigger series of waves rolled in, it required our combined efforts to hold the boats while the other carried ashore the supplies and dunnage and, last of all, the emptied boat. The zest of conflict was in our blood and we fought those demon waves for more than an hour with the same grim satisfaction, no doubt, that the cavemen felt in similar emergencies.

The city-bred man says, "Not for mine," but he is wrong. His ancestry calls for just this kind of test. If he goes at it whole-heartedly, he will be equal to it. It teaches him to draw on his latent resources — mental, physical and spiritual.

We found wood, which is scarce on Labarge, and dried out by daylight before a roaring fire. It was a beautiful clear day after the storm. All our food supplies were more or less wet, but those in the sunken freight-boat were soaked. We spread out the beans, rice and dried fruit on tarpaulins on the beach and stirred them about to get the full benefit of the sun and heat from surrounding fires which we had made. Eventually we succeeded in saving everything except the oatmeal, which in time became rancid. The flour was the least trouble of anything. The sacks may be under water indefinitely without wetting in more than a small fraction of an inch, and even this caked part is not lost. When the balance of the flour has been used, water is poured in the sack and the resulting dough may be baked into perfectly wholesome bannocks.

Most of the interior country is on edge except for the larger river valley. The thirty-mile length of Labarge lies among mountains which, especially on the east side, are irregular and so fantastic in outline as to verge on the impossible. We took the drop at Five Finger Rapids backwards, with each pair of boats headed up-stream. When the freight-boat paused in the back-wash, we rowed our lead-boats hard to prevent ramming. These rapids, for men who had been through White Horse, were a cinch.

*Time Out for Reloading*

*Shooting White Horse Rapids (Hamacher photo)
On second trip through on same
day two of the men were drowned.*

*Wreck Below White Horse Rapids — Men Overboard*

The thermometer was now from 15 to 20° below zero and our progress was seriously impeded by the mush-ice. It became increasingly difficult to get to shore to camp for the night. We could only force landings when the current of the river swung to the other side. The ice grasped us to its bosom and held us there. If the boats slipped sideways or tail-end-to they stayed, as no power of ours could move them. On account of the freeze-up, of a sudden the river grew shallow. Not only glaciers, which through melting supplied its headwaters, but even springs had congealed. We doubted that there would be water enough left in the river to float us to Dawson. The water, such as it was, was crystal clear. To look through it and see the ragged bottom chasing by gave one an uncomfortable feeling, as he thought of what would happen if the boats came in contact with it. Our safety lay in the fact that we were carried along with the greatest volume and consequently where there was the greatest depth. Once we were swept irresistibly toward a frowning cliff, where all kinds of things were happening to the ice-cakes, but before we could hit it the back-wash carried us off. If it had not been for their closely-packed cargoes, however, I feel sure the boats would have collapsed from the pressure.

We still wore our hip-boots but wrapped our legs with blankets to keep from freezing. Our oars and poles rapidly accumulated ice and they had to be pounded often to keep them at serviceable size and weight. Ice formed a foot thick on the bottoms of the boats, outside and beneath the water, and it formed on the bottom of the river itself in still pockets until, after gaining size by accretions, masses broke loose and came to the surface like breaching amphibians.

The mush-ice thickened and solidified in cakes two feet thick, circular in sections on account of the friction of the banks until the flow looked like a procession of round tables, big and little, all headed for Bering sea. Ice-jams were of frequent occurrence where these met islands or bends in the river but, as soon as the hurrying water backed up a foot or two, the jam was ripped out by its relentless force and the mass spun on again. We knew that the flow of ice would not stop until blocked by the master jam, which was even then backing up towards us from the mouth of the river at the rate of a hundred miles per day. We were on edge to beat this jam to Dawson before it got us. It was a worth-while race and we would, I think, have won except for what happened on the evening of November 7th.

Fifteen miles above the junction of the Pelly, and beginning at Wolverine Creek, the Yukon is blocked by a great number of islands and sand-bars and here on the west limit we were especially harassed by the ice. Finally, towards night, the main current took a slant toward the opposite side of the now mile-wide river and, as the ice pressure slackened and the mass separated, we succeeded in working our boats to the rim of shore-ice, which was here about fifty feet in width and terminated in deep water, like a low sea-wall. As usual, I dropped in on the lower side and did what I could to retard Mac's boats while he, from the rim, was bringing them to a halt.

There was so much floating ice, however, that the job was particularly difficult. Things looked better farther down and I was for temporizing but Mac, who could not appreciate the force of the ice-laden current, decided to stop right there and snubbed the boats by taking a turn around a snag with the result that the rope snapped like rotten twine.

We tied the broken rope and hitched the pairs of boats together and, by plain manpower, attempted to bring them to a stop; but the boats dragged both of us along the rim ice and we could not slow them up.

The shore-line ran in a long outward curve at the farther end, on which we could see a spruce grove that promised a good camp-site. Opposite this was a wide-open space free from islands; this would permit the river to spread out and so relieve the pressure. The individual boat painters were only quarter-inch rope so, fearing that even under the better conditions below they would not hold all the boats, I told Mac to get a coil of half-inch line in my boat and tie the end of each painter to it so that, when we got to the spruce, we could be sure to stop the boats. I should have done the job myself and left Mac on the rim, but I feared his over-enthusiastic snubbing might pull the sterns out of the boats.

I jogged along the ice, putting all the comeback I could on the boats until a low-cut bank was reached, where fire had toppled the trees crossways to my path. As it was impossible to get through them fast enough, I yelled to Mac that I would meet him below, tossed him the rope and detoured.

The cut-bank projected far enough into the river to hide from view things above it. When I reached the shore-ice again, I could see neither Mac nor the boats. A cold chill ran down my spine as I started to worm my way upstream among the fallen trees. Almost immediately two of our boats drifted by, followed closely by a third. They were scraping the shore and I could have jumped aboard any one of them, but I let them go because I felt sure Mac was in trouble. My thought was that he had gone overboard and that quick action was needed to save him from drowning.

I climbed under and over the trees with agonized haste, but not until I had almost reached the other end of the obstruction did I find him standing there holding a rope snubbed around a stump with only the head-boat fast to it.

I have always thanked God that in that anti-climax I had sense enough not to say anything verging on criticism. It was on my lips but my good angel must have clapped a hand over my mouth before the invective could be uttered. Even afterwards we did not discuss the incident so I have never known just what it was that caused Mac to again try to snub the boats before the better water was reached.

Night was upon us and it was useless to attempt to overtake the lost boats. Fifty yards' handicap was all the start they needed to get away from us. We unloaded Mac's boat. It contained a large tent and his blankets, cooking utensils, a 40.62 Winchester rifle and four hundred rounds of ammunition besides other things — but *not an ounce of food*. Supperless, we spread our blankets on top of the tent laid flat on the snow and turned in....

We were awakened in the morning by the chattering of red squirrels in the spruce over our heads. Taking Mac's rifle, I shot the heads off two squirrels without getting out of the blankets and a little later Mac killed another. We breakfasted on the squirrels which, for food for hungry men, went about as far as humming-bird's wings. Then we cached most of the duffle under the boat a little way back from the river and, with the blankets and rifle, started in search of the lost boats.

While we had Dawson's map of the Yukon, which was the only scale map of the river then available, and knew that the site of the old Hudson's Bay trading post of Fort Selkirk was located below us roughly opposite the mouth of the Pelly, Dawson had stated in the text of his report that the Post had been burned by Coast Indians and abandoned. We had seen no human beings for a number of days past and had no reason to believe any were in that neighborhood. We could find no gnawings or signs of porcupines. That it was starvation country was shown by the angular marks on poplar trees, wherever they occurred, from which the bark had been removed to fill empty stomachs and, through the astringent action, check the pangs of hunger.

I was thoroughly depressed. I was sure we would never find the boats. Ice was piled twenty feet high at the heads of islands and bars and, even if boats escaped destruction, it seemed likely they would be buried in the ice. Having noted the habit of the current, I also thought the boats would be drawn to the larger channels and that they might travel with the ice several hundreds of miles. Our only chance of survival seemed to be to leave the Yukon and travel up one of the tributaries to a game country. There build a cabin and so pass the winter.

Mac, however, had a hunch we would find the boats and his faith had a strong effect on my drooping spirits. Mac was not always an optimist, but he was as courageous as a well-bred bulldog and just as tenacious of purpose. He shouldered the largest pack and started down-river, and I followed at his heels.

For two days we strained our eyes looking over the accumulating ice on the bars and islands but nowhere among the flotsam did we see what we were looking for. Even red squirrels were hard to find and we rapidly grew weak from lack of food. We had reached a section where the poplar aspens did not grow or we would certainly have filled our bellies with their kind of husks. Then, just at nightfall of the second day, we both stopped simultaneously and gazed spellbound at what might have seemed to be only a dark shadow under piled-up ice, but which instinctively we *knew* was a part of the side of one of our boats.

Emotion rendered speech impossible. Together we waded hip-deep among the drifting ice, at times grasping each other and bracing our bodies while the larger cakes revolved on the fulcrum of our legs, until we reached the bar where the apparition had been sighted. It was in truth one of the boats and with a canvas cover, which meant a thousand pounds of food. We sank on our knees and thanked God. There was no water in the boat and nothing had been lost or damaged.

From the bar we could look a long distance down the river. Our attention was attracted by a light about a mile below on our side, and we made out the dim outlines of several cabins.

A half-hour later in answer to our knock on the door of the lighted cabin, a little, stoop-shouldered man, clad in hand-me-downs, moccasins and a fur cap with generous side-flaps, opened the door and peered at us owlishly. We pushed our way in and, I am ashamed to say, told him our sad story without waiting to be asked. Pitts, for that was his name, glared at us stonily until we had finished and then said, "Served you right — get out!"

The odor of boiled beans came from the direction of the stove, or otherwise we might have gone. Instead we sat down on a bench; whereupon Pitts turned upon us savagely and ordered us out for the second time. As he continued talking, however, we felt obliged to listen. We gathered from what he said that, as he had gotten there first, he claimed the country as his own and that he prized it as a place where he could be just as miserable as he wished without interference from others. Apparently the Klondikers had gotten on his nerves. He cursed the whole lot of us as ill-gotten bastards, gold-crazed and prostituted. But we were too hungry to take offense. Once he got started, there appeared to be no reverse action to the flood-gates, so we sidled back to the bench and watched tensely as he began setting the table. Then Mac's glance caught mine. It seemed too good to be true, but he had set three places! Gruffly he explained as we drew up to the table that he had no supplies except beans and condensed milk. We made no complaint and when we had finished, Pitts' weekly boiling of beans had vanished.

We got to know Pitts quite well in the days which followed. To hear him talk one would think him made of vinegar and wormwood, but once in awhile he would make a slip that betrayed a warm heart. He has been dead many years and the Indians who were with him at Selkirk are all dead and gone, but the white men who invariably first hated him and then changed their minds have given him an imperishable monument by attaching his name to the mountain which broods over the place.

We made Pitts happy by giving him several cans of butter, an article which he had not tasted for two years. He provided us with a cabin and the services of a young Indian, whom

*Spruce Rail Tramway bypassing White Horse Rapids.*

*Five Finger Rapids of Yukon River*

we called Bailey for short, to assist us in the work of carrying on our quest for the other lost boats. Bailey had a toboggan and each morning we loaded a boat on the craft and dragged it to some point on the river's edge, where we could push off to explore systematically a new series of ice-covered bars. As it happened the boat we used for these reconnaissances was the one we had cached at the scene of our disaster because the other, after bringing the recovered supplies to the mainland, had been turned over them as a shelter. We left the bulk of the supplies on a level spot under the bank, because every moment was precious and we did not want to take the time just then to sled them in to our cabin.

By a miscue, when chopping the ice from our boat, the blade of the axe had gone right through her bottom. We had no patching materials and for a moment it looked as if we would have to go back to Selkirk for canvas, needle and cement, and so lose a day. Mac suggested that as ice froze under water the same principle could be used to patch the boat. I took a piece from my handkerchief, placed it against the inner side, which was the smoothest, and splashed a little river water on it. It froze like the bark on a tree and we used the boat thereafter with no thought of other cement.

Because of a jam which had formed somewhere above us and which held longer than usual, we had one particularly good forenoon for work; this enabled us to complete our inspection of the bars above Selkirk. Late in the afternoon, as we neared the post, Bailey appeared on the shore waving his arms to attract attention. He pointed down-stream — and there under the bank we saw one of the big Yukon boats moored at the exact spot where our supplies had been cached. Four men were passing backward and forward methodically and the horrible fact assailed us that they were stealing our food.

We were too far out in the river and the current was too swift to permit landing at the scene of the operations, but we made the fronting bar and from there I waded the intervening channel and came along-side the strangers, who were loading the last of our supplies into their boat.

They were rough-looking customers, bearded and booted, but what struck me most unfavorably was the fact that each of the four wore cartridge belts with holsters dangling on their hips holding revolvers of heavy calibre. In all my experience on the trail I had not seen a party so armed. In addition, there were four rifles stacked in the bow of their boat.

I stood a moment and looked them over and then, as they paid no attention to me, I asked what they were doing. "Can't you see what we are doing?" replied the man who appeared to be the leader, with a leer, "You're not blind, are you?"

"That is all the grub we have to winter on," I said, "if you take it we will starve!" to which he replied, "Starve and be damned!"

His point was all too evident. They had the physical power that gave the right for their action from this perspective and, if this was not enough, four pistols and four rifles for good measure. The young fellow standing in the water below them and another in a boat on a sand-bar, unarmed, must have appeared ludicrous to them.

Without giving any further attention to me, they proceeded to stow the last of our supplies in their boat. They did not even try to stop me as I started down the river.

As I reached our snow-shoe trail I looked back and saw that the pirates had cut a rope and were attempting to tow their boat upstream to a point where they could gain the main channel of the river. They had apparently just realized that otherwise they would be cut off from the open water for a considerable distance and furnish an easy target for bullets from the shore. The ice had started running again and I felt sure that they could not succeed, and that we had them trapped provided the light would last until I could get a rifle and return.

At our cabin I had a moment of heart failure for Mac's rifle was nowhere to be seen. There were cartridges on the window-sill, but the gun was not behind the door, nor overhead nor yet in the bed. I tossed the blankets all over the floor.

Getting a grip on myself I thought, "Now Mac is Scotch and provident. He thinks some Indian will come in and steal the gun. He has hidden it." I looked over the bare interior systematically, eliminating places it could not be, until my eye caught sight of a base-board closing a gap next to the bottom log. I wrenched it off — and there was the rifle!

Shoving cartridges into the magazine as I came through the door, I nearly bowled Pitts over. He had scented trouble and came across to find out what it was all about. I told him our supplies had been jumped as I ran for the snow-shoe trail. I had a mile to go and it would soon be dark.

*McKercher Chopping Canoe Loose from Ice*

I watched the river as I ran, but no boat was to be seen. Before leaving the cover of the spruces I cut my gait and advanced at a stalking pace until I could see the men. Only two of the strangers were visible, sitting side by side in the Yukon boat. They were talking to Mac in our boat on the bar, and my blood boiled as I realized they were bargaining for the return of our food. The men were looking towards Mac so I walked down the shore and into the water without their seeing me, then threw the cocked rifle to my shoulder with no other thought in my head than drilling them both through with a single bullet. But in that split second I could not press the trigger. My finger simply would not set. I had the blood-lust in my heart and the right on my side. I could not understand myself until it flashed in my mind that, like potting grouse or quail on the ground, it was not good sportsmanship to kill men without giving them a chance. So I said, "Hands up!" — hoping by all that was holy that they would reach for their guns. Instead, however, without the slightest hesitation, their hands shot upward. They never even looked my way. I realized that they were tough birds used to this kind of game.

Mac waded over and began restoring the supplies to our cache. With an eye cocked to the woods for the approach of the other men, I began turning over in my mind Mac's apparent disloyalty. Then I realized that his bargaining had been only a stall to give me time to get the gun, and I warmed considerably with the memory of how he had not dropped a clue when he saw what our enemies had not seen as I emerged from the spruces.

Mac was working like a beaver, but finally he paused and called out to me that he had gotten all our supplies out of the boat — plus a couple of hundred pounds of theirs as well and wanted to know if this would even the score.

At that moment the other two outlaws appeared. Taking in the situation at a glance, they began upbraiding their companions in the boat. They asked them with excess profanity if they did not know that the loot was worth $1500.00 in Dawson — and what kind of guards were they anyway? I took a part in the discussion by telling the newcomers to get in the boat and hurried their movements a certain amount by a couple of rifle bullets fired at their feet. Even then they had the gall to tell Mac to untie their mooring line, but he cut it next to the boat, remarking that we could find use for a nice hundred-foot rope like that. The outlaws were getting excited by this time and there might have been real trouble had not Pitts appeared on the scene and put in his vitriol so effectively that they were talked to a stand-still, as their boat disappeared down-river in the darkness....

There were half a dozen families of Indians living around the Post and from time to time others came in to exchange their furs for the few yards of calico and other trading goods Pitts had remaining. The little trading steamboat which should have replenished his stock had failed to reach Selkirk during the summer of 1897. Apparently Pitts and his Indians had been forgotten in the excitement of the gold strike.

One evening our cabin was invaded by a band of Indians from one of the upper tributaries of the Pelly — people who were so primitive and so unfamiliar with white men and their ways that they were impelled to feel us over — our hair, skin and clothing. A white man resents such attention and Mac was for throwing them out on their heads. Instead, however, we had a little fun with them, which culminated in an exhibition of burning water to produce light. We had not yet taken to consuming all our bacon grease (which is the case when the thermometer falls below minus fifty) and were using some of it for illuminating the cabin. Our lamp was a tomato can. Mac had woven a broad wick from strands of cotton cloth and fashioned a burner from the bottom of a condensed milk can which was supported on a wooden float. The grease had burned down until the top of the tomato can cut off the horizontal rays of light.

During a lull in the proceedings, Mac filled a dipper with water from the pail from which the Indians had been drinking and ceremoniously poured it into the lamp, taking care not to spill any on the wick. The wick in its bath of grease naturally floated to the top and the volume of light was increased.

The Indians at once began a babel of jabbering. They were determined to find out how the magic had been accomplished. They had to be shown every detail of the wick and burner and some even sought for the supernatural in the lowly tomato can. All sampled the water again. A week later Pitts told us those Indians were still carrying on water-burning investigations and Pitts was indignant, partly because he sympathized with the simple people and partly because in their desire for knowledge they made his life miserable.

Bailey's wages were chiefly "hiu muck muck," which meant all the grub he could stow away in his india-rubber belly. A camel's capacity for storing water against a time of shortage is not in it with an Indian's capacity for anticipating starvation. I could sympathize with Mac's wistful regard of the Indian at mealtime because my father's people, like his, originated in the Highlands of Scotland. My mother's ancestry, however, was Irish, and for this fact I have often thanked God. Mac's only deficiency was his inability to see a joke on himself, or his pocketbook.

We had tired of Bailey's enjoyment of our food and were carrying on our search for the missing supplies on foot and without his aid. The temperature reached fifty below zero. Islands below Selkirk could be reached by ice-bridges and all had been explored. We had decided to move down-river thirty miles to a new base at Selwyn Creek when a momentous event happened which completely altered our plans.

# Chapter 7

## Near Tragedy for the Renaud Party and the Recovery of the Boats

I had just returned to our cabin with a sled-load of firewood and was about to prepare supper when the door was wrenched open and a man fell halfway across the floor. In reality he was a living skeleton, gaunt beyond belief and in his eyes, as we helped him up, there was a look of terror that suggested insanity. His countenance was further disfigured by black patches on both cheek-bones where the flesh had frozen and sloughed off.

"For the love of God," he said, "For the love of God, take me in, my feet are frozen!"
"Sure, Mon," said Mac, "We'll take ye in! Don't get excited!"

We sat him down in a corner by the stove and I went out for Pitts. The stranger's legs were wrapped with pieces of burnt cloth, which were continued down over the caribou-skin moccasins on his feet. Peeling the coverings off, we noted that each layer was frozen to the next, and when the flesh was finally exposed it was as white and hard as marble.

Pitts ordered a pan of snow and, when it was brought, he buried the man's feet in it and directed us to start a skillet of dried onions stewing. The man raved about inaccessible meats, rafts and canyons, and ravens and ice-jams, but we finally gathered that his name was Renaud and that he had a partner named Hanburg, and that he came from Selwyn Creek. I noticed, however, a sly look in his eye when he gave the Creek as headquarters, but at the time its significance escaped me. The only other fact we learned was that Hanburg was ill and incapable of traveling. Renaud cursed him for not accompanying him.

After the frozen feet had been immersed in the snow a minute or two, Pitts took them out and mopped them dry with a towel and then anointed them with kerosene oil. A minute or so later he buried his own hands in the snow until they were chilled and then felt Renaud's feet. When he detected any warmth to the touch, Pitts put the feet back into the snow. Meanwhile, Mac and I ate our supper and Renaud wolfed a considerable quantity of food. It required something over four hours to draw the frost. After about half that time a faint tinge of color appeared, then the flesh softened so that it could be dented. As with flesh affected with scurvy, the flesh would remain indented an appreciable length of time. Finally, when the flesh was normally soft and resilient, the onions, softened to a paste, were applied as a poultice bound on with cloths.

By the time Pitts had finished his ministrations and left, Renaud had to some extent recovered his poise, though the terror of starvation and cold shone from his eyes. To him, as to many of the others adventuring in Alaska, food and warmth were fanatically and paganly deified.

In a sly way he tried to bargain with us for food and he wanted to know how much we intended charging him for his supper, assuring us he had plenty of money. Mac and I were disgusted and gave him blankets and attempted to turn in. He begged to sleep between us for the luxury of the warmth, assuring us he was not lousy. We refused, more, I think, on account of the loathsomeness of his mind than of his body.

It was one o'clock in the morning and Mac and I were so sleepy we could hardly keep our eyes open, but Renaud brought us suddenly wide-awake by saying, "You would knuckle down if I told you where there were two dark-green canvas boats!" We asked where they were so quickly that he laughed. "Don't you wish you knew?" he jeered.

For an hour Renaud fenced with us trying to make a bargain for half the contents of the boats. Pitts had told him he would not be able to walk for at least two weeks and it was this knowledge only that made him mention the boats. We knew perfectly well that he had found them and, as he had disclosed the fact that there were several more men in his party than the one first mentioned, we feared that his companions would appropriate the food and abandon Renaud for us to support, thus imposing a double handicap. If Renaud had not frozen his feet we should certainly have lost whatever chance we had of recovering the supplies.

Renaud said the boats were on an inaccessible bar in the Yukon in the neighborhood of Selwyn Creek, so hidden in the ice that they would not be seen except by accident, and that he would not give the exact location unless we met his terms. To this I replied, "You never walked that thirty miles on feet frozen like yours! The boats are much nearer. In the morning I will follow back your tracks in the snow and find them."

With the realization of his failure the man became bestial in his chagrin. He raved imprecations one moment and the next groveled at our feet. My statement that as long as we had food we would not let any fellow-creature starve had no effect whatever. It was plain that he did not believe that kind of talk and only thought of our refusal to make a bargain. Finally, however, he wore himself out and became calm. Then we got the true story and it was fortunate that we did because he had scarcely finished when, with a roar that made the hair on our heads stand up — a roar that sounded like all the freight trains in the world were in collision — the ice-jam which had been racing up from Bering Sea reached us. The river rose in places forty feet and Renaud's foot-marks were obliterated. If the jam had come a little sooner we should, in all probability, never had known what had become of our boats.

Renaud's story made us feel much more charitable toward him. It explained, for one thing, his lack of faith in human nature. It was the story of six prospectors caught unawares by the food shortage caused by the Gold Rush. These men had spent the Summer prospecting in the Ogilvy Rockies at the head of the Klondike River, expecting to procure supplies for the Winter on their return to the Yukon but, when they got back, the forefront of the Gold Rush — men traveling with only a few days' supplies — had reached Dawson like a cloud of hungry locusts and absorbed all the food. The one thing that saved Renaud's party from immediate starvation was the fact that they had six or eight hundred pounds of moose-meat with them from an animal they had killed a day or so before, while drifting down the Klondike on a raft. This moose-meat they were able to exchange for flour and other supplies which, while totally inadequate in amount for the Winter, were sufficient, they thought, to see them through to the Coast.

They thought they could reach the Coast in a month, but at the end of two months had not won through the Upper Ramparts of the Yukon, a distance of 185 miles. The last of their supplies had been consumed nearly two weeks before Renaud reached Selkirk.

They left Dawson with poling boats, but soon the mush-ice put an effectual stop to that kind of travel and they changed to sleds. They were following the east side of the Yukon. Their little rim of shore-ice ended at every cliff, washed by a swift current and more than once they had to climb a thousand feet before they could pass such obstructions and return to the river. At times they did not gain a mile a day. They had deep, swift tributary streams to cross, which necessitated detours and the building of rafts. The weather continually grew colder and they had insufficient clothing and blankets.

As they were eking out the last of their supplies they discovered a meat boat of Jack Dalton's, black with ravens, abandoned on a bar. For two days they stayed there trying to reach this food of Tantalus, meanwhile consuming the last of their supplies. The floating ice was too open to cross on foot but too concentrated to permit navigation with a raft, and the water was too deep for wading.

The next day, when opposite Selwyn Creek, they saw two tents in the spruce flat at the Creek's mouth. Just then the ice thickened and jammed. Renaud and young Hanburg, made desperate by privation, started across. They had barely passed mid-stream when the back-up water broke through behind them and the whole jam started moving. The men ran, as men only can run with Death at their heels, leaping from temporary perches on up-ended cakes to others in unstable equilibrium but, by a miracle, they reached the west shore of the river.

The men from both tents were assembled in one of them eating dinner. I have reason to believe that one of the parties was the same which had attempted to loot our supplies, as on both occasions there was a man named MacDonald present. At least six months' supply of provisions was in sight in a cache, but the diners refused even a meal to the starving men.

Like specters at a feast Renaud and Hanburg stood inside the tent watching the men at their repast. They were ordered away but, like dying animals, would not move. At last one of the men, with an oath to the effect that he could not relish his food, asked if he could buy them off to leave with three pounds of beans. Renaud agreed and they were given the beans in a sack. He asked for a pail to boil them in and also for one of three axes he saw lying around, but at that the men left their table and forcibly ejected Renaud and Hanburg.

That night the outcasts, thinly-clad and with no blankets in the merciless cold of fifty below zero, broke off little dead spruce trees with their hands and built four fires between which they huddled as they attempted to parch beans which should have had four hours' boiling. No wonder Renaud thought decency had perished from the earth!

Late the next day they reached a spruce-clad flat, a little basin just inside the sentinel peaks that mark the termination of the Ramparts. There were islands outside in the river and the separating lagoon was frozen. It was the only smooth stretch they had encountered all day. Instead of taking advantage of it Renaud turned to his left and started toward the open water of the river. Part of the story was given by Hanburg and when he told of this event he said he was convinced Renaud had gone all the way insane. Personally, I think Renaud was just in the right condition to be affected by telepathic impulse and that he was acting upon a vaguely realized hunch.

Renaud reached one of the islands and, crossing it, found further progress blocked by the current of the Yukon. Hanburg upbraided him, saying that they had come out of there uselessly, that they were almost gone and would die unless they exercised better judgment. Whereupon Renaud cursed him and started south along the island.

When they reached its upper end, traveling in the cover of the spruces, they found they were cut off from the mainland by an open channel and would have to retrace their steps. Hanburg became lachrymose but, without paying the slightest attention to his protests,

Renaud started toward another island above and still farther out in the river over one of the flimsy ice-bridges that occurred on shoals. The ice rocked with the current and threatened to disintegrate at any moment, but Hanburg feared being left alone and followed.

Halfway across Hanburg saw the frayed end of a rope that Renaud had passed without notice. He pulled on it and some loose ice slid away, disclosing the canvas cover of the missing freight-boat. Renaud, who had stopped and was watching in a dazed way, rejoined Hanburg. They ripped the tarpaulin with a pocket knife and found that they, in this strange way, had become possessors of food beyond their wildest dreams.

They were so famished that they made no selection but seized the first food they laid hands on. This happened to be a fourteen-quart pail half-full of leached sugar from our accident in Lake Labarge, a sack of dried peaches and a sack of flour. They went ashore on the nearest island, built a fire, filled the sugar pail chock-a-bloc with the dried peaches and then, before they were much more than warmed, ate the whole fourteen quarts of peaches and sugar, besides great amounts of half-baked dough. Naturally, they got a bad dose of cramps and it was from this cause that Hanburg was still suffering. They managed, however, to get all the supplies ashore and also the contents of the boat I rowed, which they found still fast to its freight-boat. While they were at work salvaging the things, the remainder of their party appeared on the other bank of the river and were made to understand the good fortune by signals and the exhibition of the plunder. They camped, waiting for the river to close. It was our good fortune that Renaud froze his feet from a wetting received while carrying the last of the things from the ice to the island.

Mac, Renaud and I got very little sleep that night. Every little while the ice would shift as the water of the Yukon forced its way under or over, sometimes with the roar of artillery or again with the staccato of small arms. When daylight came we held a consultation with Pitts. He agreed with us that there was grave danger the others of Renaud's party might decamp with our supplies and leave the incapacitated man on our hands, but he said it would be impossible for another twenty-four hours to reach the island and that we must curb our impatience.

Mac was content to be governed by Pitts' experience and reminded me that four of the refugees were on the other side of the river and subject to the same handicap as ourselves, but I reasoned that men in their condition would be reckless of danger and was determined to reach the island that day.

First, I endeavored to persuade some of the Indians to accompany me, but they refused to go before the next day. The idea was in my mind that most of the seven miles to the island could be negotiated by land, so I started on snow-shoes across country. The first three miles were level, but then the way was barred by the westerly mountain of the twin sentinels that form the gateway to the Ramparts. The face of this mountain presented a practically unbroken rock escarpment, but there were several places where, if it had not been for the ice, it might have been scaled. All the latter part of the day was spent in testing these possible routes without success, and after one particularly dangerous slip which almost sent me over a precipice, I gave up and descended to the river's edge just at night-fall.

The ice was piled in fantastic windrows as high as houses, but between the shore and the ice was a current of rapid water averaging a hundred feet in width. I spent an hour worming my way down-stream over rocks and around buttresses of the mountain until I finally found an ice mass bridging the channel, which made it possible to gain the main body of the jam. Just before going on the ice I had secured a spruce pole eight feet long and with this I tested the ice.

It was a clear night but there was no moon and for this reason it was often impossible to see whether or not the deep shadow in a depression had substance to support my weight. Sometimes when I tested such places with my pole a half acre of brash-ice would fall in with a noise like the side of a greenhouse collapsing. At other times it might be only a few feet which gave way. The current below tugged at my pole as if it were a demon intent on pulling me in and occasionally I had difficulty holding on. Once an open place intervened which seemed to extend across the river from shore to shore. I crossed this on an ice-bridge level with the water, which rocked with the current and once slipped a few feet. My heart came up where I could bite it.

The safest place seemed to be near the center of the river and there too the light was better. About midnight the dim outline of the island appeared on my left. I made my way toward it and helloed, but could get no reply until opposite its lower end. Then a faint answer came and the dim glow of a fire appeared in the spruces. I descended from a miniature mountain of jammed ice to a strip skirting the shore smooth as a skating rink. I could drive my pole through this ice but, as there was no other way of reaching the shore except over it, I started across. It held as long as I moved rapidly but, when stepping ashore, it gave way and I got wet up to my knees.

Hanburg sat by his fire, the picture of dejection. He showed no interest in the news I brought. I stripped off my boot-gear and trousers and, with my feet in the hot ashes, proceeded to dry out socks and trousers. A steel spring thermometer from my outfit, hung on a neighboring tree, in the full light of the fire, registered forty below zero.

Unconsciously taking the key from the sick man we conversed in low tones with long pauses punctuating the sentences. Hanburg told me the smooth ice I had crossed had been open water at sunset. He said that there was no more dead spruce on the island for fuel. By the time my clothing had dried his supply was exhausted, and we proceeded to turn in as the only alternative to freezing.

They had made a sort of cubby from the tent, a small bear-den-like enclosure a couple of feet high and the length of a man's body. Into this Hanburg crawled and I followed. He worked his way into my sleeping bag, remarking that Renaud and he had slept together in it. He added, however, that two men in their condition were no larger in girth than one ordinary man and that he doubted if I could get inside. I tried it but could force my way no farther than my hips. It was so tight a squeeze that it threatened to check the circulation in both of our bodies, so I withdrew all but my feet from the bag. The only other article that could be used for covering was a very light blanket, a blanket so thin that one could see through it. I wrapped this about me and thus we passed the balance of the night, lying on the frozen ground with so little protection from the cold that men not toughened to it would undoubtedly have perished.

In the morning, when it became sufficiently light to see, I hustled some wood and prepared breakfast. Afterwards I tried to persuade Hanburg to accompany me back to Fort Selkirk, but he was not only too weak for the trip but had experienced a terrible scare when the jammed ice started to ride over the head of the island and he thought he would be buried. He said that not all the gold in the Klondike could tempt him to set foot on the ice. I knew that Mac would bring a relief party before long so I waited, puzzled that Hanburg's companions had not appeared.

About noon an odd thing happened, something which might have had disastrous results but which fortunately did not. Hanburg and I were standing silently gazing at the fire when at its center there was the loud report of an exploding rifle cartridge — and a bullet whizzed between our heads and embedded itself in a spruce tree behind. I chopped the bullet out and found it was .30 calibre. My .30-.30 carbine was in camp. As Hanburg remarked, if either of us had been killed by the bullet the other would have swung for murder. The prosecution would have made a perfect circumstantial case, with the motive a quarrel over the food supplies. The men who would have constituted a jury knew what food meant in that country.

In the early afternoon a large party of men came in sight, clambering over the ice. At its head was Mac and with him was Hanburg's older brother. The others were Indians who were drawing a toboggan to transfer the sick man back to Selkirk. We gave the refugees sufficient provisions to last them the balance of their trip from our supplies at the post, and as soon as Renaud's feet were in condition, they left. Later on we learned that all but one reached the outside world. The casualty was a jolly fellow whom we knew only by the name of Sam. He froze his gee-pole arm (used in directing his sled), died as a result of blood poisoning and was buried at the mouth of the Big Salmon River. Sam had shown us large nuggets to the value of $3,000 while at Selkirk.

As soon as our transaction with the Hanburg-Renaud party was completed, Mac and I moved to the island where the supplies were cached. We lived in a Baker tent of Mac's which we banked with snow and heated by our Yukon stove, while we built a cabin on the nearby mainland. We decided that, even though we were perfectly comfortable in the tent, we would feel more secure with a home to house our remaining supplies and as a place of refuge in case of necessity.

# Chapter 8

## Some Survival Suggestions and The Demise of Two Wary Wolves

Many of the older books dealing with Arctic explorations were written by incompetent theorists. My father had a good library of such books and as a boy I had read them all. Now, in temperatures as low as any these explorers had experienced, I had to unlearn a lot of false information they had given as fact. For example, the idea of applying snow for frostbite outdoors is murderous. Snow should only be used indoors where the temperature is warm, for the purpose of retarding the return of circulation. Used outdoors in low temperatures, snow increases the frozen area and *rubbing* with it causes ghastly sores later on. In the open the gentle application of heat is the only means by which frost can be removed. If one's nose, ears or cheek-bones develop white, hard spots, as may happen many times on a cold day when the wind is blowing, the thing to do is to simply warm them with the bare hands. When the hands become cold, put them inside your clothing on your chest and heat them up and keep repeating the process until the frozen part becomes soft and the circulation is restored. If one refrains from rubbing there will be no unpleasant aftereffects.

Another fallacy we unlearned had to do with the use of cold water in bathing. A Mid-Victorian explorer had asserted he had toughened his men to endure low temperatures by obliging them to bathe in icy water outdoors. We found that the only comfortable and beneficial way to bathe in our tent was to use steaming hot water and to do the job quickly. Even then, before one could get his clothes on, the surface of his body would be chilled and exhilarated as if by a cold plunge. One man at a time would strip and while he sloshed and lathered and rinsed his front, his companion would similarly attend to his back. We bathed regularly and this, I am sure, was one of the reasons we enjoyed good health and perfect circulation to combat the cold.

We also learned that to keep comfortable in low temperatures one must not overburden his body. He must keep clothing at the minimum and the moment the pores open from exercise, reduce the amount. At times we stripped to our undershirts with the thermometer twenty below zero.

In 1898 I wrote an article in which an attempt was made to explain why explorers had not then reached the North Pole and the action that should be taken to insure success. This was after Mac and I had made our trip back to the Coast over ice rougher than the paleocrystic ice of the Arctic Ocean, with lower temperatures, and had covered an equal distance to that acquired, for example, by Nansen from the "Fram" without dog teams and with infinitely poorer outfits and supplies. I remember that I emphasized that Summer was not the proper time for Polar dashes, because then there was continuous interruption to travel from open leads and water on the ice.

Perry's success verified many of my statements. The Klondike "Rushers" revolutionized methods of Arctic travel, but of course they did nothing more than apply methods known to Eskimos and Northern Indians from the dim past and bring them to the attention of the civilized world.

We built our cabin of dead spruce logs because green logs, being full of frozen sap, would have made the building much harder to heat. Mac took the job of sledding the logs while I put them together. He had the harder job because of the distance he had to travel, particularly when the nearby supply was exhausted. We were using a Yukon sled borrowed from Pitts. It was about eight feet long and tracked eighteen inches, built of oak and iron-shod. The cabin was ten-by-twelve inside measure and it had no window, because we had nothing we could use from which to make a window, not even beer bottles. We had some five-inch-wide photographic film, and on two occasions I cleared strips of this with hypo to give women otherwise cut off from the sight of an outside world places to look through; but it was too precious for its intended purpose to waste it on ourselves.

One of the recipients was a very pretty girl of nineteen who had frozen her feet badly because her husband was terrified by the cold, would not go outdoors and compelled her to do his work, despite the fact that she had no suitable footgear. They were wintering on the Pelly River about sixteen miles from our cabin and, together with members of the Canadian Yukon Company, were our nearest white neighbors, aside from Pitts. The men of this company, after they learned of the freezing, took the matter in hand and saw to it that both husband and wife received suitable, though not similar, attention.

As there was no volcanic ash available for the dirt roof commonly used on the Yukon, as on shacks in the Western States, on account of the hard-frozen upper soil, we made our roof of the same log construction as the walls. The day I chinked the roof our steel-spring thermometer registered fifty-seven below zero at noon. It is needless to say that I made frequent trips to the ground, where I had a fire. Most of the spruce trees had a spiral grain, but Mac had found one good straight-grained log from which he split the plank for our door. When this was hung on wood hinges and provided with a good latch and rawhide latch-string, the cabin was complete and we felt duly proud of our handiwork.

Inside we had sections of logs for stools, a table constructed from poles and splints and a spring bed. To make the bed we cribbed up a couple of courses of logs and sewed a canvas tick around longitudinal side-poles which suspended the bed. On trying it, however, we found that a center pole was also needed to keep us from rolling together. Our blankets were sewed at the edges to form a sleeping bag large enough for the two of us and we enjoyed luxurious rest. Our stove, however, was not large enough to thoroughly heat the cabin. When developing photographs the solution would freeze in any part of the cabin except on top of the stove.

While still living in the tent and before we occupied our cabin, we had an experience with a pair of old wolf mates which proved that conjugal consistency and affection is not solely a human virtue. The Yukon Valley in those days was thickly populated with wolves and foxes and other fur bearers. We had a small vial of crystalized strychnine and one morning I mixed some of it with cubes of lard and started down-river to distribute the baits where carnivorous animals would find them. I had only gotten as far as the next island when Frank Slavin, who was wintering with the Canadian Yukon Company, turned up. I buried the plate of poison cubes in the snow of the slue and returned with Slavin to our tent.

*Cabin Near Fort Selkirk*

*Interior of Burnham-McKercher Cabin*

*Burnham and Giant Wolf*

*Close-up of the Giant Wolf*

When Slavin left, Mac accompanied him as far as Fort Selkirk, while I returned to the place I had concealed the poison, intending to distribute it farther down the river's edge at points where their runways showed animals were in the habit of passing. To my surprise, however, I found that a wolf had already visited the cache. He appeared to have scented it from the mainland a hundred yards away and then left on a gallop heading towards a spot where a faint current of steam betrayed the presence of an open air-hole.

Picking up the plate of poison,[1] I followed the tracks and saw where the wolf had fallen in the snow on his side and then gotten up and run towards a part of the shore which had not before been visible. Looking in that direction I saw there ten or a dozen ravens perched in spruce trees and below them at the river's edge the body of an exceptionally large wolf. It was a beautiful animal, pure white and not yellow like many of the so-called white Arctic wolves, and he had a benign expression like a fine old Newfoundland dog; though his face was somewhat marred by a malformed tush, which showed outside his mouth. His age was attested by the worn condition of his remaining teeth and the fact that he had a few porcupine quills in his nose, thus betraying the fall in estate of the famous puller-down of caribou stags. There was a raw opening in his flank where the ravens had begun feasting on the kidney fat.

I dug a hole among three roots under the bank and again buried the poison: I did not want to waste it on ravens. While doing this the idea occurred to me that I could have some fun with Mac by placing the wolf in the narrow trail to our tent, where he was certain to run into him on his return that night. Accordingly I did not skin the wolf on the spot but started to drag him to camp. The ice was level but the snow on its surface was just the consistency to exert the maximum friction, so presently I raised the animal to my shoulders and carried him the rest of the way to cabin. I estimated the weight at 135 pounds and he measured, when frozen-stiff later on, six feet ten inches from the end of his hind legs to his nose.

Our trail from the river to the tent had been cut through small spruces which formed a jungle on either side. I cut a pole and braced it chest high across the trail and on this supported the wolf. Then, as it was too late in the day to cover the distance I had planned for the poison trail, I set to work sledding supplies to the cabin site.

On my first trip I was surprised to note the tracks of a wolf following my own made only a few minutes before while carrying in the big fellow. On my way back I passed additional fresh tracks in my sledge-trail so, puzzled at the unusual daring displayed by the animal, I slipped my .30-.30 carbine in the ropes holding the load on the sled and proceeded on my next trip, very cautiously, making as little noise as possible. As I rounded the end of an island I saw a wolf dart from my sled-trail and run like a wraith toward the next island below. The light by now was none too good, but I caught the rifle sights on her body and pressed the trigger. She was looking back over her shoulder and as the flame spurted from the rifle, made a great leap sideways and disappeared in the spruces. It was such a wonderful instance of anticipating an intention I could almost have sworn she had dodged the bullet!

I ran to the island and followed her spoor to its center and then, stopping, became aware of the fact that the wolf was circling my position as attested by the scolding of the red squirrels. Again I moved in her direction and, when I stopped, the volume of the squirrels' chattering was behind me. It was hopeless to attempt to stalk an alert animal possessed of such keen senses, with such soft and noiseless foot-pads, so I gave up and completed the embarkation of the supplies, with an eerie feeling that some ghost were-wolf at any moment might spring from the shadows. On my way I noted that the snow in the neighborhood

---

[1] Since traps were few and money from sale of furs urgently needed, Burnham resorted to poison — a practice he strongly opposed.

where the white wolf had died was a maze of wolf tracks.

The surprise planned for Mac was all too successful. He came back in the pitch-dark while I was preparing our evening meal and the yell he let loose as he ran into and grappled with the dead wolf scared me, I am sure, almost as much as he was scared. When he entered the tent, his face was white as chalk. "The creature! The creature!" — was all he could say at first, and then he told of a great hairy thing which had pounced on him. After that Mac wished on me all the trips away from camp that could not be completed by daylight, and this was my punishment. As I have said before, Mac's sense of humor was not highly developed. He could see no joke in the incident — nor can I in retrospect.

Several inches of snow fell that night. In the morning Mac went to the river to get a pail of ice to melt for water and on his return reported a fresh wolf track almost at the entrance to our tent. He said the wolf had come there to scent the dead one. We debated the subject at breakfast and came to the conclusion that the track had been made by the mate of the old white wolf I had poisoned, and that it was this wolf which had followed me the evening before on account of my clothing's carrying the scent which she had lost when I had given up dragging him. Our interest was aroused and when we had finished eating we set out on the wolf trail. The track led north straight as the crow flies to the place where her mate had died. There she lay dead herself, one paw on a crushed raven which had too rashly attempted to attack her. Quite unsullied, her glassy eyes were directed at others of the gloomy company perched above in the spruces. She was a beautiful gray wolf, younger than the other but without doubt his mate. As Mac remarked she had committed suicide the moment she found her mate was surely dead. "Her tracks show," said Mac, "that she found the poison yesterday, but the poor creature did not take it until she knew her mate was no more."......

A short distance down-river below our cabin was the overland terminus of the old Indian trail over which Jack Dalton had driven cattle from Chilkoot on the Pacific Coast for the Dawson market. At this point the cattle were slaughtered and the carcasses rafted the remainder of the distance to Dawson. The offal had attracted to the spot various kinds of meat-eating animals as well as ravens, and for the last two weeks in December I was occupied in trapping and poisoning them. Mac, unfortunately, had no interest in this kind of thing and kept to the cabin.

I succeeded in poisoning a number of red foxes in beautiful pelage and caught marten in steel traps. These marten were very dark, on a par with the so-called Russian crown sable, and had a white patch on the chest in place of the dash of orange found in their Eastern cousins. We saw them not infrequently chasing and capturing red squirrels in the spruces. Like all animals of the weasel tribe their movements are incrediby swift.

Today, marten are almost exterminated in the Upper Yukon Valley and so are the foxes, but strangely enough there has been a remarkable increase in the number of moose, no doubt due to the decrease in the Indian population. At a rough guess, the Yukon watershed must be nearly as large as the Mississippi watershed above St. Louis, which takes in a tremendous slice of the United States, and yet total present population of this great area, both Indian and White, is less than the daily population of one of many of the larger office buildings in New York City.

The chief reason for the disappearance of the marten is of course the high prices paid for the pelts, but the destruction of the spruce along the river is also an important factor. In the heyday of the Klondike the woodburning river-steamers used so much spruce that the Provincial authorities became alarmed and in the interest of forest preservation enacted a regulation prohibiting the cutting of growing trees for fuel. As a result, the woodchoppers started incendiary fires all along the river and green spruce disappeared. Marten are not rodents, nor herbivorous, but spruce trees are necessary for their existence because the red squirrels which provide their chief food must have spruce cones to survive the winter. Incidentally, spruce trees are practically the only trees which grow as far north as the locality where we were at this time. We had seen no Banksian pine after leaving White Horse Rapids, and were not in an aspen country. There were, however, a very few small white birches growing within five miles of our cabin.

A thing which interested me at this time is the apparent immunity from strychnine poisoning of marten and wolverine. A pair of the latter animals were in the habit of following my poison trail and destroying the foxes which took my baits. When one of these wolverines found a dead fox, it was his custom to throw the body over his shoulders and carry it to the thickest jungle of spruce he could find and there rend it to pieces, scattering the fur all over the area, as he consumed the animal "body, bones and hymn book too," as was the case of the missionary of "the plains of Timbuctoo." Maybe a lower jaw would be left, but precious little else besides the fur. I tried to poison the wolverines, either by decreasing and also increasing the amount of poison administered but, while they ate all that was put in their way, they did not succumb.

The one that ate the largest dose seemed to be most inconvenienced, as he fell down repeatedly. A wolf or a fox dies either the second or third time he falls, but this wolverine fell at least twenty times. I followed his trail for several hours until he had recovered from the effects of the poison and had resumed his normal gait and begun hunting again. He had not vomited and so relieved himself, but he had perspired copiously. Each time he fell the snow was stained a dirty yellow. It was apparently through his pores that he got rid of the poison.

In order to get any fur at all it was necessary to get rid of the wolverines; but while I accomplished this result, it was not in the way I had planned. I constructed a dead-fall of spruce logs, heavy enough to hold a black bear, and drove wire spikes through both the weighted log and the bed-piece so that their points projected more than an inch. A few hours after it was set a wolverine sprang it so that it fell on his shoulders, but when I got there he was not in evidence. He had lifted the great weight far enough to pull his body out, but the upper set of spikes were blood-stained and his hair and patches of skin were scattered all around. The wolverine must have presented a sorry sight to his mate! At any rate, the pair cleared out and we were not again troubled by wolverines.

The carcasses of some of our poisoned animals were piled against our cabin at the back. One night after we were asleep an animal roused us by its gnawing on the frozen meat. We held a whispered consultation. Mac thought it was a bear, but I told him all the bears were hibernating so we compromised on a wolf. The sounds seemed to indicate an animal as large as a wolf, but the quality of rending was absent. I could think of no creature of that country large enough to create such a volume of sound which would be contented merely with gnawing its prey.

We tiptoed across the dirt floor in our bare feet and secured our rifles. We knew that the wood hinges of the door creaked abominably, so, with a quick motion, we threw it open and dashed to the back of the cabin. Keyed for conflict with an unknown fury we stopped and were rooted to the spot. We looked at each other inanely, for in the bright moonlight we had seen a tiny dark creature, the size of an elongated rat, spring from a wolf carcass into a neighboring tree — and we realized that all the pother was over a marten! Strange how the still air of sixty below zero intensifies sounds!

We went back to bed, but had no more than settled comfortably when the the marten returned to his gnawing. Mac was so irritated that he crept out and took a shot at him with his rifle, but missed. Almost as soon as he returned to his bed the marten was back at his feast and there he remained until daylight. I got up once and doctored the place he was chewing with strychnine, but the marten seemed to enjoy it as some people like mustard on their ham.

The next evening, as I was following our trail from the river, the marten appeared and hopped along sociably, only a few feet in advance, almost in our cabin. It might have gone into the cabin if it had not been for a large fire Mac had built to thaw the ice out of the Baker tent. When I told Mac that the marten wanted to adopt us, he became excited and ordered me to get one of my steel traps and end the nuisance forthwith.

We had just sat down to supper when I distinctly heard the trap snap. Picking up a stick of stove-wood, I ran to the corner of the cabin and was met by the marten no longer amiable and attractive, but a little spitting demon, bent on bloodshed. I reset the trap and some time later during the night caught a second marten. Pairs are the order of the universe! "Male and female created He them..."

Although old-timers we met have told us that the trip as we planned it was absolutely impossible, we nevertheless continued to make preparations for a trip to Dawson. Two sleds were constructed from spruce poles 6 inches wide and 8 feet long, joined together with rawhide lashings and with runners shod with strips of white birch laboriously ripped from the tree with a cross-cut hand-saw. December 30th all was ready, but that day we made a complete reversal of plan. For some time Mac and I had been discussing what would happen when the big rush of miners hit White Horse Rapids in the Spring. We knew there would be ten times as many men coming down in '98 as in '97 and we foresaw a traffic glut at that point which might check indefinitely the advance of the hordes. We felt sure that anyone who could ease the jam would coin money.

I had seen a little, narrow-gauge railroad used for getting the logs from a southern cypress swamp, with rails made from round poles on which ran flanged wheels, and Mac agreed with me it would be no trick at all to build such a road the three miles around Miles Canyon and White Horse Rapids. The lodge-pole pines which grow there were straight as arrows, the soil was sandy and level for the most part and the grades at either end by no means difficult. We knew there was quite a colony of stranded men at that point who would be glad of work before the river opened, and who would not be difficult on the wage question. All that was needed was a little capital, eight or ten thousand dollars, to purchase supplies and hardware; to pay wages and obtain horses and mules for motive power. I thought I knew where I could get the money and we had about made up our minds to try this as our Eldorado when Frank Slavin turned the final trick by making us a good offer for our surplus goods. Then and there the dice were cast and on December 31st we started planning our hike to the Coast....

> [After his return to New York City Burnham received a cable from his partner informing him that Norman Macauley and Andy Hepburn had already built horse-powered tramways along both sides of the Canyon. Thereupon the resourceful Burnham countered by drawing up plans for an aerial cable device to be placed directly over the west channel of the River and the Rapids. By this method, for a fee of $25 each, about 20 boats per day could be attached to guidewires and safely lowered through the three-mile stretch of vicious whitewater which wrecked more than 150 craft and claimed ten lives during the first few days of the down-river stampede.
>
> Against a cost estimate of $90,000 Burnham anticipated a possible return of nearly a million dollars, of which he eventually expected a sizeable share.

*Although the enterprising young man succeeded in raising the required capital, the prospect of a late Spring and a necessarily shortened transportation season put the kibosh on the very viable proposition: Editor]*

*Part of the Female Klondike Contingent*

*Dog Teams On the Trail*

*Heavy Sledding*

*Wolverine Family*

# Chapter 9

**Rumors and Reports from Dawson City**

December 30th was eventful in more ways than one, for it brought us our first news of the Winter from the outside World. Three hard-bitten men, John Peche and his two half-breed companions, came in by dog-team with Canadian Government dispatches for Dawson. We were greatly surprised when they told us there was no war between the United States and Japan. How the story originated nobody knows but the war was an accepted fact in the interior that Winter. The last news we had was of a naval engagement in which Rear Admiral Beardsley's flagship, the Philadelphia, had been sunk; but the final result of the battle was in doubt and we were naturally on edge to learn if the Pacific Coast cities had been bombarded. We had heard so much about the war that it required time to rid our minds of the false information, and to realize it was a figment of the imagination of active minds of men completely isolated from a restless world.

Mac and I learned other news from the dog-team mushers who were now coming up-river from Dawson. Some of these men were from the little company who had been at Circle at the time of George Carmack's discovery on Bonanza Creek, who had "struck it rich," and were in a hurry to get out to spend their nuggets. Others were refugees who had "gone in light" the previous Fall but now, for lack of supplies, must reach the Coast or die of starvation. All alike cursed Pitts for the supplies he did not have and Pitts cursed them back with added rancor. One of the men was Behrens, who had been a packer in the Cryolite mines in Greenland. He was a shrewd Dane who had gone through with limited food supplies but filled his boat with a miscellaneous assortment of discarded junk from Bennett. He said that before his boat was made fast at the river front at Dawson, men were bargaining for the things. He sold four seventy-five cent window sashes for $400 — and the men who bought them boasted of his bargain all Winter. A twenty-five cent bottle of vinegar extract went for $75.00 and so on. He had landed at Dawson with just three cents in his pocket, which was nothing at all in a country where eight bits, or a dollar, was the smallest change, and now he was going out with capital to build a hotel at Sheep Camp in Chilkoot Pass. There were others who had cleared from $10,000 to $15,000 on a few cases of whiskey taken in on the side and who planned boat-loads for the Spring. Whiskey was a dollar a shot; cigars, a dollar apiece, and eggs the same price. A meal with ham, eggs, beans, bread and coffee or tea — when it could be had — was $15.00. Wages on the Creek were $15.00 per day and board — and what gold the man could hijack with his fingers from the pay streak. Anyone was a dub who would not double or triple his nominal pay.

They told of "Big Alex" MacDonald[1] (later the prototype hero of Jack London's "Burning Daylight") who, when he received the first news of the Klondike at Circle had the hunch that this was the big strike, and who mortgaged the future by putting all he had and all he could borrow into supplies and their transport, and how this man who could not read or write accumulated shares (or fractions) in many of the most fabulously valuable claims for messes of pottage!

They told of Antone Stander and Clarence Berry, for mankind loves winners, how the former, a foreigner who could hardly speak English and knew little about mining, wandering through the forest found a gold-bearing creek. Stooping down to take a drink, so the story goes, he saw through the clear water in the seams of a rock surface quantities of yellow pebbles which, when retrieved, proved to be abnormally heavy. He gathered what he could that day and buried them, and then for several weeks spent his time, like Diogenes, looking for an honest man. When at length he was satisfied he led the man he trusted to his find. The beauty of the story is that he had not made a mistake. The stranger showed the discoverer how to record his claim and assured his own fortune by filing on the next below. The nuggets which the stampeder had taken out with his bare hands sold for $80,000 and sluicing produced more than a million more.

Berry, it was said, was another example of Lady Luck's fickleness for the tried and true. In the Klondike, expert miners did not fare as well as the rankest Cheechako. Berry, who had been a fruit farmer in Fresno, California, went in to Circle for a lark in 1896. Being an inexperienced musher he was one of the last on the ground when Circle went crazy and moved en masse to the Klondike. He walked the entire length of Bonanza Creek and found every claim staked, and then he repeated the experience on the big side "pup" called Eldorado, four miles long. On the way back from the head of Eldorado, however, he noticed quite by accident that there were no double stakes at the limits of what should have been Thirteen Below Discovery. With his pocket knife he cut four saplings, shaved one side flat, wrote his name on the surface with a lead pencil, pushed them into the ground— and by so doing acquired the richest of all Klondike claims, one which produced more than $3,000,000. Ironically enough, several individuals had previously passed up Claim 13 as unlucky — and lived to regret that superstition.

One of the crop of new millionaires who were part of the exodus was accompanied by a very beautiful girl, who might have been Rex Beach's Cherry Mallotte. This gentleman, called Nigger Jim on account of his Southern accent, took up a cache of dried salmon dogfood left with Pitts the Fall before by a man named Barton, on a written order signed with Barton's name. Pitts was suspicious, but had to admit it appeared to be correct. Three days later, while Mac and I were at Selkirk, Barton himself appeared and demanded his salmon. When Pitts explained what had happened and showed the order, Barton threw seven fits. He was in a particularly vile humor, because one of the Indians practicing with Mac's rifle had shot the tail off his lead dog and incapacitated him. When Barton recovered sufficiently to be lucid, we learned that the lady was no lady and, moreover, an ingrate. She was called the "Kansas City Cyclone," so Barton said. He represented Boston parties who held options on Birch Creek claims near Circle City and, when going in the Fall before, in their interest had been persuaded against his will to take the girl with him. Her people were highly respectable and she had strictly observed the proprieties — and everything ran smoothly until after Barton introduced her to the best people in Dawson and left for Circle. Then, said

---

[1] Aptly described as the King of the Klondike the reticent, insatiable speculator MacDonald, with paper profits reckoned to be worth many millions, eventually died penniless and alone.

Barton, the corks of fifty-dollar champagne bottles began popping, and the deluge broke loose in all-night revelry.

On his return, Barton found his reputation with the best people worth no more than last year's birds' nests. The best people were scandalized and put all the blame on Barton instead of where it rightfully belonged. Barton's voice broke when he mentioned his lost reputation, but it grew hard and vindictive again as he recalled the stolen salmon. He wanted to know what good beef heads were for dog food — "90% bone and 10% camouflage!" was the way he characterized them, only he used a grosser word for camouflage. The girl had remembered every place he had cached the light and nutritious salmon on the way down-river, and as a result of her forged orders, her dogs were in fine fettle and widening the gap with their pursuer every day.

A man I particularly wanted to meet but failed to get in touch with was my distant kinsman, Major Frederick Russell Burnham, who has told his Klondike experiences in his classic adventure book, *Scouting in Two Continents*.

*Ancient Squaw and Smoke Spooks (Stoddard photo)*

*Kloochmen at Home (Stoddard photo)*

# Chapter 10

## More Survival Tactics and the Houtchikoo Murders

When Mac and I started our outbound trek on the last day of 1897 we each pulled a sled loaded with two hundred pounds. Of the four hundred pounds total weight, three hundred and thirty were food and seventy bedding, in the form of sleeping bags. We had toothbrushes, combs, and a few negligible extras, but no stove, no tent, no rifles; not even a change of clothing except extra socks. The only firearm was a short barrel .38 revolver which I carried in a hip pocket. Our cooking utensils were three light pails and a frying pan. We each had a tin plate and cup on which our initials were scratched to save washing. Every last ounce of non-essential was sacrificed because it was a starvation trail that reached ahead of us, as long as the distance which separated Peary's base from the Pole, and the old-timers all said that two men alone without dogs could not make it.

We could not get dogs because the Klondike magnates had run the price up even as far away as Selkirk to $500 per dog, or $2500 for the average team. We did not have the money and the dogs that were left were few in number and of indifferent quality.

The first day out we only made two miles and I developed grippe, the only real sickness either of us had in seven months. The day before I had gone into an Indian cabin to photograph a couple of ancient hags, whose exceptionally lined faces in combination with unkempt hair and a wild ensemble had fascinated me. They were squatting over a smoky fire in the center of the floor. Against an inside wall was a stack of gaily-colored bokis in diamond patterns about a foot square. I piled several of these on top of one another as a stand for the camera, not knowing that each contained the ashes of an ancestor, and then started another pile as a base from which to fire a magnesium flashlight charge. While I was doing this, every Indian in Selkirk piled in — men, women and children, 'til the place was jammed to the point of suffocation. Most of the Indians were hawking and coughing and this is how I got the grippe.

I threw a wad of paper to one side to make them look that way so as to save their eyes and touched off the flash. It went off with a "whoof" that threatened to take the roof off the cabin and hidden by the mantle of smoke, I took my leave before the Indians realized the performance was over. Not one of them, I am sure, had the faintest idea what it was all about. They all waited inside to see what kind of a spirit had been exorcised.

I soon developed a high fever. Mac was very much worried and wanted to camp until my condition improved, but this was out of the question. I was so nauseated I could not eat. Half the time we were climbing miniature ice mountains, doubling up on the sleds and sometimes having to lift them bodily, and then holding back for all we were worth to prevent their smashing on the down-grade. Our course was over a continuous succession of windrows of jumbled ice-cakes. We were over-loaded by a third. The rule of the country, developed from long experience is that a man can pull on a sled no more than his own weight, and Mac and I each weighed about 150.

I think it was the second night after leaving Selkirk that a mouse invaded our blankets and bit me on the nose. Excited by the pain I flung the blankets off my head and sat up so suddenly that Mac at my side was roused wide-awake instantly. When I told him what had happened he naturally assumed it was an hallucination and that I was delirious. "There, there, mon," he said, "don't you believe it. It was no mouse." And he put his arms about me, with the evident intention of restraining me from crazily running away. The action put a strain on my taut nerves, and I struggled with him as I told him to take his hands off. But I was weak from lack of food and physical exhaustion and also had enough sense to realize his point of view, so I soon gave up and settled down. We pulled the blankets over our heads and the deathless silence of the winter forest settled down again, a silence that only was broken by occasional pistol-like reports from the freezing sap in the trunks of the spruce trees.

Mac tried to keep awake, as I could tell from his suppressed breathing, but presently tired Nature got the upper hand. I was stanching a very real flow of blood from the end of my nose, which Mac had not observed, when of a sudden there was a minor earthquake at my side, the blankets were convulsively disrupted, and we again found ourselves sitting upright in the cold moonlight. "Drat the little creature," said Mac, as he shook his right hand and then brought it to his mouth, "the infernal pest had bitten me on the finger!"

We each reached out and got sticks of wood and then rested on elbows, waiting. Presently a chinchilla-colored woods-mouse nearly as large as a chipmunk appeared, weaving its way in and out among the forest litter back to our bed. Evidently the nose and finger he had sampled were to his liking. They were, however, the last samples of human flesh he tasted. Off-stage, as it were, I disclose the fact that he was ruthlessly assassinated.

We improved our mileage steadily up to eight and ten and then with much lighter loads to fifteen miles per day. Our best day's run was twenty-five miles across the full length of Lake LaBarge. During December and January we never saw the sun. We were south of the Arctic Circle, but in a deep river valley, and moreover, in that intense cold of fifty and sixty below zero — once in the trip the thermometer reached sixty-seven below — the air was clouded with frozen mist. Even at midday there was no clear vision. We could get no distant views and things at short distances were distorted, spectral and ghostly. Much of our travel was in the darkness. We allowed ourselves eight hours' sleep and the rest of the time, aside from making and breaking camp and eating, was devoted to travel. We started in the dark and finished the day without light except when the moon helped us. Our best days were at the time of the full moon. We feared most of all a broken leg. The footing was terribly uneven and it was not possible to see what the shadows concealed.

We had provided against starvation with the remnants of strychnine in our little bottle. Not that we intended to use the poison for self-destruction, which was farthest from our thoughts, but to secure meat for our bellies. Wolves, which ate poisoned foxes, while highly susceptible themselves to the poison, were not inconvenienced; and we had decided if our supplies gave out to try the experiment of subsisting on poisoned wolves and foxes. There were plenty of them along the river. We saw them every little while.

Sometimes as we rounded a turn we would see the wolves and foxes scurrying for the cover of the forest from a disheveled mass of torn rags, or ravens taking a more leisurely flight to their perches in the trees, and then as we approached we would find as the nucleus of the rags, the bony structure of what had once been a man. The eye-sockets were always staring and empty because their contents are the raven's favorite tidbits.

Most of the dead men were found in the stretch of the "30 Mile River" below White Horse Rapids. Some undoubtedly had met death by drowning the previous Fall, but most, I think, were from the ranks of the Dawson refugees. In severe cold a man requires considerably more food for bodily fuel than to replace the tissue consumed by physical exertion. As their food ran low they tried rationing with disastrous results. Partial starvation reduced their vitality and made them easy victims to freezing. It was a gruesome object lesson. Death paced our progress. We did not oversleep in the mornings.

Mac and I between us had three watches, but the two best had given up the ghost and could not be made to run. We were left with a cheap watch which had to be carried in a tin salve box because its crystal was broken and otherwise the hands would have been torn off. No watch that hasn't a full-jeweled movement will run out-doors in a low temperature, and even though I carried this timepiece inside my trouser-band the lubricant on its bearings would freeze as soon as we got up in the morning. With rifles it is necessary to burn the lubricant from the reloading mechanism to make them serviceable. We lost all track of standard time, but the watch was useful to keep us from oversleeping.

When our day's travel was over we would hunt for a flat place on the river's bank and then for a dead spruce tree. These factors governed the selection of our camping place. Our work was systemized. With our snowshoes we cleared the ground to an area large enough for our bed and our fire, piling the snow on all sides as a windbreak. Next we cut a six-inch log for a pillow, spread our blanket sleeping bag and stamped it flat. Then the fire was started and we changed our socks and, while I cooked the supper, Mac dried out the socks we had worn that day for use the next morning. His was by far the hardest job. We each wore four pair of socks, so there were sixteen individual socks to be looked after. These were hung in a fringe around the fire on branches stuck in the snow. As the heat of the fire varied, their position had to be constantly changed. Our pail of water, set at the edge of the fire, would be simmering on the hot side and skimmed with ice on the other side. It was the same with the socks. The plane between freezing and burning could be measured in millimeters. If kept a few inches outside this range, the socks remained frozen and, of course, undried. If brought inside it, they were burned. Every time the foot part burned we would cut the sock off with a pocket-knife and sew up the end. We started with regular Christmas stockings and ended with abbreviated half-hose.

When our meal was ready we settled down to eat with real appreciation and delight. We could conceive of no greater physical enjoyment. First, came about a gallon of mush to take the edge off. Then hot bread and bacon and stewed fruit. We wound up for dessert with a mixture of raisins and bacon grease and could not, at that time, realize that we might ever tire of such a diet. When we ate pork we merely warmed it and consumed it raw to get the full benefit of the fat. Our drink was tea. For some reason, in extreme cold, tea seems more satisfying than coffee. It is the drink of the Eskimo. We missed fresh meat, it is true, and often while tracking our sleds would think and talk for hours on end of thick steaks smothered in onions and turkeys with oyster dressing; but as an actual fact we missed most from our diet the lowly bean, red or white. If I wrote of the ecstasy evoked by this Epicurean delicacy, I should probably nauseate some of my readers, so I will pass it by; merely saying that our schedule did not permit keeping a fire going the four hours required to boil beans. Also we had no suitable coals for baking them. Several times we tried cooking them on successive fires, but they froze so hard in between that before we could start them again they burned.

*One Who Didn't Make It*

*Burnham's Watch in Salve Box Carrier*

*Packet Awaiting Spring Launching at Lake Bennett*

*Northwest Mounties and Teams*

Supper over, the watch was thawed by the simple expedient of burying it in the hot ashes until after shaking we could hear it tick. We dusted the hoar-frost from each other's backs and, having slipped the watch in next to the body, turned in for the night.

Before we reached the Coast our blankets became so stiff with ice from frozen breath that we had a hard job prying them apart to get inside. We would stand side by side with our feet on the bottom folds and, stooping, grasp the upper folds and heave. It was cold for a while inside, until heat from our bodies softened the blankets. Then we would tuck the upper folds over our heads and sleep dreamlessly.

We always had pieces of candles in our pockets for lighting fires. Toward morning I would wake and consult the watch. When our eight hours were up, with the lighted candle in my gloved hand, I would crawl out and start a fire. We slept with all our clothes on, including four pairs of socks and two pairs of moccasins, fur cap and two pairs of mittens. Dog-team travelers generally were garbed in heavy furs, but this style of clothing, unless worn the native way, next to the skin, causes profuse perspiration. Our work was heavy, but at times required agility and quick action. We added very little to our customary method of dressing, but this little was highly effective for comfort and safety. The extra wool socks on our feet and the soft-tanned buckskin moccasins were essential, as with ordinary leather or rubber foot-gear a man with the best circulation in the world will freeze his feet when the thermometer gets below minus 40, no matter how many socks he wears. On our hands we wore heavy wool mittens inside great fur gauntlets hung by rawhide thongs around our necks. Many times during the day our hands were out of the gauntlets and sometimes of course free from the mitts also, but it is essential to have a means of keeping the hands warm, as otherwise frostbite cannot be removed from one's face. Our caps were capotes which covered the entire head and neck except for the face, with the face-opening fringed with wolverine fur, the only fur that does not collect frost. We sewed on one side a horizontal strip of the same fur and an inch wide, with a button hole, to be buttoned across over cheeks and nose at times when the wind blew; thus leaving only our eyes and mouth exposed. Next to our bodies we wore two suits of light-weight Jaeger wool underwear, which is twice as warm as the same weight in one suit, and then the lightest kind of a chamois-skin shirt as protection from the wind. Over our wool trousers we added closely-woven overalls for the same purpose. Our costume was completed with heavy wool shirts, sweaters and mackinaw coats. We also had light drill parkas for use on windy days. As soon after starting as we began to feel the warmth from exertion, we would strip off the coat, next the sweater and often the shirt as well. The neck-strings of our caps would be loosened and the flaps turned up and our hands freed from the gauntlets. This, of course, was only on days when there was no wind. The North is stimulating and delightful no matter how cold it is when the air is still, and particularly so when the days grow long and the sun shines.

Stefansson, who in many respects is the most competent Arctic traveler of all times, fails in his "Friendly Arctic" to give a single line of mention to the nerve-wracking curse of the winter darkness. Any healthy man will enjoy the cold and receive physical benefit therefrom, but it takes an exceptionally well-balanced human being to come unscathed through the long night. Insanity from this cause is common in the Northland and it is the cause of many crimes of violence. The antidote is work in the open, but this work must be carried on under great handicaps.

Mac and I were obliged one night to camp on the ice, owing to the fact that a precipitous bluff of considerable extent prevented our getting ashore. We had eaten some burned and frozen beans for lunch and were quite unwell as a result. It happened, therefore, that we were both awake when sometime after midnight the faint tinkling of bells reached our ears. Our heads came out, like turtles from their shells, and we saw a dog team, accompanied by one man go by, followed after a slight interval by another dog team and man. The bells were on the first team. We realized that something dramatic was going on, but it was not until we reached the Big Salmon that we got an inkling of the meaning of the pursuit from the police at that point. One of the men was a drover for Jack Dalton, who had left Dawson with the owner of the first dog team to pass us. At Selkirk they had a quarrel and the team owner went on without the drover. After he had left, according to the drover's story, the latter discovered he had been robbed of the proceeds of his cattle sale, $15,000 or so in gold dust. Whereupon he commandeered Pitts' dog team and started in pursuit.

The drover had heard there were police at the Big Salmon and he determined to keep the man in sight until that place was reached, in the hope he could prevent his hiding the gold on the way. The other fellow made him all the trouble he could. He tried to get the jump on the drover by starting an hour after camping, keeping the bells on his dogs until ready to start and then removing them, and by other subterfuges designed to mislead and worry his pursuer and prevent his getting any sleep. But the drover hung on like a leech, and the two came to the cabins at the Big Salmon side by side. The suspected man's outfit was searched, but the plunder was not found. The general impression was that he had discovered a good place of concealment and hidden it somewhere along his route. One cynical "mounty" had a different opinion: "The drover is the man we ought to have searched," he said, "the gold belonged to Jack Dalton and not to him. That guy had the brains to cash in on his quarrel. Probably he started the row, and now is going out to spend the proceeds!"

We were on the fringe of a still more sinister affair near Houtchikoo Bluff. Rough ice at this point forced all the travel over next to the east side of the river. There was a low aspen flat on our left terminating ahead in a spruce point which the trail hugged closely. The point commanded the trail and served as an ambush for a pair of black-hearted murderers. There is good reason to believe that these men were watching us and that the lives of Mac and myself hung by a mighty flimsy thread when, following a fresh man's track in the snow, we left our sleds, climbed the bank and followed it some little distance on the flat, after it had come into a well-traveled trail. We were hungry for contact with fellow human-beings and we knew the men who made the trail were white men and not Indians on account of the large size of the footprints. After following the trail several hundred yards, however, we came to the conclusion that no cabin was near and that the trail must lead to some distant point, so we abandoned it and returned to the river. We gave up just in time. Had we proceeded to the trail's end this story in all probability would never have been written.

Little by little, as we journeyed to the Coast and afterwards, we learned all that will ever be known of the Houtchikoo murders. A week after we had passed, the police at the Big Salmon had their first intimation. A Canadian Government telegraph line had gotten that far down-river. One of the linemen had gone to Selkirk on business and had not returned. A search party found that he had safely reached Selkirk and left on his way back in company with two Klondike magnates. As none of the three had turned up at Big Salmon, the police on their return trip made a careful search of every foot of the trail. Half a mile below the ambuscade and at a distance from the trail was an open place where the swift current had not frozen, and here they found blood-stains and evidence of bodies dragged through the snow and dumped in. As they proceeded toward the spruce point, they found that fresh snow had been brushed in with boughs to cover the evidence of the charnel trail. Much time was wasted before the police located the scene of the crime, and it is probable that their quarry took advantage of this delay to make their escape.

The trail the searchers were following merged with the river trail but, seeing the tracks in the bank, they followed them across the aspen flat, farther than we had gone, and found the murderers' abandoned camp. Here were clothing and personal articles taken from victims and the ashes of the fire were full of buttons from other burned clothing. Following back on the trail to the spruce point the police saw where fallen trees had been piled to make a low barrier commanding a view of the trail for a long distance, fur robes on which the murderers had lain and with which they had covered themselves while awaiting victims, and many fired rifle shells.

There had been two beds at the robbers' camp and the signs showed that two men had lain in the ambush, but from this point on there is only evidence of one man. The theory is that, the game having been worked to the limit, one of the men finished the other with the object of doubling his winnings.

Word was sent to the police guarding the passes over the completed part of the telegraph line and in due time a big sullen man without dogs and pulling his sled, was held up and searched. His sled was loaded with gold and even the reins had been hollowed to hold nuggets and dust. The man was taken back to Dawson and held in confinement for two years and eventually executed, solely on circumstantial evidence. Possibly he was held this exceptional length of time in the hope that he would give information that would make definite the cause of the disappearance of the missing men, who could not be traced; but it is said he died without making a confession.

I am very sure that if Mac and I had reached the robbers' camp we would not have left alive. The men watching us rightly reasoned that we had seen nothing to arouse suspicion and, moreover, they could hear every word of our conversation and knew we had not grasped the significance of the situation. Even then we would not have escaped had not our meager outfit shown we were not worth robbing.

# Chapter 11

**Indian Starvation and the Last Lap of the Outbound Trek**

On the trip up-river each of us ate our weight of food in thirty days. This was the dry food which nearly doubles in weight with water added. We ate twice the regular ration of the Northwest Police. Two-thirds of this was for fuel. We pulled our sledges with harnesses that put the traction on our hips. When noon came, after sighting suitable fuel on the shore, we would shed our harness and build our fire on the ice and prepare lunch. Meat and bread freeze so hard they have to be chopped with an axe. Fire is essential to thaw food even if the food is not to be cooked. A man might have plenty to eat and yet starve without fire, because he could not chew it. Our lunches consisted of warmed-over things besides bacon and tea. It takes time to convert ice into boiling water, but we had things so systemized that we never lost more than forty-five minutes from the trail.

The first settlement of white men with which we came in contact was a temporary one of twelve or fifteen dugouts and tents at the point where the Big Salmon River joins the Yukon. It was composed of men who had been forced by ice-jams to halt their advance at this place. Some had experienced hairbreadth escapes. Most of the men were miners, but there were a few members of the Royal Northwest Police and a very interesting trio of gentlemen — Colonel Walsh, who first organized the Police; Crown Prosecutor Wade and Judge Fitzgerald, I think, who were going on to Dawson to establish for the Dominion the Provisional District of the Yukon.

We received an extremely cordial welcome from Colonel Walsh and his associates. They gave us a dinner at which Mac and I consumed, as I recollect it, about $20.00 worth of eggs at current prices. Aside from a crate or two of eggs, however, the Government-to-be of an empire in the making had little else in the way of food as most of their provisions had been lost in the ice of the river. Supplies were supposed to be on the way by mule-drawn sleds from the nearest established Police Post at Tagish Lake, but later on Mac and I saw the mules in log stables at that point apparently settled for the winter, eating their heads off on hay which had cost the Government $1100 per ton. The great part of this cost was in packing it over Chilkoot Pass on men's backs at fifty cents per pound. We spent an afternoon and night at Big Salmon. In the course of our conversation with the officials in the evening we hit upon one of those ideal kinds of bargains which proved of the greatest material benefit to both parties: we gave Colonel Walsh 100 pounds of supplies from our meager stock in exchange for a written order for a like amount at Tagish Post. Walsh's party thus replenished their nearly-exhausted larders while we were saved much physical exertion and enabled to make better time.

The Upper Yukon, or Lewis River as it is called, is a very crooked stream. One who follows it from the Pelly to the Passes probably covers twice the airline distance between these points. Only once were we able to save distance materially by a short-cut. This was at the oxbow below the mouth of the Mordeuskgold River, where a two-mile traverse through a boulé of rough ice saved us ten or twelve miles. To make it we were obliged at the start to hoist our sleds up and over some cliffs sixty or eighty feet in height.

While we were sweating at this job, we became aware of the fact that we were being watched from above by an impassive Indian youth, who volunteered neither assistance nor advice. Nobody else had tried the cut-off and I asked the Indian if it was practical and upon his assurance that it was, I directed him to help us with the sleds. He refused, pointing to his lips, which were chalky-white and saying, "No muckmuck, 'fraid poor Indian die." He was emaciated and seemed ill so we let it go at that and got the sleds up by our own power.

When we reached the river again the youth told us his village was only two miles farther on, and he tried to persuade us to go there but, as we did not want to be near either the Indians or their dogs, we made an early camp where we were. We had made good mileage that day and, moreover, had broken some parts in one of the sleds which must be repaired; so these facts salved our conscientious scruples over a lost hour.

We told the Indian to go home, but he hung around and watched us eat, repeating his stock phrase, "No muckmuck, 'fraid poor Indian die!" We had decided he was a lazy beggar, and our own chances of survival were none too bright, but finally Mac could not stand it. "I have me doubts," he said, "but we'll put him to the test: if he can eat the burned beans we have been carrying to save them this fortnight past, then I'll believe his story." It was a bright thought. We thawed out the mess and the Indian devoured it to the last smidge. So we boiled him a gallon of mush for good measure.

The next morning the Scotch in us received a severe jolt. As we came to the village of two hogans, we were met by the boy and a very old man, each of whom had a good-sized chunk of moose-meat in his hands. "The dirty liar!" said Mac, and I saw a steely glint fire his eye. Without further ado the boy began a palaver with the object of securing my pistol in exchange for one of the pieces of meat. He had seen me scratch a match on its butt the night before. We had eaten no fresh meat for a month and our tongues hung out, but we assumed indifference and were critical of the quality of the meat and told them to get something better. While Mac and I held a consultation, the boy disappeared to return presently with a piece of tenderloin, whereupon we produced a gaudy little blanket we had decided we could do without. The boy was plainly disappointed but the man wanted the blanket. We demanded all the meat in exchange. There was much haggling and finally it was necessary to go into one of the hogans to get the verdict of three woebegone old women. The trade was made and then I produced the "little gun," feeling sure we could get at least as much more meat for this treasure; but the boy, with a very sad expression, said, "No more."

Mac and I were certain that he lied. We believed his boyish desire for a pistol had been overridden by the older heads of the little community and that there was nothing to the incident beyond his personal disappointment. We would rather have parted with the revolver than the blanket and had retained it to the last as a trade subterfuge. We could not conceive as fact that human beings would part with their last food. But we were mistaken. Two days later we were overtaken by a dog team and police who told us they had found the Indians in the last stage of collapse from starvation. They had given them what food they could spare and were on their way to secure an additional supply. They said the able-bodied men and squaws of the tribe, who were hunting at the head of Nordeuskjold, had been out longer than expected and that we had taken the last of the food of the village. Even then Mac and I could not believe that statement. The police explained the potlatch custom. The Indians spend their lives to accumulate things of value so that, on a festal day, they can give them away. It must have been a fact but it was a bitter pill for us to swallow. We prided ourselves on our humanity and had frequently said we would see no one starve as long as we had food.

The police had thrown a cordon around the miners who had gotten through the Passes and were allowing none to advance beyond Tagish Lake to the interior without six months' provisions which, in Winter, was a prohibitive regulation. At different times and places we met two lone men who, of all the fifty thousand wanting to get in, had succeeded in breaking through. Both were old men, close to seventy years of age. One, McNally by name, had come direct from South Africa. He told us with pride of the subterfuge which he originated to get by Tagish. Having learned by chance that the officer in charge was an old South African acquaintance, he pulled his little sled with a swagger right up to the door of the headquarters and demanded to see him. The officer was delighted when he learned who it was and plied McNally with questions about his old friends. When the Irishman was sure he had diverted the Inspector's thoughts from his every-day job, he casually remarked that he wanted an order to clear a thousand pounds of supplies for the interior, and the officer directed a subordinate to make out the papers, completely forgetting to order that the supplies be checked. A few minutes later McNally flaunted his permit in the face of a dazed guard and that was the last Tagish saw of him. He had less than fifty pounds of food when we met him and three hundred and fifty miles to go but he was a very light eater, and with his courage and ingenuity I am sure he won out. Men of his type do not die until they get good and ready. They laugh at obstacles that to others spell finality.

The other old-timer was born in Rome, N.Y. and had just been cleaned out of a successful meat-packing business in Kansas on account of having developed gall to buck entrenched capital. He said the big packers used the railroads to effect his ruin. We gathered that he had detoured around the police in the night. In both cases three-score years and ten had accomplished a feat which had undoubtedly proved beyond the power of hundreds of younger men.

The only other men we met bound for the Klondike were three seasoned nomads who had spent nine months in an overland trip from Hazleton, British Columbia, and who reached the Yukon watershed via the Hooltalinqua River. These men had intended to spend the Winter near the Divide. They had cut their firewood and built a cabin in a good game territory but just as it was finished the game disappeared, having migrated to lower country. Their only food was one large ball of pemmican and on this they decided to winter by emulating the hibernating habit of bears. Their time was spent in bed. Once each day the man whose turn it was got up and built a fire, filled the skillet with water, added shavings of pemmican and, when the resultant soup was good and hot, served portions to his companions and himself, then returned to his bed. They told us they not only reduced physical effort to the lowest minimum but mental activity as well and that they had been successful in passing days at a time in a trance-like condition. According to their story they survived for two months on an amount of food that, under ordinary conditions, would not have lasted a day. Then they made their way to lower country, found game, and with a plentiful food supply, quickly recovered their strength. The men talked in a matter-of-fact way and left us with the impression that they had told the truth. Their story is interesting but I cannot, of course, vouch for its correctness.

Mac and I had a close call from freezing to death when we passed through the Seminaw Hills. Here again we found that accounts of the Mid-Victorian Arctic explorers were all wrong. One is not overcome with a pleasurable drowsiness — actually he knows that his meat is freezing on his bones, just as a beef carcass hung outdoors freezes in cold weather, and he is terrified. Far from being overcome with lassitude the brain is abnormally active.

Two hours before our day's stint of travel was up Mac and I passed an abandoned dugout, occupied the Fall before by a man who had waved us a cheery greeting as our boats drifted by. The door was open and fresh tracks in the snow showed that a wolf had a few moments before investigated the subterranean dwelling. The thermometer had risen quite rapidly that day from fifty to thirty-five below, which was an indication of wind. We looked longingly at the substantial shelter with all its implied comforts, but decided we must make another four miles before camping. It was an error in judgment that we soon regretted.

As we plodded along in the semi-darkness occasional spurts of wind from the flanking mountains carried little whirling spirals of snow [snow devils] across the frozen surface of the river. In each ensuing calm we were oppressed by an ominous feeling that a sinister power was toying with us, as a cat plays with a mouse so, as the gusts became more frequent, our nerves tightened and tingled in preparation for the onslaught. Through my mind, over and over again, were running the lines:

> "And only the stars are above him at night,
> And the trees that creak and groan,
> And the frozen wind swept mountain crests —
> With their silent fronts of stone."

We were following an apparently interminable wind-swept cut-bank a hundred feet or so in height and behind it was a mountain with an inhospitable front of stone, but nowhere were there trees to provide shelter and fuel.

The wind rapidly increased in volume. Built upon a thunderous monotone of sound came staccato shrieks and a howling as of jungle beasts. The air was so full of driving snow that breathing was difficult. We sensed the heat being drawn from our bodies and realized that we must find shelter or die. And still that inexorable cut-bank continued.

We came to a place where a discoloration in the snow-covered face of the cut-bank suggested that an old trail had gone up it. Mac, however, thought the streak might be due to a natural depression and as this explanation seemed quite likely, we did not at first investigate what might lie above. Instead, we left our sleds and ran ahead several hundred yards around and beyond the bulging sweep of the bank. We could find no end to it, and fought our way back to the sleds at a slow walk.

We knew that our bodies were freezing. Our muscles were sluggish, like machinery in need of oiling. It was only a question of moments when they would cease to function. Each leg seemed to have a hundred pounds of lead attached to it.

Thoughts of how to escape were racing through our minds. Our condition brought me the thought of a diver I had once seen walking on a vessel deck in his weighted diving suit and then, through suggestion, there flashed an instruction my uncle had given me years before of what to do if seized with cramp when swimming. "Don't let the cramp be your master," he said. "You can master it by will-power!"

As I started up the cut-bank, my muscles were crying out against the friction of action, and there was the urge to double up as with cramps but my mind fought the impulse. I said to my body, "I am your master, I will make you do what I want." All the time, however, I had the terrible fear that if I found wood and shelter I could not strike a match to start a fire.

I got to the top of the bank and found a nice little spruce hollow tucked between it and the wall-faced mountain behind, and a blown-over dead spruce. There was no sensation in my hands but I forced them to crumple together the dead twigs of the boughs, and to strike the match that kindled them. In a few moments in that sheltered and warmed spot the surging blood restored movement to the muscles. I went back on the trail and pulled Mac to the fire. He had gotten nearly but not quite to the top of the bank progressing on his knees and elbows. It was a close call but neither of us suffered from after-effects beyond extreme stiffness the next day.

At Rink Rapids a colony of about twenty-five people were living in dug-outs and cabins. Among their number was Willie Byrne, a Chicago lad of twelve who, while on his way to the Coast with his uncle, had walked for five days with frozen feet until he had kicked off most of his toes. We were told that the uncle was too badly frightened about his own chances to give the boy proper attention. The Rink Rapids community took the lad in and, finding that amputation was necessary to save his life, the self-appointed surgeons had given him a stiff dose of whiskey for no anesthetics were available.

Between White Horse Rapids and Marsh Lake one evening we found snowshoe tracks leading to an island and casting our eyes in that direction saw a faint column of smoke curling up from among the spruce trees. We changed our course and soon came to a cabin occupied by a man named Kelly from the state of Maine. Mr. Kelly told us the usual story: His party had been caught in the ice and had built the cabin to shelter their supplies. In this case, however, as the distance to the Coast was not great, the others in the party had gone out for the Winter leaving Kelly to guard the outfit. Mr. Kelly made us welcome and we passed the night with him.

The thing that interested Mac most in the cabin was Kelly's little sheet-iron stove. Mac suggested biscuits for supper. He had a digestion like an ostrich's but for some reason the "dough gods" he had eaten that morning for breakfast were not resting easy. For the benefit of the Cheechakos I will explain that dough gods are a mixture of bacon grease and dough, highly esteemed for food in the North. A big frying pan is filled with cold grease and, just as soon as the grease melts, chunks of bread dough the size of biscuits are dropped in until skillet is full to overflowing. As the grease heats the dough absorbs it until finally there is only enough left outside to dry the cakes and keep them from sticking to the pan. They are then fifty-fifty, dough and grease. Our culinary efforts were directed to producing food that would stay by us until the next meal, so that we would not feel famished between-times. In this respect dough gods held the supremacy. But Mac's had overstayed their welcome.

We had several disappointments over the biscuit. The top had dropped off the can of baking powder we had been using and the contents had sifted through the gunny sack that served as chuck box. We had one more can but when this was opened we realized it had been in the boat swamped in Lake Labarge, because it was cemented in a solid cake. Next, we found a big hole in Kelly's oven, as a result of which it required two hours to bake the biscuits. When they were done they were so hard and heavy you could have knocked a man down with them.

Kelly had only a small bunk in the cabin so Mac and I spread our blankets on the dirt floor. We passed a most uncomfortable night on account of the unaccustomed heat. Our blankets thawed out and were wet and soggy.

In the morning Mac was in an agony of pain from the combined effect of the dough gods and biscuits. He was rolling around on the floor with his hands clamped tightly about his stomach, and he was sure he was going to die by bursting. At first both Kelly and I thought he was joking, but we soon realized he was in earnest. In a disjointed way he told us

*Police and Canadian Customs Station at Summit of Chilkoot Pass*

*Above the Scales in Chilkoot Pass*

*Nearing Summit of the Pass*

*Typical Stampeders*

the story of one of the pioneers of Ontario who had the same trouble, and he averred that the only way the man's life was saved was by wrapping him around with basswood bark to prevent the explosion. Try as we would Kelly and I could not help laughing. This irritated Mac. He said he knew what he was talking about, that he was not afraid to die by freezing or starving or in any decent way, but that he did not want to pass out in an ignominious manner. It was the disgrace of the thing which worried him.

Mac's clear grit was shown by the fact that after Kelly and I had breakfasted, he insisted on hitting the trail. Both of us did our utmost to persuade him to lie up a day or two until he was over the attack, but he started out alone and I had to follow. He firmly believed he was about to die, but he wanted to die fighting.

All our load was in one sled now and it consisted entirely of food and blankets. As it was my turn I got in the harness and started pulling. The other man's job was to push from behind with a short pole. I could feel Mac's help for a short time, but soon realized it was lacking. Not wanting to embarrass him, I did not look back at first. When I did he was nowhere in sight. I ran back and found him rolling in the snow near the willow-bordered edge of the island. As he saw me approach he called out, "Go on, leave me to die! There's no use in our both starving!"

I said, "Mac, I was the cook that made those biscuits, and I am responsible for your condition. You must get rid of them!" "I wish to God I could!" I cut a willow twig and wrapping some tissue paper around the end, tied it on with string, making something not unlike a paint brush. "Now, stand up," I said, "and tilt back your head and open your mouth!" Mac could not straighten up, but I got my arm around him and, when he opened his mouth, I jammed the brush against his palate, with such a tickling effect that I had to jump to get out of the way of the biscuits. After that Mac felt better and we continued on our way....

We crossed Chilkoot Pass, from navigable waters of the Yukon to the salt water of the Pacific, in one day. It was fifty below zero when we left Lake Bennett in the morning and thirty-six above zero when we reached Dyea that night, a difference in temperature of eighty-six degrees. We had abandoned our sled and carried nothing with us except our snowshoes and lunch. The great difference in temperatures between the coastal air, warmed by the Japan Current, and that on the inner side of the Range — Black Sullivan at Bennett told us that the morning of February 3rd was the coldest day of the Winter — caused a terrific wind in the height of the Pass. While we passed innumerable caches, and while several thousand men were ordinarily at work in getting their supplies over, Mac and I were the only men who crossed the Summit of Chilkoot that day. Had we not been in exceptionally fine physical condition I doubt if we could have made it. It was not bad while the cold lasted but as we neared the Summit the wind rose along with the temperature to paroxysms of fury I have never seen equaled. It was a head-wind. At times it picked us off our feet and threw us backward and rolled us over and over for the loss of many yards. The last part of the distance Mac and I crawled on our hands and knees — forward in the lulls and then lying flat clung for dear life to the hard-packed snow when the cyclones hit us. Then in the lull we would crawl forward a few paces and hang on again until the worst was over. We were bruised and sore, but in no way paralyzed by the cold.

Consequently, we were not particularly worried. We had reason to know the danger signals of freezing to death.

Finally we reached the drop-off at the Summit and looked down. Four miles below was Sheep Camp. To reach it, as the saying of the day was, "All you have to do is step off." The intervening distance to within a thousand feet below was marked by a black line of toiling

*Cache of Flour or Oats*

*The 35 Degree Ordeal on Lower Chilkoot Trail*

*Near View of Line of Packers*

*Carrying Timbers for Boat Building up the Pass*

men in the otherwise unbroken expanse of white snow. Some of these men a short time later on lost their lives in an avalanche. We took advantage of the rope they had been using and descended.

We had made the trek from the headwaters of the Yukon to the tidewaters of the North Pacific in a single day, a distance that over the neighboring White Pass route had required three months to cover the previous Summer. But then we had a ton of supplies to transport whereas now, exuberant with life and hard as nails, we were traveling encumbered by little more than the clothes we stood in.

After reaching the lower level, somewhere in the drifting snow but unaware of the fact, we passed the body of an Indian woman who, carrying her baby, had dropped behind her Indian companions and lost her life. That night they brought her body into Dyea, dug from the drifts. The woman had taken off most of her scanty clothing to wrap about her baby and the infant was apparently unscathed.

In the morning we waded out in the mud and water of the tidal flat fronting Dyea to where we could get into a small boat and by this means reached a tugboat, which ferried us five miles to Skagway. Our feet in soft, tanned caribou moccasins were very wet, and the salty wind made us more chilly and uncomfortable than we had been in the dry air of the interior with the thermometer eighty or ninety degrees lower. The greatest cold we had experienced on the trip was sixty-seven below zero.

The captain of the tug told us that a small steamer, the "Clara Nevada," was due to sail for Seattle at three that afternoon. Mac had decided in any case to stay in Alaska, but as I was going out to try to raise money for the tramway the news was welcome. The captain told us that three long wharves had been built since we had last seen Skagway. The "Clara Nevada" was docked at the one next to that at which he landed.

As we rounded the last point and came in sight of the harbor the captain called us back to say that he might have been mistaken in the time of the steamer's sailing, as he could see a cloud of black smoke pouring from her funnel, which indicated to me she had steam up. Accordingly, as soon as the tug touched its dock, Mac and I jumped off and started on the run for the shore-end. There was a warehouse there and, as we were rounding it, the "Clara Nevada" blew her whistle. When we came in sight of the vessel again, the deck-hands were throwing off the mooring hawsers. We shouted and waved our arms but, while the officers plainly saw us, they did not stop. A moment later, when we were almost abreast, the vessel reached full headway. The tug captain had told us all that was necessary to insure passage on the boat was to get in sight of it. The fare was $100 and captains of tramp steamers of this type would come back five miles for a passenger. But this captain was a different kind of bird and he kept right on going.

Mac and I were disappointed and angry as we turned back to the town to look up a hotel. We could not hope to get another steamer short of three days. We had only proceeded a short distance when we encountered three men coming toward us with luggage in their hands. Surmising that they were would-be passengers on the steamer we stopped and told them it had sailed. This being a respectable story, it is impossible to give an exact quotation of their remarks. We learned, however, that each of the three had paid his passage-money in advance. Arrived at the Yule House, we found several more persons who were booked for the "Clara Nevada," and these men showed us a prominently displayed poster giving the vessel's sailing time as 3 P.M. that day. It was about noon when we reached the hotel.

Just why the "Clara Nevada" sailed more than three hours ahead of her scheduled time will never be known, in all probability, for that night she disappeared in the placid waters of Lynn Canal with no known survivors.

Shortly after dark, miners at the little settlement of Beaver's Bay saw a bright flash a mile away; this was followed almost immediately by the sound of an explosion. The next day wreckage drifted ashore bearing the name "Corwin," which was the former name of the "Clara Nevada." As the tramp had no office and carried with her the passenger lists, relatives of those lost in the disaster were confronted by great legal difficulties in establishing proof of death, and it was said some life insurance payments were never recovered. The vessel's early sailing gives a sinister aspect to the affair. It was rumored that she had $200,-000 of Klondike Gold in her safe.

I had to wait three days in Skagway for another little tramp steamer called "The Rosalie," which eventually landed me in Seattle. Of all the scrapes we were in I imagine the closest I ever came to death was the half-minute margin by which I missed the "Clara Nevada." Relating the incident to Charles B. Reynolds, the managing editor of <u>Forest and Stream</u>, he remarked, "You were certainly spared by Divine Providence — and then after a moment he added, "God took the good too good to stay and left the bad too bad to take away!"

[McKercher drowned a few years later: Editor]

*Sheep Camp — Chilkoot Pass*

*Trailside Camp in Chilkoot Pass*

# Part III

## Burnham the Adirondacker

*After his return from Alaska Burnham wasted no time in resuming his life-long pattern of energetic and varied activities — but this time on his own terms and in his preferred rural surroundings. For him the pressure-cooker existence and insatiable demands which typify most city jobs were now an unregretted and unmissed part of the past. Although he knew that it was necessary for him to go to New York in order to market his maple candy and fill numerous lecture dates, he virtually begrudged the time spent away from the Champlain Valley and its serrated Adirondack and Green Mountain vistas.*

*Like all countrymen the enterprising young man realized that he would have to handle the wide variety of daily problems and challenges by himself, so he soon became a competent example of the modern do-it-yourselfer. And like the esteemed Thomas Huxley he had long before found out that "perhaps the most valuable result of all education is the ability to make yourself do the thing you have to do, when it ought to be done, as it ought to be done — and whether you like to do it or not." Of course another condition has to be satisfied: you must also have the ability to learn how to do the thing you have to do.*

*Burnham learned fast and mostly on the job as shown by his initial success as a builder/carpenter. Moreover, he combined this experience with his inherent resourcefulness, foresight and ambitious plans for himself and his family by systematically acquiring some 10,000 acres, including land needed for the eventual construction near Essex of a large cottage colony which he called the Crater Club and, later, for his "Highlands" home.*

*When this project had been completed he turned his attention to another phase of the building trade — and became the nation's first mass-producer of pre-cut log cabins. Since he owned his own timberlands and sawmill he was able to cut overhead down to the bone, eliminate the middlemen, control the entire operation and efficiently supply the ever-increasing demand of log structures of varying sizes, for varying purposes and in many sections of the Northeast.* [1]

*Furthermore, as the largest and busiest employer in the area he became an important factor in its economy and frequently, in order to meet the payroll on which his workers depended, he took on marginal contracts which netted him either a puny profit or none at all. Such concern naturally paid off over the long haul in increased production, pride in workmanship and mutual loyalty.*

*Nor did he neglect his civic and social responsibilities during that period, as is indi-*

---

[1] *Burnham derived much personal satisfaction from knowing that every forest acre he owned had not only paid for itself and taxes but also grew more timber than before acquisition. The log cabin business provided a ready market for pines thinned to improve the stand.*

cated by his decision to accept the burdensome assignment as chief game protector of New York State in order to bring law and order to that mismanaged department. Apparently he felt that this was the most convincing way to put into practice his deep concerns and feasible concepts for improved game management and its conservation, which subsequently presented him with opportunities for even greater service and recognition on the national and international level.

Another highlight episode in the life of this many-sided man took place in 1921 when Burnham and Andy Taylor, his Alaskan guide, made the short but risky trip to the Chukotsk Peninsula of Siberia in search of a specimen of a rare breed of mountain sheep and, in the process, Burnham attracted considerably more action than he bargained for during the tense and hostile court-martial-type inquisition aboard the sinister Japanese vessel, the Daichii Toro Maru.

This James Bondish encounter and the engrossing story of the expedition and its tenuous international implications was ably recounted by Burnham in The Rim of Mystery,[1] a book approved by the Boone and Crockett Club, of which he was a member.

The American Indian expression — "Him have plenty arrows in quiver" — certainly applied to the man from "Highlands" because his social contributions to the region were important and numerous.

But even though the business of making a living took much of his time, Burnham saw to it that he had regular intervals for enjoying to the utmost his favorite sports of fishing and hunting in the Adirondacks, Canada, Alaska, Mexico and the Southwest. For him recreation was re-creation and he made the most of the seasonal occasions to recharge his physical and spiritual batteries.

As will be seen this segment of Burnham's life provides many indications and insights into the character and personality of a very eminent Adirondacker.

*[Editor]*

---

[1] *Published by G. B. Putnam's, New York and London 1929.*

# Burnham the Adirondacker

# Chapter 12

### Moving Along the Road to Success

Burnham had left New York seven months before weighing 143 pounds and in his own words — weak, spineless and beaten. Now he was returning East enjoying everything from the scenery along the Canadian Pacific to the meals in the dining car. The only trouble with the latter was the food would not stay with him. He had no sooner finished a meal than he was hungry for more. Moreover, he now weighed 165 pounds of good hard muscle and had never felt better in his life.

En route he made the acquaintance of Charley Ferris, who had built one of Skagway's hotels, the Yule House. Charley's guests provided their own blankets and paid him a dollar a night to sleep in one of the bunks in triple rows which lined the walls of his "hotel." He had made good money from his venture but, thinking the boom had blown, he had put the hotel up for raffle — five dollars a throw — and with his cash was on his way home to join his family.

"We did not go into details about personal matters. On my part I was reticent, I think, because I had not heard from my wife and was worried for the first time in months by the uncertainty. Our train had been held up by a blizzard outside of Montreal and when we parted it was a hurried hand-shake. I supposed that his home was in Montreal," Burnham recalled.

From Montreal Burnham went south on the Delaware & Hudson Railroad to the little village of Whallonsburgh, in Essex County, which he reached just before midnight. This was the nearest point on the railroad to the farm where he believed his wife and children to be, and he intended to walk there that night. The agent, George Wyland, however, told him they were not at the farm, but spending the Winter at Mrs. Strong's boarding house in Elizabethtown, the County Seat, sixteen miles away, and he kindly took him to his home for the balance of the night. In the morning Burnham took a train to Westport and the stage from that place and, as he alighted in Elizabethtown, the first person he saw was Charley Ferris! His family also, it developed, were in Elizabethtown.

The next thing he saw were the curly heads of his three children, who were looking at him from an upstairs window. On all three faces were puzzled expressions. They had received no word of his coming and yet to their two to five-year old eyes he must have looked like their Daddy. The next moment his wife was in his arms....

They moved directly to the farm on Lake Champlain and the life of a share-farmer. The money he had left with the family was gone, and while he had brought $700 back with him he felt this money must be husbanded until they could find a new method of life. He took a lease on the farm on the same terms as the former tenant, his labor balanced against the owner's investment.

The great advantage of the country over the city as a place of residence is of course the esthetic one. The whole family loved Nature, from the red squirrels and chipmunks that ran along the stone walls and climbed the nut trees to the white expanse of pure snow in Winter; the almost equally white expanse of apple blossoms in late Spring; the midsummer glossiness of the surface of the Lake; the hammering woodpeckers and the hum of bees. But even above the delights to the senses was the feeling of independence that was theirs. There was no competitor scheming to throw him out of his leasehold, and he felt sure he could stay as long as he liked on the farm. Moreover, there was no rent to pay and no staggering expenses.

Burnham knew that in average times a farm day-laborer, if thrifty and capable, could earn enough in half the working days of a year to support and clothe his family. If he was ambitious he knew he could put money in the savings bank the balance of the year; otherwise, he could travel around the country visiting or hunting and fishing. But in order to do so he had to grow most of his food in his garden, keep pigs and a cow, fodder which he cut along the roadside, and have a wife who could can vegetables and wild fruits for the Winter.

For a while, however, his previous training made him fearful of the big bad wolf he had learned to dread in the City but, nonetheless, Burnham decided to go to New York and try to land another job. Fortunately, as he later stated, his efforts were unsuccessful and he never afterward failed to thank the Good Lord for that.

In the Klondike Burnham had observed that much of humanity made idols of their grub-sacks. They figured their food to the last ounce and calculated the number of days, hours and minutes the supply would last them. They turned away hungry men to death and starvation, and some of them went insane amid their selfish plenty as their personal punishment — and all because of the fetish they had created. This was the same terror that gregarious men in cities have imposed upon themselves and their fellows.

There was another kind of man in the Klondike, however, who would strike out into the unknown wilderness with a few handfuls of food and a rifle, travel where he willed and who retained through it all health and a sound mind. It was this type of man who made the new gold strikes. Their mental poise was not a patented or copyrighted thing: they had merely possessed themselves of something that was common property but overlooked by others. So he took his own worn shoes from the New York sidewalks and brought them back to the springy soil and Fear never afterward guided him permanently city-ward.

Of course it is as hard to get a start in the country as it is anywhere else but mistakes cost less. The tuition fees in this school of experience are nominal or non-existent. One does not have to quit because his money runs out as long as he has a roof over his head and a piece of land to raise food. Wealth lies not in the greatness of riches, but in the fewness of wants. The cost of existence was low but since he wanted more than mere existence Burnham tried a great number of things to produce income — so many that he was called a jack-of-all-trades, and once by one of his French-Canadian employees, without intended disrespect, "a *Jackass*-of-all-trades."

He went down to New York when he could get a series of lectures slated, took a number of consecutive nights in Dr. Leipziger's Board of Education Free Lectures for the People series and talked about the Klondike. The fee was only $10.00 per lecture, but Burnham totaled more talks than anyone else of the hundreds of Dr. Leipziger's staff, and because Burnham had an adventurous and timely subject which held the interest of the audience, he was also used to fill in when a substitute was needed.[1] Raymond Spears, a talented writer and he syndicated the first wild-life stories with a conservation trend. Back home he also sold Aermotor windmills, Paroid roofing and a lot of other things used in a farming community; and he made and marketed the maple sugar bonbon candy concocted from his wife's recipe.

His New York lectures got him other dates at other places, and while filling these he used the days to sell the candy which was attractively packaged in a birchbark container, tied with green raffia and sealed with red wax. Almost at the start he was fortunate enough to place it with Park & Tilford, and this gave it standing with the trade. Furthermore, he was not foolish enough to place the price too low. Huyler's and Lowney's package candies were selling then for eighty cents a pound. He put the price of his at a dollar and soon built up a prosperous business based on the high quality of the product. As it melted in his mouth, if he was a good-natured person, the buyer would say, "That is a smooth piece; what does it sell for?" When Burnham told him the price his reaction was usually a mixed one: either he was a fool or else he had something exceptionally good. To find out he would ask who the customers were. This was the time when the name of Park & Tilford worked wonders. How often Burnham blessed the memory of that hero in Park & Tilford who had given him their order, a discerning and noble man who later lost his life in saving two young men from a watery grave.

His assistant in the candy business was a Dell Clark and their duties were varied. Burnham recollected that one day Dell and he, after the chores were finished, the stock watered and fed, went to the sugar-bush, collected the night's run of sap and then drew out and spread several loads of manure on the "greensward." In the course of this operation they encountered a good jet-black skunk which they killed and skinned. The receipt for its pelt paid Dell's wages for the day. Later they made bonbons to supply some accumulated orders.

While engaged in this job Dell remarked, "Maybe this candy wouldn't taste so good to the people who eat it if they knew about the skunk and the manure!"

The candy business was continued for a number of years until he got so deeply involved in conservation work he sold out to other refugees from the city who made the country their home — and for a sizeable profit.

Burnham's capital of $700 went into the construction of a summer cottage to be rented to some anticipated tenant. He figured that he could buy the lumber and other materials for the building and the furniture, stove and kitchen utensils with this money, but there was nothing left for labor or for a site on which to build it. The latter problem was solved by an agreement with the landowner that payment for the lot could be made when the rental money was received, and while he had no experience as a carpenter he was rash enough to contract the labor supply in his own person.

Pride caused the fall of Lucifer, but it also built that cottage. He had to get help on two occasions — with the framing and with the door and window question but the total outlay for assistance was the modest sum of eleven dollars.

In the building process he found out that it is some job to hold in place, 'til it can be nailed, both ends of a long board at the same time. He got to know by heart every stone in the foundation and every nail and every board in that building. Before it was finished he

---

[1] His success as a lecturer was confirmed by the following comment by one of his former professors — Dr. E. F. Johnson of Trinity College, Hartford, Connecticut:

"Mr. Burnham's lecture on the Klondike, delivered here, was extremely interesting, and held the attention of the audience better than any illustrated lecture I have ever heard. This was partly because the matter was new, and partly because it was the record of an extraordinary experience modestly and graphically told. The lecture cannot fail to give satisfaction."

spent $1.25 for an advertisement in the Boston *Transcript* and in reply received a postcard from Philadelphia, which asked for information about the cottage. He not only gave what was asked but a lot more, dwelling on the natural charm of the locality and even going so far as to tell of a local laundress and how groceries and other supplies could be had. After a further interchange of letters the Seagers rented the cottage, "sight unseen," and the youthful entrepreneur realized that the personal touch could be conveyed by letter as well as presence. Mrs. Seager told him later on that she had sent to a friend for the Boston *Transcript* with the intention of getting a place somewhere on the New England coast. She had written letters and postcards to thirteen such advertisers and then on a whim, because she had no intention of summering in the Adirondacks section of New York, she had written Burnham. The other replies had been perfunctory. His had interested her and finally won her away from her original intention....

Most people who know nothing about it regard farming as a perfectly simple, plodding kind of a job and farmers as "hayseeds" who would be failures in any other kind of occupation. They think if worst came to worst they themselves could earn a living as farmers and no doubt teach the clod-hoppers a few tricks while about it. Many of the great white-collar class ridicule whoever gets his living by manual labor. But as a man who had repeatedly stepped from one side to the other, Burnham learned that the farmer, to be good, has a longer apprenticeship to serve than in most occupations; moreover, that his calling frequently requires far more intelligence and knowledge than most people realize.....

From the practical standpoint of results accomplished the C.C.C.[1] program was a farcical failure but there was one thing in its favor: the training it gave to thousands of flabby, incapable young men and the wholesome outdoor experience it provided. However, as had been the case when the same work was given to farmers' sons, they did from ten to fifty times more work — and did it better.

For example, the average farm-boy chopped, as occasion required, either right or left-handed and the chips popped from the kerf without unneeded blows. The city-boy hit aimlessly always from one direction and left a stump that any self-respecting beaver would have disdained.

Out of charity, Burnham once gave two city-bred but husky young men a chopping job. While local men around them were earning as much as $4.00 per day, on a result basis, these boys could not earn their board of a dollar daily. They were willing to a degree and they had no bad habits, unless smoking could be so characterized, but in three weeks they cost him a loss of thirty dollars and he had to fire them. They could not even learn how to carry brush out of the way.

Pick-and-shovel work requires long experience to reach the productive stage and it is not so much muscle that counts as its proper application. There is a real and exact art in all manual occupation.

Burnham was a farmer who never learned to milk a cow. There was a reason for this, however: he hired with the fixed stipulation that if the hired man wanted to go to the County Fair or elsewhere he was to provide a substitute when absent. Cows on a farm are enshrined and sacred, and there is no greater farm crime than to leave them unmilked — unless it is to neglect the care of the horses.

Moreover, farming is one of the greatest of gambles, and therefore character building. One year from 22 acres of oats he did not even get his seed back. Human foresight can more easily predict rises and falls in the stock market than farmers can anticipate floods and

---
[1] Civilian Conservation Corps of the mid 1930s.

droughts. The farm, in their case, provided the home, but they had to look outside to get the "edge" that meant their mental and moral progress.

When he was going to Rugby Military School, J.B. boarded with a man of the get-ahead type, named John Traynor. There were two Traynor brothers, Philip and John, both of whom had been iron-moulders. About that time John had given up his wage job so that he could devote his whole attention to a growing business. The brothers had developed a business of building small houses for rental purposes. They had put up about thirty of these houses. John not only collected the rents and paid the taxes but he also kept the houses in repair, redecorated the interiors when required, evicted renters who did not pay up, secured new tenants in their place and attended to the thousand and one details involved in the looking after a community of thirty families. It was the plan by which they acquired their houses that Burnham now remembered.

The operation was simple but it had appealed to the imagination of the young boarder and seemed a merger of daring and high finance. When the Traynors had saved a couple of hundred dollars, they bought a lot and built a new house — chiefly with their own hands and after conventional working hours. Their credit was A-1 with building-supply concerns, who were always ready to give them time to finish the job before asking for payment. They built on a shoestring of actual cash, plus credit, plus their own labor and, when the house was erected and neatly painted and grass seed sown in the dooryard, the Traynors put on their Sunday clothes and invaded the domain of capital. They always came back with enough money to pay all the cost of building the particular house, which of course was secured by a long-term mortgage.

To the Traynors the lender of money on a mortgage was not an ogre, but a loved patron saint, through whose help alone their dream of independence could be realized; so the enterprising Burnham decided to operate the same way.

Among Burnham's friends were Wes Wilson and Fred Sherman, a couple of industrious fellows who owned the leading general store in Essex. Wes still kept his job as a boss mechanic in the Essex Horse Nail Company, but Fred gave all his time to the business of Wilson & Sherman. One night when both were together in the store Burnham told them of the Traynor plan. Both had the shrewd, kindly judgment of the better-class Yankee. They told him to go ahead and build more summer cottages and that as far as their money went they would back him.

This was the way the Crater Club began. Wilson & Sherman received 6% interest on their loans and also increased sales for their store from the more than 500 people who eventually made Essex their summer home. It was a wise business venture on their part, but it meant much more than that in the long run. There were plenty of seasoned investments available for their money, deals that apparently were more certain to repay principal and interest, rather than to take a chance with an untried newcomer in the community. But they sensed a new enterprise that would shake the town out of its rut and had the courage to take a chance where the welfare of their town was involved.

And so Burnham built cottage after cottage, only pausing between times until the papers were made out to warrant the next venture. He secured additional money from other sources and on the Crater Club property alone built about 75 cottages, plus others all around that neighborhood. Years later he paid off all the mortgage loans and savored a tidy profit for his labors....

The human being has always found pleasure in creative work. In the Stone Age there were those who wanted bigger and better caves and others who spent years in carving or painting decorations, and through the ages this desire of man for expression has grown

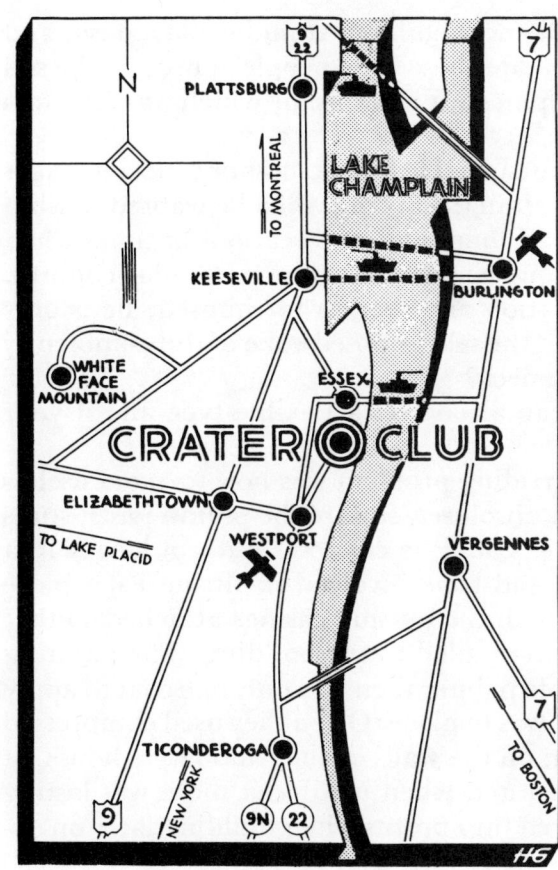

*Crater Club Map of Grounds*

*Crater Club Map (Burnham)*

*The Sawmill*

117

rather than diminished. It is the instinct that influences children to build playhouses and dam the street gutters. How absorbed in their work are these little people! Through the soil on their faces shines out the light of unalloyed happiness. It was this joy which was his when building cottages.

Moreover, J.B. had time for other congenial pursuits. He had no boss or office manager who set his vacations for him. He could take a day off in the Spring when he wanted to whip the streams for trout, and in the Fall, he always had long hunting vacations at times when conditions were right for the particular kind of game he wanted or the particular country. Of course when one ceases working for a corporation and sets up for himself, he is only exchanging one kind of yoke for another; but is not the self-imposed yoke of duty eminently preferable to the collar-design that gives one a stiff neck?

When you make the selection yourself you can always set a flexible type and if your neck gets sore take the yoke off for a while.

Furthermore, he also discovered that the overriding problem was how to avoid useless expense. He learned that if a building was laid out absolutely square the plumb joists, studs and rafters — and in fact about everything else — could be cut to a uniform length in a miter box, thus saving half or more of the cost and time involved in fitting each piece separately. He had the window frames made up with the outside casings attached so that they could be painted a couple of coats before being nailed to the building. The painting was done by a boy with a whitewash brush. A capable painter then had only one coat to apply with the painstaking care required when the frame was in place. Often they used compressed air to spray on the body color of the paint or stain on the walls of the windowless house. It was always fine to experiment with some new idea and when it worked there was lasting satisfaction. Moreover, these methods were parlayed into profits when building later on expanded his activities into log cabin construction.

# Chapter 13

## The Crater Club

While he was building cottages in the bight of the bay next to Split Rock Point, Burnham gradually worked farther north to the beautiful piece of woodland owned then by Stephen Decatur Derby, the local magnate, who was both farmer and merchant. Mr. Derby was invariably addressed as "Commodore" because of the Stephen Decatur in his name. As Burnham's means permitted he bought from him more and more ambitious slices of this choice property. The price he charged, $200 per acre, scandalized the neighborhood. If regarded solely from its soil and rock content the kind of land he was getting, compared with similar prices, was not worth more than $10 to $15 per acre. It certainly was poor farming soil for corn, potatoes or hay — the worst kind of "marginal land" imaginable. The Commodore was blamed for taking advantage of a greenhorn.

But Burnham saw things otherwise:

"I told them I was buying trees and good drainage and scenery and that the land was worth more for the purpose for which I wanted it than any other in the county. But the price per acre was four times as much as the best heavy clay soil farms were bringing so if Derby was not a shyster then I was a fool. It all boiled down to this: — Commodore Derby and I were the only men in the town of Essex at that time who not only knew beauty in Nature when we saw it, but who also realized that it had *per se* a sales value.

"I acquired the hog pasture lot and the ten-acre lot north of that, then an option on the next seventeen acres and when the Commodore died, there were 300 acres remaining in the farm and the numerous heirs decided to sell it at auction. The terms were 10% cash down and the balance in six months.

"I decided I had to have about ninety acres of the land or that all I had worked for here would be lost. The unique "Crater" hill was just beyond the land I already owned. It is the only place on the New York side of Lake Champlain, so far as I know, where from near the water an uninterrupted view can be had completely around the horizon of the higher peaks of the Adirondack and Green Mountains. It is one of the outstanding views of its kind, and I also wanted the rest of the lake frontage. My tenants were cultivated people and I feared that the beer-garden and hot-dog-stand kind might run us out.

"I could scrape together only one hundred dollars, so I journeyed over to Wadhams Mills and conferred with Dan Payne, our local Scattergood Baynes, who agreed in company with a nearby farmer to put up the cash and to bid in the Derby farm. I was to have my ninety acres on a mortgage, and the farmer a pasture lot he wanted; Dan would carve a new farm from the balance, which was all tillable land, and sell it when the opportunity offered. The understanding was merely verbal and not legally enforceable, but most such deals in the country are of this type until consummated. According to the law real estate agreements are of course only valid if in writing, but I knew that Dan Payne's word was as good as his bond. Unfortunately I did not reckon on the third party in the transaction, a man with a very different reputation.

"The day of the sale arrived and after the personal effects had been disposed of, the auctioneer announced that at the request of one of the heirs the real estate would first be divided into two parts to be bid separately, then the entire farm as a unit and that the property would be awarded to the highest bidder or sum of the bids. The heir who had persuaded the auctioneer to adopt this method had in mind getting for himself the land I wanted together with the land Payne was to take, and had only omitted as the other parcel the large pasture which our farmer partner desired. I was naive in failing to realize that this was likely to incite treachery in our camp.

"There was spirited bidding for the home farm including all the good farming land behind the ridge and the price ran up to $5,250, but when the pasture was put on the block it went begging. Our farmer partner's pocket affection was touched and he forgot all about his agreement with us and the pasture (worth the best part of a thousand dollars) was knocked down to him for $250.

"The auctioneer promptly put up the combined property for bidding, but Dan Payne only regarded him grimly and did not open his mouth. Nor did anyone else for that matter. I hurried to Dan and asked why he did not bid. 'I am through with it,' said Dan, 'that skunk has gone back on us and I'll have nothing more to do with the deal!'

"I recollected having overheard a young farmer say a short time before that if the land had been separated in a different way he would have bid for the back part of the farm, which was the part I did not want. I hurried to Fred Stone, for that was his name, in the crowd and asked if he would give $15 per acre for 150 acres. It was a bargain price for such good land and he said "Yes" without a moment's hesitation. I told him it was a deal — that we would bid in the farm for something over $5,500 and that I would pay everything over $2250, the price for his part but explained that I would have to have time to raise the money. Meanwhile, the auctioneer had received no bids under the second arrangement so, as we returned to the scene, he announced that the bidding was closed and the farm would go under the first arrangement. Fred and I tried to get him to open the bidding again. Several of the bystanders aided us by telling the auctioneer he had not allowed a reasonable time, but he was adamant until the executor of the estate, Whitney Safford, who as it happened was a brother-in-law of Stone, took a hand in the discussion. To my great relief Whitney ruled in our favor on the ground that it was his duty as executor to see that the best price possible was realized from the sale. The spirit of that decision cost me $45. As there were no others interested Fred and I had to bid against each other and, as luck would have it, it was he who reached the $5,500 bid. I knew that $5 more or 5 cents for that matter would get the property, but I felt it was up to me to do something to make the executor's reopening of the sale worthwhile, so I raised the ante by $50 — half my total capital! The executor notified Stone and myself to meet him at his office in Essex at seven that evening to make our first payment.

"When I reached Whitney Safford's promptly on the stroke of the clock, he came to the door in person and refused me admission. 'The deal you had with my brother-in-law is off,' he said. 'I will never permit my sister to live on a farm off the main road and inaccessible like that place!' I countered by asking if his brother-in-law was inside. 'Yes.' said Whitney, 'Fred is inside but he feels just as I feel and I am not going to let you see him until

*"Camp Bonnie," First Burnham Cottage at Club*

*Log House at Thirteenth Lake*

ABOVE: (left) Club House veranda; and (right) a part of the main dining room.

CENTER: (left) "Acorn"; and (right) "Lochanbrae"

BELOW: Cottages are of many types, all with lake or mountain view. Pictured (left to right) are "Juniper Lodge", "Donique" and "Wild Acres".

you agree to leave him out of the picture and handle the entire deal yourself!' I told Whitney that the transaction was between Stone and myself, that he had nothing to do with it and pushed by him and into the office off the hallway, where I found Stone.

"This was at seven o'clock in the evening of one day and not until daylight the next day did our party break up. The oil center lamp had to be replenished and many times someone or other had to be called on to lower his voice in order to not wake up the family sleeping overhead.

"Fred Stone was an honorable man. He told me that when he came to think it over he realized that while the land was fertile and a good buy, its location made it impossible for a home. It was half-a-mile off a road and there were no neighbors nor available schools. There had been no witnesses to our agreement and it was a real estate deal which is not binding unless committed to writing. Stone, therefore, was not in any way legally bound. But he had a fine sense of honesty and, when I asked him if he denied our agreement he refused to attempt evasion. Small-minded men would have side-stepped and invented misunderstandings to show that our minds had not met, but Stone admitted the agreement flat-footedly. 'Only,' he said, 'my wife cannot live there and I will not buy that farm!...'

"And so the night passed, the birds waked and one after another began their morning carols until the air was full of melody. Stone had cows to milk and Safford legal clients to meet but I refused to be thrown out on a stalemate. For the fortieth time I told Stone that he did not have to live on the farm. 'Live where you are living, rent part of the pasture to the fellow who went back on Dan Payne and me, and the balance to village people who have cows to put out. The receipts will pay taxes and most of the interest on the investment. Then you have all that fine hay-and-grain land on which to make a profit.' The stubborn look on Stone's face did not relax. "Now, look here, Fred, that soil is loam, the best of its kind, but not as strong as some of the clay farms farther west. But you know that the best of those farms are assessed at fifty dollars an acre and sell for more. This land on such a basis is worth thirty-five an acre, more than double the price you have to pay. You can hold it a while, making a profit meanwhile and when the right party comes along you can sell and double your money.' I could see an awakened interest in his tired eyes. He knew that my statement was true. I continued. 'Nobody ever gets anywhere in this world who does not take chances. Right now with my hundred-dollar capital I am taking a far greater chance than you, but I believe in your gamble just as much as in my own and I will make this proposition to you: you put your money in this farm and a year from today if you are not satisfied with your bargain, I will buy back the farm from you at the rate of $25 per acre, a profit of ten dollars per acre to you or $1500!' Stone was now looking me squarely in the eyes. Without a moment's hesitation he accepted. There was no written agreement between us, but a year later I had the satisfaction of going to Stone prepared to meet my obligation. He turned me down because he considered the land worth more than the specified $25.00 per acre. Later on he sold the farm at a much higher price.

"I paid my $100 and Stone the $455 balance of the first payment. Before the six-month period was up I had sold the lake-shore farm-house and other parcels of land to make up the $3300 payment due from me, and I had my desired 90 acres of land debt-free as a present. It is a fact that rewards go to those who work for them.

"As I write about the transaction which got me most of the Crater Club property, my mind goes back to the lesson taught me through pain and blood by Principal Alcorn of the first school I ever attended. Alcorn said I had the least persistence of any human being he had ever known, that I only picked up a thing to immediately drop it and take up something else — that I was aimless like a butterfly, an incorrigible "Wool gatherer" without concentration or purpose. I am perfectly sure that it was as a result of his criticisms that I persisted that night in Whitney Safford's law office."

The Crater Club project, which he started to develop about 1900, was triggered by his hunch that the region needed and could support a large-scale recreational development. It still operates under similar management policies and ideals. Its main purpose was to provide summer residences with a woodsy atmosphere, near Lake Champlain, for professional and business men and their families. The simple rustic life was stressed and those who demanded swanky accommodations sought them elsewhere. Originally organized as a club, the colony eventually grew into a complex of 75 cottages and camps, all within a mile of the central clubhouse. Guests were admitted only by introduction of members or by satisfactory references.

Among the members have been prominent government figures, military and naval officers, professors, writers, artists, doctors and scientists. Over the years more of the buildings were sold to members who had started out on a rental basis but later preferred to buy, remodel and furnish according to their own tastes.

Christopher Morley in his book *John Mistletoe*[1] devoted several pages to delightful memories of the Crater Club. These excerpts capture poignantly the special appeal of the place and explain why it cast such a nostalgic spell over the lives of its vacation-time residents of all ages:

*Christopher Morley (1890-1957)*

"Mistletoe remembers Lake Champlain. Sometimes he wonders if it is still there. It is twenty years since he last saw it; it must be a big lake by now, and very likely too busy to remember. But shame indeed to celebrate the Lake of Geneva or any other fluid — even Long Island Sound — and not ask forgiveness of Champlain. It is not just a body of water: it is an eternity of summer days. Does the old steamer *Vermont* still come past the stony cape of Split Rock, her paddles sounding across the still mirror of the afternoon?[2] (You could hear them best by listening under water.) At least the blue profile of Camel's Hump must be unchanged. There are red lizards on the rocks, and harebells; and pickerel to be trolled for; thunder-storms, porcupines and chattering red squirrels that dance on birch boughs after rain and shake down a crystal spatter as you pass underneath. Once he shot a squirrel with a rifle. That, and a bullet through his own fingers, cured him of any joy in firearms.

"If you make the effort to lift that lake and all its woodland shore out of the abyss of irretrievable distance, poise it tenderly in balance, you can see that the whole scene moved in a charming sentimental rhythm and below that emerged something also much more

---

[1] From JOHN MISTLETOE by Christopher Morley — Copyright 1931 by Christopher Morley — Copyright © renewed 1959 by Helen F. Morley. Reprinted by permission of J. B. Lippincott Company.

[2] Vermont III, built in 1903, became a Depression Years victim. Cut down, fitted with diesels it became a freighter on the run to New York City via Canal.

elementary. (We are concerned of course only with the pure egotism of memory.) Like the steady pound and sway of the old *Vermont's* pistons, lulling the watcher almost to a swoon in long passages on the lake, I think I discern the power of real meanings behind apparently casual recollections...

"Holding that green and blue microcosm for study I am aware of huckleberry pastures with a clank of cowbells; glades of underbrush violent with sun; and the feeling of hills. Perhaps more than any other thing physical, one whose childhood knew big hills misses them in a life too level. Men need mountains, those who have never associated with them have missed much of earth's suggestion. Also one could hear the wail of the wildcat on some of those Adirondack spurs; it was often a blow to those who imagined they liked solitude.

*Steamer "Vermont" from the book "A Century of Progress"*

*Capt. Sherman of the "Vermont"*

There was poetry as well as picnic on those unspoiled shores. No one will have forgotten Grog Harbor, or the windings of Otter Creek, where the wake of the launch sways and tosses the reeds as a strong personality draws softer creatures into its suction. There was a sandy jut, even whose name I have forgotten, surmounted by a steep plateau of pines...

"There was a road, powdered thick with dust, that ran along the lake shore. At night it was a deep channel through pine trees where a dark ribbon of sky was granulated with stars. The water below it whispered with Tennysonian delicacy. Add to this the balsam savor of the Adirondack woods, and the endearing mischief of our human race. And in those days, or nights, there were no cars on such roads. It was silence...."

Another testimonial from a prominent visitor is expressed in the following letter:

Sir Wilfred Grenfell<br>Kinloch House<br>Charlotte, Vermont

2nd September 1935

Dear Mr. Burnham:

Lady Grenfell and I want to thank you most heartily for the generous way in which you and all your other good friends at the Crater Club helped us out the other day.

We thoroughly enjoyed coming over and Lady Grenfell has told me particularly of your kind hospitality to her personally and the more than cooperative way in which you helped with the Sale.

Believe me to be,

Sincerely and gratefully yours,<br><br>Wilfred Grenfell

Koert Burnham, Esq.
Crater Club
Essex County, N.Y.

Besides the Crater Club enterprise Burnham's business reached the point where he was the country's first and largest builder of log cabins. By pre-cutting and pre-fitting logs which he felled and milled on his own property, he was able to effect economies not possible for the average builder. Also featured were pre-fabricated fireplaces — guaranteed not to smoke! His three basic cabin models — called the Mohawk, Algonquin and Iroquois — which listed for $2,000-$2,500 became popular for homes, vacation use and real estate offices throughout the Northeast. The very first of the latter type is still in use near Howard Johnson's on Route 9 in Lake George. Many other contracts, however, were for larger structures in the 20, 30 and 40-thousand dollar bracket.

Two of these were the main entrance buildings — the gift house at Polar Caves near Plymouth, New Hampshire and the Log House at Big Shanty on Thirteenth Lake, North River, New York. He also built the extension on the Main Cabin of the Camp Fire Club of America in Chappaqua, New York as well as a number of other cottages on their preserve and elsewhere in Westchester county. Still another was put up in Philadelphia's Fairmount Park, where it served as the Boy Scout Headquarters.

Needing utilities at the Crater Club, Burnham of necessity was concerned with the early water system, the telephone and electric lines. The water company had 14 miles of piping. The telephone set-up was a free and easy one. Anyone wishing a phone merely built his own line or tapped the end of someone else's. Everyone chipped in to keep up the "Central." The best tool of the "lineman" was a bamboo fish-pole with which he unsnarled twisted lines. When the Bell System took over there were 32 so-called telephone companies in Essex, three of which were Burnham-owned.

By 1900 electric light and power companies were starting in many localities, one of them on the north branch of the Bouquet to serve the Essex/Willsboro area. Hopes were high but money soon ran low. The project met resistance from those who thought that the lines would glow all night and keep them awake. Others believed that many birds would be electrocuted, while still others expressed fears that sparks from the wires would start forest fires or that radiation would endanger their cattle.

The floundering, fledgling company sought the help of Burnham, who had already provided running water and telephone service to his Crater Club cottage colony. Burnham also realized that the powerline would benefit not only his Club but also residents of Whallonsburgh, Essex, Willsboro and Reber so in 1905 he became a stockholder of the company which was incorporated that year as the Boquet (first "u" in name dropped to conform with regional pronunciation) Electric Power Co.

On Nov. 8, 1906 the Essex Town Board and Highway Commissioner gave the company the right to run its lines along the highway provided the lines were insulated wherever they crossed over telephone lines. Moreover, the company agreed "to do all in their power that could reasonably be done to avoid all telephone troubles."

The financial affairs of the company, never efficiently managed in the early years, suffered another blow when the then secretary-treasurer disclosed that he had misappropriated most of the funds which he had collected over a two-year period and had falsified his reports to the Public Service Commission.

By 1925 the company had 40 miles of mainline, nearly 100 transformers but inadequate power. Obviously, something had to be done because the day of the small independent outfits was about over. At that point Congressman Pierce of Plattsburgh was actively engaged in promoting — for a commission — the absorption of small outfits by larger corporations. When Pierce advised him that he could sell his controlling interest for a fat profit, Burnham remarked that electric and telephone companies were public service organizations. He granted that a stronger company should buy them out and serve their customers efficiently by connecting their area with the Ausable and Saranac River watersheds. "However," as Burnham explained it, "I did not assume control of the Boquet Company in order to make a profit. Therefore, I and the few others who have stuck it out will sell for exactly the amount of money we have risked."

The J. F. White Management Corporation and the Associated Gas and Electric Corporation bought out Boquet in May, 1925 for $77,000. As its balance sheet showed assets of $59,415.61, the difference included the commission fee of $15,000 plus an extra amount needed to buy out small shareholders. In the turnover Burnham was company president for a moment or two in order to handle the transaction, then he became the local superintendent.

Obviously, with all his various occupations and interests John Burnham did not have much time left in which to just sit around and twiddle his thumbs.

# Chapter 14

### The Acquisition of the Highlands Property

The Crater Club needed a lot of firewood for wood-burning cook stoves as well as fireplaces so Burnham set out to find a wood-lot to supply it. The country newspaper for several months had carried the advertisement of a farm for sale for $2500, with a hundred and thirty-three acres of well-wooded land; but while the price seemed unconscionably high, he determined to look it over. He got Pat Boyle, manager of the Essex Horse Nail Company to go with him and together they drove north into the Willsboro mountains. It was a one-trip per day route for a team and the wood could not stand such a portage cost, but the mountains ran down to Lake Champlain and water transportation was cheap. The Club was using a hundred cords per season, which was just a fair schooner load. So Boyle and he found the tenant farmer and with him located the lines of the property and inspected the timber. The land had not been cut over for many years and there was not only an ample supply of hardwood, but also a great deal of beautiful evergreen timber. They decided, however, that in this out-of-the-way locality the price was at least $1,000 too high. Such land could then be bought for not to exceed $10 per acre.

Weeks went by, but Burnham could not forget the Forbes lot and its beautiful surroundings. From the old house on the place there was an entrancing view down a brook valley of Lake Champlain 600 feet below, and the Green Mountains beyond. There were little glacial lakes all around the place nestled in the hills and the largest of these, Warm Pond, was only a stone's throw from the house. Despite its name Warm Pond was not a mud pond, but a deep crystal-clear white-water lake a mile long, with sandy beaches where the shore was not rocky, fringed with pines and hemlocks and cedars. He just could not forget the place, so one day he hitched up and journeyed there again.

This time he climbed a bare hill, called the Pinnacle, which commanded not only a view of Lake Champlain but also an outlook over all the Forbes property. The Scotch ancestry in him from his father's inheritance kept telling him not to be a fool and buy at an extravagant price, but his mother's Irish blood sent thrill after thrill through the roots of his being at the thought of owning all this beauty. He doubted if St. Anthony was more tempted. Finally the Scotch gave him a rude jolt by saying, "Where are you going to get the money?"

But the Scotch are not hardhearted, only thrifty. And the Scotch advanced a welcome suggestion, subconsciously of course. It came like the wee small voice of a singing mouse, "There is more land in this domain than is mentioned," it said, "and therefore the price is not too high." He again looked at the corners far below. He could see by a rough ledge that marked it the location of the northwest corner, and the corner south of that could be

*Willsboro Point from the Pinnacle (Courtesy of Morris Glenn)*

*Burnham's First "Highlands" Home*

placed by the little lake containing trout. The other corners were easily located nearer by. It was an L shaped piece of land and, when he had satisfied himself that he had all the lines placed properly, he got out a piece of paper and a pencil and set down in rods the distances as estimated by eye. Then he began feverishly computing the result. There was, as he had hoped, much more land than the 133 acres given in the advertisement. In fact he made the acreage to be about 250. He hurried home, and the next day returned with "Young Charlie" Stafford, the surveyor. Together they chained the lines and when, toward nightfall, he assembled his figures in the note-book and announced the result as 233 acres, he felt like whooping with joy. But the Scotch kept him outwardly calm.

The day after that J. B. visited the seller in Keeseville and told him there were a hundred acres more in the Forbes place than the owner had advertised. The owner produced the deed and also the field notes of lot 129 P.B.T. from an 1811 survey and both tallied — "133⅓ acres of land including water." He said the extra acreage meant nothing to him. The price was $2500 as is. So Burnham made a down-payment, borrowed the necessary balance and acquired the land, which since then became his home — aptly called "The Highlands."

Over the years he could not help think that that discrepancy in acreage was no mistake on the part of the original surveyor but intentional, and that the surveyor, long dead, was a crook because his notes described the land as being of poor quality, scantily timbered and poorly watered. All of which was untrue as in his day. He had intended probably to get a bargain in the land for himself or for some friend.

Burnham shipped a great many schooner-loads of wood from Port Misery, as the abandoned dock below the Forbes Place was called, to the Crater Club, but he did no cutting which involved unnecessary scars in the landscape. Other people who owned abandoned farms in this forgotten neighborhood came to him and sold him their land. He bought 600 acres including the Pinnacle and a part of the shoreline of Warm Pond for $1,000 or at the rate of $1.67 per acre. The highest he paid was $25 per acre. Eventually, he owned eleven square miles there and along Cold Brook — which was quite a territory to pay taxes on.

Despite his Yankee strain he considered himself a very poor bargainer. He could see the other fellow's side and if he really wanted to buy what he had to sell Burnham did not have the heart to lie about it and beat him down. His method was to have the seller set his price and then he looked things over and told him whether or not he would buy. He never was in sympathy with the Biblical shyster of whom it was written, "It is naught, it is naught, saith the buyer, but when he goeth his way, then he boasteth."

As Burnham described himself: "I could not be called a good businesman for other reasons. I love land as land and I love it far too much in its natural state. There are too many pieces which from a forestry and business standpoint should have been "improved" or lumbered that have been left in an uneconomical state of nature. I simply haven't the heart to spoil them. I love them till my heart aches. No one who lets beauty get the better of him can be classed a good businessman."

There was one small lot fronting on Warm Pond that cost him more trouble to acquire than all the rest of the land. This belonged to Tom Spear, a track-walker on the Delaware & Hudson Railroad, who lived several miles away. He had purchased the land for a woodlot to keep him supplied with fuel, but it was too far off and he never cut on it. Burnham offered him three times the price he had paid but he needed time for contemplation — three years to be exact.

Burnham described the progress of the transaction:

*Old P O and Tavern at Highlands Forge*

"Tom worked all night and slept during the day. To talk with him I had to adopt his habits. Winter and Summer I walked that track with him discussing the wood situation. It was not a question of price for Tom agreed I had offered him all the lot was worth, or ever would be worth, but 'Where be I going to get my wood?' I told him I had land much nearer his home and that he was welcome to all he could use, to which he would counter that I was not going to live forever and that someday he might be hard put to find wood for his stoves. The conversation ran in the same circle and, tired and sleepy, I would get home to the serenade of crowing roosters and all the other birds in creation.

"After three years of this Mrs. Spear took a hand in the matter, and one day I was dumbfounded to get word to meet them at the office of Syd Maders, the lawyer in Keeseville. When I got there both Mr. and Mrs. Spear were present and the deed was already drawn and ready for their signatures. But Tom was sick with apprehension and shaking as if with palsy. With trembling hand on my arm he led me to the window of the law office. 'Mr. Burnham,' he said, 'you see that grey mare hitched to the post? You know she's a good one. Take her and let me out of this bargain.'

"I don't want your mare, Tom," I said, "but I do want your lot and I am ready to pay for it."

'But what be I going to do with the money? You know yourself that banks ain't safe and I don't want to keep it in the house.'

"Give it to one of your boys," I said. "They're ambitious and it will give them a boost to get ahead." (Today they are leading businessmen and one of them has been mayor of Plattsburg.)

*Burnham's Second Home*

"'Tom, you old fool,' said Mrs. Spear, 'come over here and sign this paper!'

"The lawyer put the pen in his hand and in a daze Tom signed, followed by his wife. Immediately Tom was a different man. The agony of a difficult decision was over, and he was as happy as Ambrose Shappy, the French-Canadian who, at the birth of his first-born, shouted 'The deed is done, the child is born, his name is Alexander!'"

Just another example of Burnham's persistence and singleness of purpose without which characteristics he would never have accomplished any of his major personal desires and goals.

# Chapter 15

## The Wide Waters of Lake Champlain

*[Told in first person because it is such a characteristic
expression of Burnham's personal nature and concepts: Editor]*

"As the population of the world continually grows less self-sufficient and more nearly like peas from the same pod, there are fewer persons left in it who respond to primal emotions. Not only women but men also ask me with genuine lack of understanding why I am so passionately fond of hunting in spite of the hardships that accompany long trips into the wilderness. Why, for example, would it not be equally satisfying to go out in a barnyard and slaughter domestic animals? They think the killer instinct would be appeased in this way, simply because they have no comprehension of the manly exercises of their forefathers. While such people are not always by any means tender-hearted, they experience disgust over what they picture hunting to be."

*[The Guns of Autumn syndrome: Editor]*

"It is useless for me to tell such people that I get just as much pleasure on days when I do not bag game; that joy comes from the tussles with primitive nature; that the forests and mountains, rivers and seas, rain, snow and storms are all my friends; that the wilderness for me breeds peace of mind and contentment. The thought of hardship, danger, and killing nauseates them, despite the fact that the human race climbed upward over these very same stepping-stones. Obviously, they would be out of place at King Arthur's Round Table.

"Fortunately, there are still left in the world simple people who, while they have never buffeted seas or rapids or scaled dizzy heights, believe what we men of the outdoors tell them of our pleasures. For such I write about one part of my life when I frequently had to cross Lake Champlain at times when the Lake said 'No,' — not that this has to do with hunting but because it gives the setting that for men of our type goes with big game and exploring trips.

"I have always loved wide waters and have never lived for any length of time where I could not see them. When I am very old and feeble I want to sit where I can look over an expanse of water, and from morning 'til night I shall not miss other companionship. On sunny days the expanse will speak to me of smooth and pleasant interchanges, like the purring of a cat; and on stormy days, of honest conflict and adventure. Water has more moods than any woman, but it is more easily understood. It is never twice alike but the underlying principles of change are thoroughly logical.

*The "Happy Jack"*

"Champlain in this section does not freeze over until late in the Winter. Some years the broad lake does not freeze at all. In January the water becomes heavy and sullen. The waves pound like battering rams and when they climb over the combing of a boat it does not take many of them to fill and swamp the craft. When I sit and look out from my eyrie, as an old man, I shall remember the January day when Jake and I crossed the lake from Burlington to Willsboro Bay and escaped Davy Jones' locker by a small but satisfying margin.

"It was the worst blow of the Winter. Once outside the breakwater we could see nothing because of the fog clouds, and had to set our course by the current streaks. Our direction was parallel with the troughs and the crests of the waves, but mostly we headed diagonally into the waves to avoid the danger of rolling bottom-side up when balanced on their summits. There were ten miles of this exhilarating roller-coasting over the billowing, foam-flecked carpet of the lake. Our boat, the "Happy Jack," was a light, twenty-foot power-canoe covered from stem to stern with a canvas spray-hood and, as the water frequently climbed above the coaming, it was this hood alone which saved us from swamping. Despite the fact that we were in all probability not making more than six miles an hour, the rush down from the wave crests and the smother of foam provoked by the boat's passage gave the impression of great speed. We were aiming for the precipitous end of Willsboro Point. If we were carried too far to the right we could never make our destination against that wind and sea but, on the other hand, we could not afford the mistake of steering too far to the left, because then we would be smashed on the rocks of Pumpkin Reef.

"Jake and I did not have to make the trip that day. The schooner captain inside the breakwater warned us against it. There was nothing at stake except manhood. We went solely because we were confident of the seaworthiness of our boat and because of the fun of licking the Lake at its worst.

"We hit Willsboro Point square on the nose and just in time. The boat was awash with water which had come in between the coaming and spray-hood. We had no more than made the lee when water got into the carburetor and the engine went dead. In that wild fury outside it would have been impossible to have bailed out the boat and got the engine started, but here it was only a matter of a few minutes to get everything righted; and in a few minutes more we were safe at our destination.

*Split Rock Over Whallon's Bay (Courtesy, Morris Glenn)*

"Lake Champlain opposite Essex is four hundred feet deep. Its bottom is three hundred feet below the surface of the Atlantic and it could never be drained. The bodies of men drowned here seldom come to the surface. Large sums of money at times have been expended in efforts to recover bodies but almost always without result. Those the Lake claims for her own she keeps. But what better grave could a hardy man have?

"When I first came to live at Essex, John Burt, a barrel-shaped man, said he knew the Lake was deep there because he once fell in and wet his feet. Then this Yankee humorist told me the story of Ethan Allen's and Seth Warner's fishing excursion when Warner lost his powder-horn overboard in the deepest part. In these legendary stories Seth Warner is always characterized as scrupulously honest but dumb, while Allen is given the opposite characteristics. 'Now, don't you get excited, Seth, I'll have your powder-horn in a jiffy.' Whereupon he stripped off his coat and vest and dove over the side of the boat. He was gone an unconscionable long time and Warner had scratched a lot of dandruff onto his collar before he recollected Allen's reputation for untrustworthiness and, in a fever, stripped off his coat and vest and himself descended to the depths of the Lake. There he found Allen seated on a rock pouring the powder from Warner's powder-horn into his own before he should come to the surface...!

"On account of building operations which I was carrying on in Vermont I had to cross the Lake at all seasons of the year. My boat was the last to come out of the water in Winter, and for some time I had the reputation of being the first to cross on the ice and the last to come off. I have skated on the Lake the day after it closed, when there was still open water with wild ducks resting on it.

"On one occasion shortly after the Lake had frozen over, I started from Essex with horse and cutter for Mile Point, Vermont, and Edgar Safford asked to accompany me. Off Split Rock there were a number of open cracks in the ice. I swung far out but could not avoid all of them. As we crossed the longest the ice broke and the cutter settled perceptibly. Edgar wanted to get out and walk, but I would not let him because our safety depended on rapid movement. Whip in hand I kept the horse at a steady trot. We were on very thin ice. Look-

*Split Rock Lighthouse and Tower (Courtesy of Morris Glenn)*

*Room Built by Burnham Connecting Lighthouse and Tower (Courtesy, Morris Glenn)*

ing behind, Edgar told me he could see the water spout through the holes cut by the horses' caulks. I landed Edgar safely at Mile Point, but he understandably would not make the return trip with me and walked the entire distance back to Essex.

"Late one March my horse broke through a crack in the middle of the Lake. It was all in the day's work. I unhitched him from the cutter and floated him to a place where I had chopped the ice for foothold and then, after having choked him and pushed his head down, aided him on the rebound to plunge his way up to firm footing.[1] Nor was the horse any the worse for the experience.

---
[1] The reason for this is that after being choked and then released the horse gulps in great breaths which distend its lungs and enable it to ride higher in the water.

"The Narrows, south of Split Rock, freeze over long before the broad Lake closes. At times I would ride a bicycle as far as I could go and then walk out on the Point to Grog Harbor, where I kept a St. Lawrence River skiff. Here I would take to the water and row to the edge of the ice. Pulling the boat out onto the ice and mooring it to a stone cemented to the ice by means of a dipper of lake water, I would clamp skates to my feet and so, by various methods of progression, my destination was reached. Once, on my return, I found that a heavy south wind had broken up most of the hundred feet of ice that separated my boat from the open water. In a very few minutes the boat would have been lost. Quickly I hoisted my little sail, climbed aboard, cut loose from my frozen anchor and sailed off the ice and on to Grog Harbor. By the time we came to the harbor entrance the sea was so rough that I doubted my ability to take in sail without swamping the boat, but this was my lucky day: the mast obligingly snapped off short — so I shipped my oars and rowed in with comfort.

"Had I been ignorant of the idiosyncrasies of ice and water I could not have enjoyed such experiences but, fortunately, as a boy I had learned their powers and limitations, how they could be played with and when the safety margin became tenuous to the vanishing point. In freezing, snappy weather an inch of ice is safer to pass over than two inches when it is thawing. Under the former condition one can take chances with reasonable assurance. Should he break through all he has to do is to freeze his wet mittens solidly to the unbroken ice and, with this purchase, pull himself out flat on his belly to give the greatest bearing surface for support. A deer weighing two hundred and fifty pounds will walk across a thinly-frozen river that a hundred and fifty-pound man cannot cross on his feet without breaking through, because the deer always has two feet on the ice and his weight is distributed.

"If one breaks through the ice on a thawing day, however, it is a different story. Maybe you can open a channel to stronger ice and then cut hand-holds for pulling yourself out onto it, but if this is not possible about the only thing remaining is to call for assistance and meanwhile keep the submerged part of your body perfectly still, If you avoid motion the water inside your clothing becomes warmed to the point of endurance whereas, if you struggle, fresh supplies of cold water continually come in contact with your body and resistance finally succumbs. Few people realize the heating capacity of the power-plant they have in their torsos. In Siberia Andy Taylor and I went to bed at night in clothing soaked from fording glacial streams yet, by morning, we were thoroughly dry except for our extremities.

"If one has a love like the Lake he must have courage because such a mistress will not brook a weakling. When Easton and Evans capsized their tiny sailboat, rightly named "The Coffin," in the middle of Lake Champlain they were too far from shore to be seen. The water was icy-cold, and less courageous boys would soon have given up and drowned. Hanging onto it they succeeded in partly bailing out their boat time and again — only to have the higher surges undo their work. But they were not quitters and after hours of fighting they beat out the waves, won the contest, climbed into the boat and sailed home.

"In contrast to this, the night Fred McDurphy, the Kanaka, was swamped I caught with a grapple and recovered the body of one of his companions who had drowned in only four feet of water. Manning was a strong, well-knit laboring man but he lacked will-power and had pemitted a stomach cramp to double him up when, if he had had "sand," he could have walked ashore. There is only one kind of courage and that is courage that never admits defeat.

"Big-game hunters and explorers have experiences like these in greater or lesser degree. Conflicts with Nature are an inseparable part of their work. For the hunter only a few hours of each week may be devoted to the actual taking of game. No, it is not blood-lust that inspires real hunters, but something bigger that is not to be comprehended by the sophisticated."

# Chapter 16

## Surgery Survival and the Subconscious Mind

*[Told in the first person because it is so personal: Editor]*

"George Barton Cutting told his students at Colgate that social legislation 'is begging the unfit to be more unfit and inviting the fit to join the ranks of unfit. The greatest sinners,' he said, 'are probably the philanthropists and the doctors.' I think the criticism can be extended still further to those who, while they continue to be classed as fit, unintelligently avoid all personal responsibility when stricken with illness. I do not believe in leaning heavily on any living person. God provided the good earth to lie on when we are tired and there are any number of bed and couch manufacturers who need an outlet for their products. For your own good it is not wise to flop all over the doctor or surgeon. Their job is to supply their special skill in your behalf, but not as a beast of burden to carry you. There is a distinct realm in which you must do your part. Courage and intelligence on the patient's part are often more important factors for recovery than the practitioner's skill. Moreover, professional men are not always right, being human and subject to error like the rest of us.

"On one occasion in my life, having experienced some unpleasant symptoms, I went to an eminent surgeon for an examination, and the surgeon then and there tried to throw me on his operating table so that he could carve out my gizzard and withdraw some altogether imaginary gallstones. For some reason which would be hard to explain I felt he was wrong in his diagnosis. I went to another well-known surgeon and he also said I should immediately report to his hospital for an operation. The fact that two very capable and highly-recommended authorities had come to similar decisions as to the cause of my trouble, however, did not convince me that they were right — probably on account of my natural stubbornness. They were both too cocksure they were right. Experience has taught me never to give full trust to such men. A man's internal mechanism is too delicate an affair to be monkeyed with on a wrong hypothesis. I was in pain but I determined to search further for the aid I needed.

"I came back home to our country doctor and surgeon, Dr. Guy Barton of Willsboro. On exactly the same facts and conditions he made an entirely different diagnosis and he convinced me he was right, and as a result he operated and saved my life. The other men were specialists and they had less open minds than the country doctor who handled everything that came his way. When I told him, as I had told the other surgeons, that during my freshman year at college I was dangerously ill with what was then called peritonitis, he recognized this as an important clue to my present trouble; so after a physical examination and many searching questions, he decided I was suffering from adhesions, the after-effect of a ruptured appendix. Back in 1886, he said, appendicitis had not been recognized. My symptoms were characteristic of such a cause. At last I had an explanation which appealed to my common-sense.[1]

"I had a room next to a bathroom in my own home sterilized and there Dr. Barton opened me up and separated sixty inches of my intestines which were stuck to each other and to the other internal organs on my right side. The operation was so extensive that after it was over the outraged viscera refused to function. They folded up like a sensitive plant which has been touched by a rude hand and anticipated the methods of a sit-down strike. The doctor told me that if the peristaltic action was not restored within forty-eight hours it would be just too bad for me and that I would have a one-way ticket across the Styx. He told me that the orthodox practice at that time was to open me up again, sever an intestine and feed milk through the incision, but that the percentage of mortality by this method was discouragingly high. As a matter of fact right after this the Governor of Minnesota at the Mayo Sanitarium failed to survive such a treatment. Barton asked me if I was willing to have a new idea tried. He said that, while he had no precedent for such practice, he believed an irritant brought in contact with the sensitive mucous membrane of the intestine might mechanically do the trick. He used the example of the muscles of frogs' legs "Jumping" when salt was put on them. I told him to go ahead; he injected raw turpentine and almost at once peristaltic action was restored — and shortly thereafter I was restored to my family and friends a well man.

"This was a major operation in the full sense of the term. A portion of my intestines was outside my body for more than an hour, lying on my chest covered with hot cloths. I have not used the word "experiment" in connection with the use of the turpentine because to my mind that word is too often associated with enterprises destined from the start to failure. Barton's plan was based on common-sense. I have always been willing to leap in the dark on that basis. He used the irritant, the intestines jumped like lambs on a May morning and life to them and to me was restored. I have a great respect and affection for the hard-headed pioneering surgeons who are interested in every phase of their patient's cases, who talk things over and who are ready to admit the fact when they are in doubt as to procedure. A sensible patient can be of assistance, and can do things to speed his own recovery.

"The late Dr. Bromley of Danbury, Connecticut cut out a cancer from my bladder in 1930 and saved my life. The surgeon should also have imagination and judgment, an open mind, and a willingness to discuss the case with the patient. By this I mean with reasonable patients.

"I had to go to the Danbury Hospital to get the expert attention of Dr. Bromley. The reason I had the other operation in my own house was because I could more easily attend to my business there and, moreover, I am so accustomed to freedom of action that I dislike the regimentation of a hospital. When in a hospital, however, I do about as I like and commonly get away with it, though at times I have to resort to subterfuge.

"As a by-product of this case Bromley was interested in the discovery that my subconscious mind refused to be anesthetized and that I could carry on an intelligent conversation when under the full effects of ether. It had required a week's conditioning to get me in shape for the job, and when I was wheeled into the operating room I was as nervous as a cat in a strange garret. Irritation almost got the better of my control when I saw that a woman was making the preparations for administering the anesthetic. I spoke roughly to her, being in just the condition when I did not want anything new tried on me, my former experience having been with men. I told her not to choke me with the ether. She smiled sweetly and

---
[1] Date of operation: April 28, 1909.

replied that she would do her best to keep me from being uncomfortable. And so a conversation began which continued while Miss McGinley, as I found her name to be, was doing her part. She was so deft and considerate that before long she had me completely subjugated. I told her that I was falling into a comfortable sleep with no unpleasant sensations of any kind, that I should have known that women are naturally more considerate than men and not so apt to be in a rush to get a thing done, and that if ever again I had to have such an experience no one but a woman should anesthetize me. I recollect telling her 'she had a heart.'

"Dr. Bromley had been interested in the conversation with Miss McGinley and as soon as his work was over he asked me if I could hear him. In my numbed condition his voice seemed to come from a great distance, from the limits of the stellar system, but I replied. I felt like telling him to get a better 'wire,' but instinctively I knew this would sound foolish and omitted the telephone metaphor. I knew perfectly well it was Dr. Bromley who was talking and that he must be close by. 'Your job is done,' he said, and I asked, 'How did it come out?' 'I had to cut you further than I expected.' 'What was the reason?' 'I found a growth in your bladder.' 'What kind of a growth?' His voice was serious as he replied, 'I am hoping it is not malignant, but I do not like its appearance. I will send it to the Presbyterian Hospital for a report.' My reasoning mind was shackled and my subjective mind found it hard to weigh this information. I knew the word malignant meant cancer which commonly spells death, and I like a poor, wild bird trying to get out of a room through the glass of a window, was greatly troubled. I did not want to die while impotent by the power of a drug — so I said, 'In that case how long have I to live?' The surgeon, fine man that he was, immediately replied, 'A couple of years or so; you will have plenty of time to straighten out your affairs.'

"Four hours later when I woke up in my room I remembered the conversation, and through the long, wakeful night that followed I made up my mind that as far as life or death was concerned I had no worry. I do not believe in leaning on human beings, but I do believe in leaning on God... If my Maker thought the time had come to take back the life He had given it was His to decide. I have never dreaded death. At the same time I hoped to live, because in flesh and blood I love so many things in this beautiful world.

"When Dr. Bromley visited me the next morning the first thing he said was, 'You are a bird! You are the only man I ever cut up who could carry on an intelligent conversation while under ether.' I repeated for him what had passed between us and he said I had it correctly. He was not pleased that I had remembered so well. Especially, he did not like it when I mentioned the word malignant. It is a convention that cancer is not to be mentioned to a patient until the end is in sight. Dr. Bromley would not have spoken so frankly to me while anesthetized if he had thought I would have comprehended and remembered. It was not until three years later that the subject was again mentioned between us.[1]

"During my life I have had about everything going in the line of sickness, from necrosis of the jaw, caused by killing the nerves of two upper molars with a red-hot wire as a post-Klondike experience, to a bad case of blood poisoning contracted in a hospital where I had gone for a minor operation. Yet while close to the Biblical limit of three score and ten, I still have sufficient endurance to enjoy outdoor pursuits of a somewhat strenuous nature, such as road-building, shopping and hunting. Handicapped physically early in life and springing from a short-lived ancestry, I am sure the story would have been different had it

---

[1] Dr. Bromley kept a follow-up record of all his patients. Each year he would contact Dr. John Stafford of Essex regarding Burnham's progress. Apparently he was convinced that Burnham was not long for this world. However, when the usual inquiry did not arrive on schedule several years later, Dr. Stafford wrote the surgeon's Danbury office and found out that the eminent medico had himself died from the dreaded disease.

not been for the wise intelligence of my mother. At thirteen I had the same tuberculosis which had carried off my father and, a little later, my sisters; but that birthday my mother gave me my father's shotgun, a strange remedy but in my case a very helpful one. It gave me happiness and the desire to be in the woods, and though my time was spent aimlessly I must have been benefited by the tonic of the open air. She thoroughly realized the danger of a loaded gun in weak and inexperienced hands, but she believed it was the lesser of two evils. Her only stipulation was that I should not hunt in the company of other boys. With perfect unselfishness she encouraged my natural love for the wilderness and more than fifty years ago she permitted her only son and the sole other survivor of the family to go to the Far West at the youthful age of seventeen. After my return I suffered the ruptured appendix and recovered without an operation — other than the placing of leeches on my belly. I have always believed that the shotgun supplied the cure for the t.b., and that the toughening supplied by the Wyoming hunt gave me the vitality that pulled me through the year's agony caused by the ruptured appendix.

"It was another woman of vision, my wife, who when I was broken by nervous prostration as the result of overwork in New York shipped me off to the Klondike and to restored health. In 1923 I traveled twelve hundred miles through Alaska with my son, Koert, while suffering from pneumonia, and during this time was in bed but two days.[1] Nature is the great restorer; and for pneumonia, if your heart holds out, there is no better tonic than the pure air of the mountains....

"At one period in my life I was not popular with the mothers of my boy friends because I was too adventurous and got the little darlings into all kinds of scrapes. These mothers used to say to me that I was born to be hanged because I could not be killed any other way. Upon sober reflection I think they were right."

---

[1] An old sourdough friend, finding Burnham very sick in Gacona, Alaska, used an unusual remedy: Filling an improvised bathtub with woodashes and boiling water, he had his "patient" lie in it for a fairly long time. This odd treatment broke the fever.

The same man told Koert that J.B.B. was the only man he knew who could backpack his own weight 20 miles a day on muskeg, into which a person's feet sink deeply with every step.

# Chapter 17

## Some Thoughts about Prayer, Solitude, Practical Religion and the Rev. George Webster

*[This fascinating and intensely personal chapter provides many indicators and insights concerning Burnham's philosophical, social and spiritual concepts and perceptions. Convinced, as was Thoreau, that "in wildness is the preservation of the world" he often sought the solitude of lonely places and there in communion with Nature and Nature's God he found the answers to his human problems.*

*Particularly noteworthy are his keen, well-founded and sometimes slightly caustic remarks about clergymen, church attendance, private prayer and public morality — and of course his memorable tribute to the late Rev. George Webster: The Editor]*

"Probably the only thing that was original in my youthful prayers (the other things being from my mother's teaching) was that I prayed for wisdom. The urge came from the strong impression made upon me by one of the Old Testament stories. I felt guilty for this and would have been ashamed to admit it to anyone, because it was not the kind of praying I had been taught and seemed selfish — and also because no one else seemed to want it. Even the other boys who were trained in the religious families would laugh at me, I thought, it they knew I prayed for wisdom.

"When I became a man and had to match myself with other men I still prayed for wisdom, not perhaps the "ghostly wisdom" of the Christian Fathers, but the balance and good sense to carry through against men with readier tongues than mine. It came later that, along with wisdom, I prayed for mercy in the sense of merciful temperance with others.

"The boyish thought had a more spiritual foundation than the intermediate stage. During the warring years I wanted wisdom to enable me to win in the struggle for life.

"In the early hours of the morning or on lonely tramps in the woods or fields I got my answers. It is customary for men confronted by problems to get together in stuffy quarters and split the hair between the south and southwest side, pounding away at each other verbally not only by day but 'til late at night. With me such "conferences" only result in mental tiredness and unfitness. The more protracted they are the more stupid I become. Realizing that my judgment was imperative, I developed the protective policy of refusing to commit myself to a decision until I had time to get my bearings in the outdoors alone.

"Beyond the problem itself I studied the men tied up with it and their motives, or lack of motives. The human factor has always seemed to me more important than mere formulas. Good talkers are apt to be men of unreliable judgment and are generally lacking in courage. As a rule they have no time for other things than talking and framing in their minds the most effective way of saying a thing. They develop their facility at the expense of personal initiative and are lost without a George to put it over. Contrariwise, men of action are usually not noted for being glib talkers.

"It is instructive to mistrust the business or the movement where too much time is given to conferences. Humanity despises sophistry and insincerity instinctively. It knows that the trail marked by a superfluity of words leads to pitfalls, and that the words themselves conceal the perils of the trail.

"The trouble with us is that we have lost the way to the safe fortress of solitude. How many, aside from solitary prospectors and trappers, have ever cut themselves off from human companionship for a month — or even a week? Jesus spent forty days alone in the wilderness before he started his mission. Does anyone really, at first, desire only crowds, radio, jazz and the tabloids? Is there anything Godlike in sheep-mindedness and regimentation? We have become caged birds when we cease to thrill with the soaring eagle. The great prophets worked out their problems alone in the deserts and hills.

"The world's conquering races came from the mountains. It was not that the mere elevation above sea level of their homes bred in them power, but the fact that they weren't congested like the peoples of the cities on the fertile plains. They were not crowded and as herders and hunters they were alone much of the time.

"Gregariousness, like smoking or opium eating, becomes a progressive habit. It is not bad of itself but only when carried to excess. The antidote for the addict is temporary solitude. Lone prospectors and trappers generally wind up by "shaking hands with the willows," as the saying is in the Far North. Translated it means they go nutty. The antidote against insanity of this type is human companionship. There is a happy medium between the two extremes in the country. Thank God for what is called the country!

"I have heard doctors say that to have T.B. is a mark of distinction, that it is essentially a disease of the active, worth-while people. Similarly, I think, the people in the city, but not of the city, are its shining lights. I admire those who have the courage and character to retain their individuality despite the sour and senile atmosphere. Periodically such people should have the tonic of the wilderness.

"If a man is blue, or needs to orient his perspective, he should go off by himself into whatever wilderness is available and find some exercise for his body if it is nothing more than chopping wood. If his mind is blank at the start it is all the better for him. A fresh fall of snow blots out the mass of confusing details that may have spoiled a lovely landscape. As he walks or paddles or works, the facts straighten themselves out into a harmonious whole, and the high-lights stand out from the shadows. Just one practical point I can give you and this is: if you are absolutely shut off from other people for a week or more, do not fail to talk to yourself aloud, even if all you say is: 'You damn old fool!' Otherwise, the muscles that govern the formation of words will play you a trick and on your return you will have difficulty and embarrassment in talking. The vocal cords lose their facility more quickly than other muscles....

"I got disgusted with church attendance when I was a man with a family. As an Episcopalian I had to listen to too many sermons on doctrine when my soul craved truth to combat temptation. It all culminated in a rector talking himself down to the level of us less spiritual men in a social meeting. He smoked and drank beer with us, which did not shock me, but when he remarked that he had been tired out at the time of his recent visit to the City and to get relaxation had gone to a "leg show," the bottom seemed to fall out from under me.

*Rev. George Webster (1866-1942)*

"Average men who go to church go there to get help. They want bracing against the demands of their passions and their meannesses. They require a far greater degree of Godliness in their leader than in themselves. If he cannot make good his words by his example, he cannot be of help to others.

"It was a bad example that put an end to my church-going and it was a good example too that brought me back. I got to know the Reverend George O. Webster, a Baptist pastor who ministered to the Presbyterians and Methodists as well in our village. The first thing that attracted me to him was noticing how quickly the smutty talk stopped when he happened around, out of respect to a clean man and not his cloth. I had already observed evidence of the good he was doing to people in trouble and particularly among young people. He had boys and young men at his services as well as women, and those who had gotten along to the stage when they were afraid not to make their peace with God.

"I began once more going to church with my family, and anger at the way God was interpreted and distrust in the teacher left my soul. I also go to the Episcopal church with my family in the Summer when we have a rector. The truly glorious ritual of that church appeals to them in a way that by early training it should appeal to me but does not. I suppose I am all the time fearing a sermon of the type intended to show pity on other ways of worship. I like the directness and simplicity of those who do not lay store on apostolic succession.

"George Webster is[1] possibly the biggest man in Essex. He has a massive frame and he weighs 245 pounds. He is just as big-minded as his avoirdupois. He called on the Oblate Fathers when they came to town and they like him. Catholics know a good Baptist when they see him but most of them do not get the chance to become acquainted. Webster, when the opportunity offers, enjoys dropping in at a service in the Episcopal Church. He is a great lover of music and of Nature and is a fine lyric poet; but as he has had little time for

---
[1] Webster (1866-1942) died in Essex after a short illness.

anything other than serving his Master, most of his poems are religious, and they are sung from Coast to Coast. I once dug from him the story of his life.

"Webster was on his way from the lumber camp to the city, intent on nothing except blowing in the pay he had in his pocket, when he passed the lonely church at North River where his parents had worshipped. It was evening, but from the church came the sound of the organ and singing struggling with the rhythm of the swift waters of the Hudson just in front. Something not to be analyzed made him go in and take a seat next to the door. His mind was in a tumult, but apparently no one noticed his presence.

"He was roused from his revery by hearing the kindly old pastor say, 'I am glad to see that our brother, George Webster, is present. If he cares to say anything, I am sure we will be glad to hear him---.' It was too late to slink out; he had been caught; in words that did not seem to be his own Webster replied: 'I got in here by accident......All of you know what a tough character I am.... By the grace of God things are going to be different hereafter.' And they were!...

"While it is perfectly evident that church attendance has been falling off ever since Hell was renovated into a beer garden and the fear of its tortures removed, it seems to me that I find fewer atheists among my acquaintances than when I was a boy. There were plenty of them then to be sure. The majority of people today are unreligious rather than irreligious as far as my experience goes. Most people believe in God and follow his teachings up to the point of the very doors of the church. Alaskans go to the ultimate limit in practicing Christ's precept of doing good to others and so do lots of people in cities. The only thoroughly unreligious people are the young and thoughtless and the selfish. Personally, I believe that the "unforgivable sin" is selfishness.

"The trouble today is that the movies, radio[1] and tabloids have played hob with mentality and that Mankind does not think enough for itself. If it did, then I am sure people would realize that touch with God is needed through the church to combat temptation and to fit one to pass the entrance examinations for the next world. The old conception of harps and nightgowns there has gone with brimstone and pitchforks in Hell. I would rather associate with heroes than with hoboes, with honest and unselfish souls than with those who make their bellies their God. Also I love trees and clear water and animals and birds, and I don't fancy there is much of that kind of thing in Hell. I have made my Heaven to suit my better desires, and as I believe God is just as square as He is loving I feel sure He will give me the Heaven I want.

"I must say, however, that I do not like the artist's concept of Christ anymore than the concept of some churchmen. I do not believe He is sad anymore than that He is sour. I prefer to picture Him as laughing over his carpentry work in His shop, and as thoroughly enjoying His fishing in the lake, with boats for a hobby. In this light I can understand the last three years of His life — when duty called and Golgotha loomed on the horizon.

"I have a hell-roaring California friend who accuses me of being a slave to a New England conscience. 'Wake up, John,' he shouts, 'the Devil is dead; let's make a night of it!' I like Joe for his joyousness. His motto is eat, drink and be merry — for tomorrow we are dead for a long time. To this I cannot subscribe, but joyousness of itself is a fine thing, a tonic, and only prudes condemn it. Joe loves the ladies indiscriminately but with a platonic rather than a fleshly love. I think of the Master's statement: "Call nothing common or unclean." All things are good in moderation but bad in excess. Even one woman is too much for many men. But those who treat wine, women and song with a light touch are preferable

---

[1] *[Editor's note: T.V. especially is the arch-enemy of society.]*

to the morbid-minded. Pleasure and light-heartedness should be a part of life, and I have great sympathy for the dalliers so long as their practice does not harm others. I prefer, however, to find my happiness in simpler and less dangerous channels.

"I believe in God and a future life first, I think, on account of my Christian training by a devout mother and father. Next, I believe because of an implanted instinct, my conscience, which tells me that God's word is true. It has never been necessary for me to attempt to reason out a basis for belief. It is born and bred in me to have faith, and for this I am thankful, because I know that an intuitive faith is far from universal. I am so created that I do not like to talk much about religion and for a long while in my life I neglected church attendance. It was my friend, George W. who won me back, but faith was so deeply ingrained in my make-up that I never questioned or doubted the fundamentals of religion. Sin and error are so easy and with us every moment, like the germs of disease, that if we are to avoid them we must at frequent intervals be jacked up in our convictions by going to church.

"Every time I go to a service more or less evil I have done since the last time pops into my head and I refresh my resolve to try to do better. Church attendance helps keep the soul healthy to throw off the microbes of sin.

"As I get older I also realize that if I am to enjoy a future life I must fit myself for it. I do not believe that I must learn to twang a harp or be comfortable going around in a nightshirt with fancy wings on my back. Heaven will be Heaven only if it gives us happiness, if it gives us compensation for the heart and body wracks of this world, with no night and no sin and no sorrow. But on the other hand it cannot be a place of mere physical gratification. The pleasure must come from the enjoyment of the spirit. Therefore, to be fit for it so that it will be all that the term implies, one must cultivate the things of the spirit.

"I love hunting and often think of Nessmuk's[1] lines:

"Give me a heaven
Wherein the deer
Shall be more plentiful than here,
And brown October all the years!"

"I know perfectly well I can't take a rifle with me when I die and I feel very uncertain about the game laws of the Kingdom Come — there may not be any open seasons! Therefore, I am trying to cultivate in myself a greater pleasure in the other things associated with hunting rather than in bringing the game to pot. For one thing, I feel sure I can enjoy hunting even if not killing — in countries and places I have always wanted to visit. Since I was a child I have wanted to know what lay behind the next range of mountains beyond where I have been. I have always loved the crags and lakes and forests and deserts, and I know I shall enjoy the beauties of them if I reach Heaven because this conviction is spiritual. This part of the thing I have pretty well settled in my own mind. But there's a much bigger question that I have not solved and probably never shall solve, and this is how to fit myself to carry on in the shining presence of my Lord and Master. I go to church to find this out, but in life I fail so much and deny my Lord so often that I feel I cannot face His presence without a complete change. The only favorable thing about the situation is that I know I want the regeneration.

"The longer I live the more my belief in spiritual things is strengthened. We have two parts to our minds — the reasoning mind and the subjective mind. By observation I have noticed that men in trouble lean on God. Biologists who consider only what they can put their finger on commonly differentiate between man and the lower animals by giving to

---

[1] George Washington Sears (1821-1890).

man the power of reason. They leave out of account the soul — which constitutes the real difference between man and beast.[1] For this reason they are likely, I think, to depreciate the value in man of the instinctive mind. But man needs his intuitive mind more than his reasoning mind to see God. The hero does not reason when he gives his life for his friend or his country. It is the instinctive/intuitive mind, what is called heart or soul, that prompts the great heroics, the great self-sacrifices that mankind admires, reveres and honors. It is through it that God acts to influence men.

"Some of the demonstrations of instinct in animals have strengthened my belief in God because they are beyond human reason and could not have developed by chance. After all they are also God's creatures and his creations.

---

[1] *[The longer I live the more convinced I am that mankind does not have a monopoly on souls or essential spirits. Some pet cats that I have observed seem to have more than a modicum of that divine attribute: Editor.]*

# Chapter 18

## Local Politics and Politicians

*[Up to this point I have been hesitant — even reluctant — to exercise my editorial rights and privileges but since this topic — grassroots government — produces so much personal concern and emotional heat, I have decided to register my own proverbial two cents' worth of aged-in-the-wood, long-held opinions and observations. By doing so I am well aware that many if not most of my comments will ignite considerable resentment in certain circles. Nevertheless, I also know that such anticipated hostility will be effectively counterbalanced by the heartfelt approval of an ever-increasing number of perceptive people who have reached mental as well as physical maturity.*

*Obviously, I sincerely share Burnham's openly cynical attitude toward the low-caliber character and/or lack of same and the dubious motives displayed by the common and run-of-the-mill variety of local, state and national office-holders. Fortunately for us there are occasional exceptions among their ranks, but all too often they are outnumbered by the limited-horizon, devious, myopic individuals who use, misuse and abuse the political process in order to get a piece of the action for themselves or their manipulators for their own particular purposes. Not so incidentally they are also acquiring power, prestige, patronage and plunder.*

*A typical example of such tunnel-vision recently surfaced in an upper Ausable Valley town meeting when the resident supervisor protested against a proposal for a fairly strict zoning plan by complaining that it would "sure ruffle a lot of (influential) feathers! — and implied that he was not about to be a party to it!*

*Far too frequently local government means very little or no government at all — or as little as the average incumbent can get by with or get away with without jeopardizing his job. Get along and go along seems to be the slogan. Don't make waves or rock the boat! Play it cool! No sweat!*

*Regrettably often these representatives develop into a self-perpetuating machine organization which eventually becomes so ensconced and entrenched that they can arrogantly rule the roost with little fear of replacement. Such a cozy clique can then dedicate themselves not to the furtherance of the public good but to the maintenance of the comfortable and convenient status quo. They consider themselves special somebodies above the legal structure — with its seemingly contrived loopholes — which they helped concoct, conceal and condone.*

*As Burnham demonstrated, such a malodorous situation can be corrected but only by almost incredible personal effort and persistence. Men of integrity and reasonable means who aren't on the make and take, who don't feel forced to string along with the two-bit politicos can beat City Hall and have done so on occaison. But it should happen much more often! Editor]*

Continuing Burnham's story: "While I was drawn into politics by force of circumstance I am now firmly of the opinion that under our form of government everyone should take a part in this business either by running for office or else through working for the election of those they respect. There is still a lot of dirt in politics, plenty to make a level-thinking man get up on his hind legs and thrash out and this is what is needed. Get into the game and get mad and fight! This is my advice.

"You will find it a fascinating game and you will also find that honest, straight speaking will win every time. Germs and slime cannot stand the sunlight. Your only danger is being too good-natured and acquiescent in things you know are not right and not for the public benefit.

"When I started a fight on the Chief Game Protector of the State I little thought it would lead to my becoming the chief officer of my town and eventually the chief of the State job as well, and yet it was directly responsible for this outcome. On *Forest & Stream* I had learned something of conservation, and through the influence of George Bird Grinnell, the president of the company and Charles B. Reynolds, the managing editor, I had changed from game poacher to a worker for law enforcement. It was this training that made me see things that were not right when I went to live in the country. There were plenty of game laws and a force of officers to make them effective, but the enforcement was not equitable and men of influence, particularly judges and politicians broke all the laws with impunity. Essex County, where I lived, was notorious for the fact that there was no enforcement of the law prohibiting the use of dogs in hunting deer. The older "sports" came to it in droves to sit comfortably on a runway until the hounds drove them deer upon which they could exercise their marksmanship. My blood, which had for sometime been stewing, came to a boil when, as guests of John & George Stevens, the joint Fish & Game Committees of the State Senate & Assembly carried on a three-day hounding jamboree on the Chubb River, near Lake Placid. In the party was Senator (afterwards Congressman) Malby[1], the author of the anti-hounding law!

"I wrote a series of several articles which were printed in *Forest & Stream* showing up the situation in all its rottenness, and as a result the Chief Officer of the State started legal action against me in three different ways. The spear-head was a suit for libel.

"In Essex lived a remarkable man named Anthony Ross. He was a direct descendant of William Gilliland, the pioneer English-speaking settler of this part of the North, who before the Revolution had founded a manorial estate on Lake Champlain. Anthony Ross was a surveyor and a farmer and, typifying the best in our free life, a lawyer as well. It was in the latter capacity that I now sought his advice.

'This is a serious matter," he said, when he had read the papers with which I had been served. 'Where are the offensive articles which you have written?'

"We spent a number of hours going over the articles and discussing their basis. To my joy I found that Mr. Ross became as hot as I had been when he had absorbed the ugly facts, and he espoused my cause and made it his own.

'The dirty scoundrels,' he said, 'we'll make no apologies. We'll throw the gauntlet right back in their teeth!'

"Confronting us was an array of the best legal talent that our State Capitol could produce, led by Carr, Chief Attorney of the D. & H. Rail Road. They made the mistake of their lives in underestimating their country surveyor-lawyer-farmer opponent. When the clouds of battle cleared we were masters of the field and I was free to proceed as I liked.

---

[1] Later Malby told me he'd put through this law at the request of owners of large private parks who were tired of having hounds run deer off their preserves.

"The Chief Game Protector had endeavored to justify himself by saying that a law against hounding could not be enforced. I had stated that it could be enforced. I felt now it was up to me to prove my contention. There was a vacancy in the County game protectorship and I applied for the job. Walter Witherbee, a wealthy owner of iron mines, was our political leader and I went to Walter and asked him for the appointment. Walter, by the way, loved to get his deer in front of a dog.

"At first he tried to tell me I did not want the job — that it was degrading and all that kind of thing, but when he found I could not be dissuaded, he directed me to get the endorsement of a majority of the County Committee. I was so green that I had to ask what a County Committee was and who composed it.

"It required a full week's time with horse and sulky to see the ten men who constituted a majority of the representatives from the 18 towns, for Essex County is larger than some states; but in the end I sent to Walter the written endorsement of the majority. Several days later, our Essex Committeeman called me into his office. I did not like Dr. Sweatt because he had refused to give me, his own townsman, his endorsement until he found I was certain to get what I wanted without his help — and I did not like what he now had to say. He was tactless, moreover, because he called me "Johnny" — which was always a fighting name to me when I was a kid.

'Johnny,' he said as he gave me a sick cat kind of look, 'the powers that be are thinking seriously of giving you this position, but first we want your assurance that you will enforce the law *judiciously.*'

"Doc, if you have in mind that I will be somewhere else when Walter Witherbee and his friends are going hounding, you tell them I'll enforce the law damn injudiciously!"

"The next time I was called in, the Doctor tried a new tack. He told me that, greatly to his surprise, Walter Witherbee, Jim Graeff, our member in the State Assembly, and the other insiders seemed to have taken a great liking to me, and that they considered me a young man of great promise, one who would mount the ladder of political preferment several rungs at a time. Therefore, after due consultation they had determined to start me right and that I, instead of the measly $600 paid a game protector, was to be given $1200 as Excise Commissioner of the County. "Doc," I said, "I made ten thousand in my own business last year, — can't you get it through your head that there are such things in this world as service due one's country? Also that a man can have pride in proving a contention? I don't even want the perquisites of a booze-hound's job."

"One reason why professional politicians are dumb is because they actually believe every man has his price. The final olive branch was the offer of the Deputy Collectorship of the Port of Plattsburgh, the best plum in sight, paying $6,000 per year. After I turned that down, I got in so deep in a business matter I forgot about the game protector matter and after six months' desuetude Charley Barnes was given the job. Eventually I became Charley's boss through appointment as the head of the force.

"Our Town Committeeman had thrown it up to me several times during our interview that I had done nothing for the party and did not, therefore, deserve political preferment. His theory was that one should begin at the bottom of the ladder with some job like town constable and gradually work his way up. I heard that his next step, as he planned it, was to be selected Supervisor of Essex and I resolved to beat him to it. My motives, no doubt, were not of the highest, but it gave me a pain in the prat to think of him as the leading representative of our Town.

"Paris Stafford, for whom I afterwards secured the postmastership of Whallonsburgh, told me that a little clique of which he was a member always got together in advance of

Town Meeting Day and selected the slate of Town officers for which the populace was permitted to vote, so I reached an agreement with Paris to let me know the date when it was set by Dr. Sweatt. I was told the meeting would be held in Whitney Stafford's law office. The appointed evening arrived and just before the hour of 7 set for it to begin I made a business call on the long-suffering Whitney. He had not forgotten the night session devoted to settling the Derby farm matter, and his greeting was perfunctory and marked by an utter lack of cordiality; but I was now quite an important legal client and he did not have the nerve to bounce me. His face was an interesting study of mixed emotions.

"One by one other members of the coterie arrived. We conversed about the weather and crop prospects and about every other possible topic except politics. Most of them did not know that I was present without an invitation, but like typical politicians they were suspicious.

"It was Whitney who at length broke the ice. He needed sleep and he was in no mood for another all-night session. After our aimless conversation had run for about three hours, he got up from his chair and said: 'It is only a few days from now to Caucus and we must decide tonight who we are going to run for Supervisor against Meeker Tromblee.'

"Everybody looked at me so, without rising I said, "Looks as if I was out of place here; I'd better be leaving," whereupon Paris Stafford remarked: 'You're a good Republican and entitled to take part in the councils of your party.'

"I saw the Doctor cast a venomous glance at Paris, but it was an awkward situation, and no one had the nerve to be the first to suggest throwing me out. To break the silence which ensued I spoke of the question before the house and nominated myself for Supervisor.

"The meeting had been arranged to hand Dr. Sweatt the nomination on a silver platter. While the vote of the Town was overwhelmingly Republican, squabbles in the Republican ranks for the past two elections had given the office to Meeker Tromblee, a popular Democrat. Sweatt desired the office but he was a cautious man and not too well-liked, and he realized that he could only hope for success with an undivided party vote. His supporters therefore were ready to conciliate me rather than run the risk of a party row. They spent a lot of time telling me why I was not available. 'It will take $400 to defeat Meeker Tromblee and you won't pay it.'

"Why not?" I asked.

'Well, you've got to fight the Devil with fire. Tom, Meeker's brother, will be there on the stairs passing out cigars with two-dollar bills wrapped around them.'

"Now, gentlemen, you know I do not believe in buying votes, but if you can show me any legitimate way of spending it I will put up any sum you name."

"At once everyone became good-natured. They were so thoroughly convinced that Meeker could not be beaten except by outbuying him that for the moment they thought I had counted myself out of the race.

"When I could get a chance to be heard, however, I threw some more cold water on the nice dream of harmony.

"I'll take the nomination and I'll be elected without buying a single vote and this is the way it will be done. I'll arrange for some of the men who are working for me to take money from Tom, and I'll have a warrant ready and he will be thrown behind the bars so quick he won't know what's happened!" Anger and pity for my lack of sophistication showed in their faces and the terms "young" and "green" were over-used in their characterization of my remarks. But the meeting broke up without making its slate, which was the most I had hoped for.

"The next morning I announced my candidacy through a man-to-man canvass of the parts of the town where I was not known. I bought a couple of boxes of cigars at Wilson & Sherman's store and drove to Whallonsburgh, where I picked up Paris Stafford, and then we made our leisurely way back north towards Bouquet, stopping at about every farmhouse. Paris would introduce me to the farmer and I would hand him a cigar and relight my own, meanwhile telling the voter that I was a candidate for Supervisor and would appreciate his support. The next day I got another friend who was well-acquainted in Brookfield and repeated the process. Each evening I circulated around the village of Essex, getting in touch with as many voters as time permitted. I tried as far as possible to avoid arguments, and when I struck a disputatious fellow who wanted to prove I had no right to enter the lists for office I shook him without ceremony.

"My platform was a very simple one: I promised, if elected, to manage the town economically and honestly. Taxes had recently been mounting and I said they should be kept below a dollar. I also spoke of cement sidewalks to take the place of the rotten board sidewalks for Essex Village and better roads in the country districts.

"The third day, which was the next day but one before Caucus, I was in Whallonsburgh again. A boy came to me with the information that I was wanted at the railroad station. Arrived there I found half a dozen grey-beards assembled for a conference. George Wyland opened the proceedings: 'We all know you, Johnny. You are a nice boy and a clean one and under other conditions we would like to vote for you, but don't you think you are a little bit presumptuous in aiming at the head of the ticket first off the bat, without ever having held any other office?'

"I admitted the corn, and Wyland proceeded, 'We have here in Whallonsburgh Dan Stafford, an old war horse of the party, who had been Justice of the Peace for many years. He is ambitious to round out his career of service by becoming Supervisor. You know Dan. Don't you think he is better fitted and more entitled to be Supervisor than you are?'

"Sure," I said, without a moment's hesitation, "Dan is all to the good and deserves the job. All I want is to keep Dr. Sweatt out. I'll announce I have withdrawn in favor of Dan Stafford."

'Not so fast, young man. Not so fast!' Jock Mather said, 'I'm just as anxious as you are not to have the town run any longer by Sweatt and his gang, but before we settle this matter we want to be sure we've got the candidate that can defeat him. Dan is not too well-known around Essex Village and he cannot lick Sweatt unless he had the support of his son Whitney. I propose that a committee of two be sent to Essex at once to tell Whitney that John Burnham will withdraw in favor of Dan provided he will come out for his father. You will never get Whitney to break with Sweatt and support his father any other way.'

"This council prevailed, and I returned to Essex to await results.

"I did not have long to wait. I had just become engrossed in the 1851 map "Showing the Track of H.M.S. Pioneer in Search of Sir John Franklin" and was wondering why these brave Englishmen were so far off from the place where Franklin and his men perished, when the Whallonsburgh committee arrived with the information that Whitney Stafford had refused their proposal. They were fighting mad because Whitney had ridiculed them saying that neither his father nor myself had the ghost of a chance to get the nomination and that they were trying to pull his leg. They had been instructed, they said, to tell me in this situation to make the fight; and they assured me that Dan Stafford and the rest of them would take off their shirts to elect me.

"Whitney Stafford was Chairman of the Caucus. He appointed two tellers, one of whom held a derby hat into which the ballots were deposited while the other wrote the name of the voter on a yellow foolscap pad to make sure that nobody voted more than once. The voters wrote the names of their candidates on small pieces of paper torn from the same yellow pad.

"I had gotten some ballots typewritten with my name, and I went among the crowd in the hall looking for unfamiliar faces. Whenever I noticed a man I did not think I had talked with, I gave him a ballot and asked for his vote. Old Myron Tyrrell came in, his massive frame draped with a fur coat from which patches of hair had disappeared, looking for all the world like a bear just out of hibernation. Without knowing his name, I addressed him and asked for his vote. 'I don't know you, young feller,' he said as he glared at me, 'but I do know the other feller and I shan't vote for him. Give me your ballot!' and he walked up and deposited it in the hat.

"When the ballots had all been cast the tellers proceeded to count them and they finally announced to the Chairman that I had been nominated by a vote of between two and three to one. Whitney was pale but not satisfied. He had the man who kept the record of names count them up with the result that there was one name less on the written list than the number of ballots in the hat.

"A half-hour was lost in the check-up and many of the voters had gone home, but Whitney announced the vote as invalid and called for another ballot. The voters who remained knew that it was customary in a case like this to withdraw one ballot from the candidate having the largest number. They registered their disapproval of Whitney's action by giving me an almost unanimous vote on the second ballot, whereupon Whitney announced my nomination without taking any time for a second check-up.

"This was the end of the Sweatt machine. As there were no indications of Republican disharmony the Democrats, when they caucused a few days later, gave me their endorsement and I was elected without opposition.

"I served for three terms of two years each and during this time we put in cement sidewalks on all our streets and also an electric street-lighting system. For the sidewalks we got part of the money from the State and the balance from the abutting property owners. The tax rate never exceeded one dollar.

"I am proud of the fact that my town of Essex gave me good majorities every time my name was on a ballot. As a supporter of Theodore Roosevelt I followed him into the Bull Moose party. Without knowing anything about it I was nominated for Congress at a convention of the new party held in Clinton County, one of the four counties forming the largest Congressional district in New York. This district takes in the Northern part of the State from Lake Champlain to the St. Lawrence River.

"The last thing in the world I wanted was to sit in the House of Representatives in Washington. I would rather have gone to prison, for there I would have time to catch up with my reading. But I accepted out of deference to my chief and I spent $4,000 paying the expenses of speakers and for my own traveling expenses. I was running against Ed Merritt, who had just given up the Speakership of the Lower Chamber at Albany.

When the vote was counted it was found that I had carried the lake-shore side of the district by a vote greater than the combined Republican and Democratic candidates, and that I had also carried the section where Merritt lived; but I was defeated by a small majority made from the straight party vote in Franklin and Clinton Counties. All the while I knew that had I wanted it, I could win by sending money to the workers to get out the vote on Election Day. We had no organization at the polls and so lost a great many potential votes.

"Two years later, at a convention in Utica which I did not attend, I was nominated for State Comptroller. I went to Theodore Douglas Robinson, State Progressive Chairman, and asked to have my name taken from the ballot. I told him that I was poor that year, but that I would contribute a couple of thousand dollars to the war chest if my request was granted, and that if it was not I would give nothing; but he refused saying, 'Two years ago there was a chance; this time we are just standing up to be shot at!'

"The Association for the Protection of the Adirondacks took up the campaign against the Chief Game Protector of the State where I had left off. They had found irregularities in his handling of State forests, just as I had found malfeasances in game-law enforcement. The Association presented their case and Governor Higgins dismissed him. A reorganization of the Fish & Game Commission followed. Up to this time the Chief Game Protector had been about all there was to the commission in an executive way, but now James S. Whipple was appointed to be a de facto commissioner and I was asked to serve under him as head of the game department. My first year in office we secured 17 convictions in Essex County for violations of the anti-hounding law. In all the years before there had been only one conviction and that a phony one.

"Another lesson in "practical politics" came shortly after I took office. We had two very picturesque old covered bridges across the Bouquet River in the Town of Essex and one of these bridges threatened to give up the ghost during the period when I was Supervisor. Thinking it might be the best economy to put in a new iron bridge, I wrote several bridge concerns giving them the essential data and asking for prices. It was my intention to place the figures before the Town Board together with an estimate of the cost of repairing the existing bridge, and we could then determine the proper course of action to pursue. But there was a different result than I had expected: I was never able to get a proper tender and during my term we put in no iron bridges.

"A few days after I had written the letters a big well-dressed chap breezed into my office and, without other preliminaries than merely to satisfy himself that I was the Supervisor, counted out $500 in crisp $20 bills and deposited the money in front of me on my desk. Somewhat flabbergasted, I asked him what it was for. 'Oh, merely as a token of our good will and esteem,' he said, and then no doubt thinking I was not satisfied with the ante, he added, 'There will be more coming to you when the details are settled. This is merely a retainer!'

"I told him I did not accept retainers and made him put the money back in his billfold. He was genuinely puzzled. 'What's the idea?' he asked. 'Would a thousand make you feel better? I can give you anything you ask that is not too indiscreet.'

"I told him in just as plain words as I could muster with ease that what I wanted was to get a new price on the bridge with no graft attached, but he would not believe that I meant what I said. 'What salary do you get from this job?' he asked.

"Oh, about $100 a year," I replied.

'That won't buy your postage stamps!' he said with an air of scorn and finality. 'You're certainly not in it for your health only!'

"I actually labored with that man to get him to set a price on his bridges but he was so accustomed to his method of doing business that I never got his estimate. Thinking to assure me that it was perfectly safe and respectable to take the graft, he told me that his company had erected most of the town iron bridges in Northern New York, that they had always "made presents" to the Supervisor and the more important members of the Town Board, and that there had never been any comeback. He admitted that at a town in St. Lawrence County where the officers had been unusually grasping, one of the citizens had started a taxpayer's action. 'That bridge,' he said, 'should have cost about $3,000 but they ran it up to pretty near $15,000. We sent up Colonel Blank, our lawyer, and he found the skeletons in that particular taxpayer's closet and that gentleman pulled in his horns pronto!'

"The enactment of the Moreland law did much to put an end to this unsavory added income and it has now practically disappeared. To make up for its loss, however, the Supervisors are paying themselves far too large salaries. This bridge salesman, by the way, represented Senator Conger's bridge company. It was Senator Conger who started the investigation which resulted in putting the Republican party out of power for years in New York. The Bull Moose party, if it accomplished nothing else, had to its credit the awakening of civic interest and had much to do with the elimination of graft. Our campaign in Northern New York was aimed at two things — against dishonesty in both political parties and for social justice."

# Chapter 19

### The Fateful Siberian Interlude* and Some Environmental Concerns

In 1921 John Burnham, accompanied by the guide, Andy Taylor, went on an eventful expedition to the Chukotsk Peninsula of Northeastern Siberia. The stated purpose of the trip was to obtain specimens of the extremely rare mountain sheep which scientists believed existed there and thus establish a link between the Asiatic and Northern American varieties of the species.

According to Burnham "Andy and I traveled 2,000 miles to get one small sheep, thirty-one inches high and forty-one inches overall. We were five days on the sea, fifty days traveling on land, or unprofitably occupied, and fifty days on the hunting grounds. Between us we wore out nine pairs of shoes, two sets of tempers and two sets of eyes looking for sheep where they weren't. But we were satisfied because we finally got the sheep (subsequently named ovis burnhami) and established a scientific fact."

They were also treated with the utmost suspicion by both the Bolsheviks and the Japanese who, having defeated the Russians less than twenty years previously, considered themselves sole owners of the region and were busily mapping, exploring and exploiting its gold and salmon resources in total disregard for the restrictive provisions of the Portsmouth Treaty.

One day when the two Americans were hunting in the interior a native messenger arrived with an obviously phony note from a trader named Thompson, who requested that they meet him without delay. Four days later Burnham went down to see what it was all about because they were relying on Thompson's boat to take them back to Alaska. At the Coast Burnham's suspicions were confirmed: it was the Russian captain who wanted to see him.

Apprehensive but nevertheless wishing to get his status settled rather than being summarily shoved into a vermin-infested jail, Burnham put a pistol in his pocket and accompanied four Japanese sailors in European clothes who suddenly emerged from the shadow of a native hut.

At the landing, instead of offering him passage in their motorized dinghy, the Japs waited while one of the natives launched a skin boat and, once the visitor was aboard, kept just a short distance ahead all the way out to the three-masted vessel, the Daichii Toro Maru. Arrived there they clambered aboard and proceeded to hoist the gangway — a hostile action in itself but followed by even more insulting behavior. Just as the American started

---

* *Interlude*, as used here means an intervening or interruptive period, space or event. No musical or farcical denotation is intended or should be inferred.

*Andy Taylor and J. B. Burnham*

*The Unknown Sheep*

*The Base Camp*

*Interior of Chukotsk Peninsula*

to climb up the ropeladder on the side of the schooner, one of the Japs attempted to empty his bladder into Burnham's face — but the intended victim adroitly managed to duck most of the discharge. On deck he was rudely hustled into the cabin where eight men were seated awaiting his arrival.

Two of them were apparently educated Japanese businessmen; the others were Russians, one of whom spoke perfect English and was the chief interrogator. Although Burham resented their questions he realized that there was something serious about the affair and that nothing was to be gained by refusal to comply.

"So this is Mr. Burnham of whom we have heard so much. May I ask what business brought you to Siberia?"

"I did not come on business but for pleasure." Burnham replied.

"Pleasure? What pleasure can you find in such an inhospitable region?" inquired the Russian.

"I am hunting."

"Hunting with any specific object in view?"

"Yes, I'm trying to determine the nature of the mountain sheep in the area."...

More pointed questions followed until one of the Japanese asked Burnham's address in New York.

"233 Broadway," he answered.

"What building is that?"

"The Woolworth Building."

"Do you live there?" was the next question.

"No, that's my business address. I live on 72nd Street."

"How many elevators has the Woolworth Building?"

"Thirty or more," Burnham replied.

It soon became evident that these men, who were obviously familiar with New York City, were testing the visitor's veracity and they soon came to the nub and reason for the interview. They wanted to know if he was a spy-prospector. After he had assured them that he wasn't, the inquest was terminated.

Only once in the general conversation did the Japanese take special notice. That was when Burnham remarked that English was an illogical language — to which the Japs laughingly agreed.

The incident was significant because it clearly proved that the Japanese in that region in particular were not over-friendly in their feelings toward Americans. Other nationalists were treated respectfully while our citizens were spat on — or worse — by the common sailors and made subjects of suspicion by those higher up. Much of the direction of affairs in Japan, then as well as now, was in the control of the big business families and these men were and are very able, far-seeing and mercenary. As dollar-chasers Americans are not even in the same league with them.

To Burnham it seemed that the hostility of the common people, shown unmasked in that out-of-the-way corner of the world, indicated more than mere resentment at our exclusion laws. He was convinced that it was prompted from above by business motives.

Burnham later learned that his interrogator, John A. Korsookeen, an internationally known mining engineer who spoke ten languages with equal ease, had formerly had an office in the Woolworth Building. Not in sympathy with the Bolsheviks he and his fellow Russians were then working for a Nipponese mining firm which had recently made important mineral discoveries nearby and were understandably wary of any American competition.

There were many loose ends to this story and lingering doubts about the exact identity of the man who saved his life. Our State Department would not permit the publication of the full account of the manner in which Korsookeen, apparently a double agent, had been able to talk the Japanese out of the ominous situation with its potentially murderous overtones.

Interestingly enough the paths of the two principals in that "court martial" incident crossed one day in an elevator in the Woolworth Building. Mutual recognition was followed by a lively conversation during which Burnham was able to express more fully his heartfelt appreciation for the other's intervention in his behalf several years earlier.

Most of the story of this harrowing experience was told in Burnham's book: *The Rim of Mystery — A Hunter's Wanderings in Unknown Siberian Asia*. G. P. Putnam's Sons, 1929. 281pp. 60 illustrations and map.

Burnham's experiences and observations convinced him that the activities of the Japs represented a serious military as well as a trade threat to the United States since they could easily overrun the then almost defenseless Alaska. He reported his convictions to Washington and the next year, when "The Bear" made an extended flora and fauna cruise in the area, there were many government agents among the scientists on board.

While the scientists considered this a wonderful and welcome field trip, the State Department officers found ample proof that Burnham's suspicions were sound. Besides providing Washington with plenty of cause for concern, Burnham also kept records, diaries, reports and made sketch maps of the Siberian coast; he also compiled data on its tides and fog patterns which Navy intelligence found to be both valuable and urgently needed. For that reason they requested the material for duplication purposes and in due time delivered the documents to their owner. Later, they borrowed them again but this time they were never returned.

Other prominent agencies and persons made extensive use of the information, photos and experiences acquired by Burnham on his subsequent trips to the Far North. Among these was Vilhjalmur Stefansson, famed Polar explorer, who was a frequent guest at the "Highlands." Another welcome visitor was Arnold Boyd, eminent New York lawyer and the man who was mainly responsible for the availability of the *Nautilus,* the submarine used in the early summer of 1931 by Sir G. Hubert Wilkins, the venturesome Australian and his American associate, Lincoln Ellsworth. While both were renowned aviators and veterans of numerous Arctic and Antarctic expeditions, they were eager to contend with still another medium — the underwater route to the North Pole. Besides the main goal of scientific exploration they were also interested in the commercial and military potentials.

Burnham's advice and suggestions were carefully considered by the U.S. Army Quartermaster Corps and the leaders of several other Arctic expeditions after the turn of the century. His series of six articles, titled *Yukon Notes,* which appeared in *Forest & Stream* magazines from March 26th to June 18th, 1898, contain numerous details on sled dogs, clothing, equipment, firearms, hunting, fishing and trapping and general information on that region.

Over the years the many-sided Burnham gave generously of his time and knowledge to numerous men who later on achieved great prominence on the international scene.

John Burnham also made several studies in northern Canada and Alaska to determine the cause of the severe periodic fluctuations in the grouse supply on both sides of the border. As a result of this research he established that there was a close and valid relationship between the periods of minimal grouse supply and the rabbit plagues in the Arctic region. He discovered that when the ten-year epidemic almost annihilated the varying hare population

*The "Wislow"*

*Capt. Billy Thompson*

161

*U.S. Coast Guard Schooner "The Bear"*

of the Far North, the hawks and owls were driven southward by the lack of their usual prey in sufficient numbers to account for the corresponding cycles of grouse scarcity in the United States.

John Burnham was also one of the pioneer proponents of the wilderness area concern. Like Thoreau, he devoutly believed that wildness is the salvation of the world. Eloquently, in the following excerpt from a longer article, he described, defined and advocated his personal concept of such natural escape hatches:

"A Wilderness area, in the sense that Theodore Roosevelt, John Muir and their disciples would use the term, is an area just as the Creator made and left it when 'He saw that it was good.' In other words it is a place in primeval condition which civilization has not touched. Such areas must not be spoiled.

"Elevations above timber line, barren of animal and plant life, are largely self-protected and escape contamination by reason of their inaccessibility and because they furnish little loot to invite spoliation. They may safely be left in Nature's care. But the accessible places, favored with animal, plant and forest life of dim ancestry, must be saved from encroachment of commerce, be protected even from human trails.

"It is the obligation of our civilization, which has done so much to wreck beauty in Nature, to preserve forever in pristine form something at least of the varying types of wilderness, from sea-level bayous to the tree-line, forests, lakes, marshes and deserts. Nature has its rights as well as Man. For humanity's higher good there must be some sacristies beyond profanation. There must be some point where material utilization is held back with an iron hand. There must be saved some Edens where Eve and Adam reincarnated may view things as they were at the dawn..."

Needless to say, these perceptions and convictions, which were valid and cogent concerns in Burnham's era, are even more profoundly applicable to these days of ever-increasing pressures and demands on our obviously finite and fragile ecosystem. He knew what he was saying. The message is clear, the options are few — and the alternatives are obvious and frightening for all living things. Moreover, it's hard to escape the feeling that time is definitely not on our side and is running out rapidly.

# Chapter 20

## The Washington's Birthday Meetings at "The Highlands" and Burnham's Confrontation with New Deal Bureaucracy

*Mrs. Burnham in 1940*

*Burnham at "Highlands" 1935*

Over a span of more than twenty-five years, from 1914 until 1939, the year of his death, John Burnham's "Highlands" home was the scene of an annual gathering of the Conservation Committee of the Camp-Fire Club of America plus other prominent men with similar interests. This committee, one of the most powerful of its kind in the nation, was responsible for much constructive legislation on both State and Federal levels. Held each year over the Washington's Birthday holiday, the renowned host and his guests divided their time between winter sports and work for the cause of conservation. Always included were proponents of divergent views and the meetings were planned so that as many viewpoints as possible could be presented during the brainstorming sessions.

On one such occasion in 1935 there were eight Camp-Fire Club members and another thirteen men who had achieved prominence for their outstanding contributions to some aspect of conservation or preservation of wildlife and our natural environment. They were as follows: Dr. Robert Loughren, president of the Camp-Fire Club; Alex D. Walker, a former president; Karl T. Frederick, president of both the National Rifle Assn. and the U.S. Revolver Assn.; Marshall McLean, former legal advisor to the Conservation Commission; O. H. Van Norden, former vice-president of the Lake Placid Club; William B. Greeley, eminent conservationist; Joseph A. Ford and host Burnham.

Other guests were James Derieux, author and former editor of the *American Magazine;* Dr. D. W. Henderson of the U.S. Biological Survey; Hugh Terhune, executive officer of the Alaska Game Commission; Ted White, M.P. of Ottawa, Canada; Frank Hooper, mining engineer and former State Assemblyman (N.Y.); W. M. Newsom, author of *White-Tailed Deer;* Dr. A. L. Hayes, Lou P. Evans, Koert D. Burnham, Wallace Howell of the New York and Pennsylvania Co.

Dr. Gardiner Bump, Inspector Ray Burmaster, Robert Darrow, Victor Skiff and A. Shepard — all on the New York State Conservation Department staff — attended some of the meetings as did many other men who were active in the field of conservation.

Telegrams were received from Jay N. Darling, chief of the U.S. Biological Survey, who was ill; Commissioner Lithgow Osborne, detained by the Long Lake hearing and Andy Taylor, who was making an aerial survey of Mt. Hubbard preparatory to its ascent later in the Spring.

Andy Taylor,[1] a relatively unknown sourdough prior to his meeting with Burnham, had made two substantial goldstrikes and had twice gone broke. His association with Burnham on the Siberian sheephunt gave him such wide publicity that he later became the most celebrated Alaskan mountaineering guide of his time. He served as guide for the Harvard-Bradford climb of Mt. McKinley and was also credited with saving the lives of a party which had been ice-bound for 40 days in the St. Elias Range.

Burnham's own ideas on sociability are not only inherently interesting but also provide another means of understanding the nature and character of this many-sided, controversial and unusually productive man. They also reflect the depth and warmth of the affection which he imparted and received:

"I am not a sociable person in the sense that I like "small talk" nor am I dependent upon society. I have lived alone in the wilderness for days on end and never felt the need of human touch or conversation. But, despite this fact, there is little I love more in life than the society of my friends and the extension to them of hospitality under my rooftree.

"I am sure I came by a great part of this through inheritance. All through their married life my parents kept open house. Friends came and stayed as long as they liked and while there did as they liked. No particular plans were made for their entertainment and nothing in the way of compliance with strict formalities was expected of them. Guests were never made "company." Yet the niceties were observed. My mother gave and exacted in her unselfish way the service of a more courtly age than ours. She loathed bad English, indifferent table manners and slovenly dress alike with lack of deference to age and womanhood. She set the key but my father, though cast in a rougher mould, was in full sympathy with it and there was perfect cooperation between them; and thus they worked out a full enjoyment of their friends.

"I have degenerated from the ideal of my parents in the respect of niceties of good

---
[1] Andy Taylor of McCarthy, Alaska.

*Conservationists at "Highlands," February, 1919.*

| Front row l. to r. | Middle row | Back row |
|---|---|---|
| V. Stefansson | Gen. Will Greeley | Dr. E.W. Nelson |
| O. Van Norden | Warwick Carpenter | John B. Burnham |
| Marshall McLean | Clinton Abbott | Fred Vreeland |
| George Pratt | Maj. Hugh Smiley | |

*Group of Conservationists at "Highlands" in 1934*

| Left to Right: | Alex Walker | Lithgow Osborne | Karl Frederick |
|---|---|---|---|
| Harry Lee | Koert Burnham | Bob Agnew | Art Bauer |
| Fred Walcott | Hugh Terhune | John Burnham | Will Greeley |
| Paul Redington | Andy Taylor | Otto Van Norden | Seth Gordon |

manners but not, I hope, in the love I have for my friends. Grafted onto my early training has been another type of hospitality — that of the frontier, crude, coarse in expression, deteriorating into horse play, rude in manners, but essentially honest and unselfish. On the Yukon any visitor is welcome to food and lodging. There is nothing selective about it, except that the totally deficient in character never become "pardner" with the host. The frontier has a communion without any manners except in the raw fundamentals. You reach a cabin while the owner is absent, enter it and use his goods and blankets as if they were your own but, on leaving, you put things in shape, replenish the woodpile and, if possible, make some return for the food you have consumed. Thus you have complied with the simple code."...

The annual Winter meetings at "Highlands" were welcome interludes in Burnham's life. Many of the men were frequent guests, as were his long-time friends such as Dan Beard,[1] George Pratt, Capt. Bob Bartlett, Gurth Whipple, Vilhjalmur Stefansson and other distinguished sportsmen, administrators and explorers. The reliving of shared experiences in the field and the savoring again of legislative triumphs in Albany and Washington provided needed diversion during the drab Depression years which were truly "the times that tried men's souls," as Thomas Paine had so aptly characterized the crisis years of the early Revolution.

Burnham was now in his late sixties, and in spite of his utmost efforts to even break even in his numerous diversified businesses, he was becoming increasingly more discouraged. Furthermore, he was rapidly becoming intensely and outspokenly disenchanted with the ineptness, bordering on sheer stupidity, being demonstrated by wide-eyed theorists who headed F.D.R.'s so-called Brain Trust in Foggy Bottom on the Potomac. This letter is self-explanatory:

December 30, 1935

To the Editor of the New York *Times:*

I hope the New Dealers who have spent their time on Earth inventing devilish tortures for men in small business when they go to Hell will be given a dose of their own medicine. I hope I have a reserved seat, so I can watch them trying to solve their unsolvable problems. Then I want them returned to Earth and given their former places of authority. I believe that under these conditions the old U.S.A. might again be habitable for small-businessmen.

The New Dealers are never satisfied with doing a thing in a reasonable way. Commonsense is too common for them. N. R. A. would have been successful if they had confined their efforts to humanitarian betterment. Instead they had to gum the works with price-fixing. They itch to regiment business, to pull it apart and mess it up, regardless of the fact that such a process spoils perfectly good machines.

As a small-businessman, I am sympathetic with the theory of old age pensions and unemployment insurance, provided the Administration will give the benefits to the actual workers and not to the loafers. But I am not in favor of the Federal and State laws as now drafted. My business simply cannot stand the eventual six percent on gross. No law is practical which taxes an employer more than he earns.

---
[1] Dan Beard, renowned artist, author, conservationist and National Boy Scout executive, summed up eloquently the reasons why he and many other famed guests so thoroughly enjoyed the weekends at "Highlands." In a letter dated Feb. 12, 1923 here is his verbal tribute:

"It requires character to make a real man, it requires pluck and perserverance to win distinction as an explorer. It requires skill, marksmanship and woodcraft to make a real hunter.

"But to make a successful host one must possess an ability to anticipate the desires of one's guests, take joy in gratifying them and possess a big warm heart with an inborn love for his fellowmen.

"All these qualities are thine, John. Good luck to you."

*Dan Beard and Trophy, Lake Kipawa, Ont. (Photo by Joseph Van Vleck)*

*Burnham Bookplate made by Dan Beard*

But while they are killing us off they are resorting to cruel and inhuman methods of torture through their required accounting systems. There are many small-businessmen in country districts, like myself, who because our outlets are limited, have been obliged to engage in several different lines of business. If we specialized in one line there would not be enough customers within our radius of activity to make profitable our particular product or services. In order to make a living we must diversify and sell to the same people several times over. My workmen's compensation account books cover ten or a dozen different kinds of employment, and at times I have to divide the weekly payroll of one man two or three different ways.

Now come the New Dealers with their ill-considered unemployment insurance mandate and in voluminous print tell me to start a new set of accounts requiring seventeen entries and giving me only three working days before the deadline of January first. I am required to keep separate consecutive accounts of each worker including the family cook. Workmen's compensation records will not answer because wages are entered in that as paid. It is nothing to these masters that I have no bookkeeper. If they had permitted me to make my quarterly report from the compensation record, in a way similar to that I now use when assembling my figures for State and Federal income tax reports, I should have been saved endless duplication. But they are distrustful and require additional information — *seventeen* answers in all. To comply, I should at once employ an expert bookkeeper, a lawyer and a stenographer.

My business runs up to $200,000 per annum, and my net return has been as low as 1½%. How am I to hire the service for this additional accounting? It can't be done and I continue to live.

I take pride in keeping men employed during the hard times and I have taken on (unremunerative) work solely to create employment. Everywhere among businessmen I find a similar situation. We have been sufficiently patriotic to sacrifice the profit motive. But I have run myself ragged doing it and I cannot continue indefinitely. For example, I cut my bid below the grass roots to take a contract employing a maximum of 150 men because my chief competitor uses workmen from a distance, and our local laborers needed employment. The only way I could get out with my skin was my rigid economy. My working day was double that of any of the laborers. The men were opening a right-of-way nineteen miles long and were scattered along this distance. Saturday mornings I would start at one end of the line paying the men off and ten o'clock at night would find me still making out checks in the headlights of my car. The job simply would not stand the expense of timekeepers or paymasters or bookkeepers. When I found I would get through with my shirt, I voluntarily raised the wages of one class of men, about forty in number, who seemed to me to be underpaid and made the payment retroactive.

In country districts I am no exception to the rule. Employers punish themselves to keep going because they feel an obligation to their employees.

But it is beyond both my pocketbook and my physical powers to keep dancing to the pipes of these theoretical uplifters. Even if one did not have to sleep, there are not enough hours in the day for me to fill out all the <u>seventeen</u> entries, many of them complicated and split up into dissimilar sections. Frankly, I want to see them all in Hell and from an air-conditioned seat in the grandstand.

John B. Burnham

His opinion of Franklin D. was pungently stated in the following excerpt from his Letter to the Editor of the New York *Times* dated Jan. 28, 1936:

"Today I am more bitter against Roosevelt than I should be. He is certainly a bull in the china shop of American ideals, but I ask myself if he is really fired with sympathy for the underdog? He must be sincere in his desire to secure for the Common Man the "more abundant life." Is he not a patrician filled with Theodore's passion for the square deal? Amid all the ghastly failures, in the wreckage of the falling temple, I try to think of him as honest though incompetent. — And then I read Al Smith's speech. "Nuff said!"

That letter was one of many such in which Burnham registered his dismay, discouragement and virtual disbelief concerning the misdirection and mismanagement characteristic of the F. D. R. administration as it fumblingly and futilely sought to give the nation a credible, stable and accountable government. Little wonder that businessmen resented bitterly the torrents of red tape perpetrated and promulgated by the high-domed, idealistic, inexperienced and generally inept paper-pushers who harassed the already distressed taxpayers during the difficult Depression years.

Many other men shared the same frustration, simmered but suffered in relative silence. But if speaking out forcefully in support of strongly-held political, philosophical, ethical, economic and ecological issues makes a man controversial then certainly Burnham was that type of individual. For that matter anyone who goes through life dodging confrontations and conflicts has not really lived and is not worth his salt.

The truly acid tests of Burnham's character, stamina, determination and persistence are delineated in the next chapter.

A line from Plato probably best describes Burnham's attitude and basic creed: "I will live in such a way that I will prove by my life that my critics are liars!"

# Part IV

## Burnham the Conservationist

*[As has already been reasonably well established, Burnham's lifespan was an occasionally interrupted series of unusual, dramatic and sometimes traumatic episodes. His narrow schoolboy escape from drowning in the swollen Brandywine River was just a preview to subsequent events that shaped his character and colored his life. Later on, the Klondike and Siberian interludes — especially the latter with its sinister overtones — provided him with nearly more than enough touch- and-go experiences to satisfy even his almost insatiable yen for excitement, particularly in far places. Then too his frequent encounters with the unpleasant aspects of stormy Lake Champlain served as readily available seasonal challenges to his skill and sense of derring-do.*

*Moreover, in addition to these confrontations with such formidable natural forces, he also contended successfully with two frequently fatal surgical situations — adhesions and cancer.*

*While much tamer by contrast with these personal physical crises, nevertheless Burnham's record as an internationally renowned conservationist required a different but equally essential combination of attributes — patience, persistence and persuasive power. These qualities were often tested during his tenure as chief game protector and deputy commissioner of the New York State Conservation Department. They were constantly drawn on during his many years as president of the American Game Protective Association and as principal proponent of the Migratory Bird Act, Migratory Bird Treaty and international Game Refuge legislation. Since the opposition to each bill was led by powerful groups and factions even among the so-called conservationists themselves, the wrangling and in-fighting were often vicious and the campaigns seemingly endless.*

*In retrospect it is fairly easy to understand why and how the bitter feud between Burnham and William T. Hornaday generated and developed. Each was determined, resourceful, opinionated and egotistical to a degree. Each represented a diametrically opposite concept of the role and importance of conservation. While Burnham, as a sportsman, felt and reasoned strongly that wild game was a renewable resource which could be intelligently managed and harvested, Hornaday was equally vehement in his denunciation of hunters and advocated total protection of all species. The "Guns of Autumn" syndrome personified.*

*Not so incidentally these antipodal positions split the game management movement wide open and the rift persists even into the present. While Hornaday's version has been widely publicized, his adversary's viewpoints have not become as well-known to the present generation.*

*Interestingly enough Hornaday didn't always display a consistent attitude toward hunters and wildlife. In fact he admittedly derived just as much fierce pleasure from a successful shot as did the men whom he publicly despised for their primordial instincts. This is shown on page 103 of his book* A Wild Animal Round-Up — New York: Scribner's, 1925. *Here's his account:*

*"I was sorely puzzled [after a supposedly unsuccessful stalk] and began to fear that I might prove myself to be a bungling sheep-hunter. Think of the disgrace that a failure*

*would bring upon me! Just then I happened to glance up and there on the highest point of rocks stood a grand old mountain ram — statue-like, feet braced and staring in wide-eyed curiosity down at me and about 300 feet away.*

*"Quickly swinging my shoulders a quarter way round I flung up my rifle and, with a mighty quick sight on the centre of the ram's breast, let go. It was all done while you could count three. Instantly the big sheep wheeled about, and vanished....*

*"It was clear that I ought to rush forward, triumphantly bound up the nearest notch leading to the top...but I simply couldn't do it. Besides, I thought that hurrying wasn't really necessary for I felt sure that that old ram was mine! Sometimes a hunter feels that way after a shot; and it is a pretty good sign of dead game. [He rested awhile and then climbed up the ridge.]*

*"And there in the head of that notch, thirty feet below, lay my splendid mountain ram. My bullet had fairly telescoped him. Did I think him a grand sight? Truly I did, and I opine that it was better for me to gloat over him than for a mountain lion to do so later on.*

*"I am no Hindoo, and even yet I have not reached the point where I feel that it is always wrong to kill a wild-game animal, especially where such animals are yet fairly plentiful."*

Compare and contrast this incident with a similar experience narrated by Burnham, an ardent hunter, in the story of The Moose Shot 'Round the Corner *found in the Appendix (p. 251). Then draw your own conclusions.*

*From my personal point of view there is much to be said on either side of this highly debatable and fiercely emotional topic. Having been a hunter of sorts during my childhood and early manhood I can distinctly recall the thrills and pleasures of success in the field and forest. But the unforgettable experience of watching a deer in its death throes and looking in fascination at those pleading big brown eyes made me an instant non-hunter. S. R. Stoddard recalled the same mournful memory in one of his articles in his* Northern Monthly Magazine. *Therefore, I can well understand the "Bambi" and "Guns of Autumn" syndromes.*

*Nevertheless, I can equally well comprehend the feelings and attitudes of a true sportsman like Burnham, who thoroughly enjoyed just being in the wild places and didn't feel frustrated or totally dejected if he returned home with empty game-bag or creel.*

*Each of these two preeminent personalities apparently exemplified the precept practiced by Harold G. Wilm, himself a prominent conservationist and former New York State Conservation Department Commissioner: "Establish a firm wall of principle beyond which point you will not retreat. Up to that point compromise by all means — then stop!"*[1]

*On occasion, however, this apparently became a case of each of the foes being willing to compromise — but on his own terms!*

*Benjamin Franklin's basic guide to the effective pursuit of the political and diplomatic processes would also apply to their particular modi operandi. "My rule, in which I have always found satisfaction, is never to turn aside in the public interest, but to go straight forward in doing what appears to me right at the time, leaving the consequences to Providence."*[2]

*Another pertinent and pungent quotable quote came from a disgruntled farmer with the sobriquet Mt. Tom in a "Letter to the Editor" carried in* Forest & Stream *Feb. 12, 1898. In his counterattack on a so-called "gentleman-sportsman" — synonymous terms of course — who protested against posting, the incensed "gentleman-countryman" came up with this gem: "I deny the allegations and I defy the allegators!"*

*Burnham must have felt that way often during the stormy yet most characteristic and productive phase of his career — for the cause of conservation in Albany, Washington and Ottawa: Editor]*

---

[1] American Forests *November 1976, p. 14.*
[2] *Ibid.*

# Chapter 21

## The Albany Years

Although Burnham had been aware of the increasing urgency for the conservation of our dwindling wildlife resources since his boyhood experiences in Delaware and Wyoming, and through his contacts with noted men of similar interests whom he had met while on the staff of *Forest & Stream,* his first opportunity to do something really constructive came in 1899. This was brought about when the ardent young man became incensed by his realization that the game laws were being almost completely ignored or defied in his home county of Essex. Violations of the 1896 law forbidding the hounding of deer were numerous and flagrant even by the men who had been hired and sworn to enforce the regionally unpopular law — the so-called game protectors or wardens.

Burnham decided to do something to correct this intolerable situation so he wrote the following power-packed article which came out in the Oct. 28, 1899 issue of *Forest & Stream:*

### Game Bag and Gun

### Adirondack Deer Hounding

Editor, Forest and Stream:

It is generally admitted that the law which forbids the use of dogs in hunting deer has been and is unpopular in most parts of the Adirondacks.

The natives in the central and eastern portion of this region believe in the use of dogs, and liked the old law as it stood until three years ago, except that many were opposed to the early opening of the season, and it was pretty generally believed that a limited hunting season in October would be better both for the hunters and for the game.

There was consequently a strong public sentiment against the law which first came into force three years ago prohibiting hounding. It was contrary to all ideals of home rule, for it enforced a principle antagonistic to the convictions of nine out of every ten men who lived and hunted in the Adirondacks, and moreover it created hardships and pecuniary loss for many of the backwoods settlers, who were deprived of the means of securing a very desirable portion of their food supply, and who had ten, twenty or even fifty dollars of their capital invested in dogs which with the passage of the law lost all commercial valuation. From the first the law was not enforced. The game protectors realized the hardships which a thorough and effective execution of their powers would entail, and in most cases it was more than their positions were worth to buck up against public sentiment and antagonize the community in which they lived by a strict enforcement of the text.

The protectors themselves were not apt to be in sympathy with an innovation which made illegal the method of hunting which had been pursued as far back as the oldest inhabitants could remember and the necessity for which innovation was by no means apparent, so it is little wonder that the non-hounding clause in the law receives only a perfunctory and superficial attention.

Let it be noted that what has been said and what is to follow has no bearing on the merits of the law.

Personally, the writer believes that the time has come in the Adirondacks, as it has elsewhere, when such a law is not only admirable, but necessary for the continuance of any satisfactory game supply.

Public sentiment in the Adirondacks is slowly but surely coming around in favor of the law. Particularly on the outskirts of the woods, where there are witnesses to every act of hounding who may, through personal enmity, cause the hounder to suffer, the deer have increased, and they are found today in places where they had not been seen for ten or fifteen years. There could be no stronger argument in favor of the law. With public sentiment aroused by so favorable an object lesson, it would seem the protectors' golden opportunity to step in and by a sharp, vigorous campaign clinch the matter and effectually put an end to hounding. Early in the season there was reason to believe that such a policy would be inaugurated. Today, however, as far as his observation goes, the writer is convinced that little or nothing has been done to put the law on a proper basis of enforcement. Apparently the law will continue as heretofore to be a dead letter throughout a large part of the hunting country. The following facts apply particularly to Essex County and its protector, Fletcher Beede, of Keene Valley.

Mr. Beede has a large territory to look after. Essex has an area of 1,800 square miles. Deer are found over a large portion of the County, and the western side contains the roughest mountain area in the State. Beede's, which is a post office at the head of Keene Valley, is, however, at the geographical center of the region, and for the sake of not appearing to be unfair to Mr. Beede I shall only cite cases where the law is being violated within a very short distance of his home.

A certain outsider whose name can be given if required participated in a hounding expedition within three miles of Game Protector Beede's home, guided by a man who was said to be a deputy for Mr. Beede. The outsider, who had previously hounded in the Adirondacks, was unaware that the law had been changed, and wrote to the guide to procure dogs and arrange for the hunt. The outsider had only a day for the trip, and was horrified when back in the woods to learn that the law was being violated. The guide, who supposed all along the outsider knew and was intentionally evading the law, tried to relieve the outsider by saying that there was no danger of arrest as he was the man who made arrests and no one else would handle them.

The hunt was terminated then and there, however, and the guide did not receive his expected bonus.

The hounding in Keene Valley itself was never good. The nearest territory of much consequence to Protector Beede's home is in the neighborhood of North Hudson, which is about half a day's drive to the southward over a well-traveled road. At this point I am of the opinion that a protector who had the sand [guts] to enforce the law could arrest 25 men any Sunday with sufficient evidence to secure their conviction, and not walk more than two miles in making the arrests or be at any time more than a quarter of a mile from his buggy. On other days of the week he would find men breaking the law, but more are out on weekends and are bolder because of the confidence which numbers give.

On Sunday, October 8th three deer were killed by hounding within a radius of ¾ of a mile from the old bridge over the Schroon River, just below the old Sharpe place. There were 8 hounds there on that day. One deer was killed at Lindsay Brook, one on the main river and one on West Mill Brook near Mrs. Mc Auley's.

Much of the venison is sold. Early in the season it brought fancy prices; now it can be bought cheaper than beef, some of it as low as .05¢ per pound. There are two organized groups of men who do the hunting and if hounding is to be stopped these men must be taught a sharp lesson. Among themselves they say that Beede is afraid to leave the beaten road to make an arrest. They know that he is capable of doing it because the protector has high abilities as a woodsman, and he knows all about hounding and just where to go to get his men.

Last November I camped in an old lumber camp three miles up West Mill Brook. The hounds were running every day and frequently jumped the deer I was still-hunting. At the "Roll Bank" and other stands were a full quota of watchers. It was known that my sentiments were in favor of the law. The cabin which I occupied and another building and the buildings at two other camps were burned between that time and the present hunting season. Apparently I was *persona non grata*.

My sympathy is and always has been with the native hunters, for though I think the present law is best for the game, I am a believer in home rule and I think the natives should have been consulted in making their own laws.

The hounds and shooting can be heard from the road and everyone knows that the hounding law is a dead letter. When I came out with a small buck killed as the law provides, I passed a fur buyer in the outskirts of Elizabethtown (the county seat) bargaining with a farmer for some coon skins and several moth-eaten deer hides. I drew up and asked him what he would give for a deer skin.

"Where's your hide?" asked the man.

"In the bottom of the wagon on the deer," I replied.

One of the bystanders asked when and how the deer was acquired, and on my replying that he was killed still-hunting there was a general laugh.

"Yes, you'd say so," said the man who had the skins for sale, "we all understand about that. Yesterday they ran a nice buck across my place with a couple of hounds, and today the butcher is peddling his meat. The hounds had nothing to do with it though. It's against the law to hound!"

And again the laugh went around. It did not require a diagram to see the joke. The Yankee has an elastic conscience where game laws are concerned and so long as he doesn't get caught illegal hounding is a subject for jest. I knew better than to attempt to prove that I had still-hunted my deer so I joined in the laugh. Ten years ago, when they allowed still-hunting, before the hounding season commenced, I killed a deer when the woods were dry and noisy and the leaves still on the trees preventing one seeing game at any distance. It was taken for granted that dogs were used, and I got no sympathy trying to prove that I had killed it fairly and squarely as the law provides, and there was a tendency to set me down for a combination of Puritan and hypocrite.

I could give other instances of hounding at North Hudson and around Elizabethtown, but let the above suffice. At Meigsville and in parts of Lewis there is systematic hounding at the present time, and the farther one gets back in the woods the less the law is observed.

At the Sportsmen's Exposition in New York in March the Saranac guides stated that hounding began in parts of their territory in July and continued until December. It is not quite as bad as this in Essex County, and though some hounding has been done during the

Summer in the localities mentioned, general hounding did not begin until very recently. Decisive action now would put an end to it. Game Protector Beede is a man whose training and aptitude as a woodsman well fit him to be the instrument. He has been lenient long enough, and public sentiment will back him in carrying out the law he was sworn to enforce; but if he does not enforce it, it is high time he was convicted of being a traitor to his trust.

J. B. Burnham

---

Furthermore, the aroused writer generated the almost immediate attention of Maj. J. W. Pond, the chief game protector of New York State. The latter wrote posthaste to Burnham and, as the accompanying letter indicates, requested additional information and assistance — which was duly provided.

State of New York
Fisheries, Game & Forest Commission
Albany, N.Y.

October 31, 1899

John B. Burnham Esq.,
Essex, N.Y.
Dear Sir:

Have been reading an article in *Forest and Stream,* Oct. 29th over your signature, entitled "Adirondack Deer Hounding." This Department has been doing about all it could with the limited force of Protectors over the State by sending outside Protectors into Essex Co., who of course — except when clothed as sportsmen — worked to no little disadvantage in ferreting out offenses on account of not being acquainted in the localities where the violations occurred. I am, as Chief Game Protector, highly pleased with the interest you are taking and to learn of the knowledge you possess and must be able to furnish to help the Department in bringing to justice violators of the law. Will you kindly write me, giving names, day and date of the several offenses you allude to, that I may be able to commence proceedings at once. I do not wish to be understood as trying to intimidate or threaten but with the knowledge you claim to have, which you do not hesitate to attach your signature to, it will be necessary to start a court of inquiry in your county and subpoena you and all others that are supposed to have knowledge of any infraction of the law. If your communication had been in the way of a letter marked "confidential" it would have been treated so, but as many of the offenses wherein proceedings are instituted come through such articles as yours, we must necessarily avail ourselves of every such opportunity to aid us in our work.

Trusting that you will favor the Department with an early reply and arrange where I can meet you, I am,

Respectfully yours,
J. W. Pond
Chief Protector

*N. Y. S. Conservation Dept. Hdqtrs., Albany*

*N. Y. S. Game Law Codification Comm. Left & right: John Burnham, Marshall McLean, George Lawyer*

Pond then invited Burnham to join the Department; the offer was accepted. The end result was that the already busy man from "Highlands" was appointed a game protector by J. S. Whipple in 1903; chief game protector (as indicated by Whipple's letter on Jan. 9, 1906), replacing Pond.[1]

State of New York
Forest, Fish and Game Commission
Albany

Jan. 8, 1906

Mr. John B. Burnham
Essex, N.Y.
Dear Sir:

You are hereby designated Chief Game Protector — the appointment to take effect today. This appointment is made subject to the rules and regulations of the Civil Service Commission, and to an examination to be hereafter taken by you.

Very truly yours,
J. S. Whipple
Commissioner

---

In 1910 Burnham was deputy commissioner and then acting commissioner of conservation of New York State.

During his tenure in Albany Burnham was mainly instrumental in drafting measures which resulted in more efficient selection of game warden personnel, efficiency and promotion regulations and more effective enforcement procedures. He also was credited with the codification of better fish and game laws which later influenced those adopted by other states and Alaska, then a territory. By this time he had acquired a reputation which attracted national attention and distinction and paved the way for service on a much larger front.

---

[1] "An investigation conducted by the Association for the Protection of the Adirondacks disclosed that Conservation Department Commissioner Middleton and Chief Game Protector Pond (in office from 1894-1905) had for years been notoriously lax and even guilty of collusion in their enforcement of regulations governing unlawful removal of trees from State Lands. Under pressure Middleton promptly resigned but Maj. Pond, a Civil War veteran, quit office only when he knew that specific charges of misconduct were soon to be pressed against him. James S. Whipple, the new Commissioner, then appointed Burnham as Pond's successor." From Alfred L. Donaldson's *History of the Adirondacks* Century. N.Y.C. Vol. II p.p. 218-19.

# Chapter 22

## The Campaign to Protect Migratory Birds

In the early Fall of 1911 the versatile man from "Highlands" was given an opportunity to be of even greater public service. Probably acting on Burnham's suggestion Harry S. Leonard, vice-president of the Winchester Repeating Arms Co., and William R. Clark, in charge of the firm's advertising and publicity, went to William S. Haskell's law office in New York and proposed a plan that would be of great importance in preserving the nation's wildlife. They had persuaded their own and similar companies to guarantee a starter fund of $125,000, payable in five annual instalments, to be used for furthering game protection and preservation as well as for educating the public on the value of their wildlife resources.

Additional goals were these: to urge the enactment of proper and uniform laws for protection and propagation of fish and game; to cooperate with the proper authorities; organize societies, clubs and individuals to enforce such laws; to establish and maintain preserves and reserves for game; and to demonstrate that propagation is a feasible and practical means of increasing the sport and general good supply.

Haskell's responsibility was to incorporate the proposed organization under the Membership Law of the State of New York. This he did and the American Game Protective and Propagation Association came into being.

John B. Burnham was elected president of the organization because of his fine record for courage and accomplishments in the New York State Conservation Department. Among other qualifications were his skill as a sportsman, experience as a writer and effective politician, and his knowledge of game management.

Under his leadership this organization took a foremost place in the conservationist activities of the United States. He mobilized the various groups in order to secure Congressional action by which all migratory birds would be removed from state control and placed under the protection of the Federal government. This was a novel principle first suggested by George Shiras III, a Congressman from Pennsylvania, in 1903, after his home-town of Butler was confronted with a disastrous epidemic of typhoid fever. Shiras, in calling attention to the then-recent case of Mississippi vs. Illinois, in which the Supreme Court had ruled that no state could unreasonably pollute the waters of another state, raised the issue that the Federal government should also logically have the power to control and protect the movements of beneficial wild fowl and migrant fish.

The Shiras Bill was referred to the Committee on Agriculture and, although favorably received by the members and praised by Pres. Theodore Roosevelt, it required nearly ten long years of lobbying and education before it or other bills embodying its aims could become law. The subject was kept before Congress continuously and constantly publicized in all the periodicals devoted to sport, ornithology and conservation.

Rep. Weeks of Massachusetts, later Secretary of War, introduced the first feasible Migratory Bird Bill on Dec. 8, 1908. Sen. McLean of Connecticut introduced a similar bill in that body in May, 1911. Alike in character and purpose they considered only the protection of waterfowl and wading birds. Then, mainly through the efforts of the National Association of Audubon Societies, the migratory insectivorous birds were included — a provision suggested by its first president, William Dutcher.

At a hearing before the combined House and Senate Agricultural Committee in March, 1912, thirty-two organizations were represented and Dr. T. Gilbert Pearson, then secretary of the Audubon Society, urged forcefully that all migratory birds be covered in the terms of the pending bill. In doing so he faced strong opposition from many noted conservationists of varied viewpoints.

From 1908-1913 prominent supporters of the legislation were exerting their influence — the American Game Protective Assn. (founded Sept., 1911), under John Burnham and its counsel W. S. Haskell; the National Association of Audubon Societies (founded in 1901); Charles Sheldon of the Boone and Crockett Club; the Camp-Fire Club of New York and others.

In 1912 harsh criticism was aimed at the bills by Dr. W. T. Hornaday, who then advocated the removal of all migratory wildfowl from Federal protection, apparently convinced that these birds were of interest only to sportsmen and were not a valuable economic asset to the rest of the people.

Besides the professed conservationists there were three other major enemies of the Migratory Bird Bill — the organized commercial market-hunters, the "sportsmen" who didn't want to be deprived of their Spring shooting, and the legislators who for reasons honest or dishonest claimed that such legislation was unconstitutional.

Nevertheless, forty of the nation's state fish and game commissions declared themselves in favor of the Bill and several states, Massachusetts among them, passed resolutions endorsing the legislation. Interestingly enough, only Gov. Blease of South Carolina expressed active opposition.

Finally in January, 1913 the Weeks-McLean Bill passed the Senate, then the lower House and became a law of the land on Mar. 4, 1913 as a rider on the Agricultural Appropriation Act for the fiscal year ending June 30, 1914. However, after much wrangling only the piddling sum of $10,000 was allowed for its enforcement.

So after years of bitter infighting in Congress and elsewhere in the nation, including within the various conservationist groups themselves, the Federal Migratory Bird Bill was finally passed. Under the provisions of this law nearly 1100 species of birds were more strictly protected than previously under the haphazard control of the states, many of which operated on the concept that everybody's business is nobody's business. Under such unfavorable conditions migratory game birds were rapidly nearing extermination, and other birds valuable to agriculture as well as aesthetically were also without suitable protection.

This first bird law, only one page long, merely placed migratory birds under Federal custody and authorized the Department of Agriculture to formulate regulations prescribing seasons during which such birds could not be hunted or killed. But the restrictions did not provide for the power of arrest or seizure. Moreover, the puny appropriation made enforcement measures almost negligible.

Nevertheless, the Migratory Bird Law of 1913 did stop at least 75% of the Spring shooting and appreciably reduced the slaughter and marketing of song-birds in the Southern states. Furthermore, it led to a nation-wide movement among true sportsmen to obtain state laws which closed the remaining markets for commercial hunters.

Just when things were going relatively smoothly a complication reared its ugly head: in early 1914 in Jonesboro, Arkansas a judge of the United States District Court declared the new law unconstitutional. This crucial case of U.S. vs. Harvey Shauver involved the illegal killing of ducks. Fortunately, more effective legislation was passed in 1918 before this case was to be decided by the Supreme Court. Therefore, its legal status was never actually determined because that law was superseded by the treaty with Great Britain in 1916 and by the Enabling Act of 1918. So the Bird Bill's legality was never actually determined.

Since Burnham played such a major part in the passage of this landmark bill, his behind-the-scenes comments are particularly noteworthy.

"As the end of the 62nd Congress drew near, the workers for the passage of the Weeks-McLean Bill gave up hope for success. At this juncture I remembered a casual remark made by Dr. Palmer of the Biological Survey several months before to the effect that if the bill could be added to one of the Senate Appropriation measures, the action would assure its success, because such measures required the concurrence of the House. I called on several people and asked them what they thought of the idea.

"Congressman Weeks thought very lightly of it. He said that President Taft had notified Congress that he would veto any and all appropriation bills coming to him with riders. He further said that, even if the President had not given such notification, the thing was impossible because the Senate Agricultural Committee, the only committee through which action could be taken, was firmly set against riders and that Senator Gore, himself a ranking member of the committee, had failed a few days before to get them to accept his markets bill in such a way. I asked Mr. Weeks if an attempt to 'tin can' the bill through would in any way prejudice the status of our measure. He replied in the negative, but said it could not be done.

"Senator Burnham of New Hampshire was then Chairman of the Committee on Agriculture and Forestry, and after discovering that our mutual forebear had come to Massachusetts on the ill-fated Angel Gabriel in 1638, I had established very friendly relations with him. I secured through his secretary an appointment with the Senator for the next day and by telephone arranged for a delegation of half a dozen Camp-Fire Club men to aid me in keeping the appointment. This was the only organization at the time upon which I felt free to call for assistance.

"When twelve o'clock, the time of our appointment, came, the men duly introduced as supporters of migratory bird legislation by Congress, but before Senator Burnham could tell us the hopelessness of our cause I asked permission to make a brief statement. First, I requested the Senator not to reply until he had heard me through. He acquiesced. I told him we all knew and respected his great interest in the birds which were beneficial to agriculture and his desire for the success of the pending bill for their protection. I told him that there was a way to secure success and that as he had announced that this was to be his last term in Congress, he had an opportunity to take an action which would add luster to his exit from public life. At this juncture he tried to interrupt me, having evidently read what was in my mind, but I held him to his promise to hear me through, and I then sprang my little joker. 'All we ask of you,' I said, 'is that, if your committee sees fit to add the Bird Bill as a rider to the Agricultural Appropriations Bill, you will not object.'

"The Senator smiled broadly and replied, "How can I object to a bill that I heartily favor?'

"In the hallway outside I divided the delegation into units and assigned to each the duty of calling on some friendly member of the Agricultural Committee with instructions to tell him that we wanted the Bird Bill attached as a rider to the appropriations bill at the committee meeting that afternoon. I told them that their Senator would naturally be surprised by such a peremptory request, but that as it is second nature for a politician to pass the buck, his first question would be, 'What does Senator Burnham think of this?' Then all we would have to say was 'The Senator says that he will not oppose it.'

"When we met again, half an hour or so later, each of us had been successful. When the committee met we had the necessary number of votes, and the bill passed Senate and House with its rider.

"For several years I was in ignorance of the reason President Taft had not fulfilled his promise to veto such a bill, until Louis Welsh of New Haven gave the explanation. Mr. Welsh was on a committee with the Ex-President which waited on President Wilson to request his assistance in changing the proposed architecture of a new Federal building in New Haven so as to harmonize it with neighboring buildings of Yale University, and on the way back from Washington he said to Mr. Taft that he considered the Migratory Bird Law the finest piece of legislation which had been passed during the latter's administration. He said, 'I knew all about that bill. I had grave doubts as to its constitutionality. If it had come before me, I am inclined to think that I would have given it my veto for that reason.'

"It is said that our bill reached the President on March 4th with the clock turned back and President-elect Wilson waiting to enter the White House, and that apparently Mr. Taft had no time to read it."

## Chapter 23

### The Migratory Bird Treaty with Great Britain For Canada

The background events and complex maneuvers leading up to the Migratory Bird Treaty with Great Britain for Canada make a fascinating sequence. Credit for the original overture is due to the same Sen. McLean, who suggested a constitutional amendment in 1911, but Elihu Root of New York introduced the first actual bill in the Senate on Jan. 14, 1913: "Resolved that the President be requested to propose to the Governments of other North American countries the negotiation of a convention for the mutual protection and preservation of migratory birds." This, however, failed to pass.

The following April 7th the persistent Sen. McLean of Connecticut reintroduced the resolution and this time it was approved. So now the situation for real action seemed favorable because of Rep. Weeks' support in the House of Representatives and the steady backing of national sportsmen and bird-lover groups.

The American Game Protective Association, with the help of its legal advisor W. S. Haskell, prepared the tentative draft of such a treaty in October, 1913 but difficulties were encountered in the satisfactory division of the continent into zones — especially pertinent were details and seasons in Canada, which was obviously out of American territorial bounds and likely to produce only problems and dangerous international misunderstanding. Therefore, the first and far too complicated effort was dropped and temporarily forgotten.

The issue was revived, however, in January, 1914 when the Secretary of State, William J. Bryan, asked the Department of Agriculture to draft a treaty. Dr. T. S. Palmer of the Biological Survey was delegated to do the work but it is a matter of record that the lion's share of the actual preparation was done by J. B. Burnham. Their product, a very broad and comprehensive memorandum, was accepted with only eight or nine small changes.

These minor revisions were required in order to make the proposed treaty workable. One change permitted the Canadian Indians and Eskimos the right to kill migratory birds in the Spring in order to prevent widespread starvation among their villages.

Another important addition empowered the Secretary of Agriculture to permit the killing of protected species whenever they became detrimental to agriculture. Without this clause farmers and their organizations, aided and abetted by the bitter opponents of the Treaty, could easily have hamstrung its administration by simply seeing to it that the enforcement appropriation be cut off in Congress.

The necessity for these two important provisions was stressed by Dr. C. Gordon Hewitt, Dominion Consulting Zoologist, and Dr. E. W. Nelson, the new Chief of the U.S. Biological Survey.

The recommended changes having been accepted Canada was notified and Dr. Hewitt departed on his second trip to the provinces in order to secure the consent of the entire Dominion.

However, there were many obstacles in the way of Canadian ratification and some of the first attempts were very discouraging. The main drawback was that the Dominion Government had never before taken any part in wildlife administration among the provinces and was therefore reluctant to do anything about it.

After many conferences with the top Canadian officials, they agreed to forward the U.S. Senate resolution to the provincial governments in order to test their reaction, but pointed out that a favorable vote by any parliament was an unlikely possibility.

Finally the ubiquitous John Burnham proposed a way out that offered some hope of success. In minor matters the premier of each province and his various cabinet ministers can be "put on record" and thus by dealing with a small number of intelligent men instead of a confused, slow-moving legislative body an agreement could conceivably be reached. While accepting these "orders in council" in lieu of parliamentary votes, the officials involved made it plainly understood that all the provincial parliaments must give their consent — or else the deal was off. Such unanimous action would have been unnecessary had each legislative branch voted separately on the American proposal.

This step having been taken, the American Game Association (then the American Game Protective Association), in constant conference with Dr. Nelson and following his suggestions, devoted all of its energies for a number of months to presenting the case of the Treaty to individuals and officials all over Canada. Slow to become interested were British Columbia and Quebec. It was war-time and naturally there was strong disinclination to tackle anything that did not pertain directly to an early victory.

The consent was finally secured in Quebec, but not until after the death of Minister Devlin, who was bitterly opposed to the Treaty. Here the officials of the Canadian Pacific and Grand Trunk Railroads and the Associated Steamship Lines of Canada were a tower of strength.

After the consent of Quebec, Dr. Hewitt was sent on an official visit to British Columbia, where he failed to obtain results. At this point Burnham again intervened and made a hurried trip to Ottawa.

"The first I knew of Hewitt's entry in the game was through a telephone message from Dr. Nelson to me in New York, stating that he had just had word from Dr. Hewitt that he was returning from Victoria, unsuccessful, on a certain train. Nelson asked me if I could not run up to Ottawa and meet him there. I at once agreed and was in the station when Dr. Hewitt's train pulled in.

"I had only seen Dr. Hewitt once before at a meeting in Ottawa and in some way he got by me in the crowd. I returned to my room at the hotel and called up his office by telephone. He had just come in, I was told, and was booked for an immediate interview with Sir Martin Burrell, the Dominion Minister of Agriculture. I had great difficulty in getting him to the telephone and he at once said he had not time to talk as he must immediately report to his Minister. I asked him what report he intended to make and he said, "Merely one of failure." I said, 'Man, what are you thinking of? This is a crisis. Wake up!' He said, "What else can I report?" I said, 'State that you have *not yet* succeeded. The stake is the migratory birds of the continent. One province should not be permitted to interfere with their salvation!'

"Hewitt left so quickly that I could not be sure he had taken it in. But about ten minutes later I got a call asking me to come over to the office of the Secretary of Agriculture.

"Here Sir Martin received me courteously and said that Dr. Hewitt had given him my message verbatim, and he desired to know why the matter was of such great importance. He explained to me that there was apparently a strong sentiment in British Columbia against the enactment of the Migratory Bird Treaty with the United States, and that he had to stand for election from that province. He said, 'Frankly, I am not willing to endanger my political future, even to a degree, except for the very best of reasons. Moreover,' he said, 'It is my understanding that the chief threat to the migratory game bird supply comes from over-shooting in the United States. You have a very good law which takes care of the situation. We also have good provincial laws. The benefits of the Treaty seem to me more academic than actual.'

"I explained to him the necessity for the Treaty, in order to preserve the law. First I told him that the Supreme Court in the case of the United States vs. Shauver, after hearing the appeal, had, instead of passing on the constitutionality of the law, ordered a re-hearing; and that it was commonly believed this unique action had been taken as the result of a tie vote with two members absent. Furthermore, that there was good reason to believe that the absentees thought the law unconstitutional, and that when a hearing was held before the full court, the decision would be unfavorable.

"Secondly, I told him of the organized effort which was being made to repeal the law and, lastly, of the fact that the law was almost a dead-letter by reason of insufficient appropriations and that in my opinion suitable appropriations could not be secured until the law was given a strong bolster through an international treaty.

"I told him that market shooting was going on in the United States in a wholesale way and how many of the States had no closed seasons while the ducks were with them. And I painted a gloomy picture of wildfowl destruction should the Treaty fail.

"Sir Martin then told me that to the best of his information there was really no sentiment in Canada for such a treaty. He asked me who in Canada favored it. I immediately gave him a list of important persons and organizations who were on record as favoring the Treaty, and wound up with the names of the two railroads and the Associated Steamship Companies. He at once asked me if I knew George Ham of the C. P. R. and when I told him that it was through the efforts of Ham and Usher of that railroad, and Elliott of the Grand Trunk, that the approval of Quebec had been secured, he remarked that he was satisfied, and that he would give the matter very close attention and probably recommend that the Dominion Government take action without the approval of British Columbia. I had received no definite promise but had every reason to believe that Sir Martin would take favorable action because the provinces, other than British Columbia, having already approved therefore the Dominion Government could be counted on.

"It would not be possible to follow the devious fortunes of the Treaty in complete detail at this late date. There will always be a variety opinion as to just what happened and who among the many persons interested performed the hardest tasks. Later on, gold medals were passed out in England on a rather mistaken assumption, and the bitter feeling about this has not yet entirely died out.

"These are only a few of the difficulties which were encountered on the long road. Concessions had to be made at every step and one of these came about through Canada's very just objection to the lateness of our proposed open season, which in early drafts was placed as late as March 10 in a rather feeble attempt to satisfy the demands of the Spring shooters of the Mississippi Valley states. After conferences in Washington between Commissioner James White, Dr. Hewitt and Dr. Nelson, various adjustments were made, including clauses favorable to the taking of waterfowl by natives in the Far North, as mentioned before. And when all this was done, Hewitt was given the embarrassing task of making the rounds of the provinces a second time.

"It is hardly conceivable that all this work could have been done in Canada without the faith and energy of Dr. Hewitt and conservationists should honor his memory. Although he was by profession an entomologist, he became tremendously interested in the bird and mammal fauna of Canada, and I find that as far back as 1913 he was writing to Mr. Henry Henshaw, then Chief of the Biological Survey of the United States, regarding the protection of migratory birds. He died in 1920."

Great credit is also due in Canada to Hon. Martin Burrell, Minister of Agriculture; Mr. Clifford Sifton, Chairman of the Commission of Conservation; Mr. J. B. Harkin of the Canadian National Parks; and Mr. James White, Deputy Head of the Conservation Commission. Also to Mr. F. T. D. Chambers of the Bureau of Fisheries of Quebec and various officers of the great Canadian Railroads.

The actual course of the Convention paper was as follows: First, the paper was sent by the State Department at Washington to Ottawa; from Ottawa to all the provinces of Canada for agreement; then to the British Embassy in Washington, and so to our State Department again. From our State Department it took its course to the Department of Agriculture (where it was revised after permission had been obtained from Canada, as we saw above). Next it traveled back to Ottawa and all the provinces again, to obtain agreement on the changes which we have noted. And so finally to the British Embassy in Washington — where it got sidetracked somehow — before the combined efforts of Dr. Nelson, Dr. Hewitt, John Burnham and several apprehensive officials finally located the elusive document. Then it was relayed to our State Department for its second appearance there and shortly afterward to the United States Senate, where it was ratified Aug. 29, 1916 and signed three days later by Pres. Woodrow Wilson.

## The Enabling Acts

The Treaty was now an accomplished fact, but there was no machinery to enforce it and it remained to work out further details as to seasons. This was done in the so-called Enabling Act, or Migratory Bird Treaty Act of the United States Congress, which was was approved by the President on July 3, 1918. This is another long story but it can only be touched upon here.

The same object was accomplished by Canada when the Dominion Government passed their Migratory Birds Convention Act on August 29, 1917, and formulated regulations the next May (1918). Canada arrived at her goal a year before we did.

In January, 1919, a report circulated that the Migratory Bird Treaty Act had been declared to be unconstitutional. This caused a great deal of trouble, and especially in the Mississippi Valley there followed a considerable amount of law violation.

## Constitutionality of Treaty Upheld

However, the constitutionality of the Treaty Act (of July 3, 1918) was sustained by the United States Supreme Court in a decision rendered April 19, 1920, in the case of the State of Missouri vs. Ray P. Holland. Holland, then a Federal warden, arrested Attorney General Frank McAlister of Missouri for shooting ducks out of season. The State maintained that a game warden of the United States had no power to enforce a law which was not constitutional under the Tenth Amendment. The State also alleged a pecuniary interest as owner of wild birds within its borders.

When the Government won this case against Missouri, the great opposition to the Federal law in the Middle West broke down. An association known as the Interstate Protective Association, formed as a last hope by the advocates of Spring shooting, soon collapsed.

The validity of the act of the Dominion Parliament of Canada was upheld by the Supreme Court of Prince Edward Island in a decision having to do with illegal sale of game in the case of the King vs. Russell C. Clark (1920)...so thereafter the birds of North America from the Rio Grande to the Arctic Ocean were under dual guardianship.

During the long struggle to secure the necessary legislation, Burnham drew a great deal of criticism not only from opponents among the senators but also from colleagues among the various conservationist groups. At times these individuals almost succeeded in defeating the efforts of Burnham and his associates. But nothing deterred them because they were true zealots in the cause of conservation.

"It's hard to make people act in time on a conservation measure," he later explained, "probably because conservation is not sensational. It is just the opposite of that. Destruction is sensational but salvation is not. And that's one reason why it was so hard to fight through that migratory bird legislation. Many Congressmen would not even listen to us, but fortunately there were enough sportsmen among them to push the Bill through.

"One case in particular gives you an idea of the difficulties we faced. I had gone to Washington especially to see one of the leaders in the House of Representatives. He kept me waiting one night until after 12 while he played poker. Then I returned to my hotel. Next morning I again went to his office and his secretary made an appointment for me to see him in a certain committee room. I waited there long past the hour and was leaving when one of the attendants told me the Congressman had gone to the Capitol.

"I hurried back into the committee room where I had been waiting and sat down over to one side. Shortly afterward my man came in accompanied by two others, apparently from his home state. They began to talk about a certain postmaster who had seemingly not been as active as they felt he should have been during the last election. So they were cooking up charges against him in order to oust him.

"Well, I knew that I had been eavesdropping but couldn't help it. They hadn't seen me at first but when they did the leader (my man) rose and strode over to where I was sitting.

'Who are you?' he demanded — and I told him.

'What do you want?'

"I explained as briefly as I could — or at least started to explain — but he waved me aside with a grand gesture."

'When our boys are dying in France,' he orated, 'I cannot talk about birds!'

"The hell you can't!" I exclaimed, grabbing him by the coat lapels and swinging him around. "You can stay up all night playing poker, and you can frame a little postmaster while our boys are dying in France — so why can't you talk about birds?!"

"He was visibly shaken by my anger and stood perfectly still while I told him what was wanted of him.

'Yes, yes,' he said, 'I've heard about that bill. It is excellent and I'll see that it passes!'

"It did pass and when it finally became law and the long fight was ended, I experienced the greatest thrill of my life — greater by far than I ever got out of hunting. Not even that moose shot around the corner excited me as much as that legislation!"

# Chapter 24

### The Campaign for Migratory Bird Refuges

Those who had been fighting to give the migratory birds the protection of the Federal Government, as compared with cruel and farcical lack of protection by the individual states, now took up the task of providing resting places for them while on migration which should be inviolate refuges. As regarding the game species — ducks, geese, etc. — the proponents did not want to be preserve them solely for the benefit of the club owners who already were in possession of a large share of the best marshes, so they added a provision to permit the Federal Government to also acquire areas for public shooting grounds, places where the lower-income man could have his chance. The private clubs had not gotten as far south as Louisiana in numbers so Burnham persuaded Mark Alexander, the game commissioner of that state, to establish the first poor man's club of this character in the country. This, of course, was by State action. However, when it came to the Federal Bill the advocates experienced great trouble with this provision.

Dr. E. W. Nelson, the far-seeing and courageous chief of the United States Biological Survey, was the pioneer of this legislation and the Bill was drawn in his office. His Chief Warden, George A. Lawyer, solved one staggering difficulty by devising an inexpensive way for collecting the tax of one dollar per year from the gunners, who were to finance the measure. He suggested that the Post Office Department make the collections through the medium of the so-called "duck stamp" which the applicant could attach to his regular state hunting license. This was a most important contribution as otherwise the costs of collection might have consumed most of the proceeds of the tax.

The American Game Association (of which Burnham was president) was asked to take charge of the Bill, and at once he found that they were up against a hard proposition. Dr. Hornaday became highly vocal against the shooting grounds on the basis that the refuges would decoy the wildfowl to slaughter. Will Dilg, president of the Isaak Walton League, opposed the license tax, saying that the measure should be supported by Congressional appropriations. Percy Sunthers of the Booth Fisheries Company spiked it once on the ground that it would put a crimp in commercial fishing. The fur dealers' associations opposed it because trapping was not permitted on refuges, until David Mills became head of their national organization. After that they gave it their support.

Some shooters wanted no refuges, saying it would be their money that would be used in purchasing the marshes, and an equal number of ultra-conservationists wanted nothing but inviolate refuges. It seemed that there were one hundred and ten million different causes of dissatisfaction with the Bill.

Senator New introduced the bill in the Senate and Congressman Anthony in the House. The bill passed the Senate in the 67th Congress, but in the House it failed by a few votes (154 against to 135 for). Congressman Garrett, the majority leader, was strongly opposed to the stamp tax and so was the minority leader, Frank Mondell, whom Theodore Roosevelt had characterized as an anticonservationist. Just before the holiday week in 1923 Burnham saw them from the gallery sitting together eating candy from the same box. He could not hear their conversation but he had a hunch it was about the Refuge Bill. This suspicion was verified a few days later when the Bill was called up for vote at a time when Congressmen from nearby districts had gone home. The strongest support was from members from New England and the Middle Atlantic States. Garrett and Mondell knew just as well as he did the temper of the different Congressmen so they counted noses on both sides of the House and put the bill to vote at a time when it did not have a fair show.

In a later Congess, after Harry New had left the Senate to become Postmaster General, the adherents got the Bill through the House in 1925 (vote 212 to 113), but could not surmount the inertia of the Senate. A considerable majority in the Senate favored the legislation, but everything was at a stalemate and no constructive bills were brought to vote. Burnham and his associates succeeded in getting their Refuge Bill added to several administration bills which were slated for passage but, though night sessions were held, no progress was made to relieve the congested calendar.

In desperation they set about securing the necessary two-thirds of the Senate for cloture, a method of passing legislation which has only succeeded a very few times in the history of the country.

Senator Peter Norbeck, of South Dakota, was the Bill's champion on the floor. He secured promises from a goodly number of Senators on the Republican side and a number of Democratic Senators also signified their approval. Then came an unfortunate thing. An enthusiastic Senator who was not informed made the motion for cloture prematurely, and the motion was defeated by just short of the two-thirds required for its success. It was a great surprise to most of the Senators that the vote was so close.

The end of the session was only a few days off so they re-doubled their efforts to bring it up again. The day came when a very prominent Democratic Senator authorized J.B.B. to notify Senator Norbeck that the remaining necessary pledges had been secured. He hurried to the Senate Office Building stepping on clouds, only to find that an hour before Senator Norbeck had been seriously injured in a taxi accident, and that he was in a hospital hovering between life and death. Congress adjourned long before Senator Norbeck recovered sufficiently to leave the hospital, and as the pledges had been for all intents and purposes given to him the Bill failed of passage.

Later on, in an amended form and emasculated by the taking out of the stamp tax feature, the Bill was enacted into law. The American Game Association refused to accept the compromise. They thought it more honest to put the cost on the class most directly interested and the officers were not confident that sufficient and continuing appropriations would be forthcoming. In this latter respect at least their stand was subsequently substantiated, and it remained for that fine conservationist, Senator Frederic C. C. Walcott, to put the "duck stamp license bill" on the map.

*[The American Game Protective Association, later shortened to American Game Association, headed by Burnham from 1911 until 1929, made appreciable contributions to the cause of conservation.*

*In 1935 Jay N. Darling, then Chief of the United States Biological Survey, and several other men interested in the restoration of wildlife proposed that the American Game Association merge with another influential organization which had already raised a large sum of money for that same purpose. In order to avoid duplication of expense and effort the American Wildlife Institute, then being formed, would expand and expedite the programs already in operation.*

*The American Game Association agreed to this arrangement and relinquished its staff, records and publication — American Game — to the new group. There was, however, one stipulation: The A.G.A. was to continue its existence in order that the directors could manage its affairs and the income from its endowment funds in accordance with the wishes of the donors.*

*From 1935 until 1970 these residual funds were well invested and used for the benefit of wildlife. In one four-year period (1964-68) the directors purchased almost 3,000 acres of marshlands, costing $172,041.25, and gave them to the states of Minnesota, Colorado, North and South Dakota, Idaho, Nebraska, Iowa and Wisconsin.*

*In 1970 the remaining funds, over $20,000, were turned over to the New York Conservation Council and American Game Association Foundation and became part of the Karl T. Frederick Memorial Fund: Editor]*

## Chapter 25

### Burnham Versus Hornaday

*[Dr. William T. Hornaday (1854-1937), who classified himself as being a practical zoologist, had a distinguished career in the field of conservation. His fieldwork, which included jungle exploration and scientific expeditions into many regions, was followed by service as chief taxidermist for the United States National Museum in Washington, D.C. from 1882-1890. His most noteworthy contributions to natural science were undoubtedly made while he was the Director of the New York Zoological Park in the period from 1896-1926.*

*His published works, numbering more than twenty, included* Two Years in the Jungle, Campfires in the Rockies, Minds and Manners of Animals *and* Our Vanishing Wildlife.

*Given much of the credit for saving the buffalo from extinction, the subsequent establishment of the Montana Buffalo Range and the Elk River Game Preserve, he was also influential in instigating the legislative action resulting in the passage of the Bayne Law, which prohibited the sale of game, and the Fur Seal Treaty of 1911.*

*The* Encyclopedia Britannica *biographical article has him state that he carried on what he called "constant war against the gamehogs of the Atlantic Coast." In* Twentieth Century Authors *he described himself as "No mild-mannered, white-bearded scientist but rather a tireless fighter who thrived on controversy:" Editor]*

"Back in 1909 when Forest, Fish and Game Commissioner, James S. Whipple and I were codifying the game laws of New York State, Dr. William T. Hornaday sent us an edict that gray squirrels were to be taken from the game list and included in the species protected at all times from shooting. He has since then learned that squirrels not only eat nuts but animal food as well, including eggs and young birds, that a squirrel Eden would be songsterless desert in nesting time at any rate and, as a result, he has dropped this particular kind of campaign. But in 1908 he was determined to save the gray squirrels at any cost, so Whipple and I were given our orders to fix the law in such a way that gray squirrels could never thereafter be killed.

"As head of the state game protective division I wrote Dr. Hornaday that in many parts of New York under existing protective laws gray squirrels were abundant and that in a few localities, as in Watertown, they had become a plague almost on a par with starlings. Later on, I gave him other reasons why I thought it inadvisable to single them out for perpetual protection. But I told him it was our job to save bird life from extinction and, that if he would furnish the facts he said he possessed to show the supply was too low in particular

*First Shipment at "Highlands" Deer Park*

parts of the State (other than in counties already closed to shooting), we would give the additional protection required.

"Friends who knew Dr. Hornaday said that I had committed lèse majesté in that the Doctor decided such questions for himself and that he considered it improper — particularly for a game official — to attempt to debate his edicts. Jotham P. Allds, after a trial which has gone down in history, had just been severed from his seat in the State Senate.[1] The next I heard of the squirrel question was that Dr. Hornaday had labeled me the "Joe Allds of game protection" in a vitriolic outburst characteristic of his particular genius. To make the blow more effective, at the same time he had a bill introduced in the Legislature giving gray squirrels absolute protection as long as water runs and grass grows in all the counties of New York with the exception of Cattaraugus and Essex, *The Home Counties of Commissioner Whipple and myself*. The exemption of these counties was a clever political maneuver designed to put Whipple and myself in the hole. It was stated that we feared the farmer

---

[1] Early in 1910 Sen. Conger made charges of bribery against Sen. Allds, who had been connected with former land purchases by the State. Special commissioners appointed by Gov. Hughes conducted an investigation covering the management and affairs of both the Forest Purchasing Board and the Forest, Fish and Game Commission, going back over a period of 15 years, during which Commissioner Dewitt Middleton was forced to resign after disclosures of lumber-larceny under his administration.

The 425 page report showed that the Forest Purchasing Board, of which Commissioner Whipple was then a member, had paid $650 an acre for land previously offered to the State for $1.50 per acre. Although Whipple was criticized for inefficiency, extravagance and allowing his subordinates too free a hand, no charge of dishonesty was made against him or any member of the Purchasing Board.

vote in our home locality and had forced the confession that we were looking out for our own selfish interests and not for the welfare of the wildlife.

"Only a short time after this Hornaday's book, *Our Vanishing Wildlife,* was published and he sent a copy to me. It was with a feeling of genuine astonishment that I opened the book and found the following autograph: To Mr. John B. Burnham on the firing line. Army of Defense with the compliments of the author — W. T. Hornaday. Equally surprising was the discovery of my photograph, along with eleven others, whom Hornaday cited as notable protectors of wildlife. To the best of my recollection I had not seen nor corresponded with Dr. Hornaday in the meanwhile. The gray squirrel bill had not passed the Legislature and I had done nothing as far as I am aware to cause a change of opinion. I can only believe that he used his insulting language and resorted to his dishonest tactics merely for effect with the State Legislature — that he was perfectly aware of the untruth of his statements and he did not think me venal, but had no hesitancy in attempting to wreck my character to accomplish his object. Such action was inhumanly cold-blooded and I lost my respect for the man.

"The Forest, Fish and Game Commission of New York was changed by act of Legislature to the Conservation Commission. I had served as the Deputy Commissioner of the old Commission before I resigned to take up the work of the American Game Protective Association. My salary in the new job (which has never been raised) was $4,000 less than Governor Dix offered me to remain with the State Commission. I made the change because I believe in the new Federal legislation. Theodore Roosevelt, George Bird Grinnell and John Burroughs advised me to take the step. It was Dr. Grinnell who first suggested my name to the arms and ammunition manufacturers as fitted for the job. Theodore Roosevelt wrote me a long letter giving his reasons why the work was right and worth-while.

"Dr. Hornaday in one of his publications had given his version of the events leading up to the formation of the American Game Protective Association but while I received, I think, all his other reports on or about the date of publication, I never saw this statement until recently. His version differs so fundamentally from what I believe to be the facts that I am impelled to give my account, which is true to the best of my knowledge and belief.

"Allds' litigation led up to an investigation of the Forest, Fish and Game Commission. Whipple's resignation was requested and given. Then Dr. Hornaday selected Whipple as his candidate for president of the Forest, Fish and Game League, the sportsmen's State organization. He notified me of this fact and knowing my friendship for Commissioner Whipple told me he counted on my support in the approaching election. I told Dr. Hornaday that it would hurt Whipple to become a candidate for an elective office of this character at this time. It seemed probable that the friends of another contestant who was already in the field would rehash the charges that had been made against him and all indications pointed to a bitter fight. Asked if I did not believe in Whipple, I replied emphatically that he was a man of character and honor and that he had done more for the cause of forest and wildlife conservation than any of his predecessors. But I added that in addition to my desire to protect my friend from a feud, I was also opposed to his candidacy on the ground that the friction engendered might cause a breach in the State League and so retard the cause to which we were devoted.

"Hornaday refused to see any merit in my argument. He electioneered for delegates for Whipple and, just before the date of the convention, told me over the telephone in the course of another argument for Whipple that he had the promise of enough votes to elect Whipple. Also that he had secured Jerome B. Fisher, an orator of parts, to make the nominating speech. Fisher, to the best of my knowledge, was not a League member and had no interest in conservation.

"I told Dr. Hornaday that I did not like the political methods he was using. He asked me who my candidate was and I replied that I had no candidate, that I did not favor either Whipple or his opponent. I tried to convince Hornaday that my sole interest was to see the League headed by a man acceptable to the membership, one who would carry on fearlessly and effectively for progressive and better ideals.

"When the League convened I expressed this same thought, but avoided the mention of any specific name. A similar idea in the minds of the delegates caused many of them to go to Dr. Hornaday and insist on being relieved from their promises to support his candidate. Hornaday attempted to get through the convention a resolution to advance the time for the election of officers, which was defeated. Whipple did not like the way things were going and withdrew himself from the contest. The swing of sentiment seemed to be toward George Lawyer, a man of executive ability and unquestioned loyalty to conservation ideals. At the proper time Whipple put Lawyer in nomination with a speech which reached high levels and which has long been remembered as an example of lofty oratory. The delegates, keen in their appreciation of good sportsmanship, rose to their feet in an outburst of spontaneous applause and Lawyer was elected. The next instant Whipple was nominated and elected vice president.

"Everybody left that meeting happy — with the exception of Dr. Hornaday. The next day he came out in an interview in a New York newspaper attacking me, stating that I had used political methods to defeat his candidate and that I had a stranglehold on the League in the interest of the arms and ammunition manufacturers....

"In 1912 I received a letter from Dr. Hornaday asking me to attend a conference to discuss the Migratory Bird Bill. I phoned him to say that on the night selected I had to leave New York by sleeper at 8 P.M. but that if wanted under this condition I would be present. Dr. Hornaday said that this would be satisfactory so all that was required from me was a statement of the status of the Bill in Congress.

"There were about a dozen conservationists at the conference. Dr. Hornaday sat at the head of the table as master of ceremonies. He called on me to give an account of my stewardship as having charge of the campaign for the Bill. Several times during the course of my talk he tried to make me admit that the prospect of passing the Bill was hopeless. I did not agree with him in this, but on the contrary stated that I felt confident the measure would pass at that session of Congress. Nothing was said by Dr. Hornaday relative to changing the Bill.

"On my return to New York I was greatly surprised to find that the moment I had left the conference the statement had been made that the Migratory Bird Bill was at a hopeless impasse, that its only chance of success was to abandon the protection of the game species and, through the farmers' organizations, start a new campaign with a bill protecting non-game birds solely. As a justification of what might be considered treachery to a fellow worker in the conservation field, Dr. Hornaday stated that my interest had been only for the game birds and that song and insectivorous birds had both escaped being left outside the pale.[1] The convention ended on a unpleasant note."

---

[1] "Migratory bird bills had been introduced in Congress long before the American Game Protective Association was started, first by George Shiras, the father of the idea, and afterwards by Senator McLean and Congressmen Weeks and Anthony. When the Association took up the campaign for the measure, none of the bills then before Congress was framed to give Federal protection to other than game birds. Dr. Pearson suggested to me that all birds should be included, to which suggestion I readily agreed. After conference with Sen. McLean and Congressman Weeks the change was made."

To backtrack a bit in order to put their relationship into perspective Burnham and Hornaday had known each other from the late 1890's on, had occasionally served on the same committees and seemingly were on rather sociable terms. In a letter dated Dec. 18, 1908 the latter thanked Burnham for his gift of a splendid young buck to the New York Zoo. Over the next five or six years Dr. Hornaday wrote many other cordial letters.

During the next decade, however, the viewpoints of these two prominent conservationists became increasingly more polarized and invariably in direct opposition. Hornaday, the total protectionist type, had nothing but scorn for the hunters while his adversary, who loved the sport, just as ardently maintained that sound conservation methods would not only permit the annual harvesting of wildlife resources but also insure ample seed stock as well.

Knowledgeable though Dr. Hornaday was on many phases of wildlife study, he nevertheless displayed on several occasions a very superficial understanding of the issues. This was clearly indicated in one instance when Frank Norbert, Game Commissioner of California, asked him to explain the logic behind his widely-publicized statement that deer in State were on the very verge of extermination. According to Burnham:

"Dr. Hornaday told Norbert that for several years past he had been trying to secure a set of antlers and because he had difficulty in getting them he had assumed the deer must be gone. Norbert told him that the Forest Service credited California in their latest census with 185,000 deer in Federal forests alone, not to mention other thousands on State and privately-owned lands, and several for every square mile of California's surface; but many per mile when deer territory only is considered.

"He then asked Dr. Hornaday on what grounds he had similarly stated that bob-white quail had been exterminated by shooting in California. 'Didn't you know, Doctor,' commented Norbert, 'that there never were any bob-white quail in California?'

"Hornaday was then asked if he did not consider a study of the game conditions in a state a necessity before making recommendations as to what should be done for the benefit of the game. In reply he gave this remarkable answer which is quoted verbatim:

"'In a campaign covering 48 states it is impossible to study local conditions in any of these states.'"

From 1920 onward the relationship between the men became even more acrimonious and openly hostile. Unfortunately, it also generated considerable dissension in the ranks and seriously endangered the success of many important programs which required a unanimity of effort against formidable opponents of conservation in Congress and elsewhere.

Then, on Aug. 11, 1925, in an interview with a reporter for the New York *Times,* Dr. Hornaday delivered a lengthy tirade against gun and ammunition manufacturers who, he declared, were blocking bag-limit regulations. Moreover, he scathingly referred to the organization which Burnham headed as being the *"Gunmakers'* American Game Protective Association." He then charged that his opponent had exerted undue and improper influence over the United States Department of Agriculture officials and their policies.

Understandably, this attack on his character and motives was a matter of serious concern to Burnham but, to avoid jeopardizing the outcome of imminent and important legislation by public disclosure of their deep personal differences, he reluctantly decided to defer taking legal action against his persistent detractor.

Since the two men met periodically at meetings of the Camp-Fire Club of America, this personality clash also created a difficult situation for the other members. Nevertheless, aware that they were antagonizing Hornaday, one of their most honored colleagues, the Board of Governors of that organization, after endorsing the then-pending Migratory Bird

Refuge legislation, gave Burnham their staunch support by adding this unequivocal statement:

"We deeply deplore the personal attacks that have been made upon the sponsors of the Bill, particularly Mr. John B. Burnham, President of the American Game Protective Association, and upon Dr. E. W. Nelson, Chief of the U.S. Biological Survey, who will be the chief administrator of the law when passed. We know both these men well. We have a high regard for Dr. Nelson as a scientist and as a sane wildlife conservationist. His views are not the result of mere sentiment but of thorough, scientific study. His record stands as an unassailable endorsement of his policies. We believe that the matters entrusted by the Bird Refuge Bill to the Bureau of the Biological Survey will be safe in his hands.

"We know John Burnham as an honored member of the Camp-Fire Club of America, as a conservationist and as a man. He has received the Camp-Fire Club gold medal of honor for his outstanding achievements as an American sportsman of the highest type.[1] In our opinion, his achievements as a practical wildlife conservationist are second to none. The association that he created and still leads is not an aggregation of commercial interests as has been charged, but a body nation-wide that has won high distinction in the field of conservation and includes in its membership and on its governing board men of national standing as conservationists and protectors of wildlife.

"We know John Burnham to be a man of courage and of conscience, whose convictions and policies cannot be molded by an evil or untoward influence however powerful, and we believe that attacks on men of this type do far more harm to the cause of conservation than to the objects of their venom."

The awarding of the Camp-Fire Club's gold medal to John Burnham seemed to intensify Hornaday's determination to discredit him whenever possible. Although the former apparently delayed retaliatory action for many months, he finally signed a complaint against him on Mar. 7, 1927 in Elizabethtown, N.Y. C. Byron Brewster of that village, who later became a noted State Supreme Court Judge, was one of his attorneys. The libel suit opened on July 22nd in Saratoga with State Supreme Court Judge Heffernan presiding.

In view of the fact that court costs and attorney fees cost the plaintiff far more than the token $2500.00 sought by Burnham, it was obvious that he was concerned only with the protection of his name and reputation.

Dr. Hornaday proved to be a resourceful and determined adversary because the case dragged on for nearly two years. Then, when he became convinced that he was spending money heedlessly in a cause he could not conceivably win, he changed tactics. A mutual friend conferred with Burnham in order to work out satisfactory terms for a settlement. Out of deference for his adversary's greater age and lesser financial resources, John Burnham was more than willing to discontinue the action in return for a printed public apology.

To Burnham's amazement on June 6, 1929 from Stamford, Connecticut came the following statement published in the New York *Times:* "In an interview on the general subject of game conservation given by me to a *Times* reporter on Aug. 11, 1925, I discussed issues relative to the conservation of migratory game. No reflection upon the character of Mr. John B. Burnham was intended; issues discussed were solely issues of general principle and public policy and my interview should not be otherwise construed."

---

[1] Hornaday had been one of the founders and previous award-winners as had Gifford Pinchot, Theodore Roosevelt, Ernest Thompson-Seton, Dan Beard, William Dutcher and George Pratt.

Even though this somewhat grudging apology was accepted and court action stopped, Dr. Hornaday found it difficult to accept defeat as is indicated in this revealing letter:

Essex, N.Y.<br>November 8, 1930

To the New York *Herald Tribune:*

My attention has just been called to a letter written by William T. Hornaday and published in your issue of November 2nd, relative to the libel suit which I brought against Dr. Hornaday. In all good humor I think that his statement "we never could get Mr. Burnham within 80 miles of an open court in a trial" requires correction. The facts are that I instituted the action and that the initiative was mine and not Dr. Hornaday's. There were three trials in "open court." The first before Justice Heffernan of the Supreme Court at Saratoga, the second before the Appellate Division, Third Department and the last an argument on the plaintiff's part for permission to bring the matter before the Court of Appeals. In each one of these actions my attorneys were successful, and the justification of Hornaday's answer to my action was disproved.

During the course of the trials, I was approached by a friend of Dr. Hornaday's on the subject of a compromise. This gentleman represented that Dr. Hornaday was an old man and by no means wealthy, and I was asked to accept a retraction in lieu of a money recovery, which as the case progressed it seemed likely would result.

On my part I stated that my sole object in bringing the action was to clear my good name, and therefore I was willing to accept a retraction. This is all there is to the matter. It seems to me, however, essential that the statement implying that the case did not come to trial should be corrected."

JBB/M

As is quite characteristic of all unusually competent and strongwilled men, each understandably wanted to savor the pleasure inherent in having the last word. In this case, although Hornaday tried his utmost, the man from "Highlands" was clearly the vindicated victor.

Proof that Burnham was not alone in his confrontations with Hornaday is indicated in this letter:

4530 Klingle Street<br>Wesley Heights, Wash.<br>June 24, 1927

John B. Burnham, Esquire
Woolworth Building
New York

Dear Burnham,

Your present effort to vindicate your personal and official integrity, by legal proceedings, involving the continuous and unfair attacks made upon you during the long years devoted to the conservation of wild life, involves, in my judgment more than yourself. These unjust criticisms, while aimed primarily at you necessarily concern your associates in the American Game Protective Association, Biological Survey and a great many of the leading scientists who have backed up your efforts to procure proper game legislation by the States and in Congress. With this feeling, I enclose my check for $1,000 to help defray some of the legal expenses, since it would be most unjust that you should incur the responsibility and the worry of such an effort and then have to bear the financial burden incident to the preparation and trial of the case. This is the time for your friends to rally about you, for in doing this they not only help you but protect themselves from the vindictive and selfish attacks of those who for years stood in the way of getting much-needed legislation.

I thank you for your expressions of sympathy in my recent illness and the *words* of *appreciation* contained therein.

Yours very sincerely,<br>George Shiras 3rd<br>per F.P.S.

*(From a photograph by Godfrey Sykes)*

*The Members of the Expedition, on Porous Red Lava, at the Papago Tanks*

| Jesse D. Jenkins | Charlie Foster | George Saunders | Frank Coles |
| Dr. MacDougal | Mr. Phillips | Mr. Milton | William T. Hornaday |

# Chapter 26

**The Burnham — Dilg Controversy over Game Refuge Legislation**

"Will Dilg was an advertising man for St. Louis Brewers, I think, at the time he founded the Izaak Walton League. He was a little man with a head like the London *Punch's* patron saint and a hand so small and fragile that once you had taken it in yours you dropped it in the fear it would smash like an egg-shell. He always carried a cane and gloves and hung onto them during a conference as if they were needed for mental stimulus.

"Like his contemporary and associate, Emerson Hough of *Covered Wagon* fame,[1] Dilg was a self-centered genius. He was a one-man show and he could not brook competition. As long as he held the stage alone he carried all before him, but in defeat he did not shine. He was no last-ditch contender.

"Dilg was a fly fisherman and a deviser of fishing lures. Aside from this he knew little or nothing about the broad field of sport. He started his League on the basis that nothing had been done to conserve fish and game and with advertising flare he pictured himself as the Savior of wild life.

"His real achievement was that he, more than anyone else, got across to the masses, and classes as well, the doctrine of conservation. Curiously enough another similarly uninformed man, Dr. Hornaday, similarly narrow and vindictive, stands with Dilg in the limelight of their respective crusades.

"Of the two, however, Dilg's work is the more substantial. The League which he founded has gone on to enduring achievement. Dilg, like Hornaday, was not constructive. He had the power of making people distrust existing agencies and he could arouse in them enthusiasm for action, but after the Upper Mississippi Refuge scheme, he had little to offer in the way of issues. The American Game Association, which had led the successful fight for migratory bird protection, had before Congress a nation-wide measure for migratory bird refuges. It was the biggest issue in sight and apparently Dilg decided to appropriate it for himself. No other hypothesis seems tenable in view of the events which followed.

"To explain the situation it is necessary to say that the Bill as before Congress carried the provision that the money needed for financing the refuges was to be raised by a license tax on duck hunters, and that this provision was very unpopular with the members of Congress who readily visualized the rebuke of angry constituents so taxed. We who were working for the Bill were told we could have it at any time if we would consent to finance its expenditures by means of appropriations, but we had refused for two reasons: first, because

---

[1] Emerson Hough had two reasons for his constant opposition to J. B. Burnham: (1) He mistakenly believed that the latter had cost him his job at *Forest and Stream* and (2) he strongly objected to Burnham's seemingly unsportsmanlike ownership of a deer farm.

we believed it to be more honest to make the hunters who received the chief benefit pay the expense rather than the general tax-payers; and second, because we believed the license tax to be the only enduring method. After many years of fighting, the license tax method has been adopted, but at the time of which I write the Bill had failed of passage.

"Dilg, Hornaday and others held a conference at Spokane, Washington, and shortly afterward I received a letter from one of the conferees, a man I did not know, but undoubtedly a traitor — a man who evidently wanted to curry favor with whichever side should win — telling me that a trap had been laid for me to walk into and that this trap would be sprung on the occasion of the annual meeting of the International Association of Fish, Game and Conservation Commissioners in Denver, which was then only a few days off. He told me the stage would first be set by a nation-wide attack on the American Game Association on account of its receiving financial assistance from arms and ammunition manufacturers and that then, at the Convention, with my back to the wall, I was to be accused of inefficient stewardship in handling the Bill, and a new plan for financing it was to be offered — the highly ingenious plan of taxing the arms and ammunition manufacturers two per cent on their products.

"The letter was received an hour before my train was due to leave for Denver. I dictated an identical letter to all the manufacturers who contributed to the Association, telling them the plan had merit and deserved most serious consideration. I told them that I should take whatever action I thought best, but that I hoped, if the ammunition tax was adopted, it would not mean the loss of their subscription to the Association. At Denver I got frank replies from all but one of our manufacturer contributors, telling me that in no event would their contribution be withheld — that the money was given for game protection and not for selfish business reasons.

"Dilg had been attacking the American Game Association for failure to cooperate with the Izaak Walton League in the passage of the Upper Mississippi Refuge Bill, and now Dr. Hornaday issued a statement accusing the Association of the basest of ulterior motives. Later I sued Dr. Hornaday for libel, but after the preliminary court skirmishes had been won, I weakly acceded to pleas on the Doctor's behalf and withdrew my action. I have always felt that I did an unmanly thing in not carrying this fight to a finish.

"At Denver I was early on the program for a talk on the Game Refuge Bill. The air was surcharged with innuendo and attack. I had been played up as the villain, the tool of the interests. An acquaintance drew me over for an introduction to three distinguished-looking Oklahoma Waltonians. When they heard my name they simultaneously withdrew their hands. I became angry and this was my salvation. The next minute I was called on to speak.

"I told the convention that I proposed to speak on the situation they were all discussing and only incidentally on the Bill. I said that bar associations and other organizations had found it necessary to appoint committees to regulate the ethics of their membership, but that in time past conservation associations had been free from this malodorous necessity. I hoped the time would never come when action of this kind was forced upon us.

"I told them that Will Dilg had been befouling the atmosphere and that I proposed to let in a little fresh air by discussing before them his charges and giving my answers. Taking up the charge that the American Game Association had not cooperated to help the passage of the Mississippi Refuge, I first admitted that the Association had entered into an agreement with the League in the interest of harmony to side-track its own bill for the benefit of the League's bill, thus giving it a better chance of passage through Congress; the understanding being that at the next session of Congress the League would aid us with our Game Refuge Bill. Dilg had said we denied this agreement.

"Then, taking out my notebook, I gave days and dates when conferences had been held between Dilg and myself in the interest of the Mississippi Bill and described the results of each piece of work we had taken up, down to the time when "Poly" Pincknor of Kansas, the last opponent in the House, had been won over by Ray Holland of the Association.

"I saw that the delegates were listening attentively but with no particular interest to the matter-of-fact recital, but at this juncture fate played into my hands. I was galvanized by the sight of Will Dilg slouching toward one of the rear doors of the hall. "Hold on, Mr. Dilg," I called, "The worst is yet to come. I cannot go on with what I am saying unless you are present to hear it."

"Dilg waved his fist and shouted: "I demand to be heard!"

"Sit down!" I said. When I am through you will have all the opportunity in the world to be heard!" — and I went on to picture him as a Frankenstein.

In his reply Dilg was not at his best. He made an over-long speech reciting all he had done for the cause of conservation. He said nothing to controvert the proof I had given. When he had finished the session was adjourned for dinner. As we filed out of the hall Judge Miles of Little Rock, Arkansas, said to me, 'John, some of the things you said about Dilg were pretty rough and some people may think you had it in for him personally. My advice to you is to go up to Dilg, shake hands, and tell him nothing personal was intended.'

"I acquiesced, but Lee LeCompte, standing near, interjected: 'Take a brick in your other hand.'

"Dilg was just taking his place at a table with a dozen Waltonians when I walked up, shook his hand and told him that I had no personal ill-feeling but had acted to get a truthful picture before the Convention. They all joined in forcing me to sit at their table and this time the Oklahoma men shook my hand. Half the time at the meal I was defending Dilg from the criticisms of his own bunch.

"Later in the day Dilg and I accidentally met in the lobby of the hotel. In a thoroughly friendly way he said: 'You're brilliant, John.'

"You're wet," I replied.

'Not as a speaker,' said Dilg, 'but as a tactician. You've got us licked!'

"Where you made your mistake," I replied, "was that your plan was too devilish. If you had left out all the attack and simply sprung the new plan for financing the Bill, you would have trimmed us here and at Washington."

"The Convention unanimously voted confidence in the American Game Association's handling of the Bill, but asked that the merits of the ammunition tax method of financing be investigated. This was done, but Congress at that time refused to consider an excise tax of this character. That came later."

The following testimonial represents a very valid appraisal of the services of John Bird Burnham and also indicates his stature as a preeminent conservationist:

Remarks about Burnham by FREDERIC C. WALCOTT, ( UNITED STATES SENATOR from Connecticut)

**CHAIRMAN NINTH NATIONAL GAME CONFERENCE, Dec. 10, 1922**

---

...."Now I am going to take three minutes to point out to you what one man can do who has courage and vision — whose eyes are fixed on a star. About twelve years ago our game in the East had almost vanished — it was vanishing at a rapid rate all over the United States. A man without large means who had had a varied experience in the Klondike for several years came back with some very decided views on game protection and, above all, with a great vision. He must have made a resolve something like this: "I am going to reclaim the game of America." It was a Herculean task, the kind that takes great courage. He was fortunate in his associates, the pioneers in conservation in this country — men like George Shiras, George Bird Grinnell and Theodore Roosevelt. He set out almost alone on this enormous task. About that same time George Shiras, who was then in the House of Representatives, proclaimed publicly that the Federal Government had jurisdiction over migratory birds and that such jurisdiction was constitutional. The question was discussed pro and con, and finally out of all the turmoil and trouble with the persistent backing of this one man of vision and his associates, the Weeks-McLean was passed — after literally years of the hardest kind of work and many, many discouragements. Then it was declared unconstitutional, and we had to ask our sister nation to come to our rescue, to make it constitutional by agreeing to a treaty covering the subject. And I want to say that the two flags which you see before you tonight, without any dividing line between them, are truly representative of the relations existing between these two countries — relations which I know will continue for all times. We shall go together hand and hand in the promotion of all good measures.

"But the gentleman to whom I have been referring is one of the kind who is not easily satisfied, and even with the passage of the Weeks-McLean Bill and the adoption of the Canadian Treaty and the Enabling Act, his work was not done. He continued his efforts, and finally the Biological Survey joined him in the proposal for a Federal license in order that we might avoid making the mistake that England has made, where one-quarter of the people are in possession of the land and all the shooting rights. With the ideal ahead of him of protecting the interests of the one-gallus man, he kept on and on; and the thought was that if we could get a Federal license, which would necessarily bring a considerable revenue, why should we not have great national sanctuaries and free public shooting grounds, as far as that would be practicable in a largely populated country? So that stone by stone the edifice has been built; we are now near the crown, and I think you will hear tonight that the great effort must yet be made to bring about its completion. We must do our duty in this respect; we must overcome the stumbling-blocks; we must give unflinching loyalty and support to this great leader of ours, the man who has built up the American Game Protective Association, the man who has made these conferences possible — and that man is John Burnham. (Applause) I was going to say that I was sorry John is in the room, but he probably does not know what I am talking about. But John Burnham is going to lead us to even greater heights, and we are going to get what we are after!"

Further proof of Burnham's leadership is provided by this excerpt from a report by Madison Grant, himself an acknowledged authority and advocate of progressive conservation precepts and practices.

### "The Establishment of Mt. McKinley National Park"

"At this meeting it was determined that the campaign in course be entrusted to American Game Protective Association, its President, Mr. Burnham, assuming the active leadership. Mr. Burnham was duly authorized by his Association to undertake this work and the various clubs and individuals supporting the measure agreed to act unitedly under his direction. ..........effective work in Washington and elsewhere was also done by individual members and, above all, by Mr. Burnham."

Besides being one of the founders and charter members of the Adirondack Mountain Club, Burnham's activities and services included almost the entire gamut of conservation goals. He advocated and helped secure the passage of many laws for the protection of big-game animals as well as birds and assisted in codifying the game laws of several states, including New York State. He was one of the governors of the National Parks Association and was a charter member and treasurer of the National Parks Committee, which represented twenty-eight allied organizations with four million members. In addition to taking charge of the legislative work which resulted in the creation of Mt. McKinley National Park he, with others, led a successful campaign to remove from the national parks the ban placed on them by the Jones-Esch law, which permitted waterpower development within their borders.

Obviously Burnham belonged and belongs in the forefront of the leaders in the field of American conservation.

# Chapter 27

## Three Score and Ten

"At 68 I really felt old for the first time in my life when I read in a magazine a laudatory mention of my name, along with other pioneers in the field of wildlife conservation, all of whom the writer evidently thought had crossed the Styx. It is bad enough to lose one's friends and the pain reaches to the core, but there is a different feeling when one reads his own obituary. It seems to say that if you are not dead, you should be. Your work is finished; make way for the younger generation! And all the while I had been thinking of myself as of the younger generation.

"I never question the age of the men with whom I associate and I never realize the fact that my hair is white, even while shaving, except by accident. I do not think of men in terms of the years they have been on Earth, but in terms of character and accomplishment. I often think there are no friends like old friends, but from time to time I become attached to men I have not known for long and immediately I feel as if I had known them always; and they are every bit as dear to me as those I had known since boyhood.

"Age to me means nothing except as involving a loss of activity. It is not a schedule for transit to the grave. I have friends twenty years older who are just as keen mentally as they ever were. But we all have to admit that we cannot get around as well as we used to.

"I am not afraid to die, but I don't want to. Every year I live I love this beautiful world more than the year before. I have been reading up on geology, and there are all kinds of interesting things opened up by this reading that I want to investigate. I want to locate Dana's third wollastonite occurrence in Essex County, and I want to find the Algonquin's lost lead mine which supplied their musket bullets at the time of the French and Indian Wars. I want to build new roads in my mountain and there are thousands of pine and other trees that need nursing along and freeing from choking shade if they are ever to be lusty monarchs.

"Man wants but little here below — Nor wants that little long."
         Journado del Muerto (Trail of the Dead Men)

"Professor Harlow Shapley, anticipating the extinction of the human race, pictures an ant crawling out of the eye socket of an extinct man and soliloquizing: 'A marvelous experiment of Nature's. What a brain! Alas, the poor thing did not understand the business of survival. His mind destroyed him!'

"On the verge of the Biblical limit to man's life, I look back on what has gone before with pleasure, and the things which give me pleasure in retrospect are not the spectacular events of my life, nor its relative successes, but the simple things. I am glad that this is so.

"I go to bed at night turning over in memory solitary days in the woods, my plans for roads to dodge impossible ledges and yet maintain reasonable gradients, rest periods at lunch-time by snug fires in the snow, forest improvements by cutting out slash and deformed and weed trees. Such thoughts are restful, and soft comes sleep.

"While I have always been fascinated by adventure and hair-breadth escapes from death, I do not in memory live over such things as my scrape in the whirlpool of Miles Canyon of the Yukon in the days of the Klondike gold rush.[1] And no more do I dwell on the hectic days when we fought for new laws from a hostile Congress. I like to talk of such things with friends, particularly with friends who were partners in the events, but they are not the sweet intimacies of a passing life. The simple routine of the outdoors in this primitive North Country is my real love, and I am glad this is so.

"I do not go to sleep thinking of business. If business thoughts crop up I resolutely throw them out. Money-making long ago ceased to be a major incentive — thank God it never was my master. Unless one is a money-hound, business is just a means to an end. To me it means the hours out of the day or the days out of the week it takes to do the job I have contracted to do; to do it the best I know how; to soak myself in it while it lasts, without thought of the clock, no matter how long it takes on the theory that the only thing that counts is the result. Then, when it is all over, I have the balance of time to myself, and having worked to acquire this personal time it is especially valuable. And I try to make use of it in a way as far removed as possible from the business of making a living. It is necessary that I earn my living, but I use what brains I have to get through with this chore as quickly as I can so that I may enjoy myself in the woods. I owe it to my body and I owe it to my soul."

As shown by the following letter Burnham was honored just two years before his death by election to the Ends of the Earth Club, a very small and prestigious organization of explorer-scientists:

## ENDS OF THE EARTH

S. H. P. Pell
Secretary
115 Fifth Avenue
New York

October 11th, 1937.

My dear Mr. Burnham,

I take pleasure in notifying you of your election to the Ends of the Earth. There are no initiation fees, no dues, and no obligations of any kind, except to attend the annual dinner and meeting on the first Friday in December of each year, if convenient.

I am enclosing the last list of members, published in 1936.

Faithfully yours,

S. H. P. Pell
Hon. Secretary

J. B. Burnham had always maintained that it is better for a man to burn out than to rust out and his waning years gave convincing proof of this conviction. Although he remained reasonably active until several years before the end, the warning signals were never-

---

[1] Any wild-eyed white-water enthusiast who might be inspired to duplicate his feat can stop right here because a big dam at White Horse has wiped out the Rapids: Editor.

theless becoming very evident so he gradually but gladly relinquished to his son, Koert, and daughter, Rose, most of his concerns and responsibilities.

Burnham's philosophy of life, taken in the aggregate sense, was very aptly set down by a great Irish playwright — George Bernard Shaw — in the preface to *Man and Superman*. If anyone has said it better I have yet to see it and I concur completely.

"This is the true joy in life — the being used for a purpose recognized by yourself as a mighty one; the being thoroughly worn out before you are thrown on the scrap heap; the being a force of Nature instead of a feverish, selfish little clod of ailments and grievances and always complaining because the world will not devote itself to making you happy.

"And also the only real tragedy in life is being used by personally-minded men for purposes you recognize to be base. All the rest is at worst mere misfortune or mortality."

Burnham's life was varied and eventful — chockful of notable and noteworthy achievements and widely recognized distinction in many fields. But for all his versatility his greatest sources of personal satisfaction were his successes as a sportsman, explorer, Klondiker and — above all else — as a conservationist.....

When the actual end came on Sunday, September 24, 1939, the tributes to his memory came flooding in.

The New York *Times* Obituary:

### J. B. Burnham Dies
### Explorer, Author

Conservationist, 70, Fought for
Migratory Bird Treaty and
Game Law Enforcement

### LED EXPEDITION TO SIBERIA

Official of *Forest and Stream*
Magazine, 1891-97
Special to the New York *Times*
Willsboro, N.Y., Sept. 25th —

John Bird Burnham, author, explorer and conservationist, died at his home "Highlands," near here, on Sunday at the age of 70.

An outstanding figure in conservation work for many years Mr. Burnham was largely instrumental in getting the Migratory Bird Treaty ratified and legislation passed for the protection of migratory birds. He was the author of many articles on conservation and gave numerous lectures on the subject.

He served as president of the American Game Protection Association from 1911 to 1928 and was chairman of the Federal Advisory Committee to the Bureau of Biological Survey for twenty years. In 1926 he received the gold medal of the Camp-Fire Club of America.

Born at New Castle, Delaware in the house known as the Amstel House, now a museum, Mr. Burnham was the son of John and Elizabeth Van Leuveneigh Bird Burnham. He attended Rugby Military School in Wilmington, Del., and was graduated as the youngest man in his class from Trinity College, Hartford, Conn., in 1891.

He served as business manager of *Forest and Stream* magazine from 1891 to 1897, and was in the first Klondike gold rush in 1897-98.

## Helped Codify Game Law

From 1904 to 1910 he was successively chief game protector, deputy commissioner and acting commissioner of fish and game of the State of New York. He was one of a committee of three which, in 1915, codified the New York State Fish and Game Law.

Known as a big-game hunter in all parts of the United States, Mexico, Canada, Alaska and Siberia, Mr. Burnham led an expedition to Siberia in 1921 in quest of a rare specimen of mountain sheep. He traveled nearly 25,000 miles before he accomplished his mission. An account of his expedition appears in his book, "The Rim of Mystery."

Mr. Burnham, who wrote many letters to the New York *Times* on conservation and other topics over a period of years, furnished the State Department with much information bearing on the significance of the expedition that Vilhjalmur Stefansson sent to Wrangell Island in 1921-22.

He often expressed the opinion that hunters should be required to prove their fitness as sportsmen and their willingness to obey all laws before receiving permits to hunt wild game. In an article in the *North American Review* in September 1926, he wrote:

"I love Nature but I do not love it so much for the game in the game pocket as for the game in the fields and forests. I am always ready to give up the shooting when the interests of wild life demands it. In this I think I represent the attitude of all true sportsmen."

## Founded Summer Colony

Mr. Burnham's business interests were varied. He operated large timber holdings on a scientific basis and was said to be the largest builder of real log cabins in the United States. He was the owner of the Boquet Electric Power Company and the founder of the Crater Club Summer Colony in Essex, N.Y.

The first experimental fur-farm in the country was said to have been started on his estate. At his death he was interested in scientific deer farming. He was a director of the the Essex County National Bank and of the Essex Chamber of Commerce. He was a member of the Board of Supervisors of Essex County and was president of the Essex County Taxpayers Association.

Mr. Burnham was a member of thirty clubs, among them the Explorers, Camp-Fire and Boone and Crockett. He received the honorary degree of Doctor of Science of Conservation from Trinity College on June 21, 1938. He belonged to the Delta Kappa Epsilon Fraternity.

Surviving are his widow, the former Henrietta Heathcote Du Bois, whom he married on June 14, 1892, and three children — Rose Van L. Burnham and Koert D. Burnham of Essex and John D. Burnham of South Pasadena, Calif.[1]

---

*THE LUMBER CAMP NEWS*
January, 1940
Rev. George Webster
Pays Tribute To
John B. Burnham

John Bird Burnham was a quiet, unassuming, friendly man, "human" to the

---

[1] By permission of the New York *Times*.

core, staunch and fearless in his championship of any cause that appealed to his sense of right and justice. Few men of our day knew the Adirondack region better than he, or loved its mountains and forests more devotedly. He was one of the earliest of those who ventured into the Alaskan wilds and was much in demand at gatherings of men for addresses on the subject of these adventures.

This phase of his life has been written up in various magazine articles. The story of his Siberian trip was told by himself in a fine book, *The Rim of Mystery,* published by Putnams. During the later years of his life Mr. Burnham's business interests centered largely in the building of log cabins. As one who was honored with his friendship, and interested quite largely in what may be called the "Humanities," I have been particularly challenged by his interest in the men who worked for him, his devotion to their welfare and the welfare of their families. This has been much in evidence during these recent "depression years." His interest in the welfare of his workmen was matched in every way by their devotion to him. He was an official in the Protestant Episcopal Church, and was devoted to worship and work of that church, but his religious sympathies were very broad; his personal friends represented all Christian Communions, and he was not thought of as a churchman, but always as a man and a Christian.

---

## THE ASSOCIATION FOR THE PROTECTION of the ADIRONDACKS

50 Union Square
New York, N.Y.

October 20, 1939.

Mrs. John B. Burnham
Essex, New York

Dear Mrs. Burnham,
As Secretary of The Association for the Protection of the Adirondacks, I have been instructed by the Board of Trustees to submit to you the following Resolution which was adopted by the Board of Trustees, at the 306th meeting of the Board, held on October 18, 1939.

"On September 24th, 1939, at his home, The Highlands, in Essex County, New York, John B. Burnham passed from the forests and mountains he loved so well on the last great adventure. He rested, as he had asked, on pine boards cut from his own pine trees, and was carried by six of his long-time friends.

In his life and work, courage, friendship, loyalty and a love and appreciation of the beauty in Nature beyond the ordinary, were outstanding. He served the cause of conservation long and well. A keen hunter and explorer, he was yet always a leader in the battle for the preservation of the wild life of the streams, fields and forests, a hard fighter against a wrong, and a great and good friend to the right.

In recognition of his great service in the field of forest and wildlife conservation,

It is Moved that there be spread upon the Minutes of this Association this short tribute to his life and work as an expression of our sense of loss and of our sympathy for his family and friends who will miss him deeply.

Upon motion duly made, seconded and carried, this Resolution was adopted by a rising vote, and was spread upon the minutes."

Very truly yours,
Dyson Duncan,
Secretary

LCG:em

\* \* \* \* \* \*

The *Times* obituary, in spite of its necessarily factual content is nevertheless, if judged by the criterion of length alone, a very impressive cataloging of accomplishments. The warmer, more personal expression by his long-time friend, Rev. George Webster and by Dyson Duncan, add an even deeper dimension to our understanding and appreciation of the life, nature and accomplishments of John Bird Burnham — one of the most productive men of his time and ours as well.

# Part V

# Appendix

### Editorial Precede

*Admittedly and necessarily this is a rather formidable appendix but one which I felt had to be included in order to wrap up the project. Even though the text proper should have touched most of the required bases and presented a reasonably well-rounded word portrait of the man, it seemed that much first-class material was being left out because it could not be conveniently accommodated.*

*Moreover, these additional chapters, carrying as they do some of Burnham's most significant speeches and articles, deserved to be brought together and incorporated into this effort in order to make them more readily available to interested readers and researchers.*

*Furthermore, since during this era Burnham was unquestionably one of the preeminent figures in international as well as national conservation and since his important and varied contributions in that and other related fields have virtually receded into the records, basic justice required a fairly comprehensive presentation of his achievements.*

*Because there were at least fifteen essays that rated inclusion it was not easy to make the selection, but the soundest criterion seemed to call for the more noteworthy pieces covering the topics featured in the book itself. For instance — the Klondike, the Adirondacks, and those aspects of the state and national conservation scenes in which Burnham was deeply involved.*

*Friends who know the history of conservation and its heroes far better than I have pointed out that two of Burnham's speeches — "Thirty Years of Progress in Conservation" and "Conservation's False Prophets" — are considered landmark expressions of his conservation concepts, and are essentially valid even today. The well-informed also have stated that "Conservation's Debt to Sportsmen," while failing to give proper credit to the work of non-sportsmen, nevertheless is an eloquent expression of his particular viewpoints.*

*As has already been indicated the prolonged and frequently acrimonious feud with William T. Hornaday, an ardent protectionist who personified the present-day "Guns of Autumn" syndrome, eventually polarized the two diametrically opposed positions and split the entire conservation movement wide open, and the resulting rancor is evident even today.*

*While seemingly petty in some respects, especially in his estimate of F.D.R.'s character and career, the piece on the two Roosevelts nevertheless represents the candid, well-considered opinions of a man who had many firsthand opportunities to size up each of the presidents. Nor is it hard to understand why Burnham rated T. R. as the more admirable man.*

*The final three segments — "Unpopular Game Laws," "The History of the Deer in New York State" and "The Future of the Adirondack Park" — should be interesting not only to Adirondackers but could quite conceivably attract a wider range of readers as well.*

*The Editor*

# Chapter 1

## Characteristics of Klondikers

A traveler for a cigar house who spent twenty-four hours in the gateway city to the gold fields remarked on leaving that he had known all kinds of men from ministers of the gospel to Black Hills stage robbers — but that he had never had experience with such a gang of sharks and thieves as he met with at Skagway. Skagway and Dawson are a good deal alike in this respect, but their representative populations are in no way characteristic of the average men who go to the Klondike.

A large percentage of the men who go there to make their fortunes by mining are farmers or frugal, hard-working Swedes or Germans who have earned a livelihood as sailors or by other pursuits involving manual labor. A fortune may mean anything from a thousand to a million dollars, according to the standpoint of the man expressing the opinion. It is surprising how modest many of the ideals of wealth are, and it would seem that more men say they will be content with $10,000 or less than place the figures above that amount. These men, even if in their inmost hearts they dream of duplicating the millions of Alex McDonald, have taken their measure with the rich and prosperous men of the world and realize that the mention of vast wealth in connection with their names would sound ridiculous. On the other hand, they argue that a country that makes some men millionaires in a lucky moment has possibilities for everyone, and that there must be here and there little bonanzas overlooked by the more successful that will give them their opportunity. A few thousand dollars would buy these men fame or assure them a comfortable old age, and some of them really have no higher ambition.

There is another class of Klondikers whose price of contentment is never placed below a hundred thousand dollars. These are men who think in large figures. They have handled large sums or associated with men of wealth, or possibly they have been rich themselves. The number of "has-beens" in the Klondike is larger that one would suppose. It includes men who were successful as bankers, real estate and stock speculators, pork packers, commissioned men and representatives of all the leading money-making inventions. A large number of the "has-beens" came from the ranks of owners of silver-mining properties. Among the men who were sent down to Fort Yukon to winter on charity are several Colorado mine-owners who a few years ago could have their checks in six figures honored. The largest number, however, are probably old miners who struck it rich in former excitements and lost their money trying to get more, or in dissipation. The old saying "easy come, easy go" finds its verification in mining. Major Walsh, the governor of the Provisional District of the Yukon, had in his employ at the Big Salmon River last Winter a Canadian half-breed named Ambrose, who several years ago discovered rich mines at Rat Portage. He had always had an ambition to be a steamboat captain and the first thing he did with his newly-acquired wealth was to buy a steamboat on Lake Superior and install himself as her chief officer. He had other expensive hobbies and went through his money at a glorious pace. Last Fall he got a job in the Mounted Police Force, it being recorded among his other qualifications that he was an ex-steamboat captain. Governor Walsh heard this and put him in charge of one of the boats going down the River, but a single day's experience in the rough waters of Lake Bennett effectively removed all ambition to shine as a sailor from the breast of Ambrose. So he went to the Governor and applied for the job of cook as better suited to his abilities.

The man who led the vanguard of those working into the Klondike last Winter was an old-timer named McNeally, who has been at every mining excitement in the last fifty years and who came to the Yukon direct from Bulwayo, South Africa. He is nearly seventy years of age and has struck it rich more than once. When he was eighteen he had 160 men working for him on a gold proposition he had discovered, and later at the Cassiar digging in British Columbia he made a good thing at river-bed mining. McNeally is a man of temperate habits and usually well-informed and shrewd. He lost his money, he says, trying to get more. Now he seems to have no particular ambition except to earn enough to keep up with each new rush whether the discovery be made in Africa, Australia or the Mountains of the Moon. He could not settle down to anything else in his time of life.

McNeally says that the number of men who find gold is a ridiculously small proportion of the number who constitute a rush. At the Florence craze for instance, way back in the "60's, out of 20,000 men who went to the mines only two hundred found gold. A town-site promoter named Casey, who follows mining excitements round the globe as a business, overheard the remark and said that at Ronsburg in Southern California, whose fame as a gold camp is well known, the town lots alone sold for more money than the mines ever produced. Such statements furnish food for reflection for prospective Klondikers.

Another old-timer at Dawson was Tibbitts, the discoverer of the American mining district in British Columbia. He came to the Klondike from Cook's Inlet in July but in November had not succeeded in locating anything so was a thoroughly disgusted man. Dozens of claims were being filed every day with the gold commissioner, but Tibbitts declared they were wild-cat and refused to put his name to anything of whose merit he was not convinced. He characterized Dawson as the toughest mining camp he ever struck and said that the majority of the population were speculators and swindlers, that the chief topic of conversation was grub, and that to keep a thing from being stolen a man had to sit on it with a cocked rifle.

Old McNeally was alone and had nearly reached the Hootalinqua River when seen in January. The next Argonaut was also an old man traveling alone, who in January had reached the head of Lake Lebarge. He had sunk $10,000 hard-earned money in a pork-packing establishment in Iowa which was rendered unremunerative through the finessing of the big men in the trade with whom he had become a competitor. He still had some money left and hoped to retrieve his fortune as a broker in claims.

A great many lawyers, doctors and other professional men were in the crowd working their way toward the gold fields. The man who devised the method of measuring the curvature of the eyeball mechanically wintered on the Skagway trail with a judge from Great Falls, Montana. Caught by the ice at Five Finger Rapids, Colonel Samuel Ward of Helena, Montana, a millionaire mine-owner, lawyer and public character, spent the Winter chafing at his enforced inactivity. Working on Macauley's and Kline's tramway around White Horse Rapids and the Canyon are two successful physicians, one marine chief engineer with papers of unlimited tonnage, two machinists, one Salt Lake City ex-police captain, two well-known caterers from Salt Lake who ran the best restaurants in the city, two bookkeepers and stenographers and one ex-mine superintendent. These men were all successful in their various pursuits and the compensations which they expect are no doubt large.

It is not always safe to argue, however, that money is the main inducement in leading any particular man to the Klondike. Many of those from the higher walks of life were influenced by other motives. Some went as a relaxation from overwrought mental and nervous conditions; others to bury domestic griefs, and still others for the healthful excitements of the wild life. The best original motive was that influencing a lawyer from Tennessee, a man well-advanced in age, who said that he went to be where money was plenty. All his life he came in contact only with people of moderate circumstances, and his wish was before he died to see money flowing lavishly, to be in the company of men who didn't know how rich they were and who spent money with both hands and damned the consequences.

# Chapter 2

**Personal Opinions About Some Unusual Men**

As long as I can remember I have been a hero-worshipper. Despite the fact that I have found my heroes all have feet of clay they still held my admiration. To me their failings bring them closer as fellow human-beings while their strengths still make them heroes. It is the same with my friends. I love the good in my friends while knowing the worst. I think it is for that reason that I can read "debunking" books without becoming disillusioned.

I have always believed — with Pope — that the proper study of mankind is man. It is fascinating to meet people of accomplishment and study them on the basis of the first instinctive judgment. I find all kinds of stimulation and value in those to whom I am attracted, and derive pleasure and moral profit from the meeting and almost always the first impression is sustained.

On the other hand, I must admit, I have made many mistakes in under-appraising people who did not at once favorably impress me. In these cases I am very sure that the lack of perception was mine.

For years before I met him Raold Amundsen was one of my heroes. When I came face to face with him during the month we were held up in Nome for lack of steamship service, he exceeded my expectations and I could find no flaw in him — nothing selfish, petty or disgusting.

Amundsen was a finely setup man with military bearing and he had a noble head with features suggestive of the eagle. He was physically and mentally capable to a degree rarely found in combination, and he had that instinctive understanding of others that makes what is called personal magnetism. He had to perfection the quality of leadership and I am convinced if he had not been a great explorer and had the opportunity he would have been one of the world's great generals.

Amundsen had just completed the Northeast Passage, thus making him the only explorer who had circumnavigated the North Polar basin. Long before, he had made the Northwest Passage and he had been the first to reach the South Pole. His record of accomplishment has never been excelled. I was interested to find him a warm-hearted human-being and not a ruthless driver.

Charley Carpendale, the Australian, was a Siberian trader with an Eskimo wife; he realized his responsibility to his half-breed children. The cost of these results of mésalliances in the North is hard, particularly for the girls. There is no place for them except to go native or worse. Amundsen knew this, so he persuaded Carpendale to let him take his beautiful little daughter Cosconito, aged eleven, home with him to Norway, where he said there

*Raold Amundsen at Nome in 1921. (Lomen's photo)*

*Lincoln Ellsworth and Raold Amundsen over North Pole from* First Crossing of the Polar Sea *by Amundsen and Ellsworth. Doubleday 1928.*

was no prejudice against mixed blood and where she might look forward to a happy future. He also took along another little girl, as a companion for Cosconito, who looked all Eskimo, though one can never tell because the native blood is more potent than the white in controlling racial appearance. They were to be taken care of at his sister's home and educated. This kind of benevolence was very dear to Amundsen.

The men who sailed with Amundsen loved him and trusted him implicitly. This is noteworthy in view of the high percentage of mutinies and lesser insubordinations in the history of Arctic expeditions, for Winter darkness breeds ugliness in men. I met Amundsen usually in the loyal family circle of the Lomens in one of the Farthest North homes of culture in the world, and it was a delightful experience I shall never forget.

Some years later my good opinion of Amundsen had an interesting confirmation. Karl Frederick and I were trying to get permission from the Soviet Government to fly from Alaska to Mount Matassingi at the eastern end of the Stanavoie mountains in Siberia and, having been told that Grant Schley, the banker, had great influence with Moscow, I got an introduction to him. When I had stated the object of my visit, Schley put me through a course of sprouts. Did I know Amundsen and what did I think of him?

In most cases the man who asks such a question is prejudiced unfavorably against the subject. I feared I would get in wrong with Mr. Schley right at the start, but I could not temporize or qualify so I came out flat-footed despite the fact that Amundsen was at that time under a cloud. "Amundsen," I said, "is a man among men, great in his personal honor and achievement." To my relief I saw that the answer pleased Schley. "Did you know that Lincoln Ellsworth is my brother-in-law?" he asked. He saw before I could answer that I had not known this fact and immediately shot another question at me: "What do you think of Nobile?"

"I have never met Nobile," I said, "but I do not like him as a result of the controversy he is having with Amundsen."

"You are dead right in both of your judgments," said Schley. "I will tell you something. After Lincoln got to know Amundsen and they had worked out the airship plan for crossing the blind spot in the Arctic, Lincoln went to his father and asked him for a large sum of money. He did not expect to get it, but to his surprise his father told him he would let him have it on two conditions. Lincoln asked the conditions and his father said "First, that you prove to me Amundsen is a man of honor and, second, that you give up smoking.' Without batting an eye Lincoln agreed."

"It was my job to find out about Amundsen. In various ways I followed him all over the world wherever he had been, but chiefly the investigation was in his home country. My agents developed a lot of interesting stuff, but — and this is the real point — *nowhere* did they turn up one incident discreditable to the man. On the other hand they reported a lot of very fine things, which is unusual in such an investigation. The same cannot be said about the other man."

Amundsen qualified by the classical test that a man cannot be said to have lived well until he has died well. Two noble actions marked the end. A famous association awarded him a gold medal, its highest honor — and almost immediately revoked the award. Unaware of the fact, the newspapers panned Amundsen for his hasty departure from America without waiting to receive the medal, and Amundsen did not enlighten them. He preferred to shoulder the blame rather than enter into an unseemly controversy. Then he went home to give his life in an airplane search for his avowed enemy, Nobile. [See note on Page 220.]

Only the officers of the famous association know the real reason why the award of the medal was revoked, but it is a surmise that the action was taken because Amundsen visited

Dr. Cook in Leavenworth Prison. The great association had taken pride in unmasking Cook's claim to have reached the North Pole. To them Cook was all wet and they did not bother to learn that aside from an imagination that knew no limits, Cook was a pretty decent man after all. Amundsen and Cook had been shipmates on an early Antarctic trip, and at that time the Doctor had been the life of the party, keeping them in health as much by his friendliness as by his medical skill. Amundsen knew perfectly well that his action in visiting a convicted felon would be severely criticised. He knew that Cook had shoals of enemies among those who had suffered from the promotions for which he was the figurehead. He knew that Cook was a prevaricator and the butt of every jokesmith in the country. He knew that he had everything to lose and nothing to gain by making the visit, but he also knew the good in that abnormal man, his need for sympathy and he put aside prudence and personal considerations. This, I think, was the finest action in Amundsen's life out of many fine ones, and an action every man might envy.

I knew Dr. Cook, and while I laughed at him with the rest, I never could feel the bitterness against him which that unfortunate man universally provoked. He seemed to me just an overgrown boy whose imagination had gotten too much juice from the pituitary gland or whatever it is that causes abnormal growth. I have a grandson with a vivid imagination. One day at the dining table he was romancing about some impossible thing which had happened to him and his mother was about to punish him for lying, when a friend who was present interposed: "Don't put a check on the boy's imagination," he said, "just teach him to know when he oversteps the line between fact and fiction. I do not care what that boy is going to be — business man, artist or member of a profession; imagination will be an invaluable aid in his work. No one can amount to anything without imagination. The one thing the boy must learn is to differentiate between fancy and fact. Have him stern with himself on the subject of lying, and when he wants to romance require him to preface his statement with the proper label."

Cook was probably blamed for the shortcomings of his parents. They apparently let him believe in his own wild imaginings until he could not distinguish truth from falsity. If it had not been for this failure in his upbringing, Dr. Cook might well have gone down in history as a world hero instead of a Baron Munchausen. It is possible that he was the first man to reach the North Pole, but he did not have sufficient training in science to prove the fact, if fact it was. If he had been a man with reverence for the truth, on his return to civilization he would have frankly stated that he had made a long trip over the ice north of Ellesmere Island to the neighborhood of the Pole, and then he would have won respect and admiration for his daring. No one denies that he was on the Paleocrystic ice north of Grant Land, and it is certain that on the way back he made one of the most remarkable journeys in history in covering the distance from Ellesmere Island to the settlements in Greenland. This known journey alone would have given him a place in the forefront of Arctic explorers. Only Stefansson has excelled Cook in his mastery of rapid travel in the North, in his adaptability and ability to sustain life without access to the resources required by other explorers.

At the time of the Cook fiasco, as one of the Governors of the Arctic Club, I was asked by newspapers whether or not I thought Cook had reached the North Pole. Knowing Cook's failings I told them I had not the faintest idea, but I added that his itinerary was possible.

This, as I recollect, was in 1909. Ten years before I had written an article for *Forest and Stream* in which I attempted to show that the Pole could be attained without very great difficulty by following the method later used by Cook and in part by Peary. The distance is only about five hundred miles from bases explorers are able to reach with comparative ease. McKercher and I had made an equivalent distance in the winter of '97-'98 pulling our

Dr. Frederick A. Cook

Vilhjalmur Stefansson at "Highlands"

Lieut. Robert E. Peary, Arctic Explorer,
Discoverer of the North Pole, April 6, 1909.

sleds over the terrifically rough ice jams of the Yukon River in temperatures lower than those of the Polar Basin. With a dog team the thousand-mile round-trip to the Pole and back would present less difficulty.

As the land masses were left behind the ice would in all probability become progressively smoother, and on the return trip with lightened sledges distances of thirty to fifty miles per day could be accomplished. I argued that the fatal mistake previous explorers had made was to select Summer for the time of their "dashes." Then the ice is not only quite generally covered with water but it is also broken with openings which have to be detoured or crossed with boats, or on ice cakes at great loss of time. As General Greely stated two miles per day is good time to make under such conditions. Nansen could have reached the Pole but he got cold feet, figuratively speaking, and he also failed to adapt himself to conditions. For example he and his companion, instead of stripping down when exercising, allowed perspiration to accumulate on their bodies with the result that they were clammy and so miserably cold when they started to hitch up their dogs in the morning that they lost whole days. They would have to stop and wrestle with each other to start the circulation and get warmth, and meanwhile the dogs were fighting and tangling their harnesses. Nansen was a great man, and so were Scott and Shackleton, but as explorers they lacked the experience and adaptability of Amundsen and Stefansson. For ability to cover Arctic ice without support no one has ever equaled Stefansson. Rasmussen, perhaps, approached him most nearly.

No man ever confronted the unknown with greater courage than Stefansson and few with an equal mental equipment. He absorbed the experiences of other travellers and the best of native experiences and with logic laid and carried out his plans of travel. He attained such a mastery of the difficulties of the North that he called the Arctic friendly. And this was no pose on his part. He made the Arctic friendly by taming it to his own convenience.

Yet Stefansson, like other mortals, has his feet of clay. To my surprise I found this in his sensitiveness to the opinions of others. At his request I had written a review of *The Friendly Arctic* for *American Game*. When Ray Holland, the Editor, read it he asked me if I was sure my review was what Stefansson wanted. I was sure because Stef had told me he wanted something that would boost the sale of the book, and with this end in view I had controversially omitted the soft soap. I had stated things which I thought would interest people to buy the book and see for themselves, such as disasters and mutiny.

"Yes," said Holland, "you say Stefansson went North with the best-equipped expedition that ever entered the Arctic and that immediately things went to smash. I don't think he would like it." And so the article was sent to Stefansson.

Promptly I received a 16-page letter from Stefansson to the effect that he was not the only explorer whose men had mutinied. He started with Christopher Columbus and went right on down through the list, and he told many things that are not common knowledge because interested governments or agencies suppressed them. It was a wonderful letter, but I never answered it because the only answer I could have made was that in all the list (barring one or two who were murdered) Stefansson was the only man who had not man-handled his mutiny.

Next Harold Noice, the explorer, who was living with Stefansson on Barrow Street, because as Harold naively said, the name suggested Point Barrow, the northernmost part of Alaska, called on me and asked for permission to change the article. He had already, it appeared, made the desired changes in the manuscript. I looked them over and told him we would print the article in the changed form provided he would sign his name to it. He had reversed every statement I had made which was at all critical of his Master. I remember

Harold and I got into a row over the question of seal meat which had been cooked up as an article of diet. I had said that I had known tough and roughneck traders who held stick camphor under their noses while blubber-eating Eskimos were around, to prevent vomiting. I asked Harold if he had the choice when hungry between seal meat and anything else he had ever eaten, if he would not take the other thing in preference to the seal meat, and he parried the question by asking if I had ever eaten dog. I would not reverse my opinions and Harold would not sign the article, so it ended by our giving Harold forty dollars to write an entirely new review of the *Friendly Arctic*. It was a good one at that.

In spite of the strong difference of opinion Stefansson, as indicated by this letter, remained on reasonably friendly terms with Burnham over the years.

Vilhjalmur Stefansson<br>36 Bedford Street<br>New York

March 9, 1929.

Dear Burnham:
    Didn't I give you several of my books?
    And even if it be overpayment, or payment with compound interest, haven't I one coming — your "Rim of Mystery?"

Stef.

*Note: Nobile, designer and pilot of the airship Norge on the Amundsen-Ellsworth North Pole flight on May 12, 1926 later repeated the trip, crashed on May 25 but was rescued.*
*Amundsen led an air search for the Italian but was never heard from again.*

# Chapter 3

## PIONEERS and EXPLORERS

Pioneers and explorers are chips off the same block. In one way they are typified by Kipling's uneasy fellow who heard a voice, an "Everlasting whisper day and night repeating. Something hidden, Go and find it. Something lost behind the ranges, lost and waiting for you, Go! Yes, your never-never country. Yes, your edge of cultivation." Rowland Robinson, our dear old sage of North Ferrisburg, Vermont, puts it differently through the mouth of Sam Lovell, "It comes nateral for me," says Sam, "to run in the woods..... The air o' the woods tastes good ter me, fer't haint ben breathed by nuthin but wild creeters. I luffter breathe it 'fore common folks has."

"The smell o' the woods smells good to me, dead leaves 'n' spruce boughs 'n' rotten wood 'n' it don't hurt none if it's spiced up a leetle bit wi' skunk an' mink an' weasel an' fox p' fum 'ry. An' I luffter see trees 'at's older'n any man, an' graound 't wan't plowed ner hoed, a-growing' nat'ral crops. 'N' I luffter hear the stillness o' the woods, for 'tis still there. Wind a-sythin, leaves a-rustlin', brooks a-runnin', birds a-singin'. Even a blue jay a-squallin' haint noises. It takes folks an' waggins an' cattle an' pigs an' sech ter make a noise."

It was such inspirations that moved our ancestors to go out and settle the wilderness and enjoy the hardships of a rough life, and today the curiosity as to what lies behind the ranges and the love of air that has not been contaminated motivate the explorer.

My friend Clarkson Cowl says that the average city dweller today has had his brain prostituted by jazz[1] the movies and the tabloids and that he has lost his initiative and his judgment, that he has become sheep-minded and is interested only in being wet-nursed by the Government.

This type of man certainly cannot understand the motivation of a Stanley or an Amundsen. Hardship is just what he does not want, and he cannot be shown the attractions that Kipling and Robinson told of.

Henry Van Dyke, in his noble poem, "Hudson's Last Voyage," likewise wrote: "One sail in sight upon the lonely sea,
   And only one! For never ship of mine
Has dared these waters,"

Hudson soliloquizes, as from the small boat in which his mutinous sailors have marooned him to die, he looks at his departing vessel. He watched his ship until —

---
[1] Add T.V. — For obvious reasons. The Editor

"Look, — there she goes — her topsails in the sun
   Gleam from the ragged ocean edge and drop clean out of sight!"
Then he turns to his little son in the boat leaning his head against Hudson's knee and reminds him of a former voyage —
"It was then I vowed
   My sailor-soul and yours to search the sea
Until we found the water path
   From Europe into Asia."
Van Dyke has him say,
"I believe that God has poured the ocean round his world,
   Not to divide, but to unite the lands.
And all the English captains that have dared
   In little ships to plough uncharted waves,
—Davis and Drake, Hawkins and Frobisher, Raleigh and Gilbert, —
   All the other names, —
Are written in the Chivalry of God
   As men who served His purpose.
I would claim
   A place among that Knighthood of the Sea;
And I have earned it, though my quest should fail."

The poem ends with words that I profoundly wish could be burned into the wavering minds of present-day Americans:
"We'll keep the honor of a certain aim
   Amid the peril of uncertain ways,
And sail ahead, and leave the rest to God."

    There you have the answer: The sheep-minded ask of explorers, "What's the use?"

    The first settlers had hardships, but every hardship had its compensation. Their first job was to build comfortable log cabins. Next, they made clearings in the forest and burned the slash. The following Spring they started their farm by going among the blackened stumps and with an old axe making gashes in the soil, into which they dropped kernels of seed corn, completing the job by closing the gash with their feet. They planted potatoes and maybe some small grains. Then they went hunting till the crops should ripen. Some of them had cows at pasture on neighboring beaver-meadows and possibly a horse. They were masters of all they surveyed. Their life taught them to be ingenious and resourceful, and bred that rugged individualism that made our country an outstanding nation of men.

    It is not hard to believe that if America had started in the cities we would be no better off now than is China. Unfortunately, we cannot forever live on the results of the hardships and sacrifices of our ancestors. We must renew the vital strain. To do it we must go back to the good earth — to the untainted air....

    The C.C.C. was founded on a good idea but like most of its companion measures it was sissified and tainted with the thought of giving the people security. That kind of security is the last thing that a vital people wants — particularly young people. What they need for their souls is good <u>insecurity.</u>

    The C.C.C. was founded on an idea of the late Professor William James of Harvard and expressed by him in one of his essays.[1] His idea was character building through hardship and dangerous pursuits — not providing jobs for young men. He argued against war,

---

[1]. James, William, "The Moral Equivalent of War" — *Memories and Studies*. Boston: Longmans, Green, 1911 pp290-1.

but he wanted to provide a substitute for war that would teach young men some of the lessons of war — to be courageous and self-reliant and friendly, and tolerant of their fellows. William James proposed a universal conscription of the young men of the nation without regard to their social standing or wealth at a time in their formative manhood, and he proposed making them carry on the toughest and hardest jobs to be found — such as tunnel diggers, ship's crews, laborers on construction projects, mining and mucking. While I have not too much sympathy for C.C.C. as carried on, I would give my right hand to see James' unprostituted idea put into effect.

I would like to see men developed who, if occasion required, could amputate one of their own limbs, as was the case with one of our Western pioneers. Finding that no one else was willing to cut off his gangrenous leg, this man got a saw, and a knife and an old rifle barrel which he heated in a fire for cauterization purposes. Then he cut back the flesh above the knee, sawed the bone off and turned back the flesh to cover it. He made such a good job of it that he recovered and lived to an old age. That was rugged individuality for you! The kind that pulls out of almost any kind of trouble <u>and</u> is not built up by security or soft living.

Why does mankind thrill to accounts of heroism, saving sailors from a wreck at sea for example in the face of death, if this kind of thing is not a birthright? And, conversely, why does everyone despise a man who saves his life at the expense of ignominy? Self-sacrifice and courage, thank God, are still ideals worth striving for. As long as such ideals endure, over and above food and clothes and security, there is hope....

# Chapter 4

**The Subjective Mind**

When the elder Pierrepont Morgan stated before a committee of Congress that he would lend a man a million dollars on his looks alone, he testified to the powers of his own intuition which were the next thing to infallible. I have a theory that intuition, which is a faculty of the subjective mind, should be cultivated. Training in school and in life is centered on the reasoning mind, and no attention is paid to the part behind consciousness. Most people at the end of life have a less serviceable subjective mind than when they started life. I think they can get more from living if both parts of the brain are carried along on something like an equal basis.

The subjective mind governs the involuntary actions of the body such as breathing and the circulation of the blood, but it also has many diversified functions, telepathic and the like, which can not be claimed as automatic. It is the mind of animals. When we speak of animals being governed by instinct and not by reason we express the difference, which also points to the fact that man, possessing both kinds of mind, registers contempt for one part and calls himself a reasoning being. I think man has made a mistake on this, as great a mistake as when he fails to make use of his latent capacities.

Did you ever watch a startled flock of sandsnipes skimming low along the water's edge and notice how in a split second the direction of flight is changed, with every bird keeping his place in the compact body? Compare this with airplanes flying in formation and one of the marvelous achievements of man's reasoning mind has to take second place — and a low second place at that. The tiny sandsnipe instantly responds to a mind development of which man is incapable, largely, I think, because he refuses to utilize a power which he has by inheritance.

When my four children were young I could not lose them. I tested this out by taking them into strange woodlands and, after they had wandered all around looking for flowers or other objects of interest, I would ask one the way to go in returning; the child never failed to point in the right direction. I doubt if they could do it so unfailingly today, simply because an unused faculty atrophies.

Birds, fish and animals in their migrations cover the uncharted ways of the world without error. Salmon which spend their lives in the Pacific Ocean come back to spawn and die in the same stream where they were born. One of the bird families migrates from near the North Pole well to the Antarctic and returns in order, no doubt, to get maximum sunshine through the year. Bees carried miles away in light, tight boxes, return to their hives. Why should not men be equally capable if the doctrine of evolution is true? The fact that certain persons can do almost as well as the lower orders in tests like these shows that mankind by the large has thrown away its birthright.

Most people will at once say that the sense of direction is not a worthwhile asset in our modern life, but sometimes a fellow goes off on a hunting trip and gets lost!

The sense of direction, however, is but one of the manifestations of the subjective mind. There are others equally important. How did Pierrepont Morgan keep his money when, as he testified, he would lend a man he did not know a million dollars without security? He could not reason out that the individual was a safe risk without facts as premises on which to base a conclusion, so the subjective mind was called into play to determine the man's character. Morgan formed an intuitive judgment. You can get close to crows when you haven't a gun but, believe me, they know when you have designs on their lives.

When the country banker lends an individual money without collateral, he does so because he feels sure the man will repay the loan. The borrower gives either a written or an oral statement of his assets and hopes, but the really good banker pays less attention to this than to sizing up his customer on the basis that character cannot be as easily faked as figures. If the banker has a well-developed subjective mind he rarely makes mistakes in granting loans, and he becomes famous for his judgment of character.

This same intuition plays a part in all the affairs of business. Thousands of plans for promotions, consolidations and reorganizations were submitted to Morgan for his approval or rejection. We may be sure that to the reasoning minds of his subordinates these plans all had their merits and that the balance sheets passed the bookkeeper's tests. Otherwise, they would have been thrown out before reaching the court of last resort. Some of the plans which pleased those who had recommended them Morgan accepted, but others the great man disapproved for reasons the bankers could not fathom. It is said that even if he had wanted to do so Morgan could not have explained why he had rejected these plans. He had acted intuitively in the same way he formed his opinions of character.

No man can be a success as a gambler in a game that is not entirely crooked unless he has a highly-developed subjective mind. Reasoning alone never brings the hunches that cause a man to wager his all on the turn of a single card to win a fortune.

I believe that no one can be great in any line of human endeavor who has not a well-developed dual mind. The saying that poets are born, not made, is sound because experience has taught us there are limits to cultivation of the reasoning mind. Imagination is a function of the natural mind and it is not acquired by reasoning. Business men, poets, artists, scientists, writers and gamblers — in fact all of us are as brass and tinkling cymbals without it. Curious that the logical thinkers have little of a favorable nature to say of the subjective mind and seem to regard it as a moronic quality. But I suppose this is only natural to those who have pride of intellect. These cultured ones will laugh when I say that I believe the subjective mind is the seat of the soul.

All religion is primarily founded on faith and faith is not a property of the reasoning mind, which has to be shown. Nor is conscience a reasoned process. Love without thought of reward, childlike hope, charity, abnegation and self-sacrifice are not gems of the intellect. All the basic qualities of Christianity and of the soul which prompts it, including the so-called qualities of heart come from the subjective mind. So also in this mind is the zest of that mysterious quality of telepathy, which is so important in life to a thorough understanding between people. You enjoy a friend who can read your thoughts. I believe that the true love of Nature comes from a telepathic interchange between the inanimate and the animate. The printed page is telepathic and it gives one pleasure to understand what the author has in mind before he says it. In business it is valuable to read through the mind the motives which lie behind and are never mentioned. The major pleasure of a great painting or any work of art lies in its suggestion. Those who miss all this are to be pitied.

When I come to write about this kind of thing I particularly realize the limitations of my reasoning mind and I wish I had it better trained; also that I knew the rudiments of psychology, for then I could make a stronger case for something I intuitively know to be true. Intuitively, I know I am right and my experience supports my statements. I have led an adventurous life and many times I would have cashed in my chips or failed of my objective except for the hunches of the subjective mind. Nothing in the world except instinct tells you how far you can with safety press a dangerous man who is shooting at you. The first shots, like the Indians' war whoops, are likely to be intended to terrify; but as you keep closing in it is important to know just where the point is reached when the gunman either loses his nerve or else decides to kill.

A vivid personal experience convinces me of this amazing mental faculty. At seven o'clock one clear August evening "Jake" Mussen and I stood among the spruces that clothed the valley of the Koidern River below the Nutzotin Mountains in Yukon Territory and debated whether or not we would be able to find our packs of food and blankets which we had thoughtlessly left that morning without checking the location. The day had been spent looking up a moose which Mussen had killed 24 hours before. With a marvelous place memory, Mussen had followed his devious hunting track for miles over moss which had retained no record of his passage until, just as night was upon us, he had found the carcass. Now with the tenderloins in our possession the problem confronted us of returning to our packs in a bee-line across five miles of wilderness in the dark.

Here was a case where the most accurate surveying instruments and the best calculations of the reasoning mind would not have helped us. With unknown local attractions and other uncalculable factors of error it would have been remarkable if any surveyor could have run a line across that five miles of terrain and come within a hundred feet of the objective, but to find the packs in the dark no error whatever was permissible. They had to be hit directly on the nose or not at all. So we started, governed by pure instinct and dismissing any slightest attempt to reason out our direction.

After a mile or so our course brought us out from the spruce forest into a burned foothill country which extended for many miles between the Nutzotins and the White River. Every acre of this country was just like the other acres, a monotonous succession of low gravelly ridges with no distinctive features of any kind. Mile after mile of burned and blackened skeletons of trees, and regularly recurring windrows of glacial boulders. No individualistic masses of rock in place that might have served as landmarks.

About eleven that night, while I was temporarily held up by a slash, Mussen took the lead. Almost at once I told him he was going too far to the left. He stopped and, pointing to a tree with a broken top, said: 'We passed that tree on our way out this morning. That proves I am right!' I began an argument with him but cut it short. "Jake," I said, "if I try to reason the thing out I shall lost my hunch. Your memory is infallible and I do not for one moment doubt your identification of that tree, but that means nothing to me. You go your way and I'll go mine. When I find the packs I will build a fire for a signal." I had to speak confidently because one must have implicit faith in his hunch to make it operative. Just befor midnight I found the packs by falling over one of them, finding that it was softer than a rock and realizing that the objective had been reached. I lit a fire, fired my rifle, and had supper nearly cooked before Mussen came in.

Dr. George H. Wright of New Milford, Connecticut and I were years ago with a hunting party camped on Trout Brook, in Northern Maine. We decided to take a three-day exploratory hike on the legs of a triangle. We spent the first night out at the Webster camp on Courdnahunk Lake. The next day we traveled "by guess and by God" to the Finch lumber camps near Talos Lake, finding them at night at ten o'clock with the thermometer at 22 below zero and our trousers frozen so that they slatted and rattled at every step. The third day we headed for our camp on Trout Brook, but an hour after we started Wright wounded a nice buck we were not able to secure until four o'clock on a November day.

The deer had pursued a most erratic course and we had no idea where we were. Neither of us had ever before been in this part of the wilderness. After dressing out the saddles and head and leaving them sitting up on the ground, we set out for camp by instinct. Again our way was through a monotonous brulé (burned-over) country with no landmarks. It had been snowing fitfully through the afternoon, but now the flakes fell faster and soon our vision was limited as we could not see with surety where to make the next step. There was no wind, however, and the storm was not a blizzard. Seven hours later, without any change in direction, we walked directly into our camp, a river-drivers' open lean-to tent....

When we waked in the morning it was to find that more than a foot of new snow had fallen during the night. Old Jock Darling, the famous guide who was with us, like most woodsmen and all Indians, had a place memory, reasoning type of mind, said: "Well, boys, your deer is lost just as much as if it was sunk in the middle of Moosehead Lake. You cannot follow back your tracks and you have no landmarks to go by in that brulé." Wright, however, was anxious to get the head and the venison and so we started.

First, however, we went a couple of miles up Trout Brook with DuBois and Hoisington to show them where I had a deer hung up, which they had agreed to drag back to camp; and then Wright and I started seven miles across country by a new route on what the others all thought was a wild-goose chase. About one o'clock I kicked up blood in the snow — and there within two feet was the saddle and head looking for all the world like snow-covered stumps....

In northern Bering Sea magnetic variations are extremely erratic. At times the compass goes crazy; there are uncharted coasts and other sea-lines where mariners have nothing more accurate to depend on than the hasty observations of Vitus Bering and Captain Cook. Currents are strong and changeable and for days on end the sea is blanketed with fog. Ship captains who are not "psychic" simply don't last. Yet there are captains having the instincts of walruses and polar bears who year in and year out keep off the reefs. Wiley Post flew "blind" the 2200 miles from the big bend of the Amur River and hit Nome square between the eyes. Ben Eileson flew from Point Barrow to Dead Man's Island in Evalbang Archipelago by instinct, refusing to let Wilkins check up by landing.

The fact that there are men who can do this kind of thing proves the value of the subjective mind.

# Chapter 5

## Personalities of the Two Roosevelts

T. R. cleaned the Augean stables at Albany while Frank's most notable result as governor was the hundred million deficiency he left behind. Over the years I had contact with both President Roosevelts, "Teddy" and "Frank," and I think Theodore was infinitely the greater man. I prefer the Square Deal to the New Deal. Franklin Roosevelt is a loveable man of high principles who courageously overcame a physical handicap that would have floored most men. He is too recently in the picture to give a final estimate of his character. As the Greeks said, "A man cannot be said to have lived well until he has died gloriously."

I first knew Franklin Roosevelt when I was Deputy Fish and Game Commissioner under Thomas Mott Osborne, whom I succeeded as Acting Commissioner under Governor Dix of New York. He had been elected to the State Senate and the politicians regarded him first as a joke and then as a nuisance.

In deference to his family name, he had been given the chairmanship and worked with the conservationists, but soon the hard-boiled senators of both parties got together and his chairmanship became only an empty title. This was at the time when August Silz, the big-game dealer, was supplying John W. Gates and his questionable crowd with illegal game for campaign dinners, and when Silz was riding high and pretty at the Capitol as a result of a $25,000 campaign contribution. To give the atmosphere: I was working late one evening in my office checking for possible errors and engrossed in a copy of a codification fish and game measure when an Old Guard senator came in and, seeing what I was doing, sniffed contemptuously: "That bill is not worth the paper it is printed on!" He said: "Let me tell you something" — and proceeded to show me that the engrossed copies of the measure due for passage the next day had been altered to give the game dealers what they wanted. This senator must have been overlooked when the pop was distributed, for his sole idea now was to get the bill passed in proper form. John Wilson of the bill-drafting department had told me a while before he had been offered a thousand dollars a word to change the bill, so I was ready to believe the senator, who happened to be "Joe" Allds. "I'll spike their gun. I'll get correct copies substituted for the crooked ones and they'll never know the difference until the bill is passed!"

This kind of man and Roosevelt did not mix any more than water and wine so when Roosevelt arranged a joint committee hearing for several hundred conservationists from over the State, all the senators and assemblymen of his own party and most of the Republican legislators absented themselves in order to humiliate the chairman.

*F.D.R. as Secretary of Navy April 4, 1917 (Courtesy of F.D. Roosevelt Library)*

The regulars wanted "Blue-Eyed Billy" Sheehan for U.S. senator, but Thomas Mott Osborne and Roosevelt built up an opposition that defeated him and resulted in the naming of the more statesman-like O. Gorman.

Years later when I was president of the American Game Association and the World War was on, I received a pathetic letter from a former office boy telling me that he had been convicted of desertion from the Navy and sentenced to three years in Leavenworth Penitentiary. "I am here in the 'jug' at the Brooklyn Navy Yard," wrote the boy, "waiting until they send me to Leavenworth. I am a gun pointer on a merchant vessel. We docked Saturday night and the first news I got was that my mother was in the hospital for an operation and that she wanted to see me. I spent Sunday with her at the hospital and when I reported back Monday morning I was arrested and tried. It turned out that I should have applied for individual leave, but I was excited and did not think to get it."

Roosevelt was Assistant Secretary of the Navy. I dictated a heated two-page letter to him telling the circumstances as given by the boy and vouching for his honesty. I told him of the time when the boy had come to the office with a pair of black eyes and I had asked him if he had been fighting.

"Yes, sir," said the boy.

"I suppose you licked the other fellow."

"No, sir, he licked me."

To let him down I said, "I suppose he picked on you and you had to fight him?"

"No, sir," said John, "I've been thinking it over, and I got just what I deserved."

I told Roosevelt that a boy so frank as that could not lie any more than could George Washington, and I said the whole affair was a stinking travesty on justice. Next day I received a wire from Washington, "If you will tell me the young man's name, I will see what I can do for him."

I was so mad that I had forgotten to give the name in my letter. Two days later John came into my office with a broad grin on his face to thank me. "My honorable status is restored," he said, "and all I got was my pay docked for two months and the Judge let me do that myself." It appeared that he had been summoned before a new board and asked if he did not think when his shipmates secured leave he should himself have applied for it as they had done. He had replied in the affirmative and the presiding officer had then asked him if he did not think in time of war a man going off without leave should be punished for an infraction of regulations. John again agreed with the point and the officer said, "Since you have admitted your offense, I will let you sentence yourself. What shall the penalty be?"

John replied, "I don't want to be dishonorably discharged from the Navy and I don't want a jail sentence. How would it do, sir, to dock me two months' pay?"

"You have written your own ticket," said the officer, "but don't make the same mistake again, my son!"

The exchange of correspondence after the court-martial decision is of considerable interest and indicates that Burnham's opinion of F. D. R. rose several points on the Richter scale:

---

OFFICE OF THE SECRETARY.
FILE 26251-13489:1
A.-S.

DEPARTMENT OF THE NAVY,
WASHINGTON. 26 July, 1917.

My dear Mr. Burnham:-

In further reference to the case of Edmund J. Brunner, I have to inform you that he was recently convicted by general court-martial of "absence from station and duty without leave," and "conduct to the prejudice of good order and discipline." He was sentenced to confinement for three years, dishonorable discharge, and accessories, but the Department in taking final action on this case decided to place this young man on probation for a period of one year. If he successfully completes his probationary period he will be in an honorable status in the service and may by his own efforts earn advancement. During the probationary period he will be on half pay.

In view of the serious nature of the offenses of which this young man was convicted, the Department feels that it has exercised most unusual clemency.

Sincerely yours,

F. D. Roosevelt
Assistant Secretary of the Navy.

Mr. John B. Burnham,
The Protective and Propogation Association,
Woolworth Building,
233 Broadway, N.Y.

*F.D.R. at Lake Placid September, 1935*

*Teddy Roosevelt on Campaign Trail*

I knew Theodore Roosevelt before he was chairman of the Board of Police Commissioners of New York. *Forest and Stream* published or handled over three hundred books, among them *The Book of the Boone and Crockett Club,* which was an annual compilation of stories of big-game hunters. Owen Wister cut his author's teeth writing for this book. Theodore Roosevelt, Boies Penrose and others had founded the Club. Roosevelt and George Bird Grinnell were editors of the book.

Once a year for a month or so Theodore Roosevelt made daily visits to our office to go over manuscripts and to attend to the make-up of the book. He would start talking the moment he came in and carry on with pithy comments until the door closed behind him. Everything, however, was direct and to the point and the most informed and intelligent remarks I had heard up to that point in my life. I was so impressed with his knowledge and power that I then predicted he would be President of the U.S. before he died. The sub-editors all laughed at this prediction. Even then the flash of his teeth and the way he screwed out his words seemed funny to them, and they failed to note the great head, so deep from front to back, and that which emanated from it.

When Roosevelt became a police commissioner Roundsman Petty (afterwards Captain) and I worked out a plan for police revolver practice which was put into effect for the first time in the history of the Department. My fight to get the Chief Game Protector punished came just before Roosevelt relinquished the governorship of New York. In connection with it occurred one of the two instances in our entire acquaintance when Roosevelt failed to reply to a letter I wrote him. I had asked for the head of the Chief Game Protector. It seemed to me I had furnished ample proof to warrant the removal of the officer, and in my own mind I was very critical of his motives. I thought politics had got another good man———.

Then Charles B. Reynolds, the managing editor of *Forest and Stream,* asked me to report the annual meeting of the Vermont Fish & Game Association at Burlington. The feature that made the meeting worthy of a special report was the fact that Vice-President Roosevelt was to be present together with Senator Proctor, Winston Churchill, the author, and other celebrities.

It started with a reception at the old Van Ness Hotel. A couple of thousand of us got in line to shake hands with the Vice-President. I was out of sympathy with Roosevelt and would not have joined the line except for the fact that the men with whom I was conversing pulled me in. The fellow just ahead of me was a Spanish War veteran and the moment T. R. clapped eyes on him he was enthused. He held on to his hand and apparently would have talked with him the whole time allotted for the reception had not those around him urged the veteran along. Still, holding him with one hand Roosevelt reached out his other hand to shake with me. I took the hand in a limp kind of way and with a lightning sweep it was instantly discarded, and his hand extended to the man beyond me in the line. He never looked at me and he did not know who it was, but intuition in a flash had shown him my hostility. I felt as if I had received a stinging slap in the face. Moreover, I began to see that I deserved it. The action was clean and honest, even if impulsive. For the first time I realized that Roosevelt had not acted in the Chief Game Protector [Major Pond] matter for good reasons. The latter was a Democrat, and he did not have time to make a proper investigation before leaving the governorship. That he did not doubt the truth of my statement was shown years later when he served as one of the Advisory members of the American Game Association. A man of standing who was very bitter against me wrote each member of the Advisory Board a letter relative to an action of the Association which he said was prompted by ulterior motives. Hearing of what had been done I wrote a letter to the man, giving the exact facts. Roosevelt answered, "My dear boy, nothing in this world could convince me that you would do a dishonorable deed. Faithfully — T.R." No wonder those who came in contact with Theodore Roosevelt loved him![1]

Ex-Lieutenant-Governor Fish entertained the Vermont Fish & Game Association at his home on Isle La Motte. Dinner was served for a thousand men, who had come by steamboat, in a big circus tent. All the speakers had something to say about Roosevelt which in some form or other predicted his becoming President. Maybe there was something psychic in this. The event which made Roosevelt President was taking place while they spoke.

When the meal and the speaking were over Roosevelt and his party went to Governor Fisk's old mansion while the rest of us gathered on the lawn in front, which sloped to the lake shore. There was to be another reception before the meeting broke up. The minutes passed and nothing happened. The conversation turned to surmises as to the cause of the delay. Finally Senator Proctor came out on the portico escorted by several members of the house-party. He raised his hand for silence and said, "My friends, I have a painful duty to perform." His voice broke and he wiped his eyes with his handkerchief. The crowd sensed tragedy and the silence was so great that I could distinctly hear the little wavelets washing the beach. Recovering his poise the Senator continued, "At noon today, in the Temple of Music in Buffalo, our beloved President was felled by an assassin's bullet!" He turned and re-entered the house. A sigh went up from the crowd and then every man swore. McKinley did not die, however, until some time later. Roosevelt was at Aiden Lair in the Adirondacks when he received the news of the last act in the drama.

The other letter I wrote Theodore Roosevelt which did not receive a reply was sent him to offer my services as a volunteer in his proposed regiment at the time of the World War. A few days before at his invitation I had lunched with him at the Harvard Club to discuss some information I had about an unpleasant situation in Mexico. General Harbord was present and I learned for the first time about Colonel Roosevelt's plan for overseas service.

I got no reply from Roosevelt, but in due time I received a blank for filling out from Captain Dame, who was his recruiting officer in New York. I supplied the data and returned the form to Captain Dame, only to have it sent back to me by the next mail with a blue pencil circle drawn around the date of my birth, 1869, and carried to the margin where the word "rejected" was written in a good bold hand. I called the Captain up and secured an appointment with him at four-thirty the same afternoon.

I told Captain Dame that age was only a relative term and that it should not be confused with physical unfitness. Some men, I said, were old in that sense at any age, that I had just returned from Mexico where in thirty days I had walked three hundred miles and ridden a mule an equal distance, that I was physically fit and could stand the gaff. He smiled and replied that the older a man was the more he knew and the more opinionated he became, which was not so good for discipline. He said they wanted young men who could not know enough to question orders. He added that I had no military experience and he could not see where I could be of any value to the outfit. I told him that I had attended a military school and had not only worked up to be the colonel of the two companies, but that for my last year I had been the instructor on the recommendation of the Regular Army officer who was leaving.

Captain Dame had become very fidgety and I could see that he wanted to go home. "Do you mean to tell me that some kid who has spent a month or so at Plattsburg would be more valuable than a man who had handled a hundred men on a contracting job and put it

---

[1] That the admiration and respect were mutual is indicated by an excerpt from another letter from T.R. a few years later: "John, I don't know what your proposition is but if you are for it — I am too!"

through ahead of time? A fellow like me has learned something of human nature and how to get results from his men.".......Captain Dame broke in, "You're not going to take no for an answer, are you? Where's that blank?" I handed it to him and with the same blue pencil he struck out the word "rejected," wrote above it "accepted," shoved it back to me with the remark that I was the oldest man he had passed and that he hoped he had not made a mistake.....

There was a lot of fun in the first Bull Moose campaign. It was a joyous crusade for most of the leaders, for we were fighting to right the very glaring wrongs which had grown up in both of the old boss-ridden parties, and everywhere a head rose we whacked it. But the second campaign was a tragedy. The glamour had worn off and our forces had crumpled and we knew before we started that we were licked. It took a lot of courage to stand up and be shot at without the possibility of victory.

It was then that I learned to love Theodore Roosevelt. In defeat he was greater than at any other time. One has to pass through the valley of the shadows before his place can be assigned. It is only the soundly great who can achieve defeat gloriously.

Roosevelt threw his all into that final battle. To the public he showed a serene and confident front. He was equally courageous in his talks with his followers but he permitted them to have no illusions. It was only when he was practically alone that on occasions the bitterness of the situation came to consciousness. But many times I thought of Christ in the Garden of Gethsemane.

In this last campaign Roosevelt traveled everywhere and worked day and night. In Essex County I had been running ahead with my car making arrangements for the speeches, but as we approached our night engagement at Plattsburgh, I dropped back for a word with the Colonel and Roosevelt invited me to ride with him. Speaking of the stop at Keeseville he said: "They think I am a mountebank. Many of those people came out expecting me to shoot off a pair of six-guns and yip like a cowpuncher." I reminded him of the preparation the New York newspapers had given for Lincoln when he came East, calling him uncouth and a gorilla and stopping at nothing to discredit him with the people; and I thought to myself that I had never seen him at better advantage than at this time, clothed with the dignity of high resolve.

As we crossed the bridge at the head of Ausable Chasm, I called his attention to the 80 foot drop of Alice Falls and told him that Francis Law had gone over the falls in a flat-bottomed boat as a stunt in the movies and had survived. "Marvelous!" said T.R. and he took from his pocket a book and proceeded to regain his serenity through the comfort of reading.

During my lifetime I have come in contact with only one man who had a memory in any way approaching Roosevelt's. That was an uneducated French-Canadian-American, Charley Blungie by name, who never forgot anything from his boyhood days on so far as we could tell. When Roosevelt recognized a man he had met years before the name instantly flashed to his consciousness. More remarkable, however, was his power for remembering what he read. This was shown by his Oxford lectures given on his way back from Africa and without the benefit of a library. His scientific facts were exact and one at least of the lectures is the classic today on its subject. But watching him read no one who did not know him would think he was assimilating and laying by the provender.

Roosevelt read paragraphs and pages as the ordinary person would read sentences. By the time we reached Plattsburgh he had finished the book. I had just read the same book, taking a week to do it, but that night I found he knew much more about the book and its bearing than did I, who had given it plodding attention.

The last time I saw Roosevelt alive was at a dinner of the Boone & Crockett Club in New York when the end was plainly written on his indomitable features. It was an informal dinner without speeches and Roosevelt, who had evidently been at some other function, came in about ten o'clock in evening clothes. Acting on common impulse, we reversed our chairs from the tables, made a circle and began a discussion of the World War and our part in it.

There were two high-ranking army officers present and these men, knowing the esprit de corps of the Club and that it was a privileged occasion, talked freely about their troubles with the War Department and of coffins being sent overseas for our men instead of badly-needed shoes. Roosevelt said: "I have the highest respect for Newton D. Baker. He is a man of high character and integrity and of very marked ability in certain lines, but as Secretary of War he is a ghastly mistake. In appointing him Wilson has again shown his lack of insight of character. Baker is a sociological leader and should be given that kind of job. If I were Mayor of New York I would put him in charge of children's playgrounds. A Secretary of War should not have a repulsion for his trade." He then gave us some inside information which had come to him of tragic folly. One of the listeners said, "Colonel, it is your duty to let the country know of this!"

Roosevelt replied with bitterness (which was foreign to his character), "It would do no good. I am discredited. They would only say it is a case of 'sour grapes.'"

"But," said the man, "you can have some of your friends give out the information to the public."

Roosevelt looked at him quizzically. "You remind me," he said, "of a story told of Ben Harrison when he was President of the United States. You know, gentlemen, that Harrison was the most lonely figure that ever occupied the White House. On one occasion Senator Ingalls of Kansas visited him to request the appointment of a constituent as a postmaster. Harrison sat at his flat-topped desk thrumming its top with his fingers as if he was playing a piano and never looking up while Senator Ingalls, standing opposite, recounted the qualifications of his candidate.... When Ingalls had finished, Harrison looked at him and said, 'Senator, under other circumstances I would have appointed your man, but I have a personal friend to whom I intend to give the place.' Ingalls drew himself up to the full extent of his lanky length and retorted, 'Mr. President, *if* you have a personal friend, for Heaven's sake give him the appointment!'"

The party broke up in a decidedly low tone of mind. I prefer to think of the great Roosevelt in his characteristically happy frame of mind.

# Chapter 6

### Conservation's False Prophets

I firmly believe that the greatest danger to the cause of conservation in America today is conservation's false prophets. It has been characteristic of this type of men to gain attention by pessimistic prophecies of game extermination, combined with attacks on conservation methods and policies and individuals promoting them. The taste of the public for sensationalism has been catered to, sportsmen as a class have been pilloried as selfish and blood-thirsty brutes, and leaders in conservation have been recklessly accused of dishonest motives. The result has been that a large part of the public who know nothing about shooting, and sad to say some who do, have become prejudiced against the lovers of the field sports; so that we face the danger of laws that will put an end to our sport. We must take stock of the situation, because if we do not meet it with sound educational logic we might as well put up our guns and take to playing golf or pitching horseshoes. Game and the opportunity to take it will be gone.

The forces against us are led by a sour-minded man to whom Horace Walpole's criticism of Dean Inge might well be applied. Walpole said: "He has made a specialty of attracting attention by constant hysterical pessimism. Most of his gloomy prophecies have been refuted by events almost as soon as they had been uttered. He has found that the more hysterical his writing the more attention he gets."

This man and the four or five others associated with him in the assault on field sports have a double-threat line of attack, first by direct action to cut shooting opportunities to the vanishing point through arbitrary and unscientific reductions in bag limits and shooting seasons; secondly, by interference with necessary constructive policies. An illustration of the latter is the opposition to the Federal Game Refuge Bill which through a filibuster prevented its passage at the last session of Congress. One of their school has challenged the right of the sportsmen not only to sit on boards making decisions regarding regulations, but also their right to draft laws and to work for their passage in legislatures.

These men are no more friends of the game than they are friends of the sportsmen. They are deadly enemies to both. If their plans succeed we will not only have no shooting but no game.

History shows that the whole conservation movement originated with sportsmen and that to their work is due the existing constructive game protective methods which have saved our wildlife. Game has disappeared before the agencies of civilization and commercialism but never as a result of sportsmen's actions. Let us follow up this statement and see what we shall find.

We have had game laws in this country ever since the West India Association in 1625 gave hunting privileges to persons who founded colonies in the New Netherlands, but for nearly 250 years these laws were chiefly important for giving business to the printers who published them. They certainly were not effective in saving game. The reason for this was that they were founded on Old World principles for benefit of the landowner and were highly unpopular and practically unenforceable. There were no game commissions and no sentiment for game protection. Only a minor fraction of the game was hunted by men who would today be called sportsmen. In the latter part of this era probably 90% of the game was killed as a matter of cold dollars and cents by market-hunters or men of their type. It was as a result of this condition that in 1840 Frank Forester predicted the complete extermination of American game within the next 50 years. Forester was by all odds the best-posted man of his day on the wild-life situation. There is little doubt but that his prophecy would have been realized and that the beginning of the present century, to quote his words, "Will see the wide woodlands, the dense swamps, and the mountainsides, depopulated and silent." Except for the fact that the sportsmen suddenly woke up to the situation and realized that the responsibility for game protection was theirs, and that it was their duty to provide the means for law enforcement and a game code suitable for a free country. Poor Forester committed suicide in 1858 and did not live to see the salvation of the game brought about through an organization which he had helped to found four years before his death — the New York Association for the Protection of Game, which is still in existence and which has the honor not only of being the oldest game protective association in America but also the one through whose efforts the foundation of all existing practical game protection was laid. To Forester is due the credit of stirring the sportsmen to action, but it was 30 years after its organization before the New York Association made more than a local impression by its work.

Fifty years ago the situation as regarding game preservation was certainly desperate in this country. There were few people who believed that there would be any game left for more than a decade or two. The country near centers of population was completely stripped of woodcock, grouse, quail, deer and the more desirable varieties of game. Frank Forester himself had seen the extermination of the wild turkey and heath hen, or Eastern prairie chicken, in the country he chiefly hunted in New York and New Jersey. Since 1785 New York state has had a law protecting heath hens and there were also paper laws protecting the turkeys which had been proved equally defective. The only place where any game remained in quantity was in remote localities where it was not commercially profitable to assassinate it. Over all the older parts of the country there is more game today than during the period in question.

In 1875 *Forest and Stream* was founded by Charles Hallock. The Old *Spirit of the Times,* no longer in existence, had even before this printed hunting articles and done something by way of advocating good sportsmanship. The little band of able, farseeing sportsmen from the New York Association for the Protection of Game, including Royal Phelps, Charles E. Whitehead and others, were beginning to see daylight in their problem. Reports of their conclusions were published. Suddenly the little leaven permeated the whole mass and the sportsmen of the country simultaneously appeared to realize their responsibility to protect the game. In the Winter of 1874-75 nearly 100 sportsmen's organizations sprang into existence all over the country with ten or twelve state associations and one national association. Thus was our present-day sportsmen's movement inaugurated 52 years ago this Winter. As regards the conservation of game this movement in its way is comparable with the great human movements of the Magna Carta or the American Revolution.

I can only briefly touch on the accomplishments of the sportsmen's movement. You can see the best evidence of it any day when you walk in a game cover. Without this movement there would have been no game in the country during the present century.

First, the sportsmen set themselves to secure game law enforcement. As there were no game commissions in existence, they put their hands into their own pockets and paid the expenses of game wardens. Next, the principle was carried further and state game commissions were created through sportsmen's initiative. The sportsmen have always been the prop on which game commissions have been supported.

They were not content merely to protect game birds but from the start were even insistent on the protection of non-game birds and harmless wildlife in general. Frank Forester believed in all wildlife protection. George Bird Grinnell, who went on the staff of *Forest and Stream* in 1876, ten years later founded the first Audubon Association. Ever since, the sportsmen have stood firmly to protect wildlife in its entirety.

The sportsmen's organizations fought the game hog. Having learned moderation themselves, they inaugurated and composed the laws creating bag limits. They early realized that commercialism in game meant its annihilation. Back in 1894, when at the suggestion of its managing editor, Charles B. Reynolds, *Forest and Stream* adopted the slogan, "Stop the Sale of Game," the idea was considered utopian but experience has since demonstrated its wisdom and practicability. The passage of the Migratory Bird Law and later the Migratory Bird Treaty Act made universal (as regards migratory birds) prohibitions against their sale and was the final step in the protection of non-game birds.

Sportsmen originated and put to practical use game sanctuaries, the only 100% assurance for the continuation of wildlife. Sportsmen were largely responsible for the setting aside of nearly 12,000 square miles of our territory in National Parks constituted as game sanctuaries. By executive order of March 14th, 1903 and March 4, 1909, one of our greatest sportsmen, Theodore Roosevelt, established 51 bird reservations in 17 states and territories; and it was the same sportsman-President who gave to the world conservation in all that the term now means. This subject could be expanded almost indefinitely, but I think sufficient has been given to show the debt America owes to sportsmen.

To recapitulate for a moment: the Colonial era, from the time the country was settled up to about 1875, was a time of paper laws and wildlife protection through the medium of prohibitive laws and law enforcement through which the doom of the game was averted. We are now in the constructive period. We have not thrown over old measures which have proved good, but to meet the onrush of modern development we must do things in a bigger way than ever before, and replace natural sanctuaries with ones created by both state and national action and through administrative areas. We must put the right kind of game on the right kind of land or, lacking this, we must adapt the land to the game, which means providing suitable food and cover.

I have spent a lifetime in game protective work and, as a result of my experience, I am satisfied that we can have all the game in this country for which the country is adapted. There is nothing obscure or difficult about the problem. It is simply a question of intelligent work backed with sufficent money. I am not, however, nearly so sure that we can continue free shooting. This is the problem today demanding our most serious attention and one of the vital reasons for the passage of the National Game Refuge Bill. We must secure great areas of cheap land both by national and state action or otherwise, no matter what amount of game we have, the ordinary fellow will have no available place to hunt.

I am fully aware that the chief of the attackers on sportsmen has made far-reaching claims to the effect that he was responsible in time past for many of the good results achieved in game conservation. I can only say now that his claims will not warrant a thorough investigation. The names of the men who really accomplished the progressive steps upon which was built the system which has saved our game are all a matter of record, and each one of them has been a sportsman at heart and recognized as such by his fellows. Moreover, each one has been an optimist. The only way to get anywhere is through optimism. Optimism is a creative force while pessimism is shriveling and destructive. Pierpont Morgan was right when he said, "You will go broke if you are a bear in America."

The pessimists charged the sportsmen with the extermination of the parakeet and the Labrador Duck and presumably the buffalo and passenger pigeon as well. What rot! When was the parakeet a game bird? The Labrador Duck had a limited range and a restricted diet. It was not hunted as game and the common belief is that it disappeared from natural causes. In our long list of waterfowl it is the only duck which has become extinct. The detractors have nothing to say about the work of the sportsmen in saving all the other ducks through action which culminated with the passage of the Migratory Bird Law. The buffalo and the wild pigeons went because of commercialism. It was not the sportsmen who stripped the hides from countless thousands of bison for conversion into coats and lap robes or who netted and shot the millions of pigeons for the markets. Such doctrine is a foul miasma based upon ignorance and prejudice.

The pessimists have a habit of picturing our country at the time of its settlement as everywhere swarming with game, and then contrasting it with present conditions so that they can lay the blame for game disappearance on the sportsmen and thereby swat them! Let us for a moment investigate this proposition and see first what was the actual condition at the time of the discovery of America, and then try to place what blame there is for the reduction of game where it actually belongs.

In the first place every student of history knows that when the white man came to our shores there were large areas of gameless country and periods even in good country where meat-eating Indians and carnivorous animals starved. Unbroken evergreen forests were deficient in all kinds of game because lacking in game food. Wolves and other carnivores under certain conditions were altogether too abundant and depopulated the game resources of other areas. Disease also played its part. It was only in limited areas, compared to the total, that game was abundant and these areas with teeming game were the best and most productive part of the land. More game food grows on good land than on poor land and, by the same token, more human food.

As our country was settled it was natural that the best game-lands were taken for farming. The necessities of agriculture have constantly reduced the game areas and driven the game to poorer sections incapable of supporting as large a total as the better areas.

It is true that with primitive cultivation certain kinds of game benefited, such as quail, but when modern methods came in vogue even these species were driven from the good land. Game birds cannot nest where the mowing machine runs, where barbed wire and woven wire have replaced rail fences and the wooded spots have been cleaned up. There are no breeding places or shelters left. The plow has been one of the most destructive agencies in creating gameless areas.

Cities and towns have expanded. Miles of factories have been added to other miles, fouling the air and water alike. Summer resorts and barbered parks have wiped out game covers. Drainage, mining operations and certain phases of lumbering and forestry have lessened available habitat, and — worst of all — the country is gridironed with good roads so that over most of our area there is no longer any hinterland, no natural sanctuaries, no places where a part of the game can live secure from interference by man. Note here two facts: (1) the sportsmen are not to blame for this situation; (2) the sportsmen alone are working to remedy it by restoring sanctuaries.

There are barren wilderness areas today in the remoter parts of the Americas, Asia and Africa where the rifle and shotgun, or for that matter bow and arrow, pitfall or poisoned dart have had nothing to do with the situation. Sir John Franklin and his men would not have starved to death if they could have found the caribou. Once in about every ten years the varying hare of the North, through disease, dwindles from countless numbers to practically none at all. But first they eat the willow, to such an extent that the moose, the largest meat animals of the section, are at times forced to migrate or starve. When the rabbits disappear the ptarmigan and grouse go with them either through disease infection or because the carnivora concentrate on them for sustenance. Lastly, most of the lynx perish of starvation. In Africa the tsetse fly depopulates vast areas of game territory. Men capable of supporting themselves on game from time immemorial have faced starvation in wilderness fastnesses. So comparisons of past and present game abundance as commonly made require qualification.

We can gain courage for the future through the knowledge of what has been accomplished in the past. If the pioneers of the conservation movement of 50 years ago had contented themselves with gloomy prophecies on the one hand and destructive prohibitions on the other, we certainly would have had a gameless America today. Instead, they met problems as the problems developed, optimistically and constructively. Their accomplishments point the way to our success. We have several million shooters in this country who have opportunities for sport which are denied to most of their fellows in the Old World. The engines of game destruction have multiplied, including the automobile. Every year the game and shooting areas are reduced. Old methods no longer suffice to maintain the supply. Leave it at that and there is only one conclusion possible — that of the pessimists. But there is another and brighter side to the shield, and recollect that the polished surface is only secured by hard rubbing. The brighter side is the actual game condition in America today. Would there be seven million men hunting if there was nothing for them to shoot?

Deer were exterminated in Vermont shortly after the Civil War. They have been restored to their old range and Vermont has become one of the best deer-hunting states in the Union. In Pennsylvania it is estimated that the meat value of the wild game exceeds the total value of all their domestic livestock — sheep, cattle, horses, hogs and poultry; and Pennsylvania is one of the important livestock states in the country. All of the states which require reports of the game killed show amazing totals which are always understated because many men fear to give the exact figures through ignorance of season bag limits. Moreover, if one man in a party of four kills four deer and divides them with the other members of the party, usually only one deer will be recorded as having been killed. Ever since statistics have been published, the pessimists each year have raised their voices in horror and proclaimed that the supply has been annihilated. But nothing of the kind has happened for the reason that we have not stood still, thank God, in this country in improving our game administrative methods.

Since the sportsmen's conservation movement began, we have lost no game species and none in future will be exterminated. Under our modern game-protective system if there were no other factors to be considered, we could have buffalo everywhere today. The thing that stands in the way is the farmer and the stockman and the demand of our population for the food these classes produce. It is the same with the antelope. Mountain sheep, goats, elk and mule-deer in the West, and Virginia deer and wild turkeys in the South all need better administrative care from game departments; but particularly as regards the Western species. The chief danger to their continuance comes from lack of suitable range. In a large part of their habitat they have been driven from their old haunts to the barren sides of mountain ranges and they are fenced out from winter pastures.

It can be stated as an axiom that the game for which we have suitable habitat today does not disappear except when well-recognized conservation principles are disregarded, which generally means when game laws are not enforced. Saving the game is not a cause for throwing fits, but for executive action.

Nearly 80 years ago, William Henry Herbert (Frank Forester) wrote: "I began to despair — to feel that there is no hope for those who would avert the evil day when game shall be extinct and the last manly exercise out of date in the United States of North America." Herbert was not a pessimist but he did not have the background which is ours to give him encouragement.

To quote an *Outlook* editorial: "If you will study the course of history, you will find that no dreams are ever entirely achieved. You will find that liberties are never won, that democracy is never attained, that no ideal is ever so secure that its opponents may be ignored and its possession ranked as a permanent asset of mankind. The war for liberty, democracy, and social ideals — game protection for example — is a continuous war. It is a war in which many victories may be won, but a war in which there can be no final victory. Triumph perches on the banners of the leaders of this way only so long as they remain on the firing line. Defeat is the portion of those who lay down their arms to rest." In other words, we must keep on the job.

# Chapter 7

### Thirty Years of Progress In Conservation

(Speech made in 1933)

John B. Burnham

I am glad that your President has permitted an extension to the scope of my remarks beyond the "thirty years' experience in conservation," even though it is not to be compared to Uncle Joe Cannon's in another direction. One night after 'Uncle Joe' had trimmed a bunch of newspaper correspondents playing poker one of the men said to the others it was no wonder the Congressman knew the game as he had learned it playing with Methuselah! "Not by a damn sight," said Uncle Joe, "the fellow I played with was the boy's grandfather!"

Fifty years ago, in 1886, when as a boy of seventeen I had my first big-game hunting in the West, I had never heard of game laws: there were certainly none in force at that time in the territory of Wyoming. For several months I was the "meat-hunter" for the ranch which later on furnished the scene for the novel *The Virginian.* There were no closed seasons and no bag limits or other forms of game laws, and wild game was served the cow punchers in order to save the beef steers for the Chicago stockyards. At that time all I learned of conservation was a strong dislike for the wastefulness of the buffalo hide-hunters. Five years later, having gone through college, I landed on the staff of *Forest and Stream* and there, forty-five years ago, I got my first knowledge of the rudiments of game preservation.

*Forest and Stream,* under the leadership of George Bird Grinnell and his able editor, Charles B. Reynolds, was leading a pioneer movement for conservation. At the head of its editorial column for years it printed the slogan, "Stop the Sale of Game." It carried that slogan until the principle was adopted, first by Texas and later on by the other states. Grinnell with *Forest and Stream* founded the first Audubon Association and he secured early national parks and many of the laws which are now fundamental parts of our system of wild-life protection.

In the state of New York we have had game laws ever since Colonial times. But they were not game laws in the present sense of the term. They were based on the royal prerogative that the game belonged to the sovereign. They were in effect laws against trespassers. Game belonged to the land on which it was found and the owner of the land had the sole right to take the game. All early game laws were founded on this theory.

It was not until 1892 that we actually secured a code of the modern type. The legislature in 1889 had passed an act providing for the appointment of a commission for revising and codifying the fish and game laws and, because they represented an organization which had been carrying on an aggressive fight for better conditions, General Richard U. Sherman, Hon. Robert B. Roosevelt and Edward G. Whitaker were named as the committee. No men ever were better fitted for the task they had to perform.

Recollect that at this time New York had no game commission. Way back in 1868 the same Robert B. Roosevelt then, I believe, a state senator, had gotten a bill through the Legislature creating a state fish commission, and in 1885 an entirely distinct forest commission had been formed, but there was no official commission charged with the protection of game and no protection except through local or private agencies. The law of 1892, while it continued the Board of Commissioners of Fisheries, five in number, made the body for all intents and purposes a game commission as well, with twenty salaried game protectors and a workable code of game laws. One hundred seventy-nine chapters of state laws back to 1851 were repealed to make way for the new law.

Just a word about the organization which secured this result — The New York Association for the Protection of Game. I do not think I am exaggerating when I say this association has the most interesting and valuable record of any sportsmen's association in history. Started in 1844 "to protect sporting dogs from the oppressive laws then in force" it soon found its mission and chief interest in improving game laws and enforcing them. It was a fighting organization. It hired its own game wardens and the lawyers in its membership prosecuted the violators. Many of its cases were carried to a final decision in the higher state courts and some to the Supreme Court of the United States. These private citizens assumed the functions of a negligent government.

When I was president of the American Game Association, a worthy successor to the pioneer organization, I was so impressed with the achievements of The New York Association for the Protection of Game that I had a search made of the files of *Forest and Stream, Turf, Field and Farm* and similar publications of an older generation which established the fact to our satisfaction that there had been no other game protective associations in this or any other country antedating the New York Association, and that it had set the pace for all that followed. We unearthed the fact that shortly after this association began its militant career scores of similar organizations sprang up all over the United States as well as in the colonies of the British Empire. There can be no doubt that the New York Association was the inspiration, for there is concrete evidence that the new organizations were patterned after it in the fact that they adopted similar constitutions and by-laws, and carried on after the same fashion. It was this Association which secured from the highest court the decision establishing the principle that the ownership of the game is in the people.

It was not until 1895 that the official conservation interests of the state were formally brought together in the Fisheries, Game and Forest Commission, the title of which was changed in 1900 to The Forest, Fish and Game Commission. Prior boards had quite generally consisted of five commissioners, but the last-named commission was limited to three members and provision made to reduce the number to one after two years. For a short interregnum there was a single commissioner before James W. Whipple took office in 1905, but Whipple was the first real commissioner of the state. His administration marks the start of the present vigorous and efficient handling of conservation problems. Before this time individuals and organizations had carried on the brunt of the conservation work. Under Whipple for the first time the State assumed its full responsibility.

As I look back, I should say that we have had three great commissioners who stand out above the others — Commissioner Whipple, Commissioner Pratt and our present Commissioner, Lithgow Osborne. In between commissioners had been mediocre, though some have been sufficiently interested in their work to rank well, (only one administration could be unfavorably criticized), but from my viewpoint no others have rated with the three I have named.

In 1908 I assisted Commissioner Whipple in drafting the next codification of the game law after that of 1892, a codification which gave a two months' uniform open season for most of the game of the State. This, I think, was the first game law of New York based on entirely democratic principles. We worked nights and holidays and finally got the bill introduced and, with the help of the sportsmen, passed. As a matter of fact the generation of sportsmen then in the saddle had not developed their full measure of helpfulness. Most of the steam for passing the bill came as the result of a dinner given by the Commission at its private expense to selected members of the Legislature. There were few of these legislators who knew the first thing about conservation before the dinner, but Whipple fired their interest in the novel subject and secured their support. We did not get everything we asked for in the 1908 session, but it's worth noting that practically all the things lost then were secured later on.

During Whipple's administration the present system of forest-fire control was inaugurated, including fire-towers, oil-burning regulations for the railroads in the Forest Preserve counties and the forest-ranger organization. Top-lopping of conifers was also put into effect and various types of forest disease and forest pest control established. An extensive system of tree nurseries was established, and State lands were planted with trees (though in 1908 private land-owners set out eleven times as many trees as the State.) The sale of game was prohibited. The resident hunting license law was secured. For the first time the State started propagating game at its game farm at Sherburne, under Harry Rogers. Law enforcement was placed on a business basis, and the protectors and rangers given civil service protection. Prior to this time the enforcement of conservation laws had been conducted on a haphazard basis. Many laws were violated with impunity. Great lumbering operations were in progress. It was customary for the smaller jobbers to serve their men venison instead of beef. In season and out on Sundays many of the lumberjacks hunted for the five dollars they received for the deer carcass. There was elsewhere well-organized business in game bootlegging for the city market. Many thousands of dollars' worth of State timber was stolen each year. An end was put for all time to this wholesale law violation. The result was accomplished by organization and business methods in the police work.

The first step was the divorcing of the game protectors from other employment of a private nature, which in those days was the rule rather than the exception, and getting rid of the worthless and untrustworthy. At this stage the most frequent callers at the office were the old-type politicians in behalf of their protégés. The State was separated into divisions under division chiefs, who were not only in close touch with their protectors but also with headquarters at Albany. These chiefs served nearly two years without legal recognition or increased pay because a certain Senator failed to get the man he was interested in promoted. Each month the men in the various divisions were called together at the division headquarters for the consideration of their work, and later in the month the chiefs were brought to Albany to report. Once each year the entire force was assembled at the Capitol for additional training. A system of rewards and punishments was inaugurated, increased pay being given to the best protectors from ratings based one-half on the man's success in apprehending first violators and one-half on his success in securing his community's support for law observance and game preservation. We had three ratings then and the men in the lowest grade understood they were in line for dismissal if they did not soon show improvement. An otherwise good man who, for example, had committed a bad error of judgment had his salary docked a month's pay. New York was the pioneer in thus organizing its game protective force and its example has been pretty generally followed by other states.

To the ancients wild nature was repellent. They enjoyed seeing cultivated fields and formal gardens and that kind of thing. Nature was their enemy. In this country the first settlers were of like mind. They cut down forests and burned them to get land for cultivation and they shot the "varmints" — bears, deer, cougars — as interfering with themselves and their crops. The feeling seemed to be that forests and wild-life were leagued together against the settlers and that both must be gotten rid of if the settlers were to survive. The idea persisted long after there was any excuse for it. The task of educating the people to a different viewpoint was the toughest job of the Whipple administration.

I talk about this because we lived and slept with a sort of proselyting enthusiasm. When we began weeding out from the Adirondacks the deer-hunting dogs, we were up against primitive passions. But we accomplished this without the loss of a man and in this respect fared much better than Maine, for instance. It was a time for enthusiasm. Conservation was something bright and new in history. It was a kind of renaissance: new ideas and new men came to the front, and a great many rather revolutionary concepts developed — ideas considered old-fashioned today or at any rate merely orthodox. It is hard to realize now that fighting was required to secure them!

In 1911 we had our last codification of the game laws. In 1892 formulation had determined the closed seasons during which fish and game could not be legally taken. The 1908 draft stated the legal open seasons. The 1911 law was the first notable example of a permissive system by blanket clauses — everything not specifically permitted was prohibited. From the technical point of law enforcement this was a noteworthy advance. The new codification also broke fresh ground in that it prohibited the killing of other than buck deer. Quite largely, however, the changes made were designed to close loopholes and to strengthen law enforcement. This set of regulations became a model form for other states, and its principles have been widely copied.

The word "codification" is a misnomer as applied to the laws of 1892, 1908 and 1911. In reality all the so-called codifications of the game laws in New York have been new legislation and not merely decodings or reclassifications of prior laws. This is as it should be. Public opinion advances, new methods are discovered and become operative, old methods are discarded. There is nothing static in this world and a game-law overhauling would be of little value if it did not give us a better law than before.

For example, since the time of the last codification a great volume of land formerly open to sportsmen has been closed to hunting and fishing. The posting situation has become acute. The next "codification" should implement the law through which the Conservation Department may be provided with means for solving the situation. When a citizen pays for a license there is at least the shade of an implied obligation on the part of the state which sells him the license that he shall be provided a place where he can exercise the right granted by the license, and this on no socialistic basis. The committee selected to draft the changes should give painstaking study to this and similar problems which have arisen since 1911, and the law which they develop should be in step with the age.

# Chapter 8

**Conservation's Debt to Sportsmen**

by

John B. Burnham — Reprinted from the

**NORTH AMERICAN REVIEW** September, 1928

It was the hunters and fishermen who first learned to love the charm of God's unspoiled handicraft and who, reveling in the poignancy of wild beauty, taught others the same joy. More than a hundred years before the discovery of America that good sportsman Count Gaston de Foix wrote to prove that "the life of no man that useth gentle game and disport is less displeasable unto God than the life of a perfect and skillful hunter, or from which more good cometh." He shows how the hunter is saved from the Seven Deadly Sins, and he paints this lovely word picture of dawn to prove that "hunters live in this world more joyfully than other men." "For," says he, "When the hunter riseth in the morning and he sees a sweet and fair morn and clear weather and bright, and he heareth the song of the small birds, which sing so sweetly with great melody and full of love, each in its own language in the best wise that it can according that it learneth of its own kind. And when the sun is arisen, he shall see fresh dew upon the small twigs and grasses, and the sun by his virtue shall make them shine. And *that* is great joy and liking to the hunter's heart."

Read similar passages from Izaak Walton, and then pause and think of the debt we owe these men and others like them. Half the joy of life would be missing if it were not for the appreciation of Nature first taught by sportsmen. Have you ever stopped to think that this love of Nature is a comparatively new thing in the world, and that its conservation arrived only yesterday? The writings of the ancients show that mankind feared or hated what we now love; hunting was battle, Nature an enemy. Pleasure was found only in what man had wrested from Nature — houses and streets and cultivated fields. The antithesis of the sportsman is typified by Browning's Italian person of quality who complains of the whine of the bees in the resinous firs on the hill, but grows enthusiastic over the city:

"Bang, whang, whang, goes the drum; tootle-te-tootle, the fife:

Oh, a day in the city square, there is no such pleasure in life!"

The change in man's attitude toward Nature is one of the greatest of all spiritual advances and compares favorably with the change from Paganism to Christianity. It provides the antidote to our complex civilization, the means of preserving our mental and bodily health.

No doubt hunters learned to love the mountains and forests and seas and deserts through the chase, and conversely they learned to love the wild animals and birds and fish through their association with Nature. The history of events shows that the sportsmen not only took the initiative in conservation but also have developed and carried it on. I am writing to disabuse the minds of those who still hold the Colonial New England view, that a sportsman is a man too lazy to have the mid-Victorian idea of old Webster's dictionaries — that sportsmen are jockey or gamester types skilled in field sports; also those of a later day who class them as bloodthirsty assassins of wildlife. None of these classifications will fit George Bird Grinnell, William Dutcher, George Shiras, Theodore Roosevelt — men who have worked to save wildlife and wild nature in this country. While others have scoffed, sportsmen have made their designation a title of honor through unselfish devotion. Good people are confused because the term is too loosely applied. As regards the chase, no one can today be called a sportsman who has not cultivated the ethical side of the thing and developed *noblesse oblige*.

I love hunting; but I do not love it so much for the game in the game pocket as for the game in the fields and forests. I am ready always to give up shooting when the interest of wildlife demands it. In this I think I represent the attitude of all true sportsmen. Without legal prohibition, the sportsmen of Massachusetts voluntarily stopped shooting grouse when the supply was threatened. The intelligent application of closed seasons has always been through sportsmen initiative. It was so in Minnesota last year.

In unintelligent contrast, consider the taking of a game species from the game list in Ohio. Quail were made "song-birds" there by legislative enactment, successfully promoted by a man entirely in opposition to the wonderful conservation movement of today. This man employed an accomplished cartoonist[1] to work upon the feelings of the public with harrowing pictures of wildlife persecution such as only he could draw, and he calculatingly fanned into flame the smoldering resentment of farmers against wanton trespassers on their lands. His success was achieved by arousing antagonism against sportsmen, and for what end? The sportsmen suffered and nothing gained, not even the quail, as is shown by their abundance in the neighboring state of Indiana, where shooting is permitted. Only pot-hunters and vermin profited.

This apostle for classifying quail improperly was the man who fifteen years ago tried to remove the protection designed to be given game-birds by the original Federal migratory bird legislation. He argued that the Bill was too heavily loaded, and that it could not be passed to protect both game and non-game-birds, and that the game-birds should be sacrificed. The crying conservation need in this instance was protection for the game-birds and not the others. Thanks to the Audubon Association, the safety of others had already been assured. But the migratory game-birds were on the verge of extinction. Many persons in 1912 believed they were doomed.

The great wintering state of Texas had no closed season, and many of the other states along the more important migration routes permitted ducks to be killed at all times when they were present. Market-shooting was in full swing without bag-limit restriction. The sportsmen had lovingly included all other birds in their programme, but this man was willing on a mere question of mistaken policy to sacrifice the valuable game species to the ogre of commercialism, the Moloch which has swallowed up so much of the world's wildlife! Fortunately for the birds his plan did not succeed.

There is still a conflict of opinion between those who stand for the prohibitive system of saving game by constantly cutting bag-limits and shortening shooting seasons to the vanishing point, and those who go about conserving and building up the supply by con-

---

[1] Jay N. ("Ding") Darling won Pulitzer prizes for his cartoons in 1924 and 1943.

structive methods; but the conflict has largely narrowed down to a matter of scolding on the part of the former. The critics assert that we have wasted our heritage to such an extent that to save the remnants we must pile the prohibitions of Pelion on Ossa.

The verboten system has been with us since the first settler set foot on our shores. Colonial game-laws naturally were patterned after those of the Old World, and particularly after the England of hereditary privilege, the England which taught the ordinary folk to say, "God bless the squire and his relations. and make us know our proper stations" — and which hanged the man found hunting on land that did not belong to him. The game saviors of that day framed these laws with considerable severity. They were determined to save the game willy-nilly, by restriction. It was under this type of law that practically all of our game disappeared. Something was wrong with the system, but for nearly two hundred years nobody could find out why with perfectly constructed statutes the game continued passing over the brink. An uninspired Jeremiah in Philadelphia a hundred years ago sounded the warning to save the remnants. In a way strangely reminiscent of a more modern school, he demanded additional prohibitions, and he lambasted Tom, Dick and Harry for not observing their proper stations.

Thirty years later another equally hopeless prophet arose, but this man had sufficient vision to see part way into the fog. He realized what others had not grasped, that the union of monarchial laws with an anti-monarchial sentiment made an impossible marriage, and that in America drastic prohibitions never could be as effective as in England. The American says, "To hell with the squire and his relations!" The thing that Frank Forester failed to envision was the possibility of a new system adapted to a country of equality. And so from a fullness of experience never excelled, he predicted the complete extermination of American game in from ten to forty years, depending upon the variety.

Another twenty years passed before, something more than fifty years ago, we began the foundations of our present system. The development came without fanfare of trumpets, and the men who brought it about had no genius for self-advertisement. Instead of fulminating, they went to the root of the matter and set about Americanizing the misfit plan. In England the incentive for conservation came from the value of game to the landowner as personal property, and the landowner naturally saw to it that the laws made for his benefit were enforced. Here, there was no corresponding incentive. But clear-headed sportsmen showed that with game as the common property of all the people, it was the individual's obligation to preserve the asset. It was upon this basis of personal obligation that the problem was solved. Otherwise, the predictions of game extermination would long ago have been realized.[1]

The first and for a time the only game protective association in America was the New York Association for the Protection of Game. This organization had on its rolls the most intelligent of the New York gunners, including some very able lawyers. Its name is written large in the history of conservation, because the little group which directed its energies combined action with vision. They originated most of our basic game-laws and secured fundamental decisions of the higher courts establishing the laws. But first they set in motion a campaign for law enforcement through an educational barrage to show their fellow sportsmen that it was their job and no one else's to save the game. They showed that sport was committing suicide, that when a man shot out of season he was taking another's share of the game owned in common. They insisted that the hunter must first observe the law himself, and then see to it that others followed suit.

---

[1] For the record: Many equally dedicated non-hunters should also be given their due credit for their significant assistance in the work which resulted in the successful passage of the Migratory Bird Protection legislation: Editor

The doctrine was rudimentary but new. No one before had felt personal responsibility to save game. The idea spread like wildfire. In 1874 there were one hundred, including ten or twelve state organizations. A way had been found. Optimism took the place of pessimism, and the doom of the game was averted.

For a time these sportsmen's organizations contented themselves with law enforcement. They carried on campaigns of education, and employed game wardens at their own expense, for no public funds were then available. There were no heroics in the movement, but it was practical, and it produced results. Essentially it was democratic. The big thing which only a few realized was that the fiery enthusiasm aroused for game-law enforcement was bound to bear fruit in other directions. One product was something entirely new in the world's history, though not then having a name, that which is now known as Conservation was born. The New York Association evolved as its motto, *"Non nobis solum,"* which to them meant that wildlife was to be protected not only for the benefit of men of present and future generations, but for its own sake as well. It was the first expression of an obligation of guardianship of the wild creatures by man. It has become a principle recognized by all sportsmen.

Conservation was not only born of sportsmen but owes to them much of its subsequent development. They stopped the commercialism of game and enforced moderation through bag-limits. They shackled themselves and their fellows for the benefit of the wildlife. They started the game commissions of the various states. They deprived themselves of shooting grounds to establish sanctuaries. They gave their best energies that there might be national parks. It was one of their number who brought Conservation in its fullest development to the conscience of all mankind[1], Theodore Roosevelt.

We are now in the constructive era. We have learned the fundamentals of game administration, and we know how to put our experience to practical use. As a result in some of the older states there is more game than when our fathers hunted. While individual bags are much smaller, there are more game animals and birds in the territory which Frank Forester hunted eighty years ago than when he passed away. No American game species has disappeared since this time, and none will now become extinct. Where we have failed, aside from destruction of habitat, the fault can be found in disregard of well-known conservation principles.

I have been quoted as saying that wild game is more plentiful in the United States today than ever before. I never made the statement, and it is of course untrue. The best of the game land has been taken for farming and industrial uses, the game has been driven to areas which are incapable of producing the maximum of food, and therefore we can never again have the primitive abundance. But just as Vermont and Pennsylvania have increased their supplies over those of fifty years ago, it is evident that with the same intelligent effort other states can build up their stocks. It is a much more serious problem to secure the land on which to hunt, and it will constantly be more difficult for the average man to get away from trespass signs. But the science of game preservation is so thoroughly founded that from the standpoint of shooting it is merely a question of how much we want and, sad to say, what we are willing to pay for it by hunters' license fees or otherwise. In this country of more than one hundred million population we can no longer rely for our game solely upon the bounty of Nature. The *verboten* system is a sucked orange. All its good has been extracted. It is now realized that game protection is a "do," not a "don't."

---

[1] Although T.R. admittedly entertained the proverbial bloodlust at times, he nevertheless was also one of the nation's great exponents of enlightened conservation.

# Chapter 9

## The Moose Shot 'Round the Corner

"It was a beautiful Winter day, so still you could hear a man forty rods off breaking the crust. Stubbs and Staples took the east side of the ridge and Jock Darling[1] and I the west. We knew it was impossible with the noise we were making to get within sight of the moose, but we gambled that one party might drive the moose to the other. Every little while we would stop and listen.

"At noon we swung on top of the ridge and ran into Stubbs and Staples boiling tea. None of us had seen any tracks. Stubbs and Staples said they were fed up on moose-hunting and were going over to the Wadleigh bog for caribou. They actually bagged two that afternoon. They invited us to stop and drink tea, but Jock and I refused.

"We dropped back on our side of the ridge and had hardly gotten out of hearing of the others when we sighted a bull moose crossing our line of direction from east to west. He had either heard the men on top of the ridge or been startled by the smoke of their fire. There he was: a gaunt, rangy, pre-historic-looking creature, black against the snow, seven feet high, with his shovel horns laid flat on his withers, trotting and not jumping like a deer. It was an easy shot for a man accustomed to moving game, but old Jock had come from an age when powder and ball was precious and he believed in taking no chances. As I threw up my rifle to fire he jumped squarely in front and blatted to stop the moose. The effect was the same as if he had blatted at the Congressional Limited; the moose went right on and disappeared into the thicker growth of the forest.

"I looked at Jock and he looked at me, and presently he said, 'There's more than one moose around: you work along the side of the ridge and I'll take a circle and maybe I can start another your way!'

"I climbed a knoll in the black growth and got on top of some fallen trees. Most of the bigger spruces had been blown over and in place of the original cover a thick mass of small balsams had sprung up so that the view to the north was extremely limited. I had no more than taken my position when I heard a moose below me in the balsams but I could not see him. He would trot a little distance and then stop and listen. To the east on their way to the bog, Stubbs and Staples were conversing — or rather Stubbs was shouting to Staples, who was very deaf, telling him just what he thought of his wife's relations; while from the west Jock Darling was calling to me to join him. The moose did not know which way to turn.

---

[1] Jonathan (Jock) Darling, renowned guide and owner of hunting camps at Nicatous Lake, Maine died at home in Lowell, Me. on Jan. 5, 1898, aged 68.

"Just then far down the slope, I caught a glimpse of the bull as he passed beyond a couple of large spruces not over eighteen inches apart. I fired instantly through the opening between the trees, but at once realized I had missed because there was no after-result, nothing but breathless silence. Stubbs stopped in the middle of a sentence. It was as still as the chancel of a church at midnight.

"I knew that once the moose got under way he would not stop short of ten miles and I wanted to shoot quickly again, but the "saw-log" shell of my old 40-82 stuck and I had to drop the rifle to my hip before I could get sufficient purchase on the lever to make the shell let go. So when I threw up the rifle again and fired down the opening between the trees it was a hasty shot. It had the desired effect, however, for now there came the sound of a wildly plunging animal terminated by a crash as he fell.

"The bull was not a particularly large one but Jock was hearty in his congratulations. He pointed to a gaping wound on the right shoulder and said, 'That's where your slug came out.' "No," said I, "that's where it hit him, he was passing me from left to right." Jock contended no bullet could make such a hole, three fingers wide, when first hitting its target, and to settle the argument we pried the moose over and found the bullet just under the skin on the left shoulder. 'It must have key-holed,' he said, but he was plainly nonplussed.

"We followed the track to the point where the moose, on being hit had reversed his direction and developed the remarkable fact that the animal had been killed 'round a corner,' as Jock expressed it. The moose had stood behind the earth and gravel-filled roots of a fallen tree which made a perfect barricade against a direct shot. He could only have been reached by a carom off the left of the two spruces between which I had seen him as he passed to stop a full rod further on — and sure enough this tree bore the mark of the glancing bullet! I went back to the place from which I had fired, Jock took the moose's position and I could see nothing of him even when he put his hat on the end of his long Bullard rifle and waved it as high as he could reach. I always felt that this freak shot brought its reward solely because I had worked so hard to get the moose."…..

His preferred quarry was the mountain sheep, which he claimed to be the best-tasting meat of all. Down in Lower California, while on a hunt for that elusive animal, he made what he always considered to be the finest shot of his career.

"That's the driest country in the world," he related; "There is no dew east of the Pinals. The mountains, shaken by earthquakes, are so unstable that sometimes a careless step will send tons of loose rock down into a chasm. Late one afternoon, as I was walking along a treacherous ridge, I heard the clatter of stones on the opposite mountain. With my binoculars I saw two sheep mount and then disappear before I could get my rifle on them. But just then a third sheep appeared and before he could reach the summit I leveled at him, taking in the full height of the front sight in my allowance for distance and elevation.

"Somehow I knew I was going to get him even before I pulled the trigger. It was one of those flashes of instinctive knowledge that come to a hunter — one of those hunches that all veteran hunters experience. Well, that sheep toppled backwards right after the crack of my rifle and fell down the steep side of the rotted mountain. It made me sick to see that body of flesh and bones falling so far…

"The climbing was bad and it was dark when I reached the carcass. Then next day one of the men went out with me to measure the length of the shot. We made two measurements, taking two hours for each."

'How far was the sheep when you fired?' asked the interviewer (James C. Derieux for *Field and Stream* May, 1929.)

"I'd rather not tell you," said the hunter; "Better men than I have been labeled liars for describing shots that were closer than that one; so I'm going to play it safe. But I will say that the animal was so far off that he was hidden from my eyes by the sight on the end of the rifle barrel and looked no bigger, when the rifle was lowered, than a pencil dot on white paper."

Besides being remarkable in an era that produced many remarkable men, Burnham was also one of the most resourceful businessmen of his time. Moreover, although he maintained that he could make a good living practically anywhere, he consistently refused to let the lure of money crowd out the finer things of life — which to him meant wild creatures in the continent's wildest places.

*Burnham and Mexican Mountain Sheep, 1917*

*Burnham on Mexican Hunting Trip*

# Chapter 10

## Unpopular Game Laws and the Hunter's Questionnaire

Chazy Lake, New York. September 28th, 1909

"No, sir," said the hotel proprietor, "you will have to offer more than $35 to make me part with that hound."

The chance visitor coming out on the veranda from the dining room of the country hostelry looked around curiously. He was something of a sportsman himself and had an idea that since the passage of the law prohibiting the use of dogs for hunting deer the bottom had dropped out of the hound market, but here were figures that smacked of the palmy days of the sport.

He waited a moment 'til he heard the hotel-man set his price for the slouching, bleary-eyed parcel of dog meat at $100; then he walked over to the country store and, purchasing a cigar, entered into conversation with the proprietor.

"Hounds are up again," admitted the storekeeper. "For a while you could buy good dogs cheap, but the market has been pretty well cleaned out and now a hound's a hound again."

'I see,' said the stranger, 'but the law against hounding hasn't been repealed, has it?'

"No," said the storekeeper, "There was talk of repealing it but for some reason it didn't go. It's against popular sentiment, something like this Vermont liquor law, and there are a good many who don't observe it. These Dannemora Prison Guards are great fellows for sport and that has helped raise the price for good dogs. Two years ago the game protector at Mooers came down on them and bagged eight guards and keepers at one time, and they had to pay $250, which was a pretty good round price for fly-blown venison, according to my way of thinking. They're dead game though, and at it now just as bad as ever.

"The Frenchmen at the north end of the lake are in it with the keepers. They start the deer for them, and since they've cut the voices of their dogs it's next to impossible to convict them. What do they do to the dogs? Oh, I don't know exactly. They have a way of cutting out their tonsils that they say makes them dumb as a thief in a strange henhouse. It's better than the old way of letting the dogs run muzzled."

"The Frenchmen net lots of trout too, against the law, and sell them at the Prison. Old Ben St. Germain, who used to crust deer himself, turned informer last year and had some of them arrested, but it didn't stop the illegal netting. The Frenchmen built a stone fort on Halfway Point in Chazy Lake and defied the game protectors. St. Germain and his boys tried to arrest them, and the two sides had a pitched battle one night with stones at first for missiles and afterward, rifle and revolver bullets. The netters got the best of it and I guess

St. Germain has let them do as they please since then. There isn't much in it anyway for him. A year or two ago the State allowed $5.00 apiece for seized nets over 200 feet in length, but now there's no bounty and not much inducement for the game-law protectors.

"The same gang of Frenchmen that net in Summer and hound in the Fall put in their time in Winter crusting deer. Philip Sawyers is one of them — name doesn't sound French, but it's the nearest we can come to their lingo. Sawyer followed a deer on the crust out in the clearing back of St. Germain's. He stood just inside the woods and shot the deer and dropped it in plain sight of the house. Sawyer saw that the people there were watching to find out who killed the deer, and he knew if he walked out to get it as he was he would be recognized. So he made a mask, put that over his head, stripped off all his clothes, slid 'em on the snow and walked out there as naked as the day he was born. Then he got the deer and dragged it back to the woods.

"The game might have worked with another man but it didn't with Sawyer, for he had a walk you could tell from Jerusalem to Jericho, two towns in Clinton County just north of us, you know, — and besides, St. Germain's folks knew nobody but Phil Sawyer would have thought of doing such a thing. So old Ben got on his trail, and now Sawyer's rusticating at Saranac Lake.

"The Sawyer crowd had it born in them to break the game-laws, and every other law for that matter they could make five cents out of by fracturing. Old Sawyer lived by breaking laws, you might say. He snared partridges, crusted deer and netted trout and between times smuggled wine in from Canada. He had sort of a canteen arrangement that was hung by shoulder straps and fitted close around his body under his coat, and many's the time he's gone north on the Ellenburg road with it empty and come back with it full, and himself full too in the bargain. He dasn't ship his netted trout by the railroad and so he generally brought them down to the Prison himself to sell. He's had all kinds of trouble with game constables and one thing and another; he had a sour, crabbed temper, and he used to talk there in the Prison against the State and cuss it out 'til they got to calling him a dyed-in-the wool, sure-enough anarchist.

"It tickled the prisoners to hear old Sawyer talk and swear, and the word was passed around that whenever any of them made a break old Sawyer's was the place to strike for, because he'd be sure to see them through on account of his enmity to law and order. Well, one night three fellows came to Sawyer's place, let him know they'd given the Prison the slip and wanted him to help them over the Line. Sawyer said he'd need a little money for expenses so they gave him what they had and then waited for him by a haystack till he went into the house to get his canteen arrangement; for he told them he wanted to kill two birds with one stone and bring back some high wines on the return trip. When he got to the house, instead of doing as he said, he sent over for Charlie Turner. Next old Sawyer and Turner got their guns and the first thing the convicts knew Sawyer had captured them and was marching them back to Dannemora Prison over the mountain. Sawyer got the regular reward of $100 a head for the captured men, and since then he's left off his anarchist talk and thinks himself that he's one of the pillars of the law and a leading citizen.

"Talking about the game laws," continued the storekeeper, "they are not held in any too much respect in this country. A good lawyer can get a man off under almost any circumstances, provided the man has the price of a retainer in his clothes. There was the case of the fellow over at Clintonville who was arrested for catching trout through the ice in Trout Pond. Lawyer Boynton of Keeseville defended him, and he had him acquitted, though it was proved up to the hilt that the man was guilty. The prosecution showed that the man had been fishing through the ice and that he had caught six trout, and the identity of the fish was proved beyond the shadow of a doubt. Boynton, when it came his turn to argue, says, 'I admit everything the prosecution has tried to prove but,' says he, 'their case is incomplete. The statute reads that fishing shall not be done through the ice in waters inhabited by trout. The prosecution has presented no evidence whatever to show that Trout Pond was inhabited by trout after my client caught the six which were taken from it. Since it has not been proved to be a trout water, inhabited by trout, I move that my client be discharged!' And discharged he was, for the sympathy of folks up here is mostly with the men who hunt and fish even if they don't get their game just as is prescribed, and against the protectors.

"The game-laws are unpopular because we believe the city people make them without regard to our interests. Take the law against hounding, for example. If it was put to popular vote today, nine out of ten men in Clinton County would vote for its repeal. Their fathers and grandfathers used hounds for hunting deer, and these men can't see why they should be stopped from doing the same thing. It isn't any too pleasant a job to be game constable under the circumstances. They say this man Cameron over at Saranac Lake gave up the job because it was too trying on his nerves. The story goes that he was peeking in at a window one Winter night watching to catch a man cooking some venison he had killed contrary to law, and the fellow saw him standing outside there in his fur coat. Says he, 'Either that sneaking, low-lived constable will leave here mighty quick or else he won't!' — and without waiting to open the window he fired through the glass at the man outside, and put the ball through his fur coat between his arm and his body. The game protector left P.D.Q., and the next day he sent in his resignation. Since then he has minded his own business just as if he was paid to do it.

"Say, here's a funny thing that appeared in one of our newspapers the other day," said the storekeeper, as he produced a copy of the *Republican*. The local correspondent at North Hudson in Essex County sent this note:

> There is a gentleman stopping at D. Laymond's claiming to be a game protector sent here by the Fish, Forest and Game Commission. He has been here for the last two years and what we would like to know is if the Commission can't find men in our own state to fill the place without going into New Jersey and hiring such men to come up here and try to put up a game of bluff, dodging here and there pretending to be watching parties when actually he is somewhere else either hounding deer or hunting over somebody's camp to see if he can't find some fishing tackle to catch trout when it is out of season.

"Then in the same issue of the paper only in another place, it says:

"State-protector J. W. Pond is stopping at D. Laymond's, North Hudson."

"Now that sounds very funny to me because it seems to identify the head of the game protective department in this state with the suspicious individual who, according to the local correspondent, has been breaking the laws while pretending to enforce them. Of course, Pond was there for another purpose, but he either fooled those people badly, or else the correspondent had a grudge when he wrote the note.

"Major Pond, as I happen to know, is a hard-working official and a capable man, but on account of his job of stopping hounding and game-lawbreaking in general, there isn't a more unpopular man in certain parts of the woods. When I was over at Saranac last Winter they had a joke on Pond that tickled the boys. Now Slater is a first-class guide and a man who has the reputation of being one of the best still-hunters in the Adirondacks, and at the same time one who never knows when to stop killing as long as there is a deer in the woods. He has a camp at Grass Pond in a fine game country and last year some people said he killed forty or fifty deer for sportsmen or food in his camp or one thing or another. Along the last of the season, Pond, who was on his way down from Malone, met Slater on the train and asked him where he was going. Slater told him that he was going out to his camp to kill a deer or two for his Winter's meat. Pond didn't like that for the law prohibited having venison in possession after a date that was only a few days off. He suspected Slater of killing more than the two deer allowed by law and had had constables out in the woods more than once trying to get a case against him, so he bristled up a little and says, 'Mr. Slater,' says he, 'how many deer have you killed this season, anyway?'

'Couldn't say within one or two,' says Slater, cool as a cucumber, 'but it's somewheres in the neighborhood of fifty.'

'Well,' says Pond, as he chewed on the words and swallowed 'em hard, 'I guess a couple more won't make much difference!'

"Pond couldn't say anything else for he realized Slater's beautiful cheek, and that it was nobody's fault but his own that he'd run up against it.

"The law used to be that half the fine for convictions for breaking the game-laws went to the informer. I knew of a man who under those circumstances informed on himself. He'd shot four or five great big trout on the spawning bed without knowing it was against the law, and he felt very proud of the fish and walked along the main road showing them to everybody he met and telling them the cute way he had secured them.

"After a while one of the men he met informed him that there was a fine of $5.00 apiece for shooting trout. The fellow, whose name is Albert Winch, was taken all aback for he realized that every man who had a grudge against him in town would know the facts before long, and that he was likely any minute to be in the clutches of the game protector who lived less than a mile away. He reasoned that as he was in for it anyway the half of the fine that went to the informer would be a good deal more comforting in his own pocket than if it was presented to someone else. So he hurried to the game protector's house, told on himself and got off by paying $2.50 each for the trout instead of $5.00."...

## The Hunter's Questionnaire

This appeared in the Sun Dial section of the New York *Sun* on Dec. 11, 1928, and shows another aspect of Burnham's nature — his command of sizzling sarcasm. It epitomizes his scorn for all those so-called hunters who take to the fields and forests every Fall with practically no preliminary training and experience. Their annual depredations and disgusting lack of manners and common courtesy evoke the wrath and indignation of landowners, true hunters and everyone else as well.

Even though it sounds like facetious spoofing Burnham was deadly serious when he composed this devastating diatribe:

1. — Do you hunt any specific game or will you take anything?
2. — How long have you been a menace to innocent bystanders?
3. — What is the difference between a partridge rising from the bushes and a farmer, the father of six children, stepping on some dead limbs in a thicket?
4. — In what respect does a doe with a white face differ from a hired man with a wheelbarrow?
5. — Give three distinguishing marks between a deer and a student of woodcraft.
6. — What is the difference between the sound made by a deer crashing through a thicket and a party of Ford picnickers opening a box luncheon on a stone wall?
7. — Describe a milch cow.

8. — Describe a moose.

9. — Are you sure you are not mixed up?

10. — Give a fifty-word description of a buggy-horse grazing peacefully in a field thirty yards away and state the difference, if any, between its appearance and that of a deer in full flight.

11. — Describe a farmhand walking across a woodlot with a rake over his right shoulder, whistling "Crazy Rhythm," and tell how you distinguish him from a quail sitting on a log calling to its mate.

12. — If raccoons resemble cider-mill proprietors with chin whiskers, make a cross here ...... but if a farmer's prize sow is a dead ringer in your estimation for a pheasant draw a circle here.......

13. — Does a flock of sheep in your opinion strongly resemble a herd of elk? A covey of bob-whites? A pheasant and six chicks?

14. — What's wrong with this sentence: A rabbit is a four-legged animal resembling a shepherd dog, although it is easily mistaken for a bull, drafthorse or man chopping wood?

15. — Give the errors in this statement: A deer has two legs, belongs to the Caucasian race, wears overalls and cowhide boots, has a very sunburned neck and is found on most any farm?

16. — State how many hunting trips you made last year and give names and addresses of victims.

17. — Do you make a habit of shooting at curious noises and riddling tourists in open cars?

18. — Do you go duck hunting, and if so when did you last blow a hole in the bottom of the boat?

19. — Give names of three oculists who will certify that you are not suffering from astigmatism.

20. — What will you take to put away your gun in the interests of society and become a safe citizen to be at large?

Sign here..................................................

# Chapter 11

## The History of the Deer in New York State (1920)

The history of the deer in New York State is an interesting one for several reasons, not least among which is the illustration it affords as to what is taking place in some of the older states, and also because of the check-up afforded by Forester's observations seventy-five years ago. Today, in this state of ten million people, there is hardly a county, excepting the metropolitan area, where wild deer are not found. While in the northern part of the state where conditions are most suitable, I believe there are more deer today than ever existed in that section. When I first went to the Adirondacks thirty-eight years ago, I talked with Mose Ames, Smith Beede and many of the old-time woodsmen who were pioneers in this section and they told me that prior to the Civil War, the wolves which infested the region harried the deer to such an extent that they were nowhere abundant. When hunting on the snow it was the rule rather than the exception to find wolf tracks following the tracks of deer.

After the wolves were exterminated or migrated to lower Canada, no one knows exactly what happened, the deer were beset by a new danger, for market hunting developed on a large scale and the deer were given no chance to increase. All the old roads penetrating the heart of this natural sanctuary were opened by market-hunters. It was the custom of these men to go back into the woods with the first snows in the Fall and to kill deer all Winter. The deer were shipped out on sleighs to Albany and other points having a large consuming population and, after the bottom dropped out of the roads with the Spring thaws, many of the hunters remained to carry on their merciless war of extermination for the fifty or seventy-five cents they received for the hides of the poor animals. When a deer-yard was located these butchers ran the animals down on snowshoes and killed them with clubs to save the expense of ammunition. Under such conditions the deer were completely exterminated in Vermont and all but wiped out in Northern New York.

The market-hunters, teamsters and market-men in the cities had a very considerable political influence and the hardest fight the sportsmen of the day had to make was to save these Adirondack deer. After the legislation was secured prohibiting the transportation of venison for sale, the deer slowly increased for a time; but the practice of hounding became increasingly popular and, had it not been for the creation of large preserves which afforded asylums in different parts of the woods, I believe that the last of the Adirondack deer would have been taken at this time. I know that in 1886 it was difficult through most of this wooded country to find deer tracks for a "start." In addition to hounding, other destructive methods were employed, such as jacking and shooting at salt licks. When lumbering operations on the spruce commenced on a large scale, most of the lumber camps were supplied with venison, as it could be obtained, in order to save the expense of purchasing meat. The crews of the lumber camps were encouraged to hunt on Sundays and holidays and some of the camps employed professional hunters.

Twenty years ago, when I became Chief Game Protector of the State, good laws had been enacted and under them I succeeded in stopping the most flagrant abuses. Today in New York, we have a Buck Law, which absolutely protects the does and fawns at all seasons of the year. A hunter is permitted to take one buck during the four weeks' season from October 15th to November 15th. Under this law which insures the maintenance of breeding stock, the Adirondack deer have tremendously increased until now in the wilderness proper, the food capacities of the section have been reached and in some places passed. On the south branch of the Moose River, for example, the winter food which is the test, is not sufficient to sustain the present deer population so that the Conservation Commission is obliged to provide wild hay and cut hardwood trees for browse. In severe Winters many deer die in the Adirondacks from starvation. It would be as unwise therefore to stop deer-hunting under such conditions as it is unnecessary. State ownership of forests with constitutional prohibition against cutting reduces food.

I have alluded to the extermination of the deer shortly after the Civil War in the state of Vermont. They were restored to the state by sportsmen. In 1878, twenty citizens of Rutland and Bennington Counties raised a fund and secured seventeen deer from the Lewey Lake section of the Adirondacks; these were released in Vermont and protected by law for nineteen years. Then these Vermont sportsmen, who were hard-headed Yankees, evolved the principle of the "Buck Law." They declared an open season in 1897 during which bucks could be hunted, and this open season has been continued each Fall since that time. From 1897 to 1900 a total of only four hundred and sixty deer were killed or an average of one hundred and sixteen deer per hunting season. During the next six years, the number taken averaged twenty-seven hundred and sixty-three deer per year. Since then some seasons have shown very much larger numbers of deer taken by the hunters. Vermont has applied common-sense principles to deer preservation longer than any other state in the Union. The result is what might be expected — there are more deer to the square mile in Vermont today than in any other state, and this despite the fact that fifty years ago the coverts had been completely stripped of this kind of game.

# Chapter 12

### The Future of the Adirondack State Park
### John Bird Burnham in THE NATIONAL PARKS BULLETIN — December, 1938

It is, I suppose, because in time past I have spent many moons in Washington fighting for National Park standards that I cannot get it out of my head that any park, state as well as Federal, should warrant its existence by conforming to some set of recognized values in the selection of the lands to be included. In New York, with the largest so-called park in the world no such standards have been established. The term "park" is more or less of a misnomer, for while the area in question embraces much that is up to standard from any viewpoint it also includes a miscellaneous hodge-podge of lands, good, bad and indifferent. The general impression of the cognoscenti is that the label "park" has been misused. It is difficult to escape the conviction that in buying lands undue emphasis has sometimes been placed on quantity rather than quality. Those responsible for the park are naturally proud of the fact that it is the largest state-owned park in the country, and perhaps this has led them to look on mere size as the great desideratum.

I have the highest respect for the men at present responsible for the Adirondack Park, but I think they should call on expert outside advice and formulate a plan embracing standards before they acquire any more land. The administrators are handicapped more than they realize by precedent. The park had a double genesis. One was the report of the Sargent Commission recommending the establishment of such a park, but the realization of this recommendation was undoubtedly assisted by a desire of the Adirondack lumbermen to have a market for their logged-off lands which might otherwise have gone to the state for taxes. The one subsequent expansion of the "Blue Line" in 1931 was made at the request of various conservation associations, but again it had the ardent support of lumbermen who wanted the park to embrace lands in which they had a financial interest. The quality of the extension has been little considered, aside from stumpage values. By various extensions of the Blue Line the area of the park has grown until at the present time it includes one-seventh of the State of New York.

In view of the fact that the trees may not be cut, why should the State consider stumpage values at all when making its purchases? Should not the aesthetic values be the sole criterion? I believe this situation is due to the unfortunate parentage of the "park." The State simply cannot get away from the lumberman's perspective.

One of the governing principles of management which had its dangerous aspect is the State's desire to connect and consolidate its holdings. This principle would be admirable with a compact park conforming with park standards, but when the area embraced sprawls over a considerable part of the state and when the Blue Line location has been ill considered, the policy leads again to the purchase of land without regard to quality.[1]

I am a believer in Article VII, Section 7 of the State Constitution[2], but I think the area so controlled (by regulations more severe than those applied to National Parks) should be selected to conform to principles applicable to first-class parks. If the restrictions were less severe, greater latitude in the selection of lands would be permissible. Severe restrictions imply exacting selection. It should not be otherwise. Therefore, it is my contention that the Conservation Department of New York[3] should at once secure the services of a committee of park experts and adopt a policy consistent with their recommendations, and that no further purchases of land be made until this is done.

---

[1] Burnham's comments apply only to the Forest Preserve lands in the Adirondacks — about 42% of the total 6 million acres. The remainder consists of private holdings not subject to State controls until the advent of Adirondack Park Agency in 1972: Editor.

[2] Now designated as Article XIV, Section 1.

[3] Now called Department of Environmental Conservation.

## Partial List of Published Material By and About John Bird Burnham

About:

1. Spears, Raymond S., N.Y. Chief Game Protector, *FOREST AND STREAM,* Nov. 25, 1905
2. The New York Game Protector, *FOREST AND STREAM,* December 2, 1905
3. Christaboro, C., Strenuous Game Warden, *FOREST AND STREAM,* December 9, 1905
4. Derieux, James C., John Burnham, *FIELD AND STREAM,* May, 1929
5. Derieux, James C., There'll Never Be A Time, *AMERICAN MAGAZINE,* May, 1932
6. John B. Burnham Dies, *AMERICAN WILDLIFE,* November-December, 1939
7. Webster, George C., Essex Resident Pays Tribute to John B. Burnham, *THE LUMBER CAMP NEWS,* January, 1940
8. Kranz, Marvin, *Pioneering in Conservation, A History of the Conservation Movement in New York State (1865-1905).* Doctoral thesis published by Syracuse University Press. Kranz cites Burnham collection as especially valuable primary sources.

By:

1. Pseudonym Jay Bebee, Ascent of Marcy, *RUGBY MONTHLY,* October, 1885
2. Campfire Flickerings, *FOREST AND STREAM,* December 3, 1891
3. A Sociable Bear (re Hi Benham of Saranac Lake) New York *Sunday Recorder,* August 9, 1893
4. The Adirondack "Caribou" — *FOREST AND STREAM,* October 14, 1893
5. Adirondack Deer Law, *FOREST AND STREAM,* July 29, 1893
6. de Bois, Gens (pseudonym), A Winter Hunt with Jock Darling Parts 1 and 2 *FOREST AND STREAM,* January 5, 11, 1896
7. Exotic Game in American Preserves, *FOREST AND STREAM,* 1893-1897
8. Winter Camp on Wadleigh Brook, *FOREST AND STREAM,* January 30, 1897
9. Haps and Mishaps, *FOREST AND STREAM,* February, 1898
10. Yukon Notes (series of six), *FOREST AND STREAM,* Started March 26, 1898
11. Fishing in Northern New York, *FOREST AND STREAM,* June 11, 1898
12. Skagway, *FOREST AND STREAM,* June 18, 1898
13. It Depends Upon the Bear, *FOREST AND STREAM,* July 28, 1898
14. Lake Champlain Fishing, *FOREST AND STREAM,* August 27, 1898
15. Boquet River, *FOREST AND STREAM,* September 10, 1898
16. Adirondack Deer Hunting Conditions, *FOREST AND STREAM,* September 24, 1898
17. Error in the Official Adirondack Map, *FOREST AND STREAM,* October 22, 1898
18. Adirondack Deer Law, *FOREST AND STREAM,* November 12, 1898
19. Guy Brittell, *FOREST AND STREAM,* January 7, 1899
20. Guy Ferguson, *FOREST AND STREAM,* March 11, 1899
21. Gens des Bois, *FOREST AND STREAM,* May 6, 1899

22. Maine Bear Trappers, *FOREST AND STREAM,* August 26, 1899
23. Adirondack Deer Hounding, *FOREST AND STREAM,* October 28, 1899
24. Adirondack Deer Hounding, *FOREST AND STREAM,* November 18, 1899
25. Two Days' Hunt at North Hudson, *FOREST AND STREAM,* December, 1899
26. Told at the Sportsmen's Show, *FOREST AND STREAM,* March 17, 1900
27. George Mc Bride, *FOREST AND STREAM,* March 24, 1900
28. Echoes of the New York Show, *FOREST AND STREAM,* April 7, 1900
29. Elijah Simonds, *FOREST AND STREAM,* May 12, 1900
30. Martin Van Buren Moody, *FOREST AND STREAM,* June 2, 1900
31. Simeon J. Moody, *FOREST AND STREAM,* September 8, 1900
32. Plumadore, *FOREST AND STREAM,* October 6, 1900
33. Obituary of Rowland E. Robinson, Blind Vermont Author, *FOREST AND STREAM,* October 27, 1900
34. James M. Wardner, *FOREST AND STREAM,* Nov. 10, 1900
35. Eastern Adirondack Winter, *FOREST AND STREAM,* February 16, 1901
36. Spring in the Adirondacks, *FOREST AND STREAM,* April 27, 1901
37. The House for $350.00, *LADIES HOME JOURNAL,* May, 1901
38. Joseph McGuire, *FOREST AND STREAM,* May 4, 1901
39. The Ice in the Yukon, *THE WHITE WORLD,* Lewis, Scribner & Co., 1902
40. Outing in the Snow, *FOREST AND STREAM,* April 5, 1902
41. Maple Sugar, *FOREST AND STREAM,* April 19, 1902
42. Adirondack Notes, *FOREST AND STREAM,* August 16, 1902
43. Lake Champlain Pollution, *FOREST AND STREAM,* January 2, 1904
44. Adirondack Animals, New York State *FOREST, FISH AND GAME COMMISSION, ANNUAL REPORT,* 1907-1908-1909, p.372-79
45. Panthers in the Adirondacks, *FOREST AND STREAM,* September 6, 1909
46. Men I Have Worked With, *FOREST AND STREAM,* September 6, 1913
47. Common Sense in Game Protection, *JOURNAL OF AMERICAN MUSEUM OF NATURAL HISTORY,* 1916
48. Call of the Hunter, *DU PONT MAGAZINE,* January 19, 1920
49. Hunting and Conservation, *BOONE AND CROCKETT CLUB,* Yale Univ. Press, 1925
50. Shall the Blind Lead the Blind?, *OUTLOOK,* October 14, 1925
51. Our Game Izaak Walton League, reprinted from *OUTDOOR AMERICAN,* November, 1925
52. What Are the Facts? *OUTDOOR LIFE,* January, 1929
53. Plimsoll Line, *JOURNAL OF MAMMALOGY,* February, 1929
54. *The Rim of Mystery,* A Hunter's Wanderings in Unknown Siberian Asia, G.P. Putnam's Sons, 1929 — 60 illustrations, Map, 281 pp.
55. A Hunting License Test, *FOREST AND STREAM,* January, 1930
56. Back to Log Cabin Days, *HOUSE AND GARDEN,* June, 1933
57. On the Track of the Unknown Sheep, *Explorers' Club Tales,* Dodd Mead, 1936
58. Agni, the Fire, *FIELD AND STREAM,* December, 1936
59. Progress of Conservation in New York State, N.Y.S. *SPORTSMAN,* September, October 10, 1937
60. Burnham Urges Creation of Lake Champlain Authority, *ESSEX COUNTY Republican,* September 17, 1938
61. Future of the Adirondack State Park, *NATIONAL PARKS,* December, 1939
62. Natives of the Chukatch *NATIONAL GEOGRAPHIC* n.d.

# Index

ABIQUI, New Mexico 17
ACME FOLDING CANVAS BOAT COMPANY, Miamisburg, Ohio 54
ADAMS, Samuel Hopkins 13
ADIRONDACK MOUNTAIN CLUB 201
ADIRONDACK MOUNTAIN RESERVE 30
ADIRONDACK PARK 12, 210, 260
ADIRONDACK PARK AGENCY. Blue Line. 12, 260, 261
ADIRONDACK STUDY COMMISSION 12
ADIRONDACKS, THE (mountains) 13, 110, 111, 115, 119, 126, 127, 172, 173, 207, 209, 233, 245, 255, 258, 259, 260, 261
AFRICA 240
AIDEN LAIR 233
ALASKA 31, 33, 35, 37, 75, 108, 110-111, 142, 160, 177, 206-207, 216, 219
ALASKA. Game and Fur Laws 17
ALASKA GAME COMMISSION 164
ALBANY, New York 166, 171, 177, 228, 244, 258
ALCORN, Professor 25, 124
ALEXANDER, Mark 187
ALGONQUIN INDIANS 203
ALICE FALLS 234
ALL SOULS (chapel) 30
ALLDS, Senator Jotham P. 191, 228
ALLEN, Ethan 136
*AMERICAN FORESTS* (periodical) 17, 171
*AMERICAN GAME* (periodical) 189, 219
AMERICAN GAME ASSOCIATION FOUNDATION 189
AMERICAN GAME PROTECTIVE AND PROPAGATION ASSOCIATION 9, 12, 170, 178, 179, 182, 183, 187, 188, 189, 192, 193, 194, 195, 197, 198, 199, 200, 201, 205, 227, 232, 243
*AMERICAN MAGAZINE* (periodical) 16, 164
AMERICAN REVOLUTION 237
AMERICAN WILDLIFE INSTITUTE 189
AMES, Mose 258
AMSTEL HOUSE 19, 205
AMUNDSEN, Raold 214, 216, 217 219, 220, 221
AMUR RIVER 227
"ANGEL GABRIEL" (ship) 20, 180
ANTARCTIC 217, 224
ANTHONY, Congressman 193
APPOQUINOMINK FARM 20, 21
ARCTIC 94, 160, 216, 219
ARCTIC CLUB 217
ARCTIC OCEAN 81, 186

ARIZONA. Sonora Desert and Ghost Ranch Museums 17
ASIA 240
ASPEN, Colorado 40
ASSOCIATED GAS AND ELECTRIC CORPORATION 128
ASSOCIATED STEAMSHIP LINES OF CANADA 183, 184
ASSOCIATION FOR THE PROTECTION OF THE ADIRONDACKS 155, 177, 207
AUDUBON SOCIETY 28, 238, 242, 247
AUSABLE CHASM 234
AUSABLE RIVER 128
AUSABLE VALLEY 149
AUSTRALIA 33, 212

BABYLON, New York 30
BAILEY (Indian) 72, 74
BAKER, Newton B. (Secretary of War) 235
BALTIMORE, Lord *See* Calvert, George
BALTIMORE AND OHIO RAILROAD 22
BARNES, Charles 151
BARROW, Point 227
BARTLETT, Captain Bob 166
BARTON (miner) 90, 91
BARTON, Dr. Guy 139-140
BAYNE LAW 190
BEACH, Rex 90
"BEAR" (ship) 160
BEAR MOUNTAIN STATE PARK 17
BEARD, Dan 166, 195
BEARDSLEY, Rear Admiral 89
BEAVER'S BAY 109
BECK, Thomas 12
BEEDE, Fletcher 173-175
BEEDE, Smith 258
BEETLE, David 13
BEHRENS (packer) 89
BENNETT, Lake 40, 41, 51, 54, 55, 62, 89, 106, 212
BENNETT TRAIL 47, 53
BENNINGTON COUNTY, Vermont 259
BERING, Vitus 227
BERING SEA 58, 76, 227
BERRY, Clarence 90
BIG SALMON RIVER 80, 98, 100, 211
BILLY THE COP 47-48, 54
BIRD, Elizabeth Van Leuveneigh *See* Burnham, Elizabeth Van Leuveneigh (Bird)
BLANK, Colonel 155
BLEASE, Governor 179
BLUNGIE, Charley 234
BONANZA CREEK 33, 89, 90
BOOK OF THE BOONE AND CROCKETT CLUB 232
BOONE AND CROCKETT CLUB 111, 179, 206, 235

BOOTH FISHERIES COMPANY 187
BOQUET ELECTRIC COMPANY 13, 128, 206
BOSTON TRANSCRIPT (newspaper) 115
BOUQUET RIVER 128, 153, 155
BOYD, Arnold 160
BOYLE, Pat 129
BOYNTON (lawyer) 254-255
BRANDYWINE RIVER 22
BREWSTER, C. Bryon 195
BRITISH COLUMBIA 183, 184, 212
BRITISH EMBASSY 185
BROMLEY, Doctor 140-141
BROOKLYN NAVY YARD 229
BRUNNER, Edmund J. 230
BRYAN, William J. 182
BULL MOOSE PARTY 154, 156
BULWAYO, South Africa 212
BUMP, Doctor Gardiner 164
BURLINGTON, Vermont 135, 232
BURMASTER, Ray 164
BURNHAM, Eliza 20, 21
BURNHAM, Elizabeth Van Leuveneigh (Bird) 19, 205
BURNHAM, Major Frederick Russell 91
BURNHAM, Henrietta Haines (DuBois) 29-32, 206
BURNHAM, John (father of John Bird Burnham) 20, 205
BURNHAM, John (son of John Bird Burnham) 200
BURNHAM, Koert D. 11, 13, 18, 31, 54, 127, 142, 164, 205, 206
BURNHAM, Lucy 21
BURNHAM, Rose Van Leuveneigh 13, 205, 206
BURNHAM, Senator 180-181
BURNING DAYLIGHT, by London, Jack 90
BURRELL, Sir Martin 183-185
BURROUGHS, John 192
BURT, John 136
BUTLER, Pennsylvania 178
BYRD, William 19
BYRNE, Willie 104

CALIFORNIA 33, 194, 251
CALVERT, George (Lord Baltimore) 19
CAMEL'S HUMP 125
CAMERON (game constable) 255
CAMP FIRE CLUB OF AMERICA 9, 163-164, 179, 180, 194, 195, 205, 206
CAMPFIRES IN THE ROCKIES, by Hornaday, William T. 190
CANADA 13, 17, 35, 111, 160, 182, 183, 184, 185, 186, 206, 254, 258
CANADA. Commission on Conservation 185

265

CANADA. Migratory Birds Convention Act 185
CANADIAN INDIANS 182
CANADIAN KLONDIKE 33
CANADIAN NATIONAL PARKS 185
CANADIAN PACIFIC (railroad) 112, 183, 184
CANADIAN YUKON COMPANY 82
CANNON, Joseph 242
CARIBOU 43
CARMACK, George W. 33, 89
CARMER, Carl 13
CARPENDALE, Charley 214
CARPENDALE, Cosconito 214, 216
CARR (chief attorney of the D & H Railroad) 150
CARR, William 17
CASEY (town-site promoter) 212
CASSELMAN, William 17
CASSIAR 43, 212
CATTARAUGUS COUNTY, New York 191
CHAMBERS, F.T.D. 185
CHAMPLAIN, Lake 12, 112-113, 119, 125, 129, 134-138, 150, 154, 170
CHAMPLAIN VALLEY 110
CHAPPAQUA, New York 127
CHAZY LAKE, New York 253
CHIEF GAME PROTECTOR. New York State 150-151, 155, 175, 232
CHILKOOT PASS 33, 35, 41, 58, 85, 89, 100, 101, 102, 106
CHILKOOT ROUTE 37, 41, 54
CHILLICOTHE, Ohio 29
CHIPPEWA INDIANS 30
CHUBB RIVER 150
CHUKOTSK PENINSULA, Siberia 111, 157
CHURCHILL, Winston 232
CIRCLE 33, 90
CIVIL WAR 29, 240, 258, 259
CIVILIAN CONSERVATION CORPS (CCC) 12, 115, 222, 223
"CLARA NEVADA" (ship) 108-109
CLARK, Dell 114
CLARK, Russell C. 186
CLARK, William R. 178
CLEMENS, Samuel 26
CLINTON COUNTY, New York 154, 254, 255
CLINTONVILLE, New York 254
"COFFIN", THE (boat) 138
COLD BROOK 131
COLGATE UNIVERSITY 139
COLORADO 189
CONGER, Senator 156, 191
CONNECTICUT 182
COOK, Doctor Frederick (explorer) 217, 227
COOK'S INLET 212
COOPER UNION 30
"CORWIN" (ship) See "Clara Nevada" (ship)
COURDNAHUNK LAKE 227
COVERED WAGON, by Hough, Emerson 198
COWL, Clarkson 221
CRAIG, James 17
CRATER CLUB 17, 110, 116, 119-129, 131, 206

CRATER HILL 119
CROSSETTE, George 17
CUNNINGHAM BROTHERS 48, 51-53
CUTTING, George Barton 139

"DAICHII TORO MARU" (ship) 111, 157, 159
DALTON, Jack 77, 85, 98
DAME, Captain 233-234
DANBURY, Conn. 140
DANNEMORA PRISON 253, 254
DARLING, Jay N. "DING" 12, 164, 189, 247
DARLING, Jonathan (Jock) 227, 250-252
DARROW, Robert 164
DAWSON, Sir John William 69
DAWSON CITY 33, 62, 64, 68, 74, 76, 77, 85, 87, 89, 95, 98, 99, 100, 211, 212
DEAD MAN'S ISLAND 227
DELAWARE 20, 172
DELAWARE AND HUDSON RAILROAD 112, 131, 150
DELAWARE BAY 23
DENVER, Colorado 199
DERBY, Stephen Decatur 119
DERIEUX, James C. 16, 17, 164, 251
DESORMO, Maitland 13, 18
DEVLIN, Minister 183
DILG, Will 187, 198-200
DIX, Governor 192, 228
DONALDSON, Alfred L. 177
DUBOIS (fellow hunter) 227
DUBOIS, George Washington 29
DUBOIS, Harry 31
DUBOIS, Henrietta Haines See Burnham, Henrietta Haines (DuBois)
DUBOIS, Maria Coxe (McIlvane) 29
DUNCAN, Dyson 208
DURANTS (Dr. Thomas C. Durant, William West Durant) 13
DUTCHER, William 179, 195, 247
DYEA 37, 106, 108

EASTON 138
ELDORADO 90
ELIZABETHTOWN, New York 17, 112, 174, 195
ELK RIVER GAME PRESERVE 190
ELLENBURG, New York 254
ELLIOTT (of the Grand Trunk Railroad) 184
ELLESMERE ISLAND 217
ELLSWORTH, Lincoln 160, 216, 220
ENCYCLOPEDIA BRITANNICA 190
ENDS OF THE EARTH CLUB 204
ESKIMOS 182, 220
ESSEX, Massachusetts 20
ESSEX, New York 11-12, 110, 116, 119, 128, 136-137, 141, 145, 150-151, 153-154, 155, 196, 206
ESSEX COUNTY CHAMBER OF COMMERCE 200

ESSEX COUNTY, New York 112, 150-151, 155, 172, 173, 174, 175, 191, 203, 206, 207, 234, 255
ESSEX COUNTY NATIONAL BANK 206
ESSEX COUNTY TAXPAYERS ASSOCIATION 206
ESSEX HORSE NAIL COMPANY 116, 129
EVALBANG ARCHIPELAGO 227
EVANS (sailor) 138
EVANS, Lou P. 164
EXPLORERS CLUB 206

FAIRBANKS, Alaska 33
FARIBAULT, Minnesota 30
FEDERAL GAME REFUGE BILL 236
FERRIS, Charley 112
FIELD AND STREAM (periodical) 251
FISH, Lieutenant-Governor (Vermont) 233
FISHER, Jerome B. 192
FISK, Governor 233
FITZGERALD, Judge 100
FIVE FINGERS RAPIDS 66, 212
FORBES PLACE (lot) 129, 131
FORD, Joseph A. 164
FOREST AND STREAM MAGAZINE (periodical) 9, 28, 29, 31, 32, 34, 109, 150, 160, 171, 172, 175, 198, 205, 217, 232, 237, 238, 242, 243
FOREST, FISH AND GAME LEAGUE 192, 193
FORESTER, Frank See Herbert, William Henry
FRANKLIN, Sir John 240
FRANKLIN COUNTY, New York 154
FREDERICK, Karl T. 164, 216
FREEDMAN'S POINT 62
FRENCH AND INDIAN WARS 203
FRESNO, California 90
FRIEDLANDER, Paul 13
FRIENDLY ARCTIC, by Stefansson, Vilhjalmur 97
FULTON MARKET 28
FUR SEAL TREATY 190

GACONA, Alaska 142
GARRETT, Congressman 188
GARRETT, Frank 23
GATES, John W. 228
GENEVA, Lake 125
GILLILAND, William 150
GLACIER NATIONAL PARK 28
GLENN, Morris 17
GORE, Senator 180
GORMAN, O. 229
GRAEFF, Jim 151
GRAND TRUNK RAILROAD 183, 184
GRANT, Madison 201
GRANT LAND 217
GRASS POND 255
GREAT BRITAIN 182
GREAT FALLS, Montana 53, 212
GREELEY, William B. 164
GREELY, General Adolphus Washington 219

266

GREEN, Judge 53
GREEN MOUNTAINS 119, 129
GREENLAND 89, 217
GRENFELL, Sir Wilfred 127
GRINNELL, George Bird 28, 150, 192, 201, 232, 238, 242, 247
GROG HARBOR 127, 138

HAINES, Henrietta 29
HALL, Robert F. 11, 13, 18
HALLOCK, Charles 237
HAM, George 184
HAMACHER 59
HAMILTON COLLEGE 13
HANBURG (miner) 75, 77, 78, 79, 80
HANSEN, Harry 17
"HAPPY JACK" (boat) 135
HARBORD, General 233
HARKIN, J.B. 185
HARRISON, President Benjamin 235
HARVARD CLUB 233
HARVARD CRIMSON 27
HARVARD UNIVERSITY 222
HASKELL, William S. 178, 179, 182
HASTINGS HOUSE 17
HAYES, Doctor A.L. 164
HAZLETON, British Columbia 102
HEATHCOTE, Colonel Caleb 29
HEFFERNAN, Judge 195, 196
HELENA, Montana 212
HENDERSON, Doctor D.W. 164
HENEY, Michael 40
HENSHAW, Henry 185
HEPBURN, Andy 87
HEPBURN, John 42, 43, 51, 62
HERBERT, William Henry (Frank Forester) 237, 238, 241, 249
HEWITT, Doctor C. Gordon 182-185
HIGGINS, Governor 155
"HIGHLANDS" 16, 110-111, 131, 160, 163, 166, 177-178, 205, 207
HIGHLANDS GAME PRESERVE, Willsboro, New York 9
HISTORY OF THE ADIRONDACKS, by Donaldson, Alfred L. 177
HOCHSCHILD, Harold 13
HOG BACK MOUNTAIN 40, 43
HOISINGTON (fellow hunter) 227
HOLLAND, Ray P. 185, 200, 219
HOOLTALINQUA RIVER 102, 212
HOOPER, Assemblyman Frank 164
HORNADAY, Doctor William T. 170-171, 179, 187, 190-196, 209
HOUGH, Emerson 198
HOUTCHIKOO BLUFF 99
HOWELL, Wallace 164
HUDSON RIVER 146
HUGHES, Governor Charles Evans 191
HUXLEY, Thomas 110
HUYLER COMPANY 114

IDAHO 189
IDITEROD 33
IMMANUEL CHURCH, New Castle, Delaware 21
INDIANA 247

INGALLS, Senator 235
INGE, Dean 236
INTERNATIONAL ASSOCIATION OF FISH, GAME AND CONSERVATION COMMISSIONERS 199-200
INTERSTATE PROTECTIVE ASSOCIATION 185-186
IOWA 189, 212
IPSWICH, Massachusetts 20
IRELAND 19
ISAAK WALTON LEAGUE 187, 198, 199
"ISLANDER" (steamer) 35

J.F. WHITE Corporation 128
JAMES, William 222-223
JAPAN 89, 159
JAPAN CURRENT 106
JERICHO, New York 254
JERUSALEM, New York 254
JOHN MISTLETOE, by Morley, Christopher 125
JOHNSON, Doctor E.F. 26, 114
JONES-ESCH LAW 202
JONESBORO, Arkansas 180

KANSAS 102, 200, 235
KEENE HEIGHTS, New York 30
KEENE VALLEY, New York 30, 173
KEESEVILLE, New York 16, 131, 132, 234, 254
KELLY, Mr. 104, 106
KENYON COLLEGE 29
KILPATRICK'S 23
KING (The) vs. Russell C. Clark (lawsuit) 186
KIPLING, Rudyard 221
KLONDIKE 11, 13, 31, 32, 33, 54, 79, 85, 90, 91, 93, 102, 113, 114, 141, 142, 170, 200, 209, 211, 212, 213
KLONDIKE GOLD RUSH 32-33, 35-109, 204, 205
KLONDIKE RIVER 76
KOIDERN RIVER 226
KORSOOKEEN, John A. 159-160

LABARGE, Lake 65-66, 78, 94, 104, 212
LAFAYETTE, Marquis Marie Joseph Paul Yves Gilbert du Motier 19
LAKE GEORGE, New York 127
LAKE PLACID (village) 150
LAKE PLACID CLUB 164
LAMBERT, General John 17
LAMOTTE, Isle 233
LARAMIE, Wyoming 13
LAW, Francis 234
LAWRENCE, Richard W., Jr. 13
LAWYER, George A. 187, 193
LAYMOND, D. 255
LEADERS IN AMERICAN CONSERVATION 17
LEAVENWORTH PENITENTIARY 229
LECOMPTE, Lee 200
LEECH LAKE 30
LEIPZIGER, Doctor 113
LEONARD, Harry S. 178
LEOPOLD, Aldo 12

LEWEY LAKE 259
LEWIS, New York 174
LEWIS RIVER 101
LINDERMAN, Lake 41, 58
LINDERMAN TRAIL 45
LINDSAY BROOK 174
LITTLE ROCK, Arkansas 200
LOG CABIN 45, 53-54
LOMENS (family) 216
LONDON, Jack 47, 90
LONG ISLAND SOUND 125
LOUGHREN, Doctor Robert 164
LOUISIANA 187
LOWNEY COMPANY 114
LUMBER CAMP NEWS 206
LYNN CANAL 108

MacAULEY, Norman 87
MacDONALD, "Big Alex" 90, 211
McALISTER, Frank 185
McAULEY, Mrs. 174
McCARTHY, Alaska 164
McDURPHY, Fred 138
McGINLEY, Miss 141
McILVANE, Rev. Charles Pettit 29
McILVANE, Maria Coxe See DuBois, Maria Coxe (McIlvane)
McKERCHER, Donald 43, 47-109, 217
McKINLEY, President 233
McKINLEY (mountain) 164
McKINLEY (MT.) NATIONAL PARK 201-202
McLEAN, Marshall 164
McLEAN, Senator 182, 193
McNALLY (miner) 102
McNEALLY (miner) 212
MADERS, Syd 132
MAGNA CARTA 237
MAINE 104, 226, 245
MALBY, Congressman 150
MALONE, New York 256
MAN AND SUPERMAN, by Shaw, George Bernard 205
MARSH LAKE 104
MARQUIS, Don 25
MASSACHUSETTS 179, 180, 247
MASTIC, New York 30
MATASSINGI (mountain) 216
MATHER, Jock 153
MAYO SANITARIUM 140
MEIGSVILLE, New York 174
MERRITT, Ed 154
MEXICO 111, 206, 233
MIDDLE LAKE 41, 43, 52
MIDDLETON, Commissioner Dewitt 177, 191
MIGRATORY BIRD ACT See U.S. Department of Agriculture. Migratory Bird Act
MIGRATORY BIRDS CONVENTION ACT See Canada. Migratory Birds Convention Act
MIGRATORY BIRD REFUGES 187-189, 194-195, 198-199
MIGRATORY BIRD TREATY See U.S. Department of Agriculture. Migratory Bird Treaty
MILE POINT, Vermont 136, 137
MILES, Judge 200
MILES CANYON 57-64, 87, 204
MILHOLLAND, John 13
MILLS, David 187

267

MINDS AND MANNERS OF ANIMALS, by Hornaday, William T. 190
MINNESOTA 189, 247
MINOR, Robert 30
MISERY, Port 131
MISSISSIPPI VS ILLINOIS (lawsuit) 178
MISSISSIPPI RIVER 85
MISSOURI (state) vs. Ray P. Holland (lawsuit) 185
MONDELL, Frank 188
MONTANA BUFFALO RANGE 190
MONTREAL, Quebec 12
MOOERS, New York 253
MOOSE RIVER 258
MOOSE SHOT ROUND THE CORNER, by Burnham, John Bird 171
MOOSEHEAD LAKE 227
MORELAND LAW 156
MORGAN, J.P., Sr. 30
MORGAN, Pierrepont 224-225, 239
MORLEY, Christopher 17, 125
MOSCOW 216
MUIR, John 162
MUSSEN, Jake 226

NANSEN, Fridtjof 81, 219
NARROWS, The (Lake Champlain) 138
NATIONAL ARTS CLUB 31
NATIONAL ASSOCIATION OF AUDUBON SOCIETIES 179
NATIONAL GAME REFUGE BILL 238
NATIONAL GEOGRAPHIC MAGAZINE (periodical) 17
NATIONAL PARKS ASSOCIATION 202
NATIONAL PARKS COMMITTEE 202
NATIONAL RECOVERY ACT 166
NATIONAL RIFLE ASSOCIATION 164
"NAUTILUS" (submarine) 160
NEBRASKA 189
NELSON, Doctor E.W. 17, 182-185, 187, 195
NESSMUK See Sears, George Washington
NEW, Senator Harry 188
NEW CASTLE, Delaware 19, 20, 21, 205
NEW DEAL, The 166, 168
NEW HAMPSHIRE 180
NEW HAVEN, CONNECTICUT 181
NEW JERSEY 237, 255
NEW MILFORD, Connecticut 226
NEW NETHERLANDS 237
NEW YORK CITY 9, 28, 85, 110, 112, 113-114, 142, 159, 178, 193, 235
NEW YORK (city) ZOOLOGICAL PARK 190, 194
NEW YORK (state) 12, 111, 119, 182, 202, 206, 237, 242, 243, 244, 245, 258, 259, 260, 261

NEW YORK (state) ASSEMBLY 150
NEW YORK (state) CONSERVATION COUNCIL 189, 259
NEW YORK (state) CONSERVATION COMMISSION 192
NEW YORK (state) DEPARTMENT OF CONSERVATION 164, 170, 177, 178, 245, 261
NEW YORK (state) FISH AND GAME COMMISSION 150, 155, 175, 177, 190, 191, 192, 243, 244, 255
NEW YORK (state) FISH AND GAME LAW 206
NEW YORK (state) SENATE 12, 150
NEW YORK AND PENNSYLVANIA COMPANY 164
NEW YORK ASSOCIATION FOR THE PROTECTION OF GAME 237, 243, 248, 249
NEW YORK HERALD TRIBUNE (newspaper) 196
NEW YORK SUN (newspaper) 256
NEW YORK TIMES (newspaper) 194, 195, 205, 206, 208
NEW YORK WORLD (newspaper) 40
NEWSOM, W.M. 164
NIAGARA FALLS 58
NIGGER JIM 90
NOBILE, Umberto 216
NOICE, Harold 219, 220
NOME, Alaska 33, 227
NORBECK, Senator Peter 188
NORBERT, Frank 194
NORDEUSKJOLD RIVER 101
NORGE (airship) 220
NORTH AMERICAN REVIEW (periodical) 206, 246
NORTH DAKOTA 189
NORTH FERRISBURG, Vermont 221
NORTH HUDSON, New York 173, 174, 255
NORTH POLE 81, 93, 160, 217, 224
NORTH RIVER, New York 127, 146
NORTHERN MONTHLY MAGAZINE (periodical) 171
NUTZOTIM MOUNTAINS 226

OBLATE FATHERS 145
OGDENSBURG, New York 30
OGILVY ROCKIES 76
OHIO 247
OHIO (11th) REGIMENT 29
OMENACRE 43
ONTARIO 106
ORMOND, Florida 21
OSBORNE, Lithgow 164, 243
OSBORNE, Thomas Mott 12, 228-229
OTTAWA, Canada 171, 183, 185
OTTER CREEK 128
OUR VANISHING WILDLIFE, by Hornaday, William 190, 192

PACIFIC OCEAN 58, 85, 106, 224
PAINE, Thomas 166
PAINES, (old Willsboro family) 13

PALMER, Doctor T.S. 180, 182
PARK AND TILFORD COMPANY 114
PAYNE, Dan 119-120, 124
PEARSON, Doctor T. Gilbert 179, 193
PEARY, Robert Edwin 82, 93, 217
PECHE, John 89
PECKHAM, Rufus 29
PELL, S.H.P. 204
PELLY RIVER 68, 69, 74, 82, 101
PEMAQUID, Maine 20
PENNSYLVANIA 240, 249
PENROSE, Boies 232
PETTY, Roundsman 232
PHELPS, Royal 237
PHILADELPHIA, Pennsylvania 20, 115, 127
"PHILADELPHIA" (ship) 89
PIERCE, Congressman Wallace 128
PINALS (mountains) 251
PINCHOT, Gifford 16, 195
PINCKNOR, "Poly" 200
PINNACLE (hill) 129, 131
PITTS (trader) 70, 73-76, 78, 82, 89-90, 98
PLATTSBURGH, New York 132, 151, 233, 234
PLYMOUTH, New Hampshire 127
POLAR CAVES 127
POND, Major J.W. 175-177, 255-256
PORTLAND, Oregon 33
PORTSMOUTH TREATY 157
POUND, Ezra 13
POST, Wiley 227
PRATT, Commissioner 243
PRATT, George 166, 195
PRESBYTERIAN HOSPITAL 141
PROCTOR, Senator 232-233
PULITZER, Joseph 40
PUMPKIN REEF 135
PUNCH (periodical) 198

QUEBEC (province) 183, 184
QUEBEC (province) BUREAU OF FISHERIES 185

RABBIT CREEK 33
RAMPARTS (mountains) 77-78
RASMUSSEN, Knud 219
RAT PORTAGE 212
REBER, New York 13, 128
REID, Frank H. 37
REMINGTON ARMS 28
RENAUD (miner) 75-80
REPUBLICAN (newspaper) 255
REYNOLDS, Charles B. 109, 150, 232, 238, 242
RIM OF MYSTERY, by Burnham, John Bird 9, 111, 160, 206, 207, 220
RINK RAPIDS 104
RIO GRANDE (river) 186
RISING SUN BREWERY 25
ROBINSON, ROWLAND 221
ROBINSON, Theodore Douglas 154-155
ROCKY MOUNTAINS 28
RODNEY, Caeser 19
ROGERS, Harry 244
ROME, New York 102

RONSBURG, California 212
ROOSEVELT, Robert B. 243
ROOSEVELT, Franklin Delano 12, 166, 168-169, 209, 228-230
ROOSEVELT, Theodore 16, 154, 162, 169, 188, 192, 195, 201, 209, 228, 232-235, 238, 247, 249
ROOT, Elihu 182
"ROSALIE" (ship) 109
ROSS, Anthony 150
ROYAL NORTHWEST POLICE 100
RUGBY MILITARY ACADEMY 22, 25, 31, 116, 205
RUTLAND COUNTY, Vermont 259
RYE-ON-THE-SOUND, New York 30

SAFFORD, Edgar 136-137
SAFFORD, Whitney 120, 124, 125
ST. ELIAS RANGE 164
ST. GERMAIN, Ben 253-254
ST. HUBERT'S, New York 30
ST. LAWRENCE COUNTY, New York 155
ST. LAWRENCE RIVER 30, 154
ST. LOUIS 85
ST. LOUIS BREWERS 198
ST. MICHAEL RIVER 33
SALT LAKE CITY, Utah 213
SAN FRANCISCO, California 33
SARANAC LAKE, New York 254, 255
SARANAC RIVER 128
SARATOGA, New York 196
SAWYER, Philip 254
SCARSDALE, New York 29
SCHLEY, Grant 216
SCHROON RIVER 174
SCHWATKA LAKE 64
SCOTT, Robert Falcon 219
SEAGER, Mrs. 115
SEARS, George Washington 147
SEATTLE 109
SELKIRK, Fort 69-70, 72, 74, 76, 79-80, 84, 93-94, 98
SELWYN CREEK 74-77
SEMINAW HILLS 103
SEWARD PENINSULA 33
SHACKELTON, Sir Ernest Henry 219
SHALLOW LAKE 41, 51-52
SHAW, George Bernard 205
SHEEHAN, "Blue-Eyed Billy" 229
SHEEP CAMP 89, 106
SHELDON, Charles 179
SHEPARD, A. 164
SHERMAN, FRED 116
SHERMAN, General Richard U. 243
SHIRAS, George 178, 193, 197, 201, 247
SIBERIA 9, 138, 157, 159, 160, 164, 170, 205, 206, 207, 216
SIFTON, Clifford 185
SILZ, August 228
SKAGWAY 32, 35, 37, 43, 47, 54, 108, 109, 112, 211, 212
SKAGWAY RIVER 40, 44
SKIFF, Victor 164
SKOOKUM, Jim 33

SLATER (guide) 255-256
SLAVIN, Frank 63, 82, 84, 87
SMITH, Alfred E. 169
SMITH, Jefferson R. 37
SOUTH AFRICA 33, 102
SOUTH CAROLINA 179
SOUTH DAKOTA 189
SOUTH POLE 214
SPEAR, Tom 131-133
SPEAR, Mrs. Tom 132
SPEARS, Raymond 114
SPIRIT OF THE TIMES (periodical) 237
SPLIT ROCK POINT 119, 125, 136, 138
SPOFFORD, A.R. 17
SPORTSMEN'S EXPOSITION 174
SQUAW RAPIDS 62-63
SQUIRE, H.C. 28, 29
STAFFORD, Charlie 131
STAFFORD, Dan 153
STAFFORD, Doctor John 141
STAFFORD, Paris 151-153
STAFFORD, Whitney 152-154
STAMFORD, Connecticut 195
STANAVOIE MOUNTAINS 216
STANDER, Antone 90
STANLEY, Sir Henry Morton 221
STAPLES (hunter) 250
STEFANSSON, Vilhjalmur 97, 160, 166, 206, 219, 220
STEVENS, George 150
STEVENS, John 150
STODDARD, Seneca Ray 171
STONE, Fred 120, 124
STORY OF THREE TOWNS, by Glenn, Morris 17
STRONG, Mrs. 112
STUBBS (hunter) 250-251
SULLIVAN, Black 106
SUMMIT LAKE 41, 43, 47, 51-53
SUNTHERS, Percy 187
SUPERIOR, Lake 212
SWEATT, Doctor 151-154

TABLET, The 27
TAFT, President 180-181
TAGISH CHARLEY 33
TAGISH LAKE 55, 100, 102
TAGISH POST 100
TALOS LAKE 227
TAMARAK, Captain 64
TAYLOR, Andy 111, 138, 157, 164
TENNESSEE 213
TERHUNE, Hugh 164
TEXAS 247
THAYER, Abbott 30
THIRTEEN BELOW DISCOVERY (claim) 90
THIRTEENTH LAKE 127
THIRTY-MILE RIVER 65, 95
THIRTY YEARS IN THE GOLDEN NORTH, by Welzl, Jan 64
THOMPSON (trader) 157
THOMPSON-SETON, Ernest 195
THOREAU, Henry David 143, 162
TIBBITTS (prospector) 212
TOOSHI MOUNTAINS 41
TRAYNOR, John 116
TRAYNOR, Philip 116
TREFETHEN, James B. 9, 17

TRINITY CHURCH, New York City 29
TRINITY COLLEGE, Connecticut 9, 26, 114, 205, 206
TROMBLEE, Meeker 152
TROMBLEE, Tom 152
TROUT BROOK 226-227
TROUT POND 254-255
TUCSON, Arizona 17
TURF, FIELD AND FARM (periodical) 243
TURNER, Charlie 254
TWAIN, Mark See Clemens, Samuel
TWENTIETH CENTURY AUTHORS 190
TWO YEARS IN THE JUNGLE, by Hornaday, William T. 190
TYRELL, Myron 154

UNITED STATES 35, 85, 89, 162, 184, 200, 206, 249
U.S. ARMY QUARTERMASTER Corps 160
U.S. BIOLOGICAL SURVEY 164, 180, 189, 194, 197, 201, 205
U.S. BUREAU OF BIOLOGICAL SURVEY 17, 182, 185, 187
U.S. CONGRESS 12, 178-182, 185-186, 188, 193-194, 198-201, 204, 224
U.S. CONGRESS. Committee on Agriculture 178
U.S. DEPARTMENT OF AGRICULTURE 194
U.S. DEPARTMENT OF AGRICULTURE. Advisory Committee on the Migratory Bird Law 9, 238, 248
U.S. DEPARTMENT OF AGRICULTURE. Migratory Bird Act. 170, 178-181, 193, 201, 238-239
U.S. DEPARTMENT OF AGRICULTURE. Migratory Bird Treaty. 9, 12, 17, 170, 180, 182-186, 205
U.S. DEPARTMENT OF POSTAL SERVICES 187
U.S. FOREST SERVICE COMMITTEE ON GAME IN THE NATIONAL FORESTS 9, 194
U.S. NATIONAL CONFERENCE ON OUTDOOR RECREATION. Committee on Game and Fur-bearing Animals 9
U.S. NATIONAL MUSEUM 190
U.S. REVOLVER ASSOCIATION 164
UNITED STATES VS. SHAUVER (lawsuit) 184
UPPER MISSISSIPPI RIVER WILDLIFE REFUGE 17, 198
UPPER YUKON RIVER See Lewis River
USHER (of the Canadian Pacific Railroad) 184
UTICA, New York 154

V.R. RANCH 27
VAN DYKE, Henry 221
VAN NESS HOTEL 232
VAN NORDEN, O.H. 164
"VERMONT" (ship) 125, 126

VERMONT (state) 136, 240, 249, 253, 258, 259
VERMONT FISH AND GAME ASSOCIATION 232-233
VICTORIA, British Columbia 183
VIRGINIA 19
VIRGINIAN, by Wister, Owen 27, 242

WADE, Crown Prosecutor 100
WADHAMS MILLS 119
WADLEIGH BOG 250
WALCOTT, Senator Frederic C.C. 188, 200
WALKER, Alex D. 164
WALPOLE, Horace 23
WALSH, Colonel 100
WALSH, Major 211-212
WALTON, Izaak 246
WARD, Colonel Samuel 212
WARM POND 129, 131
WARNER, Charles Dudley 26
WARNER, Seth 136
WASHINGTON, George 19
WASHINGTON, D.C. 154, 160, 166, 171, 184, 185, 190, 200-201, 230
WATERTOWN, New York 190
WATSON, Elkanah 13
WEAVER, John V.A. 13
WEBSTER, Rev. George 143, 145-147, 206, 208
WEEKS, Congressman 179-180, 182, 193
WEEKS-MCLEAN BILL See U.S. Department of Agriculture. Migratory Bird Act
WELSH, Louis 181
WELZL, Jan 64
WEST INDIA ASSOCIATION 237
WEST MILL BROOK 174

WESTOVER (Byrd family home) 19
WESTPORT, New York 12, 112
WHALLONSBURGH, New York 112, 128, 151, 153
WHALLONSBURGH (New York) Grange 12
WHIPPLE, Gurth 166
WHIPPLE, James S. 155, 177, 190-193, 243-245
WHITAKER, Edward G. 243
WHITE, James 184-185
WHITE, Ted 164
WHITE HORSE GULCH 40
WHITE HORSE RAPIDS 57-59, 62-66, 86-87, 95, 104, 212
WHITE PASS 33, 35, 37, 43, 47, 48, 51, 54, 58, 108
WHITE PASS AND YUKON RAILWAY 40, 41
WHITE PASS RAILROAD See White Pass and Yukon Railway
WHITE RIVER 226
WHITEHEAD, Charles E. 237
WHITE-TAILED DEER, by Newsom, W.M. 164
WILBUR, E.R. 28, 29
WILD ANIMAL ROUND-UP, by Hornaday, William T. 170, 171
WILDLIFE MANAGEMENT INSTITUTE 17
WILKINS (pilot) 227
WILKINS, Sir G. Hubert 160
WILLIAMS (chief packer) 53-54, 65
WILLSBORO, New York 9, 12, 13, 128, 129, 139, 205
WILLSBORO BAY 135
WILLSBORO POINT 135, 138
WILM, Harold G. 171
WILMINGTON, Delaware 22, 205
WILSON, John 228

WILSON, Wes 116
WILSON, President Woodrow 181, 185, 235
WILSON AND SHERMAN (store) 153
WINCH, Albert 256
WINCHESTER REPEATING ARMS COMPANY 178
WISCONSIN 189
WISTER, Owen 27, 232
WITHERBEE, Walter 151
WOLCOTT, Alexander 13
WOLVERINE CREEK 68
WOODSTOCK, New York 30
WOOLWORTH BUILDING 159 160
WORDEN HOTEL, Saratoga 21
WORLD WAR I 229, 233, 235
WRANGELL ISLANDS 206
WRIGHT, Doctor George H. 226-227
WRISLEY, Alton 11
WYLAND, George 112, 153
WYOMING 27, 43, 142, 172, 242
WYOMING, UNIVERSITY OF. Conservation History and Research Center 13

YALE UNIVERSITY 181
YUKON NOTES, by Burnham, John 34, 160
YUKON PROVISIONAL DISTRICT 100
YUKON RIVER 33, 37, 54, 57, 58, 66, 68-69, 72-73, 76-79, 82, 85, 87, 100, 102, 106, 108, 166, 204, 211, 212, 219
YUKON TERRITORY 33, 211, 212, 226
YUKON VALLEY 82, 85
YULE HOUSE 108, 112